The
Language
of Blood

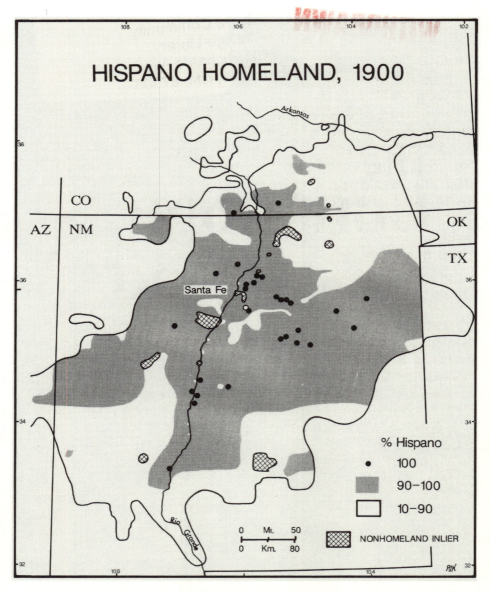

HISPANO HOMELAND, 1900

Arkansas

CO

AZ NM

OK

TX

Santa Fe

36

34

% Hispano

•   100

    90–100

    10–90

Rio Grande

| 0 | Mi. | 50 |
| 0 | Km. | 80 |

NONHOMELAND INLIER

RLN

Frontispiece. "Hispano Homeland, 1900." Adapted from Richard L. Nostrand, *The Hispano Homeland* (Norman and London: University of Oklahoma Press, 1992), Map 10.4. © 1969 University of Oklahoma Press. Reproduced by permission.

The
Language
of Blood

The Making of Spanish-American Identity in New Mexico, 1880s–1930s

John M. Nieto-Phillips

University of New Mexico Press ⵣ Albuquerque

© 2004 by the University of New Mexico Press
All rights reserved. First paperbound printing, 2008.
Printed in the United States of America

14   13   12   11   10   09   08   1   2   3   4   5   6   7

PAPERBOUND ISBN: 978-0-8263-2424-5

LIBRARY OF CONGRESS CATALOGING-IN-PUBLICATION DATA

Nieto-Phillips, John, 1964–
The language of blood : the making of Spanish-American identity in
New Mexico, 1880s–1930s / John Nieto-Phillips.
        p. cm.
Includes bibliographical references (p.   ) and index.
ISBN 0-8263-2423-1 (alk. paper)
   1. Spanish Americans—New Mexico—History.
   2. Hispanic Americans—New Mexico—History.
   3. Mexican Americans—New Mexico—History.
   4. Spanish Americans—New Mexico—Ethnic identity.
   5. Hispanic Americans—New Mexico—Ethnic identity.
   6. Mexican Americans—New Mexico—Ethnic identity.
   7. Racially mixed people—New Mexico—History.
   8. Ethnicity—New Mexico—History.
   9. New Mexico—Ethnic relations.
  10. New Mexico—Race relations. I. Title.
  F805.S75N54 2004
  978.9'0046872073—dc22

                              2004411626

Design and composition: Maya Allen-Gallegos
Typeset in Bembo 11.5/13.5
Display type set in Abbess and Caravan LH 1

Para mi madre,
Matilde Elena Nieto,
y a la memoria de mi padre,
James Robert Phillips (1930–2006)

Contents

List of Tables and Graphs

Tables

Graphs

nos·tal·gia
nä–'stal–jǝ

1: the state of being homesick
2: a wistful or excessively sentimental yearning for
return to or of some past period or irrecoverable condition

Preface

I was seven years old when my father was laid off at the machine shop in El Monte. It was 1972. Southern California's economy had slid into a recession, and the nation was at war. Today it amazes me that my parents managed to feed and clothe seven children on a part-time nurse's salary. But they could not shield us from their mounting worries. As spring became summer, my father was still jobless and grew visibly anxious and tense. Evening meals, once boisterous, chaotic events, became solemn rituals to be avoided. But as they inevitably do, things changed.

One day, my father drove up behind the wheel of a giant GMC delivery truck that read, in large white letters on navy blue canvas, "Los Angeles Times." He parked it in our front yard. Within days he had stripped the truck down to its chassis and welded onto it the metal carcass of a whale, or so it seemed. Over the next three months he worked day and night, stitching it with electrical wiring, then wrapping it in plywood and metal siding. He cut out windows like gaping eyes, transforming the thirty-five-foot mass into our gleaming new home on wheels. When he was finished, neighbors gathered round and gawked at the largest camper they had ever seen. Who knows how he managed to pay for it. What everyone wondered was where he would park it, if not right where he built it, on the dirt patch that was once a carpet of grass. It was a monstrosity.

The next year, early August, my parents piled everyone inside and set off for New Mexico. My mother had made a *promesa* to return to Bernalillo for the three-day fiesta that honors San Lorenzo, her hometown's patron saint. She was intent on dancing again among the Matachines. At least one dance, she said, to remember our ancestors and to thank God for our health. When she told me this I knew what was coming next. The story.

I knew the story by heart. I had learned it on my mother's knee. Among our families the story was so often recited, it took on the lyrical qualities of a prayer. It flowed from my *bisabuelo*'s lips in Spanish, from my grandfather's in Spanglish, from my mother's in English. The story was as familiar as Christmas posole and Grandpa Tomás's thick, handmade tortillas. It bored me.

> *In 1540 the brave* conquistador *Francisco Vázquez de Coronado came looking for the Seven Cities of Gold. He camped near Bernalillo and claimed New Mexico for the king of Spain. But he found no gold. Disappointed, Coronado retreated to Mexico. Next came Don Juan de Oñate. In 1598, he and hundreds of settlers conquered the land and tried to Christianize the Indians. When the Indians resisted, he punished two dozen of them by cutting off their right feet. There was a long drought and starvation until, in 1680, Popé led his fellow Indians in a revolt that sent the Spaniards running for their lives. Thirteen years later, Diego de Vargas returned accompanied by Spanish settlers and soldiers. He made peace with the Pueblos. To celebrate the* reconquista *of the region, De Vargas and his followers danced the Matachines in Bernalillo on* el dia de San Lorenzo, *August 10, 1693. And it has been danced there each year ever since.*

I rolled my eyes each time I heard it. I recall once asking my mother who cared about all these events, since it was so long ago and all those people are dead now. In a flash she grew indignant, then almost sullen. She answered that *she* cared and that I had better care if I wanted to know my roots. This is *your* history, she said. Whatever, I thought.

Though for years to come I wanted to erase such stories from my memory, their imprint on my young mind was deep and lasting. They also caused me a great deal of anguish and posed dilemmas that would plague me through my childhood and into my adult years. Why does my mother's family keep on insisting we are Spanish? Most of our neighbors were from Mexico, and I couldn't possibly go around our neighborhood proclaiming *we* are Spanish and not Mexican—as if we were somehow better than them. We were all working-class families with lots of kids. The better-off kids lived across the Pomona freeway. Maybe *they* were more "Spanish" than us, I thought. Plus, if I ran around boasting we were Spanish, Big Mary (María L.) across the street, a bilingual teacher proud of her

Mexican roots, might get offended. And that would be the end of tamales and cookies at her place.

To complicate matters, I had often heard it said that we were also part Indian, that Nano (Luciano Nieto, my great-grandfather) was orphaned and raised at Sandia Pueblo. The lore was that somewhere in our family tree there was a forgotten Indian branch and that's what explained why our skin got dark brown every summer. This information presented me with yet more quandaries. How could we be Spanish and Indian at the same time, but not Mexican? How could Spaniards have made it to New Mexico without first mixing with the Indians? And what did all this matter anyhow? Our regular pilgrimages to Bernalillo never rendered any answers.

As a child, I felt trapped by our supposed "Spanish" heritage. I was cursed with it. Double-bound by the pride I was supposed to possess and by the impossibility of speaking about "our history" among my friends, I grew ashamed of my family and our history. The source of that shame was the unspoken truth: that the grandeur of the past bore little relation to our humble, working-class status. One symbol of that status was the "mud house" my mother grew up in, which we visited almost every year, as if it were a shrine to our ancestors. Situated in the ancient section of Bernalillo called Las Concinitas, the house was but a few sections of adobe walls, cracked and melting into earthen mounds. Because of the shame, I pushed down all questions of my identity, pushed them into a sort of abyss of painful dilemmas. I submerged these questions for years and tried to ignore them, tried to forget them. I learned French, became a high school All-American athlete (sports were my ticket to college), and generally tried to blend into the ethnic patchwork of Los Angeles.

But there came a day in my late teens that I stared into the abyss and, as Nietzsche once wrote, the abyss stared back. When my Grandpa Tomás died, I was suddenly afflicted with a serious case of nostalgia. For reasons that have become only somewhat clearer to me with age, I yearned to revisit the dilemmas of my childhood, to recover that which I had repressed or forgotten—as well as that which never really existed. I became a collector of memorabilia of all sorts, saved museum tickets and brochures, scanned newspapers and magazines for articles on history and lore, and suffered to know every name and date that defined my family's past. I sat for hours with great uncles and great aunts and listened to tales of their lives—

usually the long versions. After my visits, I would write everything down, every story or anecdote. Many times in my excitement, I would forget important details or jumble them and have to reconstruct bits and pieces in subsequent visits. Or I would invert the sequence of events. When I did not misremember names, I made them up entirely. Such is the nature of memory, especially when one is afflicted with nostalgia.

ःん

This book is part of my migration back to New Mexico. It is my effort to come to terms with the contradictions of my family's lore that were the source of my shame and confusion as a young Chicano raised on tales of Spanish glory. I do not presume to offer a complete picture, but rather vignettes, mere fragments of a much larger story, specific sites and moments in which "the Spanish past" was imagined, written down, reshaped, commodified, contested, deployed, and passed down. This book, ultimately, is about memory and recovery from nostalgia.

Acknowledgments

Many people have helped me in completing not just this book but the journey of my education. As a junior at UCLA two decades ago I wandered into Norris Hundley's office and gazed at the hundreds of books that lined his shelves, each of them neatly catalogued. I wondered if he had actually read them all. (He had.) Norris has been a kind and steadfast supporter of my pursuits from the outset, and a model of the scholar I wish I could be. At various points during my undergraduate and graduate careers at UCLA, Melissa Meyer, Sylvia Rodríguez, Edward Telles, Vilma Ortiz, and Valerie Matsumoto read portions of my manuscript in dissertation form and were instrumental in urging me to think about issues historical and contemporary. George J. Sánchez, especially, drew me into the field of Latino history, nurtured my curiosity, and made sure I had the wherewithal to complete my education. Among my graduate school comrades, Jeffrey Rangel, Linda Nueva-España Maram, Miroslava Chávez, Cathy Ceniza Choy, and Dwight McBride have offered their continued support and friendship. Thank you all.

I had the privilege to teach at New Mexico State University (NMSU) from 1995 to 2003, where a number of colleagues and students nourished my mind and enriched my life. I particularly want to thank William Eamon, who has been a friend, critic, and mentor as I pondered life's predicaments. I could not have asked for better colleagues than those in the History Department at NMSU. Iñigo García-Bryce, Marsha Weisiger, Margaret Jacobs, and Jon Hunner read and commented on portions of my work. Joan Jensen deserves special mention for graciously offering me files from her vast archives. For their collegiality and friendship, I also want to thank Andrea Orzoff, Elizabeth Horodovich, Ken Hammond, Margaret Malamud, Jamie Bronstein, Nathan Brooks, Ray Sadler, Charles Harris, Darlis Miller, Kevin Roberts, Matt O'Hara, Jeff Brown, Edgar Newman, Jo Bloom, Mark Milliorn, Dietmar Snyder, and

Patsy Montoya. In ways both professional and personal, Cynthia Bejarano, Hermán García, Jesús Barquet, Cecilia Vázquez, Jeff Shepherd, Darío Silva, Luis Vázquez, Hermán García, and William Flores have been tremendously supportive. Thank you.

A number of people read and commented on portions of the manuscript at different stages of development, or as conference presentations. I particularly wish to thank Erlinda Gonzales-Berry, David Maciel, María Montoya, Phillip Gonzales, John Kessell, and Chris Schmidt-Nowara. Other colleagues offered insights by way of our conversations about New Mexico's past, including Dennis Trujillo, Erika Bsumek, Estevan Rael-Gálvez, Bob Himmerich y Valencia, Adrian Bustamante, Ramón Gutiérrez, Sarah Deutsch, Suzanne Forrest, Gabriel Meléndez, Rep. J. Paul Taylor, Frank Wimberly, Steve Fox, Margaret Espinosa McDonald, Vicki Ruiz, Denise Pan, Delilah Montoya, Francisco Benítez, and Marcus Embry. Special thanks to Silke Hensel, Werner Lamottke, and Catherine Lejeune, whose friendship and intellectual companionship I treasure.

Several institutions made research for this book possible by generously providing funding. They include the Ford Foundation, the National Endowment for the Humanities, the Spencer Foundation, UCLA's Institute for American Cultures, the Del Amo Endowment at UCLA, and the Smithsonian Institution. The College of Arts and Sciences at NMSU gave me much-needed leaves from teaching, as well as two mini-grants to carry out research.

I would like to thank the many archivists and librarians who helped me in my quest to recover "voices" from the past. At the New Mexico State Records Center and Archives (NMSRCA), Al Regensberg and Sandra Jaramillo were particularly helpful; at the Center for Southwest Research (CSWR) at the University of New Mexico, Beth Silbergleit, Nancy Brown, Kathlene Ferris, Ann Massmann, and Stella de sa Rego. Martha Liebert at the Sandoval County Historical Society has been a joy to know all these years and a fount of historical wisdom. At NMSU, Molly Molloy, Latin American librarian specialist, was my link to every obscure article or electronic resource. My research assistants Nancy Shockley and Jorge Porrata helped me organize and transcribe many of the sources for this book.

Many thanks also to David Holtby at the University of New Mexico Press and, especially, to my editor Jill Root, whose expert eye caught many errors and whose patience I admire. Of course any faults that remain are mine.

My journey has taken me on a few detours. I had the good fortune to spend two years at the Center for Puerto Rican Studies at Hunter College to undertake a comparative study of education and "Americanization" programs in New Mexico and Puerto Rico. During my stay in New York, a number of Puerto Rican scholars welcomed me into their lives and nurtured my new interest in Puerto Rican history. That experience launched my work in a new direction by pointing to both the confluences and differences that define Latina/o historical experiences and civic identities. I especially want to thank Iris López, Arlene Dávila, Juan Flores, Gabriel Haslip-Viera, Clara Rodríguez, Féliz Matos-Rodríguez, Virginia Sánchez-Korrol, Nélida Pérez, Miriam Jiménez and Caridad Souza *por su bondad y amistad.*

My new home institution, Indiana University, has graciously given me the time off and the resources to see this book through to its completion. I especially want to thank Jorge Chapa and John Bodnar for their warm welcome.

Finally, *no tengo las palabras, ni en francés, para agradecer a mi familia*— my parents and siblings, and the Aguilar, Nieto, and Aragon families, particularly Charles Aguilar—all of whose love and sustenance have never wavered. Corinne, my wife, has been eternally supportive, loving, and patient as I have tapped out these final words. And looking over my shoulder is our son, Shanon, eagerly waiting for me to rejoin his world of dinosaurs and coloring books.

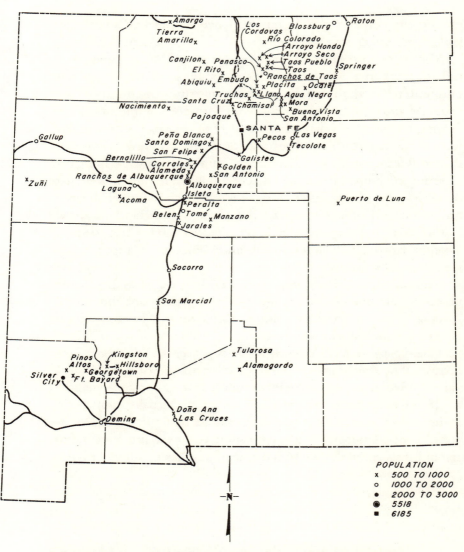

POPULATION
x   500 TO 1000
○   1000 TO 2000
●   2000 TO 3000
◉   5518
■   6185

PRINCIPAL TOWNS AND RAILROADS 1890

Principal Towns and Railroads. Source: Warren A. Beck and Ynez Haase, *Historical Atlas of New Mexico* (Norman: University of Oklahoma Press, 1969), map 53. © 1969 University of Oklahoma Press. Reproduced by permission.

Introduction

When the United States declared war on Spain in 1898, rumors abounded throughout the Southwest and the nation that the Spanish-speaking population of New Mexico secretly sympathized with the enemy. Sporadic outbreaks of treachery were reported. In Española, a riotous crowd was said to have unfurled the Spanish flag at the church of Santa Cruz de la Cañada and boastfully paraded it about the plaza during the feast of Corpus Christi. This is pure fabrication, declared the parish priest in a letter to Governor Miguel Antonio Otero. "We have no Spanish flag here in the Church of Sta. Cruz . . . [for] the people [of Española] are truly Americans."[1] The perception held by many Anglo Americans, however, remained to the contrary. Despite a half-century of U.S. citizenship, New Mexico's "Mexicans," warned the *New York Times* as the war ended, still "professed a deep hostility to American ideas and American policies." Rather than assimilating into the nation's cultural and political mainstream, the newspaper noted, these Mexicans stubbornly clung to their habits, political affiliations, and semipagan religious practices; they abhorred all things "American" and had little resolve to show their patriotism during the war, a view supported by the fact that fewer than three dozen Spanish-surname New Mexicans had enlisted in the Cuban and Puerto Rican campaigns. Most disturbing, these Mexicans seemingly refused to speak the language of the body politic. As long as Spanish remained the primary language of public instruction, the *Times* admonished, "the majority of the inhabitants will remain 'Mexican' and retain a pseudo-allegiance [to Spain]."[2]

The perception of Spanish-speaking New Mexicans as "un-American" was broadly shared. For more than sixty years, it fueled a steadfast resistance in all corners of the nation to New Mexico's formation of a state government. Even after statehood was granted in 1912, certain Americans continued to allege that "Mexicans in New Mexico" were secretly conspiring to rejoin the state to their "motherland" to the south.[3] Such allegations of disloyalty, coupled with the widely held views that all Mexican peoples were racially nonwhite, were of mixed (Spanish and Indian) blood, and were "unfit" to assume the rights and responsibilities of full citizenship, inspired powerful reactions among the Spanish-speaking people of New Mexico; together, they help us to understand the national context in which many New Mexicans contested and elaborated their "Spanish American" identity. That identity—its evolution and deployment—is the focus of this book.

Spanish American identity took root in both national and local contexts, most noticeably from the 1880s to the 1930s. It had its origins in diverse struggles against political and social marginalization, and was nurtured by a burgeoning tourist industry, a Hispanophilic cultural movement, and locally authored histories and scholarship. Marginalization came in the form of Congress's refusal to admit New Mexico into the Union, citing the territory's mixed-blood population, "inferior" cultures, fervent Catholicism, and broad use of Spanish. New Mexico's Spanish-speaking population (hereafter referred to as *Nuevomexicanos,* a term often invoked during the period in question) set out to define their racial identity as Spanish, in part by resurrecting archaic notions about "purity of blood" that dated to the conquest. For their part, Anglo Americans, sometimes in collaboration with leading Nuevomexicanos, transformed New Mexico into the tourist capital of the Southwest, a Mecca for "American" immigrants and visitors who delighted in Spanish and Indian cultures. Boosterism encouraged—among Anglo Americans and Nuevomexicanos alike—a growing fascination with the Spanish colonial past. By the 1910s, Spanish-speaking New Mexicans began to take pride in their legacy of conquest and colonization, began to defend their right to use Spanish in public realms amid campaigns to abolish the language, and made known their pluralist vision of the American polity, albeit one that confirmed, and did not challenge, the "white" racial prerequisite for full citizenship. Spanish history and language emerged as enduring symbols of their "Spanish" (white) racial identity, twin wellsprings of pride and empowerment.

Though long regarded a central feature of New Mexico's ethnic topography, Spanish American identity remains somewhat of an enigma to students of Mexican American history, and Latina/o history more broadly. But it has not gone unnoticed. In the past six decades, the very mention of Spanish American ethnic identity has sometimes sparked sharp disagreement over the validity of Nuevomexicanos' claim to Spanishness, the precise degree of their racial mixture (or *mestizaje*), or their presumed Spanish phenotype or folk culture. These sorts of exchanges have intensified ever since George Isadore Sánchez cautioned Nuevomexicanos not to be swept away by their chivalric European legacy, which he so colorfully articulated in his 1940 work *Forgotten People: A Study of New Mexicans.* That legacy goes something like this: "The settlement of New Mexico forms a thrilling chapter in the history of the New World. That adventure in exploration, in conquest, and in colonization was indeed spectacular." New Spain's inhospitable climate, vast distances, and difficult terrain, wrote Sánchez,

> combined to thwart the *conquistadores* and colonizers in their trek northward. . . . [T]he New Mexican suffered untold hardships and disappointments. Holding forth against these forces through the centuries, he comes to us today a victim of circumstances beyond his control. We find him now still struggling with his surroundings, still seaking [*sic*] to reap the fruits of his conquest.[4]

Sánchez pointed out what he believed to be the crowning irony of New Mexico's history: that the travails suffered by the conquistadores paled when compared to the hardships endured by Nuevomexicanos since the dawn of U.S. occupation. Dispossession, poverty, political exclusion, undereducation, and poor federal land management, he argued, posed greater threats to Nuevomexicanos' survival than did the ravages of the colonial frontier. Sánchez admonished Spanish Americans not to forget their Spanish forebears and urged them to hold close the valuable lessons of their own history.[5] *Forgotten People* was thus his rallying cry for Nuevomexicanos to organize around such causes as land and water struggles, political rights, and bilingual education.

Since the appearance of *Forgotten People,* Mexican American scholars have, for the most part, regarded Spanish American ethnicity with apprehension, often viewing it as the basis of an assimilationist ideology that has always stood inimical to Mexican American interests and, more recently, Chicana and Chicano consciousness. Other observers have questioned whether it constituted an "identity" at all, or have dismissed it as a kind of false consciousness. To be sure, the ubiquitous "Spanish" heritage among modern-day Nuevomexicanos has not gone ignored, but until very recently, neither has it been extensively examined within its historical, political, or cultural settings.

Folklorist Arthur León Campa associated the rise of Spanish American identity with a "problem of nomenclature." New Mexicans' claim to a Spanish legacy, wrote Campa in 1946, could be understood as a reactive impulse to racism, prompted by a general antipathy among U.S. citizens toward Mexicans and Mexican Americans, and founded in the belief that all persons of Mexican descent were: (1) racially not white, seemingly the illegitimate progeny of Spanish and Indian racial mixture; (2) both racially and culturally inferior to white U.S. citizens; and (3) recent immigrants to the United States and, therefore, not U.S. citizens (in the legal sense) and incapable of meeting the culturally defined standard for U.S. citizenship. "The New Mexican's first reaction, as a result of this 'American' attitude," Campa theorized, "is to dissociate himself from anything that carries a Mexican implication. To do this he must insist on his difference in origin." Hence the "Spanish American" label served three purposes: "[I]t lifts [him] from the opprobrium of being a Mexican; it makes him a member of the 'white' race; and expresses his American citizenship. . . . The problem with 'Spanish-American' is that, while it suits the New Mexican in the abstract, there is little in his appearance and origin that upholds the distinction he is trying so hard to make."[6] Campa, a native of Mexico, viewed Nuevomexicanos as racially and culturally Mexican, yet natives of the United States. The problem of nomenclature would resolve itself, he said, if both Anglo Americans and Spanish Americans would simply "reject race and nationality as a criterion" in the naming process and let the "folk" name themselves.[7] In Spanish, New Mexico's folk spoke of themselves as *nosotros, nuestra gente, la raza, manitos, mexicanos, neomejicanos, nuevomexicanos,* or *hispanoamericanos.* In English, however, there seemed no suitable designation. The terms "Mexican" and "New Mexican," Campa acknowledged, proved inadequate, since each held broader, unintended meanings; the former suggested a Mexican national identity, and the latter embraced all of New Mexico's residents, including so-called Anglos and Indians. Despite Campa's best intentions, the "problem of nomenclature" did not resolve itself. Instead, the "Spanish" label continued to evoke rather visceral invectives among Mexicans and Mexican Americans. Clearly such labels, far from being strictly a matter of semantics, tap into highly charged associations with history, memory, language, and ideology.[8]

In his venerable work *North from Mexico*, Carey McWilliams in 1949 unmasked Spanish American identity as a "fantasy heritage," which undoubtedly had been foisted upon the Southwest's Mexican-origin population by Anglo American tourists and boosters, and by *ricos* (or wealthy self-styled "Spanish" families) of California, Texas, and New Mexico. McWilliams postulated that New Mexico's ricos

> had experienced little discrimination or prejudice; while the poorer class, being segregated by poverty and geographic location, had partially adjusted to a bicultural [Anglo–Nuevomexicano] relationship. But the middle-class elements, small in number, lacked the social prominence to win exemption from discrimination and, at the same time, sought to distinguish themselves from the 'Mexican' lower class.[9]

Much to his credit, McWilliams drove readers straight to the nexus of race, class, and national ideology. But then he left his readers to ponder: Did Spanish American identity, in fact, succeed in winning Nuevomexicanos "exemption from discrimination"? Did the fledgling "middle-class elements" thereby succeed in setting themselves apart from the "'Mexican' lower class"? Indeed, was driving home that distinction their primary objective in declaring their *hispanidad,* or Spanishness? My initial forays into researching the subject focused on Pueblo Indian, Anglo, and Nuevomexicano relations in and around the town of Bernalillo, where additional interethnic dynamics were at work, such as land disputes, tourism, and Anglo immigration. But several scholars had already made deep inroads into "Hispano" ethnicity in northern New Mexico.

During the 1980s, geographer Richard L. Nostrand sparked a lively debate when he argued that New Mexico's "Hispanos" possessed an objectively verifiable "homeland" centered in the upper Rio Grande basin. He was quickly taken to task by various scholars for, among other things: employing the term "Hispano"; asserting that, because their ancestors "came more directly from Spain," Hispanos were "culturally distinctive among persons of Spanish-Indian or Mexican descent"; and stating that Hispanos "reject that which is Mexican."[10] Some critics accused Nostrand of propagating the "two myths": that there exists a distinctive "Spanish-derived, non-Mexican [Hispano] subculture" centered in New Mexico, and that there exists a "real and discrete geographic region" that could be called "the Hispano homeland."[11] Without retracing the exchange that ensued, it will suffice to say that Nostrand's thesis proved a catalyst for a much-needed discussion about race, region, and ethnicity in New Mexico.[12] What became apparent in the "Hispano Homeland debate" was that Nuevomexicanos' "distinctiveness," or lack thereof, was commonly conceived in terms of cultural content or genealogy, rather than in relation to the specific moments and sociopolitical contexts.

In the past fifteen years, however, a noticeable shift in this direction has occurred. Anthropologist Sylvia Rodríguez, for example, in her ethnographic studies has shown "ethnic boundaries" between Nuevomexicanos, Pueblo Indians, and Anglos to be, in good measure, a product of forces regional as well as local, such as face-to-face relations, tourism, and resource struggles. Taking a cue from Fredrick Barth, Rodríguez views these boundaries as both situationally defined and structurally maintained.[13] With a similar emphasis on context, sociologist Phillip B. Gonzales has examined the political moments in which Hispano solidarity has been manifested, such as in spontaneous public protests—or *juntas de indignación*—against perceived and real social injuries or injustices.[14] His close reading of particular political contexts has shown the Spanish heritage to be, at times, a vehicle for ethnic mobilization. Although their influence on my thinking has been significant, I do not wish to associate Rodríguez, Gonzales, or others mentioned here with my own conceptual deficiencies or errors of fact or interpretation. But having read their works, the pivotal question, to my mind, has markedly shifted from "Are Nuevomexicanos culturally 'Spanish' or 'distinctive' relative to Mexicans or Mexican Americans?" to "How has the ethnic difference and—more specifically, the discourses of Hispanophilia and hispanidad—functioned in particular interethnic contexts and historical moments?"

Though my question has been framed, in large measure, by the work of Rodríquez and Gonzales, it has also been informed by a vast body of scholarship on ethnic relations in New Mexico.[15] Ramón A. Gutiérrez's scholarship, for example, looms large over historiographical landscape and has shed light on the Spanish colonial contexts that gave rise to what I have chosen to call "the language of blood."[16] In their respective studies of literature and popular texts, including Spanish-language newspapers and autobiographies, Erlinda Gonzales-Berry, Doris L. Meyer, A. Gabriel Meléndez, and Genaro M. Padilla have unearthed examples of historical agency as well as loss in the literary record of Nuevomexicanos and Nuevomexicanas.[17]

Padilla, for example, has explained the Spanish colonial discourse evident in Nuevomexicanas' writings between the 1930s and 1950s. In the course of conquest and dispossession, he writes, Anglo Americans became intent on subverting the subordinate group's ideological consciousness, by drawing into their power structure the dispossessed Nuevomexicano elite and by providing that elite with the socioideological discourse that "not only accedes to their dispossession, but actually becomes the official cultural discourse through which the subjected group makes sufferable its subordination."[18] By sublimating the romantic past and subverting the abysmal present, the Spanish ethos served as a discursive tool of Anglo American romantics, tourists, and Hispanophiles; *these* individuals, it would seem, were the real beneficiaries of New Mexico's Spanish enchantment. (In many respects, Sánchez warned Nuevomexicanos against falling prey to precisely this sort of wistful complacency.) More recently, Charles Montgomery has eloquently recast McWilliam's "fantasy heritage" argument in contemporary terms. The "modern Spanish heritage" that evolved in New Mexico between the 1880s and the 1930s, Montgomery writes, "functioned as a shared idiom, a common vocabulary for talking and thinking about the upper Rio Grande." Prominent Hispanos and Anglos manufactured that heritage "to change the way outsiders, and they themselves, imagined New Mexican society." That shared idiom nourished an entire tourist industry and served as a rhetorical means of setting Nuevomexicanos apart from "mixed-blood" Mexicans lurking in the shadows of the body politic. It also served to redraw racial boundaries to figuratively include Nuevomexicanos in the circle of whiteness, while providing hollow recompense for their declining political and economic fortunes. (Each of these developments is exquisitely described in Montgomery's *The Spanish Redemption*.) But, Montgomery adds, "the Spanish heritage did not constitute a particular cultural or ethnic 'identity'. Though fueled by private memories, it had less to genuine nor spurious—but "invented." What makes it so compelling a subject is not the question of its legitimacy, but its articulation and its deployment in contexts of resistance and accommodation.[20]

From as early as the 1850s, Nuevomexicanos were keen to Anglo American racial perceptions of them, and to their own dreams of self-government. Never able to disown the epithets "greaser" and "mongrel" or "persons unfit for self-government," lettered and landed Nuevomexicanos (and Anglo newcomers) understood that their statehood hopes hinged largely on convincing Washington lawmakers that New Mexico's "Mexicans" were racially white—or white enough—to merit full inclusion in the body politic. So they turned to things familiar yet archaic. In the annals of their forebears, Nuevomexicanos found an array of symbols and words that helped to clarify their arcane racial genealogy to Easterners. Anglo newcomers, seeing in that history an opportunity for development, seized upon it with a passion. There was much collaboration, but also palpable resistance as Nuevomexicanos vied for control over symbols of their identity: their land, history, and language.

This book develops several themes. A principle one, described in chapter 1, is the language of blood purity, or *limpieza de sangre,* which had its roots in medieval Spain and made its way to New Mexico during the colonial period. Propagated by civic and ecclesiastical authorities, limpieza served to enforce consanguinity (marriage and procreation within a particular group) and was a defining element of one's identity for the better part of the colonial period. The notion of blood purity evolved into a highly regulated set of castes that served to identify individuals based on their parentage, and that later collapsed during the Mexican period into two distinct racial entities: so-called *españoles* and *indios.* This bifurcated society—though internally fractured further by class distinctions—persisted well into the U.S. period and became the basis for American legal and racial distinctions between the two groups.

Reclaiming one's "Spanish blood" took on particular importance in the context of the statehood movement, which is the subject of chapter 2. During New Mexico's sixty-two-year quest for self-government, references to blood alluded to more than white racial identity or biological relations. The mention of "Spanish blood" conjured up an entire history of conquest and settlement with which Americans could readily identify and that they could even admire.

Tales of Spanish adventures found their way into tourist brochures, as we see in chapter 3. The advent of the railway prompted many changes in New Mexico in the 1880s, not least of which was a dramatic increase in immigration and tourism. In an effort to attract as many settlers and visitors as possible—in part to aid New Mexico's bid for statehood by projecting an image of growth and prosperity—territorial officials initiated a booster campaign that disseminated dreamy images of Pueblo Indians and Spaniards living in relative harmony, presumably as they had for centuries. Railway companies, motivated by a desire for more passengers, often collaborated with New Mexico's officials in making and selling this benign "biracial motif."

Another theme of this book is the cultural movement of Hispanophilia—broadly conceived as "a foreigner's love of all things Spanish." Chapter 4 examines how two Anglo authors both generated and appropriated the Spanish conquest narrative to suit their own particular agendas. Motivated both by high idealism and practical objectives, Hispanophiles Charles Fletcher Lummis and one-time governor Lebaron Bradford Prince labored fastidiously to recast the racial landscape of New Mexico in the American (and Nuevomexicano) imagination. Their lives and works offer a window into the personal and organizational networks—stretching from New Mexico to "mother Spain"—that sustained the regional fascination for things Spanish.

The final chapter examines what is, in many respects, the ideological bone of contention in the Hispano Homeland Debate: hispanidad. By the turn of the century, self-identified "Spanish Americans" had begun to lay claim to their Spanish heritage. The historian whose works gave voice to hispanidad was Benjamin Maurice Read, the son of an "American" father and "Mexican" mother. His writings, together with those of renowned Stanford linguist Aurelio Macedonio Espinosa, the son of a shepherd, gave Nuevomexicanos a "scientific" rationale for their claims to Spanishness. By the second decade of the twentieth century, with the rise of Americanization programs in the schools, a growing contingent of Nuevomexicana educators, including Aurora Lucero-White and Adelina Otero-Warren—two women known foremost for their associations with Hispanophiles—undertook to remove the stigma that had been attached to the Spanish language. By the 1930s, however, the irony was plain: it was one thing to parade about as Queen Isabella during the Santa Fe Fiesta, but wholly another to teach Spanish in the public schools.

The making of Spanish American identity offers a sometimes discomforting glimpse into the making of whiteness.[21] It also suggests one way in which ideological fissures between mexicanos are made chasms. But this book is just a fragment of a much larger and more complex story—a story of longing and inclusion, cooperation and discord, memory and oblivion. The silences and omissions are many. Yet I hope that it contributes something to our understanding of how historical identities—among Nuevomexicanos, and Latinos more broadly—correspond to both the centripetal force of nation-building (blood, whiteness, and citizenship) as well as the centrifugal pull of local politics and social relations (immigration, tourism, and appropriation).[22] In these interconnected contexts the "heritage" is decidedly a language of empowerment or, from another perspective, coercion.

Chapter One

The Language of Blood

There are only a few families among the ricos who pride themselves upon not having Indian blood in their veins. The great mass of the population are very dark, and can not claim to be more than one fourth or one eighth part Spanish. The intermixture between the peasantry and the native tribes of Indians is yet carried on, and there is no present hope of the people improving in color.

—*William W. H. Davis, 1857*[1]

Many of us New Mexicans have dreamed of our Conquistador forefathers as some sort of knighted gentry—to the secret, and sometimes disguised, mirth of our non-Spanish neighbors, who wrongly believe them to have been nothing but peons and convicts.

—*Fray Angélico Chávez, 1973*[2]

ःλ Raza Conquistadora

On October 26, 1901, six hundred Nuevomexicanos took to the streets of Las Vegas, New Mexico, to denounce a newspaper editorial bearing the title "The Spanish American." Its author, the Protestant missionary Nellie Snyder, had reportedly slipped her text into an issue of the local weekly, *The Review,* while the journal's editor was out of town. Snyder's editorial attacked New Mexico's Spanish-speaking residents as slovenly and semipagan, degraded and superstitious, of mixed ("Indian and Iberian") blood, a people who lived in mud huts and slept on piles of rags for beds. On reading the piece, Ezequiél Cabeza de Baca, editor of the Spanish-language newspaper *La Voz del Pueblo,* called on Nuevomexicanos to converge on the county courthouse and express their indignation. A *junta pública* (public commission) was hastily convened that drafted a resolution proclaiming Snyder an "ingrate, hypocrite, and demagogue" who, having enjoyed the hospitality of their community, had paid it back with slander and infamies.[3] Snyder, now nowhere to be found, was branded persona non grata and banished from Las Vegas. The junta invited the bespeckled young lawyer Eusebio Chacón to step forward and address the crowd in Spanish.

> Said author begins to astonish us by saying that the Spanish American or Mexican is part Spanish and part Indian; that he resembles his Spanish and Indian ancestors in language, customs, appearance and habits. How she has twisted the linguistic canons to combine the Spanish and Indian tongues is a mystery to us. . . . I am Spanish American as are those who hear me. No other blood circulates through my veins but that which was brought by Don Juan de Oñate and by the illustrious ancestors of my name. If there is any place in Spanish America or in the former Spanish colonies that has conserved the physiognomic traits of the *raza conquistadora* it is New Mexico.[4]

Chacón's fiery discourse captured the spirit of the moment, but it also fueled indignation among Nuevomexicanos throughout the region. In the days that followed, the speech was reprinted on the front pages of Spanish-language newspapers such as the local journals *El Independiente* and *La Voz del Pueblo.* Chacón was widely heralded as an eloquent and fearless defender of the people's honor.

From an early age, Chacón had distinguished himself as an exceptional orator. Barely a teenager, he delivered lectures at gatherings of *mutualistas* (mutual aid societies). His eloquence set him apart from his classmates both in the public schools and at the Jesuit College in Las Vegas, New Mexico; it earned him laudits in speech contests as well as invitations to speak before international audiences, such as the Pan American Congress that took place in St. Paul, Minnesota, in 1889, the year he received his law degree from the University of Notre Dame. Chacón later employed his language skills in a variety of capacities: as an author of fantastical novels in Spanish that spoke volumes about local culture; as an English professor in Durango, Mexico; as an interpreter for the Court of Private Land Claims in New Mexico; and as a member of the Colorado and New Mexico bar associations. His education and contacts placed him among an informal cadre of bilingual professionals who wielded both political and economic influence in the territory, and who brokered social and cultural relations between the ascendant Anglo Americans and Spanish-speaking villagers. Chacón was comfortably ensconced among the social and intellectual elite. But he was also a person who identified with the folk.[5]

Born in 1870 to Rafael Chacón and Juana Paez de Chacón, Eusebio was the sixth of eleven children, nine of whom survived infancy. His father was a seasoned war veteran who had witnessed the American invasion in 1846 and, nine years later, joined Kit Carson's campaigns against the Utes and the Apaches. After marshalling the Spanish-speaking Company K during the Civil War, Capt. Chacón collected his meager pension and relocated with his family to Trinidad, Colorado. There he homesteaded, raised sheep, and eventually earned a small fortune, only to lose all of it through speculation. The Chacón household was bustling with children in the 1870s, and was filled with stories, folklore, pious traditions, and memories of conquests. It was during these formative years that young Eusebio was reminded time and again of his "illustrious lineage," which presumably dated from the arrival in 1710 of the marquis de la Peñuela, Admiral Don José Chacón Medina y Salazar y Villaseñor.

Contemporary research does not bear out the Chacóns' claim of direct descent from the marquis. Records suggest the marquis was "without issue," or childless. Yet the idea of an unbroken link to Spain and to the conquistadores remained a vital part of the Chacóns' identity. Despite their "illustrious" pretensions, the Chacóns were not, in fact, the landed ricos that historians have often associated with Nuevomexicano families that claim to have "Spanish blood" in their veins. On the other hand, neither were they members of the impoverished and landless *jornaleros* (day laborers) who occupied the lowest rungs of the agricultural economy. Instead, the Chacóns were one of a growing number of families who had attained sufficient education and status (often via military service) to operate in both English- and Spanish-speaking worlds in New Mexico.[6]

When Eusebio Chácon stepped before the crowd that fall afternoon in 1901, he did so not foremost as an exercise of his class privilege, though certainly his education and social position were not lost on protestors. Rather, he was a defender of the people's honor, selected for that purpose by the junta pública. In the context of the moment, Chacón was speaking with the consent of, and in solidarity with, his audience. He identified with the village traditions, cultural practices, and religious beliefs that Nellie Snyder had condemned. What makes Chacón's 1901 speech so historically momentous is that it encompassed a wide range of civic ambitions and concerns, cultural symbols, and historical referents that were familiar to the audience and that momentarily transcended class and political boundaries.[7] Chacón's defense of Nuevomexicanos' "Spanish blood" was more than a visceral response to Snyder's claim of miscegenation; it was an assertion of identity rooted in a conquest heritage and fervent Catholicism. Chacón's speech embodied several components of a "Spanish American" vernacular that can be thought of as a "language of blood."

"Blood" was but a code word for identity. It conjured up a lexicon of symbols, historical referents, social relations, and racial suppositions that were fundamental to Nuevomexicanos' self-perception and self-definition. Blood was also a convenient tool for fashioning and deploying collective memory. Chacón's invocation of his "Spanish blood" was less an affirmation of biological truth than a pronouncement of his identification with the conquistadores. "Blood purity," Chacón conceded, was perhaps more an ideal than a reality: "Some mixture [between Spaniards and Indians] has occurred, true but so slight and in such rare cases that to say that we are, as a community, a mixed race is neither proven by history nor stands up to scientific analysis. But even if it were true that we are a mixed race, there is nothing dishonorable or degrading in that."[8] At the dawn of the twentieth century, Nuevomexicanos were painfully aware that their racial identity mattered, particularly if they wished to enjoy social and civic equality with Anglo Americans. To claim "Spanish" blood was to declare one's difference from "Indian" and "Anglo" American neighbors; it was to lay claim to a European (read: racially white) heritage; it was to aver one's historical attachment to the land (by way of conquest); and it was to distinguish oneself from the maligned, mixed-blood Mexican immigrant.

We can trace the language of blood to its medieval antecedents. For centuries, blood had been a criterion for defining social categories on the Iberian Peninsula. In New Spain, blood would gain new uses.

⠶ Limpieza de Sangre

Blood has conjured a constellation of meanings dating to antiquity. The loss of blood was commonly associated with themes of violence, contamination, dissipation of power, and death. But bleeding also connoted fertility, loss of virginity, and reproduction. Conversely, the containment and preservation of blood were signs of power, honor, fortitude, and prestige. Some of these symbolic equations were apparently universal, but their origins remain a mystery. The linguistic record suggests that early Indo-European societies gave tremendous importance to blood and linked it to birth and kinship. Lines of descent were often depicted in natural terms, such as a tree whose sap (blood) nourished and allowed it to thrive, expand, and reproduce. Hence the visual portrayal of lineage often took the form of the "family tree." Bleeding was often linked to women through menstruation and birth. However, the social value of bloodlines—their integrity, regulation, and maintenance—most often accrued to men and were a measure of one's manhood. In the words of one historian, "the representation of men's social power, the determination of origin and ancestry by patrilineal descent (that is, the very principle on which Indo-European society depended), relied on blood as its dominant symbol: a man's lineage or clan membership was signified by blood."[9] Although the precise social meanings varied across time and space, generally speaking, they pervaded Europe by the Middle Ages.

On the Iberian Peninsula, blood was believed to capture the essence of one's spiritual purity and nobility. Blood positioned an individual among the social strata. Those of Spanish/Catholic blood proclaimed themselves superior to those of Indian, Moorish, or Jewish blood. Religious converts and individuals of mixed blood were scrupulously labeled and positioned according to their degree of blood mixture, or *casta*. Families and individuals reinforced their sociopolitical standing by claiming to have pure, "untainted" blood. Hence, the notion of limpieza de sangre, or "purity of blood," gained popularity as the Spanish kingdom flourished, and it defined relations of power and social status both on the Iberian Peninsula and in the New World. As early as the thirteenth century, reigning families of the Hispanic kingdoms invoked a language of blood to arrange power relations and marriages among groups of people competing for resources, and to assign military, social, and political status. Dominant families claimed to possess blood that had not been debased by the mixture of families of inferior religious beliefs, languages, military allegiances, and the like. Blood was therefore a symbol of endogamy, or marriage and procreation within a proscribed group. Endogamous marriages coalesced and conserved both families' resources, whereas exogamous ones tended to diminish them. The maintenance of limpieza de sangre through strategic marriages also implied the preservation of honor, military prowess, social rank, and/or nobility.[10]

Declarations of limpieza de sangre had both Christian and Jewish precedents, according to the renowned Hispanist Américo Castro. One document authored circa 1300 by a Barcelona rabbi pronounced two brothers, David and Azriel, eligible for marriage, declaring them to be "of pure descent . . . and eligible to marry among the most honorable families of Israel." Nowhere in their lineage, maternal or paternal, was "impure blood" to be found, recorded the rabbi. Meanings attached to blood reveal a great deal about the societies that produced them. In the case of these bachelor brothers, purity of blood served as a badge of their superior faith, honor, and social status. It was deemed so important to their marital future that friends and relatives testified before the rabbi that the brothers did indeed possess pure Jewish blood. Though initially a metaphor for faith, blood was frequently mentioned in reference to nobility and military conquest.[11]

Spain's Middle Ages were replete with references to bloodlines. Bloodlines served to fashion groups of men into cohesive military orders, or *cofradias*. An integral component of society, warrior fraternities required members to marry and procreate within the group's families, so as to safeguard the group's blood quality, identity, and honor. Endogamy, in this instance, reinforced the social boundary between knighted soldiers and the lay population. In addition to military cofradias, there existed professional and plebeian cofradias, analogous to modern guilds, whose purpose it was to create a sense of community based less on bloodlines, perhaps, than on mutual economic interest and occupational affiliation. It comes as no surprise, therefore, that, as Christians began reconquering the peninsula in the name of their god and kingdom, divisions should emerge among them in the form of "old" and "new" Christian orders.[12]

The growing concern for limpieza de sangre in Spain coincided with the Christian persecution of Jews and Moors in the fourteenth and fifteenth centuries. During this period, the killing of non-Christians became more and more commonplace, and statutes limiting their religious traditions and occupations began to gain both royal and ecclesiastical sanction. With the Iberian Reconquest came conversion campaigns and discrimination against *conversos* (converts) on the part of self-labeled *cristianos viejos* (Old Christians). Cristianos viejos claimed a long, pure ancestry. They believed their lineage to be unblemished by intermarriage with so-called heretics; thus they claimed to possess pure and untainted blood. Whether or not one had descended from a long line of Christians, or could prove it with documentation, it was commonplace to make this claim, particularly when public suspicions had indicted one's family name or individual honor. But claims to pure blood relied more on conviction than on credentials, since the very notion of purity was founded in the mystical. Because blood purity defied natural observation, institutions such as the Church and the Crown elaborated complex systems for naming, credentialing, and regulating groups based on their bloodlines, and documents relating to blood and lineage gained greater importance. Not every family could pay an official to authenticate its lineage. But the nobility could and often did.[13]

For a fee, families of dubious origins could produce documents that, effectively, purified their bloodlines by the mere assertion of blood purity. This practice was rather commonplace among the nobility who, despite claims to the contrary, "had been impregnated with Jewish blood." Jews and Moors who had converted to Christianity, known as conversos or *cristianos nuevos* (New Christians), numbered among the wealthiest and most influential families in the kingdoms of Castile and Aragón. In part because of their gaining power, public resentment toward conversos grew widespread. Rival

Old Christian families seized on this resentment and invoked rhetoric about blood purity as a means of dislodging New Christians from ecclesiastical and civic posts.[14]

The persecution of conversos proved most virulent and sustained in the city of Toledo. In that bustling and diverse Castilian capital, Old Christian forces, led by the Toledo *asistente* (supervisory official), Pedro Sarmiento, seized on the fragile state of the monarchy of Juan II in 1449 to issue a statute prohibiting New Christians from occupying civic office as *regidores, escribanos,* or *mayordomos.* The statute had little measurable impact locally, as only fifteen Toledo New Christians were expelled from their posts, but its implications rippled throughout the countryside. Anti-converso sentiment gained in villages and towns in the central provinces, as well as in Andalucía to the south. Sarmiento sought royal and papal support for his statute, but he was met with scorn by Juan II and Pope Nicolas V, and he was dismissed from his post.[15]

The conversos' reprieve from Old Christian persecution in Toledo proved short-lived. Less than twenty years later, the city was again rife with conflict between Christians old and new—the former marshaled by the Ayala family and the latter by the Silvas. Animosity between the factions soon grew violent. In 1467, anti-converso riots resulted in a tragic fire that destroyed sixteen hundred homes and left large numbers of conversos dead in the streets. Many more found themselves dispossessed, expelled from their civic posts. Conversos nonetheless rebounded from their defeat. Within a few years, they had rebuilt their homes and were reinstated in public positions by royal decree.

The disturbances that rocked Toledo, and similar ones in Seville and throughout the peninsula, demonstrate that the fixation with purity of blood permeated all levels of Spanish society. Blood purity was not the cause of the nobility alone. Rather, both in principle and practice, anti-converso discrimination reflected the common sentiment of a people living under a succession of tenuous monarchs during an era of intense economic duress. Both by the Old Christian nobility and by the populace at large, prominent conversos would become feared for their power, despised for their "tainted blood," and envied for their property.[16]

The marriage of Ferdinand II of Castile to Isabel I of Aragón in 1469, and their ascent to the throne five years later, promised a new era for the Spanish kingdom, one marked by unity, conformity, and empire. The *Reyes Católicos* (Catholic monarchs) wasted little time in moving to unify their Christian subjects. In 1478, they established the Spanish Inquisition to investigate cases of "insincere conversion," whereby converts proclaimed a Christian faith but secretly preserved their Jewish or Muslim texts and practices. In fact, such instances were not uncommon. Crypto-Jewish communities thrived in Spain and would continue to do so in the Americas, despite centuries of oppression. As elsewhere in Christian Europe, those tried and convicted of heresy met a swift and often violent end. Spanish Inquisitors, for their part, were themselves not free from tainted blood. Conversos ranked among the most zealous prosecutors of infidels, a fact that hints at their otherwise precarious social standing amid a fractious society. Indeed, the inquisitor general himself, Tomás de Torquemada, is said to have possessed Jewish antecedents, as did his successor, Fray Diego de Deza. Conversos were among the most ardent supporters of the Crown and filled many important positions therein. It is thought that their position of authority and their righteousness removed them from suspicion of heresy.[17]

Though professed Jews and Moors were not the initial object of the Inquisition, inquisitors soon targeted these communities. The Catholic Monarchs' campaign resulted in the mass conversion of Jews and Moors and, ultimately, in the expulsion of the Moors from the peninsula. The year 1492 thus signaled not just the spiritual "purification" of the populace, but also the revindication of Catholicism—first by way of the recapture of Granada from the Moors and second by way of the "discovery" of a new world of "infidels" awaiting conversion and exploitation. Purity of blood, therefore, had become equated with conquest; it was the defining symbol of Spanish Catholic identity, and would remain so for the better part of three centuries in the New World.[18]

Economic motivations notwithstanding, the Americas presented the royals an opportunity to craft a more idyllic Spanish society, one presumably uncorrupted by Jewish or Moorish blood or beliefs. For this reason, successors to the Reyes Católicos implemented stiff restrictions on the passage of Spaniards to the New World. In the sixteenth century, whatever Jews or Moors remained in Spain were prohibited from embarking for America, as were conversos and their kin. Naturally, for every rule there were as many exceptions as money could buy, but by law the persecution of conversos persisted in civic as well as ecclesiastic realms. The Inquisition's much-feared *autos de fé* (trials of faith) continued in Spain unabated, as did strict *estatutos* (statutes) regarding blood purity for civic and ecclesiastic office. Though the so-called New World was steeped in indigenous civilizations, it afforded Spaniards new lands in which to carry out their spiritual and economic missions. Consequently, the American Inquisition varied markedly from its Spanish counterpart.

In America, the Inquisition was not established until 1570 in Lima, and 1571 in Mexico City. It was neither founded in the same circumstances nor carried out with same rigor as the Inquisition in Spain. Many Spanish conversos and crypto-Jews had circumvented the Crown's ban on their emigration to America; and although they comprised a significant portion of the émigré population, their presence was not widely acknowledged. They ensconced themselves rather effectively among Old Christian compatriots in the New World, and thus became an invisible minority within Spanish colonial society. Their assimilation was so thorough that, from 1570 to 1831 (the duration of the American Inquisition), less than one hundred are said to have been sentenced to death for "heresy," a fraction of the number so punished in Spain.[19] Unlike Iberian autos de fé, the American Inquisition was hardly concerned with questions of sincerity of faith, purity of blood, or the depth of one's Christian ancestry; rather, individuals were more likely to be put on trial for their deeds and alleged moral transgressions—such as bigamy, witchcraft, and licentious behavior on the part of clergy—than for their "insincere" faith.

Whatever Spain's spiritual or economic agenda, it is clear that its exploits produced anything but an idyllic colonial society. Indigenous America proved far more diverse and expansive than the Iberian Peninsula, and the conquest of this immense new world proved immeasurably more challenging. If a Catholic/Spanish peoplehood was born on the peninsula, it was wholly transformed by the processes of conquest and colonization in America. Spain's colonies were populated by diverse indigenous peoples, whom Spaniards uniformly identified as indios. Indians represented the new infidels of Christianity. Collectively they symbolized the heathen "other" that Spaniards would seek out to vanquish through conversion, colonization, or extermination.

ꝑ Casta and Calidad in the New World

In Spanish America, as on the peninsula, blood purity was a mark of one's faith, parentage, and caste. But the language of blood that had evolved in Spain became more complex in the New World. The initial "contaminant" of Spanish blood in America was "Indian" blood; however, with the spread of African slavery, so-called *negros* (blacks) also became an additional referent against which Spanish identity would be cast. Like Indians, African slaves were diverse in origin and culture, yet, in Spanish eyes, they too were seen as a singular, inferior people. The objectified Indian and African represented the antithesis to Spanish spiritual, racial, and cultural identity. Individuals who were not born to Catholic, white, and Spanish parents were deemed inferior and were therefore subject to conversion, enslavement, or some other form of exploitation. Colonial relations were premised on the dichotomy between Spaniards and their subjects.[20]

Spaniards' identity was no less complex than that of their indio and negro subjects. Just as the latter groups were composed of a multitude of peoples possessing very distinct regional origins, cultures, and beliefs, so did Spaniards possess diverse roots on the Iberian Peninsula. The Spaniard who ventured to America in the name of God, gold, and Crown strongly identified with the province of his birth. The attachment to one's *patria chica,* or "small fatherland," led Spaniards to proclaim themselves *estremeños* (Extremadurans), *gallegos* (Galicians), *catalanes* (Catalans), *castellanos* (Castilians), *andaluces* (Andalucians), and so on. If united in their Christian zeal, Spaniards were highly differentiated by their respective places of birth, or patrias chicas. The comprehensive notion of Spanish "citizenship" or "nationhood" had not yet taken root among colonizers of the New World.[21] The attachment to place of birth led to a distinction between Spaniards born in the New World (*criollos*) and those born on the Iberian Peninsula (*peninsulares*). Peninsulares held higher rank than American-born criollos in both civic and ecclesiastic office—a trend that mirrored the distinction between "Old" and "New" Christians. By the nineteenth century, antagonism between peninsulares and criollos fomented social and political unrest that contributed to independence movements throughout the hemisphere. Nonetheless, for three centuries, to be either a peninsular or a criollo made one a Christian, a conqueror, and an español.[22]

Spaniards thought of themselves as not just superior to Indians and Africans, but as progenitors of the One True Faith. The spiritual dichotomy between Christians and non-Christians was articulated in terms of righteousness and education. According to the conquistadores, there were those who had acquired the faculties of Western Christian thought and those who had not. The former were referred to as *gente de razón* (literally translated as "people of reason"), and the latter as *gente sin razón* ("people without reason"). To be a person "of reason" meant that one had adopted a worldview that was distinctly Western and Christian, in the words of one historian, "to achieve the same split of body and mind that their civilizers accepted." Reason implied discipline and control over one's body and actions, while acknowledging one's divine Christian destiny. For Indians, such a worldview was acquired only through total spiritual and cultural conversion. Only as neophytes, or converts, could Indians' souls be redeemed in the eyes of their colonizers.[23]

But even spiritual redemption did not make them equal to Spaniards. In New Mexico, Hispanicized Indians, or *genízaros,* were never fully accepted by the self-proclaimed españoles, even though they had acquired the same manners, language, and beliefs. For this reason, it has been posited, genízaros established their own communities on the geographic and social margins of Spanish settlements. The divide that separated Spaniards from their Indian subjects was only nominally narrowed through conversion and Hispanization. Pueblo Indians resisted colonization and conversion in myriad ways. They "compartmentalized" their religious beliefs and practices, rendering the appearance of Catholicism while preserving in secret their traditional religions. They also openly, sometimes violently, resisted Spanish oppression, thus reinforcing the divide between Spaniards and Indians. The simple designation *español* alluded to one's legacy of Christianity and conquest.[24]

In New Mexico, as elsewhere, conquest had its privileges. The Spaniards who settled on New Mexican soil—those who comprised Juan de Oñate's 1598 expedition—were awarded noble titles and the right to exact labor from their Indian subjects. One important example was the *encomienda*. Drawing on tradition dating to the Iberian Reconquest, King Philip II, in 1575, ordered all those Spaniards who would participate in the "pacification of the American Indies" (that is, Indians) to be given the title of *hijo dalgo* (a contraction of *hijo de algo*, which literally translates as "the son of someone/something"), so that they might "enjoy the honors and privileges according to the customs and laws of Spain." These privileges were passed down to the male heirs of the conquistadores so long as the conquered land remained occupied.[25]

In the Hispanic diaspora, consanguinity determined one's identity and social position. Purity of blood in New Mexico implied not just spiritual purity, but the preservation of Spanish privilege, power, and honor. Families of high social standing proclaimed themselves "pure-blood Spaniards." "Our families," insisted Joseph Romo de Vera and Angela Valdez in 1745, "are Old Christian Spaniards, descendants of such, and pure of taint with the bad races—Moors, Jews, and those newly admitted to the flock of Holy Mother church." To be an español was to be an "Old Christian" and a conquistador—part of the dominant political, religious, and social apparatus. In America, as in Spain, blood remained the axis around which social identities were fashioned. As Spanish and criollo settlers mixed and married with the Indian and African populations, their progeny presented ruling Spanish authorities with predicaments of spiritual, racial, and social identity.[26]

∴ The Demography of Mestizaje

Throughout the colonial period (1598–1821) and into the Mexican period (1821–46), New Mexican society was regulated and stratified by (among other things) *casta* (caste or race) and *calidad* (social status or honor).[27] Not absolute or fixed, these concepts overlapped and varied in importance according to the social contexts and historical periods in which they were invoked. Like the notion of purity of blood, casta and calidad figured centrally in the daily operations of civic and religious institutions; they served to describe individuals according to their racial phenotype, honor, and wealth. The notion of casta reaffirmed the Spanish fixation with blood and parentage. It gave order and structure to an increasingly "mixed-blood" colonial society. Historian Ramón A. Gutiérrez notes that casta was something akin to race or raza, which the first edition of the *Diccionario de la Lengua Española* (published in 1737) defined as "The caste or racial status of origin. When speaking of persons, it usually means illegitimacy. Also, stain or dishonor of the lineage."[28] As used in northern New Mexico, *casta* generally referred to mixtures of Spanish, Indian, and/or African "races." Thus, censuses of the eighteenth and early nineteenth centuries employed the three categories "españoles," "indios," and "castas" when enumerating the population. The term *color quebrado* (broken color) was also used as a synonym for someone of mixed race and phenotype. According to Gutiérrez, "Mixed color was a sign of illegitimate birth associated with illicit sexual unions. The racially mixed progeny who resulted from concubinage and adultery ultimately led to the blurring of racial phenotypes in the population, and this, particularly after the 1760s, necessitated a stricter racial classification of the population. Without such categories, the aristocracy's claims of racial purity and honor had no significance."[29] In order to monitor their own presumed purity of blood, españoles elaborated in the eighteenth century a formula of castas by which individuals would be identified at birth, at marriage, by the courts, and in censuses (table 1.1).

As previously noted, caste labels were derived from one's parentage and referred either directly or indirectly to three racial archetypes: español (person of Spanish origin), indio, or negro (person of African origin). For example, the child of a Spanish parent and an Indian parent was deemed a *mestizo* or *mestiza*. That of a Spanish parent and mestizo/a parent was a *castizo/a*. And the offspring of a Spanish parent and a castizo/a parent reclaimed his/her Spanish identity and was deemed an español or española.[30] This last example demonstrates that blood was something which, in the context of colonial relations, could be redeemed through greater procreation with Spaniards. Thus identity alluded to the proportion of Spanish and non-Spanish blood that one possessed, and blood was measured in terms of family lineage, or consanguinity. Although lineage represented the formal means by which castes were defined, appearance or phenotype often corresponded to one's caste. Dress, hairstyle, and skin color differentiated an español from a mestizo, and a mestizo from a castizo, and so on. In the same subjective manner, casta often corresponded to one's occupation, or *clase*. Those who worked with their hands (typically indios and the mixed castas) were held in lower esteem by administrators and government officials, predominantly self-labeled españoles.[31]

The rates at which Spanish, Indian, and African-origin populations mixed varied over time and space. Some scholars have

Table 1.1

Select Caste Designations According to Parentage

Father	Mother	Offspring
Español	India	Mestizo
Español	Mestiza	Castizo
Español	Castiza	Español
Español	Negra	Mulato
Español	Mulata	Morisco
Español	Morisca	Albino
Español	Albina	Torna atrás
Español	Torna atrás	Tente en el aire
Indio	Negra	Cambujo
Chino cambujo	India	Lobo
Lobo	India	Albarazado
Albarazado	Mestiza	Barnocino
Barnocino	India	Sambaigo
Mestizo	Castiza	Chamiso
Mestizo	India	Coyote

Source: Aguirre Beltrán, Colección Larrauri Montaño (n.p., 1946), as quoted in Hensley C. Woodbridge, "Glossary of Names Used in Colonial Latin America for Crosses among Indians, Negroes, and Whites," *Journal of the Washington Academy of Sciences* 38, no. 11 (15 November 1948), 355.

Note: Beltrán's study, though published in 1946, focused on caste identities that appeared in seventeenth- and eighteenth-century documents.

attempted to gauge the extent of their mixture. Writing in 1946, Aguirre Beltrán concluded that persons of mixed racial parentage in New Spain comprised just 0.44 percent of the population in 1570; 22.6 percent in 1646; 36.6 percent in 1742; 38.7 percent in 1793; and 39.5 percent in 1810.[32] The validity of these numbers, it should be said, is premised on the faith that "race" represents a discrete scientific category that can be measured by tracing "bloodlines." It thus ignores the way in which "race" was politically or socially defined, or how the importance of race gained or declined over time.

Race was not a fixed, constant idea. Consequently, an individual's casta could change over his or her lifetime, especially if one had the

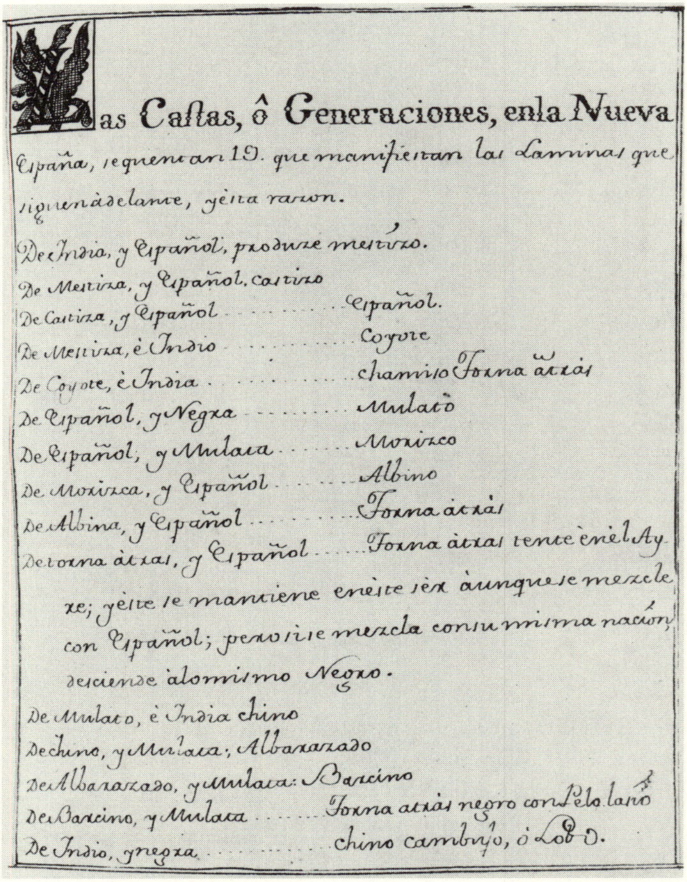

Las Castas, ô Generaciones, enla Nueva España, se quentan 19. que manifiestan las Laminas que siguen adelante, yesta razon.

De India, y Español, produze mestizo.
De Mestiza, y Español, castizo
De Castiza, y Español .... Español.
De Mestiza, è Indio .... Coyote
De Coyote, è India . ... chamiso Torna atras
De Español, y Negra .... Mulato
De Español, y Mulata .... Morisco
De Morisca, y Español .... Albino
De Albina, y Español .... Torna atras
De torna atras, y Español .... Torna atras tente en el Ayre; yeste se mantiene en este sex aunque se mezcle con Español; pero si se mezcla con su misma nacion, desciense alomismo Negro.
De Mulato, è India chino
De chino, y Mulata, Albarazado
De Albarazado, y mulata: Barcino
De Barcino, y Mulata .... Torna atras negro con Pelo lano
De Indio, y negra. .... chino cambujo, ô Lobo.

Figure 1. "Las Castas, ô Generaciones, en la Nueva España . . ." (The castes, or generations of New Spain), from Joachin Antonio de Barafás's manuscript, *Origen, costumbres, y estado presente de mexicanos y philipinos* (1763). Courtesy of the Hispanic Society of America, New York.

economic or political means to redefine one's official racial designation by purchasing a *gracias al sacar*.[33] In some instances, the drift was downward, reflecting the individual's desire to marry at the expense of his or her social status.[34] For males, notes Gutiérrez, this was called *hypergamy*. More common, however, was the tendency to adopt a higher caste upon marriage, thereby uplifting one's self and family in the racial hierarchy of colonial society.[35] For males, this was *hypogamy*. Caste formulas were not etched in stone.[36]

Figure 2. "De Mestisa I Indio sale Coyote" (Mestiza and
Indian Make Coyote), from Joachin Antonio de
Barafás's manuscript, *Origen, costumbres, y estado presente
de mexicanos y philipinos* (1763). Courtesy of the
Hispanic Society of America, New York.

Caste labels more often than not corresponded to local naming
practice. They varied from region to region and social context to
social context. Where regions possessed high numbers of African-
origin populations, such as the Caribbean, officials had constructed
many terms to describe the exact degrees of African blood that an
individual possessed. In regions where African slaves were less prevalent, such as New Mexico and the Californias, officials employed just
one term, *mulato,* to describe individuals who possessed any degree
of African blood, and abandoned the term *negro.* Although mulatos

numbered among the original settlers of New Mexico, they comprised a relatively small proportion of the population, and thus their "official" numbers were often diminished over time by civic authorities.[37] Mulatos comprised 2.6 percent of New Mexico's population in 1790, but by 1812 officials were not acknowledging their presence. That year, in a report read before the Spanish Cortes in Sevilla, Pedro Bautista boasted erroneously that "[i]n New Mexico, there are no castes of people of African origin. New Mexico has never known any caste of people of African origin."[38]

Caste labels also varied across time within New Mexico, and gradually diminished in complexity and number during the nineteenth century, reflecting the declining significance of bloodlines and the rising significance of class and individual wealth in stratifying society. As with the term "mulato," many caste designations that once permeated colonial record books were phased out in the nineteenth century.[39] Censuses and marriage records suggest that officials began labeling individuals less according to their casta than their residency (in the town or parish) or their calidad (often alluded to by reference to one's "legitimacy" of marriage or birth). The collapse of the caste structure coincided with the increasing use of two predominant categories to enumerate individuals in civic and ecclesiastic records: español and indio.[40] From 1790 to the 1840s, civic and religious officials employed various labels in enumerating their respective constituencies. Censuses and marriage records bear out this change.

In 1790, prompted by an order of the viceroy, civic authorities throughout New Spain set about enumerating their respective jurisdictions according to family, age, caste, occupation, and sex. The censuses they produced remain some of the most extensively studied documents of the colonial period, for they reveal the particular concerns and social categories that officials felt were necessary to document at that time.[41] Alicia V. Tjarks has produced a most thorough analysis of the 1790 New Mexico census, which included numbers for the four largest population centers: El Paso, Albuquerque (Río Abajo), Santa Fé, and Santa Cruz de la Cañada. As Tjarks's data suggest (table 1.2), the term "español" was the most frequent in the censuses for non–Pueblo Indian communities in northern New Mexico. Noting the large proportion of españoles and castas to indios, Tjarks suggests that "[t]he growth of the Spanish and caste towns contrasts markedly with the decadence of the Indian villages."[42] The declining

Table 1.2

Ethnic Structure of Northern New Mexico, 1790

PLACE	Spanish No.	%	Indian No.	%	Mestizo[c] No.	%	Mulato No.	%	Undetermined No.	%
Albuquerque	2,079	46.6	621	14.5	1,703	38.2	7	0.2	23	0.5
Santa Fe, Tesuque, and Pecos	1,476	53.8	456[a]	16.6	706	25.8	70	2.6	33	1.3
Santa Cruz, San Juan, and Picuris	2,525	58.6	590[b]	13.7	1,113	25.8	–	–	83	1.9

[a] Santa Fe (163), Tesuque (142), Pecos (151).
[b] Santa Cruz (13), San Juan (352), Picuris (225).
[c] This category includes those labeled coyotes and color quebrado.

Source: Adapted from New Mexico State Records Center and Archives, Spanish Archives, Santa Fe, Local Census Reports (1790), as cited in Alicia V. Tjarks, "Demographic, Ethnic and Occupational Structure of New Mexico, 1790," *The Americas: A Quarterly Review of Inter-American Cultural History* 35 (July 1978): 83.

"integrity" of the Indian communities, says Tjarks, was due to three factors: miscegenation (between Indians and non-Indians), the decrease in birth rates among Pueblo Indians, and high mortality. Whatever the reason for their decline, the Indian pueblos of northern New Mexico were viewed as discrete entities separate, and yet intimately related to, Spanish and caste neighboring communities. They were therefore enumerated as separate entities, whereas numbers for "Spaniards" and "castes" were often lumped together in census summaries. Indeed, the 1790 census represents one of the foremost official documents making distinctions among the various castes (that is, mestizos, *coyotes, lobos,* mulatos, and color quebrado).

Expanding on Tjarks's work, Adrián Bustamante offered his own data collected from the 1790 census, which differ from Tjarks's numbers, especially where enumeration of castas is concerned. Bustamante's data indicate that officials used seven caste categories to classify individuals: español, indios and *vecinos* (Indians and "neighbors," or residents), mestizos, coyotes, color quebrado, genízaros, and mulatos (see table 1.3.).[43] Of the nearly three thousand residents of Santa Fe, the largest portion of the population (57.1 percent) was classified as españoles. Significantly absent from the census is any reference to "Spaniards" by place of birth; that is, there was no differentiation between peninsulares and criollos. Since those classified as españoles were not born in Spain, but, rather were the descendants of native Spaniards, the term "español" had come to refer to family lineage, as opposed to place of birth. The next most numerous caste was color quebrado, at 13.7 percent. Its meaning is less precise, since it alludes to anyone of "broken color," which is to say, any person of an unknown degree of mixed blood. Whereas Tjarks found fewer than 2 percent of the individuals in her study to be of "undetermined" caste, Bustamante found that 13 percent of the population in Santa Fe were of "undetermined" caste. Mestizos, according to Bustamante, comprised 7.4 percent; indios and vecinos, 3.8 percent; mulatos, 2.6 percent; genízaros, 1.6 percent; and coyotes, 0.66 percent. Taken together, the works of Tjarks and Bustamante point to the prevalence of the term "español" in enumerating the non–Pueblo Indian settlements in northern New Mexico. According to Tjarks, the 1790 census indicates "a clear predominance of the white or Spanish element over the half-breed population."[44]

When compared to data collected for all of New Spain, it is evident that officials in northern New Mexico recorded a much higher proportion of "españoles" to people of recognized mixed blood. Whereas in New Mexico españoles represented more than 50 percent of the non–indio population, a 1774 ecclesiastical census found that españoles comprised just 20 percent of the non–indio population for all of New Spain, and just 9 percent of the total population of New Spain (including indios).[45] This does not mean, however, that racial mixture, or mestizaje, between Spaniards and

Table 1.3

Population of Santa Fé, 1790 by Caste

Españoles		Indios y Vecinos		Mestizos		Coyotes		Color Quebrado		Genízaros		Mulatos		Undetermined	
no.	%	no.	%	no.	%	no.	%	no.	%	no.	%	no.	%	no.	%
1,719	57.1	113	3.8	225	7.4	20	.7	411	13.7	49	1.6	79	2.6	394	13.0

Source: Adapted from table 3, Adrian Herminio Bustamante, "Los Hispanos: Ethnicity and Social Change in New Mexico" (PhD diss., University of New Mexico, 1982), 53.

non-Spaniards did not occur; rather, the label "Spaniard" held a meaning other than "of pure Spanish blood."

Tjarks proposes that those who called themselves españoles were neither born in Spain nor necessarily "pure-blood" descendants of the conquistadores. Many Spaniards enumerated in the 1790 census, she writes, were "Spanish in name only," since their forefathers who had participated in the 1693 reconquest of northern New Mexico were "half-breed families from New Spain," who were "already miscegenated."[46] The persistence of the term "español," Tjarks posits, was due to the "cultural assimilation and the social prestige implicit in the status of the first settlers."[47] Bustamante reaffirms Tjarks opinion: "español was the highest category where status mattered. Since this is the case, it is safe to assume that individuals would strive to achieve this identity. This category would include those who were genetically Spaniards and those who achieved that identity by claiming to be Spaniards and being accepted as such by the true Spaniards."[48] Although Tjarks and Bustamante do not state it explicitly, both view the category "español" as a social construction, a category not based on strict genealogy or "pure" bloodlines. Indeed, it would be fallacious to attempt a genealogical reconstruction of those who appeared as "españoles" in the 1790 census and to trace their origins to Spain, since the very notion of Spanishness was rooted less in principles of biology or documented genealogy than in the social construction and regulation of "Spanish" culture in New Mexico. Whereas the former consisted of strict documentation of consanguinity, the latter consisted of fervent Catholicism and the ideology of honor and conquest.

After the 1790 census, reference to specific castas, such as coyote, mestizo, and mulato, declined. Increasingly, both civic and ecclesiastical authorities classified individuals in one of three categories: españoles, indios, or castas. This was the case in 1794, when Governor Chacón reported 7,502 españoles, 4,343 indios, and 1,941 castas in New Mexico.[49] Similarly, in 1808, Fray Josef Pereyro enumerated 4,734 "españoles y castas" in the Villa Capital de Santa Fé, and no "indios who pertain that jurisdiction."[50] In his 1812 *Exposición Sucinta y Sencilla de la Provincia del Nuevo México,* Pedro Bautista Pino described the region's population as consisting of "26 Indian populations and 102 Spanish plazas."[51] Pino made no mention of "castas" or mixed-blood persons in New Mexico, except in reference to four communities—Cinecú, Isleta, Socorro, and Real—whose "castes of people . . . are from the Indian nations that surround these commu-nities."[52] Written while Pino was in Spain to persuade the Spanish Cortes to address the underdeveloped condition of New Mexico, the *Exposición* boasted the absence of "castes of African-origin peo-ples," proclaiming, "Perhaps my province is the only one that can make this claim in all of Spanish America. Spaniards and pure Indians (who can hardly be distinguished from us) are those that comprise the 40 thousand inhabitants."[53]

While some colonial officials reduced the population to two racial archetypes—Spanish and Indian—others varied widely in their description of New Mexico's population. Fray Antonio García del Valle's inconsistency in caste labeling makes clear this point. From 1811 to 1818, he employed "español," "mestizo," "indio," and, occa-sionally, "vecino," which refers rather ambiguously to "residents" of the place in question. In 1814, he referred to José Miguel Brito of San Miguel del Vado as an "Yndio," although three years earlier, García had labeled Brito a "vecino." In 1808, Brito was listed as a "genízaro" by García's predecessor. Even "Spaniards" were victim-ized by the officials' inconsistent labeling. In 1804, Spaniard Ramón Archuleta was mistakenly registered as a genízaro by Fray Francisco Bragado, where four years earlier he was an español, according to another friar, Diego Martínez.[54]

By 1820, the collapse of caste categories in northern New Mexico was complete. A parish census of that year listed but two "castas": "Indios" and "Españoles y Gentes de otras Clases" (Spaniards and people of other classes).[55] No effort was made to define those "of other classes." In 1822, a church census of Santa Cruz de la Cañada listed all parishioners as either "españoles" or "indios," with no ref-erence whatever to "other clases" or "other castes."[56] Those who were not clearly "indios," or Pueblo Indians living within the corporate pueblo as accepted members, were deemed "españoles."

What were the social implications of one's caste identity? How did the decline of the caste system reflect changes in social values, in marital patterns? To arrive at answers about casta and identity, we must explore the related concept of "calidad," for one cannot discuss the notion of "casta" outside the notion of "calidad." Together, they comprised the social identity of the individual between 1693 and 1846. "Calidad" referred literally to one's "quality," or social status. The *Primer diccionario general etimológico de la Lengua Española* defined this term as "the various qualities which constitute the essence of a person or thing, that which constitutes the status of a person, his nature, his age and other circumstances and conditions."[57] According to Robert McCaa, "Color, occupation, and wealth might influence one's calidad, as did purity of blood, honor, integrity, and even place of origin."[58] Ramón A. Gutiérrez equates calidad with social status, which determined how one was treated under the law: "Whenever anyone came before a legal tribunal, whether civil or ecclesiastical, the judge was always eager to determine the person's calidad or social status. . . . [P]unishment was meted out differentially according to one's status. Thus, legal documents always began with a formulaic statement to the effect that *Fulano de tal*'es de calidad mestizo, obrero, hijo legítimo de tal y tal y cristiano nuevo' (John Doe's social status is mestizo, laborer, the legitimate son of so and so, and a New Christian)."[59] One's calidad, therefore, implied the overall social status of the individual, including his or her "legitimacy," which was premised on marriage within the Church and procreation in the "legitimate" marriage. Marriage, then, represented "the most important ritual event in the course of life," because it involved "the union of two properties, the joining of two households, the creation of a web of affinal alliances, and the perpetuation of a family's symbolic patrimony—its name and reputation."[60] In marriage, the honor of the family preceded all other considerations, and therefore marriages were usually arranged by the families in question. Individuals and their families aspired to marry into families of equal or greater social standing, so as to preserve not only the family's cumulative resources, labor, and power over subordinate castes, but also to enhance their own honor and reputation. Thus, according to McCaa, "Homogamy was the basic rule."[61]

In colonial New Spain, three dimensions of homogamy prevailed: selection by race, status, and birthplace. "These factors acted together in a simple—though not absolute—fashion," writes McCaa, "like marrying like; the combined effect was to constrict sharply the size of the mating pools from which people seeking to marry made their choices."[62] Even when individuals married outside their particular social group, they aspired to the highest possible racial standard; thus, in half of all mixed marriages in Parral, Mexico, between 1788 and 1790, "either the groom (or more likely the bride) changed racial status at marriage."[63] Marital partner selection, in this case, depended more on caste/race than on occupational status. That being said, the Church continued to play the leading role in determining who were appropriate and inappropriate marital partners, and it delineated two classes of canonic impediments to marriage. The least frequent were known as preventative impediments. These could be circumvented by dispensations from the local clergy. The more frequent and severe were known as dire impediments, and these required papal or episcopal dispensations. Dire impediments included, among other things, consanguinity, or marriage to a relative between the first and fourth degrees.

Gutiérrez's study of marital records, or *diligencias matrimoniales,* of the Archdiocese of Santa Fe shows that consanguinity and affinity represented the most common reasons for dispensations in New Mexico between 1694 and 1846. Of the 250 consanguinity dispensations granted to New Mexicans, none pertained to the marriage of immediate siblings (brothers and sisters); rather, all were for marriage between relatives of the second degree (first cousin), third degree (second cousin), and fourth degree (third cousin) of consanguinity. Marriages between close cousins occurred more often among the nobility, who had submitted 160 of the dispensation requests. Endogamy preserved the nobility's blood purity, honor, and social status, and protected the families' material interests from outside intrusion. Gutiérrez's study shows that Spanish men in the Albuquerque area tended to marry Spanish women at a rate of 78.8 percent in 1750, and at a similar rate in 1790. Tjarks's study confirms that endogamic marriages were the norm in Santa Fe as well, comprising some 71 percent of marriages there in 1790. After 1800, as caste categories were collapsed into "Spanish" and "Indian" groups, endogamy rose, such that those who were now deemed "españoles" or "españoles y castas" married among themselves at a rate of 97 to 100 percent, according to Gutiérrez's data. This figure is likely exaggerated due to the small percentage of marital candidates who declared their race. Conversely, exogamous marriages were evident among the "popular classes," writes Gutiérrez, "due to the blurring of racial boundaries."[64] With the rise of liberal principles and the establishment of the Spanish Córtes in 1808, concepts of civic equality and citizenship had begun to erode the need for subtler caste distinctions.

The decline of mixed-blood racial designations in the early years of the nineteenth century rendered new meaning to the terms "español" and "indio." By 1820, they referred less to degrees of blood purity or racial mixture than to cultural, ethnic, and geopolitical boundaries that separated Pueblo Indians from the amorphous vecinos (previously known as españoles and castas) that resided near them. Ethnic and cultural distinctions were evident in parish membership, religious traditions, languages, governments, and legal designations. In his meticulous study of vecino culture, Ross Frank concludes that decades of intermarriage between Pueblo Indians and castas had wrought the emergence of a distinctive vecino culture and civic identity, "defined in large part in contradistinction to that of the Pueblos."[65] Though unified by a common culture, economic divisions persisted and grew among vecinos themselves, as already prosperous families acquired more wealth and power by consolidating their grasp on land and political offices.

ジ Ascendant Vecinos, 1821-1846

Individual identity during the Mexican period was rooted in family relations, one's native community, one's class, and the dynamic of Pueblo–Spanish ethnic relations that were unique to New Mexico.[66] These distinctions, combined with the relative isolation from, and poor communication with, central Mexico, mitigated whatever affinity with the Mexican capital developed between 1821 and 1846. New Mexico's most remarkable social divisions during this period, in addition to sexual and gender divisions, were between the ricos and the *pobres,* and between the indios and the amorphous and numerically dominant population of vecinos.

Mexican independence from Spain in 1821 did not significantly alter the ethnic consciousness of northern New Mexicans, nor did it instill a profound and pervasive Mexican consciousness rooted in national sentiment. It did, however, diminish the use of caste referents in civic documents and accelerate the growing liberal notion of civic equality among all categories of people. For "españoles y castas," equality presented them with an opportunity to gain access to previously protected Pueblo Indian lands and resources. The liberal movement toward legal equality between Spaniards and Indians was aided by legislation of the Cortes in 1811, which removed old legal distinctions between Spaniards and Indians, and in doing so also removed special legal protections for the latter as wards of the Crown.

When this legislation was forwarded to New Mexico in 1821, Governor Facundo Melgares wrote that the Pueblo Indians should be considered "as Spanish in all things."[67]

On achieving independence, Mexican authorities, including those in New Mexico, sought to implement the principles of legal equality, but often with less-than-auspicious intentions. According to the Constitution of 1824, all Mexican citizens, including Indians, were made equal before the law.[68] Thereafter, assemblymen in New Mexico began to refer to Pueblo Indians as *hijos, naturales,* or *ciudadanos* instead of indios. Priests were instructed not to record an individual's caste in their parish records; with increasing regularity, they began invoking the term "vecino" (literally, "neighbor") in lieu of the terms "español" and "casta." As already mentioned, the term "vecino" denoted both a cultural and a civic identity, rather than caste or race. Gutiérrez's study of marriage records reflected this change in nomenclature. While "vecino" was the most common designation for the calidad of marital candidates between 1690 and 1759, "casta" became more frequently used in referring to one's calidad between 1760 and 1819. During this period, more marital candidates were labeled by their caste than by the civic term "vecino." Between 1820 and 1846, however, "vecino" once again became the most frequent designation for calidad. Nonetheless, 678 individuals were registered as españoles between 1820 and 1839, while 2,510 were "vecinos" and 384 were "residentes." Between 1840 and 1846, no individuals were classified as españoles, according to Gutiérrez's data, while 1,679 vecinos registered for marriage, and only 9 mexicanos did the same.[69]

One must use caution in interpreting these calidad designations, since the ecclesiastical documents that contained them were products of the clergy elite, and since Gutiérrez's sample size varies dramatically from one period to the next; yet from these data, it may be deduced that a fervent "mexicano" national identity did not flourish in New Mexico during the Mexican period. This deduction helps to explain why the twenty-five years of Mexican rule in New Mexico did not become etched into the historical identity that "Spanish Americans" later would articulate in newspapers and academic writings.

Civic designations supplanted racial ones during the Mexican period and widened the ethnic divide between Pueblo Indians and vecinos. What the two communities shared was equality before the law, albeit an equality that seldom translated into equality in social and political terms. If anything, legal equality opened the door for greater access to Indian land on the part of vecinos, thereby exacerbating historic tensions between the two peoples over land and water. In the view of dominant vecinos, if the new nation's "three guarantees" of the 1821 Plan de Iguala—independence, equality, and unity—were to be fully achieved, the integration of Pueblo Indians and their lands with those of other Mexican citizens was necessary. Independence thus exposed the Pueblos to vecino land grabs.[70] By 1821, vecinos had encroached on the pueblos in unprecedented numbers, and by 1823, vecinos outnumbered Pueblo Indians in fourteen pueblos.[71] As G. Emlen Hall and David J. Weber have noted, "With the coming of Mexican Independence, legislation began to undermine the sanctity of the square league of the Pueblo Indians."[72] Equality implied the destruction of legal protection of communal Indian land.

By 1824, the threat to Indian lands had become real. On February 16, eighteen non-Indians submitted three different petitions to the seven-member *diputación* (presided over by the governor) to occupy and own farmland (*tierra de labor*) belonging to San Felipe and Santo Domingo pueblos. The petitioners based their claim on the premise that the "surplus" communal lands lay dormant and, under a Spanish law of 1812, were subject to settlement by non-Indians. The diputación decided that the Indians were entitled to individual ownership of their lands, and could thenceforth sell or lease their allotments as each individual saw fit. It is not known how many petitioners gained access to the two pueblos' lands; however, as Hall and Weber state, such litigation made one thing eminently clear: "Liberalism had clearly come to the Pueblos."[73]

Problems of encroachments on other Indian lands did not abate. The following year, when "naturales" of Pecos Pueblo complained to the diputación that non-Indians had been wrongly granted land that encroached on their league, commissioners replied that "just as their [the Pecos Indians'] obligations have ceased, so have their privileges ended. They are equal to one another, to all the other citizens who with them form the great Mexican family."[74] The diputación firmly supported the liberal concept of individual land ownership among the Pueblo Indians, and the distribution (at the diputación's discretion) of supposedly unoccupied or "surplus" communal lands. It sent a two-man commission—José Francisco Ortiz and Matias Ortiz—to Pecos with instructions to distribute surplus lands among ten families at the pueblo, so that the Indians might exercise their right to sell or otherwise dispose of their allotment. According to Hall and Weber, lands that remained unassigned were then parceled out to eleven families of "non Indians who were 'absolutely desolate.'"[75]

By September 1825 the liberal mandate of the diputación was being less vigorously enforced. The diputación, under the leadership of the new governor of New Mexico, Antonio Narbona, temporarily retreated from its earlier decision to redistribute Indian lands and referred pending Indian land questions to central authorities in Mexico City. The authorities' response apparently discouraged further allotment of Indian lands, since both requests and allotment efforts diminished after 1825. Meanwhile, the Pecos Indians sought the restoration of their original communal lands. It appears that vecinos had already begun to sell off their allotments, and additional encroachments had occurred. These problems continued for four years, until the diputación, in 1829, decided to restore the communal status of previously allotted surplus land while simultaneously upholding the rights of Indians to hold property either in common or individually. In short, the Pueblo Indians argued successfully for equal status with non-Indians, and for the right to own and/or sell their original lands, as earlier granted them by the Spanish Crown. "By appealing to their rights as citizens," write Hall and Weber, "the Pueblo Indians staved off the liberal threat to their communal property in the 1820s, even though they could not always protect themselves from squatters or resist the impulse to exercise their new rights to sell land."[76] Though equal citizenship, for Pueblo Indians, had both benefits and hazards, the law more often lent itself to the objectives of vecinos during the Mexican period.

Among vecinos themselves disparities of wealth wrought the occasional reminder of old social distinctions based on bloodlines. Though church and civic officials were ordered not to make reference to caste in official records, many apparently defied the order. Some families sought to remind others that theirs was pure, untainted Spanish blood. This was the case in 1822, when "Don Francisco Ortiz" and his wife, "Doña María García de Noriega," appeared before the Santa Fe mayor, Pedro Armendáriz, to answer questions as to their limpieza de sangre. The occasion was the nomination of their son, Rafael Ortiz, as a candidate for priesthood. To prove his purity of blood before church officials, Ortiz saw it necessary to formulate a list of five questions, which he asked be put to his three witnesses, who came from "the oldest families in this city": the illustrious Pedro Bautista Pino, Juan Cristóbal Vigil, and José Armijo. Each stepped forward to answer the mayor's interrogatories, which, loosely translated, read:

1. Can you confirm that Don Rafael Ortiz is the legitimate son of Don Francisco Ortiz and Doña María García de Noriega?

2. Can you confirm that during the marriage of said parents, they raised, educated, and presented Rafael as their son, and addressed him as such, and he addressed them as his parents?

3. Can you confirm that the grandparents of said son are Don Antonio José Ortiz, Captain of the Militia, who was the son of Don Nicolas Ortiz, Lieutenant of this Company, and his wife Doña Gertrudes Paes Urtado, daughter of Don Juan Paes Urtado, re-conqueror of this province . . . ?

4. Can you confirm that the mother of Rafael is the legitimate daughter of Captain Don José García de Noriega and Doña Rosalia Velarde del Villar . . . both of whose families have obtained honorable positions, and have been recognized as families with the best calidad, and as descendants of the first conquerors?

5. Can you confirm that these families are Spaniards of pure blood, free from all bad castes of Indians, Moors, and others who are not entitled to honorable position, or to serve in Ecclesiastical positions, or have been sentenced by any tribunal of the Inquisition . . . ?[77]

To each of the questions the three witnesses answered in the affirmative, emphasizing repeatedly that Rafael and his parents were "descendants of the conquerors and reconquerors of this province, privileged and characterized by their majesty with the title of *hijos dalgos*, of known origins," and were "pure-blood Old Christian Spaniards."[78] Both Rafael and his twin brother, Fernando Miguel, would go on to become prominent priests in New Mexico, as had their cousin, Ramón Ortiz.[79]

Such explicit claims about purity of blood were rare during the remainder of the Mexican period, but a few are to be found interspersed among the marriage petitions.[80] There is the additional example of José Antonio Vallejo, a "mexicano" who, in June 1833, sought a dispensation for the dire impediment of consanguinity. His bride-to-be, María Gertrudis García, also a "mexicana" according to their petition, was related by "the third and fourth degrees of consanguinity, transverse line." The petition sought a dispensation for consanguinity based on their mutual love and their desire to maintain their pure Spanish blood and social status in their community. "Both [candidates] are related to all or at least two thirds of the families of equal status, for having always preserved themselves pure as to blood, and with honor and mutual love." According to the pastor, there were three classes in his parish, "superior, medium, and lowest," and these families in question belonged to the first, for they had not tarnished their blood by mixing with the lower castes.[81] To prove this claim and gain the sympathy of the archbishop, the priest forwarded to the archbishop in Durango a family tree.

It should come as no surprise that the Ortiz and Vallejo families would attempt to remind their less wealthy and less powerful compatriots of their noble Spanish ancestry. According to Ruth R. Olivera and Liliene Crété, Mexican society remained highly stratified by race, in spite of declarations of "equality": "[T]he mention of whites, Indians, and *castas* was still found on official documents and in statistical tables, and the social hierarchy, according to foreign visitors, remained roughly the same as always. [In central Mexico,] [i]t was divided into six general groups: whites or Creoles (those who prided themselves on their descent from the Spanish, yet who might be of mixed blood), mestizos, mulattoes, zambos (descendants of Negroes and Indians), Indians, and Negroes."[82] In spite of proclamations to the contrary, New Mexican society also remained highly stratified. However, the rise of liberalism and the rhetoric of caste equality, combined with greater economic and social mobility and competition wrought by trade with the United States and Mexico, likely heightened insecurities among elite vecinos about their social position. Perhaps they felt the need to reassert their position by continuing to make reference to their purity of blood, but any insecurities defied substantiation in fact. Rather, during the Mexican administration, ricos—such as the landed Ortiz family—actually amassed more wealth and land than during the previous 128 years under Spain.[83] As elsewhere in Mexico, those families that occupied positions in the government, the military, and the Church aided one another in procuring land grants and circumventing trade laws. The Ortiz family, in particular, benefited directly from its political positions. In the Pecos land dispute, the diputación awarded Matías Ortiz and José Francisco Ortiz plots of "surplus land" at Pecos Pueblo for their service in parceling out Indian land among Pecos residents.[84] In short, the reigning self-identified españoles of northern New Mexico who traced their lineage to Spanish conquistadores and hidalgos were well entrenched in the most powerful echelons of Mexican society in Santa Fe, from church to civic to military realms; and they aided one another in maintaining their grasp on wealth and power, often at the expense of Pueblo Indians and less well-established vecinos. The story of the Ortiz land grant eloquently shows how ricos prospered under Mexico.

History speaks of a Mexican peasant who had the habit of herding his mules in the vicinity of El Real de Dolores, twenty-seven miles south of Santa Fe. It was there, one day in 1823, that this mule-hand made a remarkable discovery. He came upon a glistening stone that resembled those of his native Sonora. On closer inspection he saw that it was laden with particles of gold. When word reached Santa Fe that this Mexican had unwittingly discovered a gold placer, it caught the attention of everyone. Hundreds of prospectors flocked to the site from all parts of New Mexico and beyond. They set up small family operations out of which they eked a meager living; within a few years, the Dolores placer was the most productive in all of New Mexico. It was not long before mining at Dolores fell into the hands of the elite Ortiz family of Santa Fe and, ultimately, into the hands of Anglo Americans.[85]

As it happened, the Dolores placer, situated on unclaimed state domain, also caught the attention of Lt. José Francisco Ortiz, who had profited handsomely from his duties as land commissioner in the Pecos land dispute in 1825. As a lieutenant of the local militia, Ortiz

was stationed at Dolores and witnessed the flurry of mining excitement that followed the placer's discovery. By September 1833, Ortiz
himself became afflicted with gold fever. That year, he and a cohort,
Ignacio Cano, purchased the nearby "Santa Rosalia mine" from José
de Jesús García and Rafael Alejo, and shortly thereafter petitioned
the "Constitutional Mayor" in Santa Fe, Francisco Baca Ortiz (of no
direct relation), for possession of the land surrounding the mine. "In
the name of the Mexican nation," pleaded Ortiz and Cano, they
wished permission "to work it for silver, gold, copper, or whatever
God may be pleased to grant us."[86]

In December of that same year, Baca Ortiz granted the pair their
request, giving them not just rights to the mine, but "the privilege
of necessary water supplies and issues, for the working of machinery
and the pasturage of the cattle that are to work on the farm or farms
of the mine ... without detriment to third persons."[87] The two were
also given rights to the Oso spring that lay contiguous to Ortiz's
dwelling, as well as rights to "other springs, which may be granted
to them in the direction of the east, and as pasture commons, [one
league] for each of the four cardinal points of the mine."[88] In other
words, Ortiz and Cano had just been awarded four square leagues,
or about a hundred square miles, to be used in common with others,
for as long as the mine was in operation by Ortiz and Cano or their
families. By an agreement of 1833, Ortiz bought out his partner,
Cano, and became the sole owner of the mine. Between 1833 and
1846, the Ortiz mine produced the most gold bullion of any mine
in New Mexico and was the envy of Mexicans and Americans
alike.[89] Like many of his contemporaries, Ortiz showed little apprehension for Anglo American newcomers. When a U.S. delegation
marched into Santa Fe in 1846 to meet with Governor Manuel
Armijo, Ortiz warmly greeted them and offered his residence at
Dolores as a site for secret negotiations. Two years later, Ortiz died
in Santa Fe, leaving his estate to his wife.[90] Although, under Mexican
law, ownership of the mine and use of the four square leagues surrounding it were contingent on the mine's continuous tenure and
operation, widow Ortiz assumed full possession of both on her hus-
band's death and sold her interest to Indian agent John Grenier in
1853.[91] A year later, Grenier sold out to the New Mexico Mining
Company, with connections to New Mexico's territorial legislature.
Contrary to the spirit of the original Mexican grant, the mine and

surface rights to the land surrounding it were viewed by the U.S. surveyor general as a single grant. On the surveyor general's recommendation, the Ortiz grant of 64,458 acres was confirmed by Congress in 1861.

The Ortiz land grant illustrates how ricos profited from their positions and connections under Mexico's administration. By allying themselves with a small number of Anglo American officials and merchants, the ricos would maintain some of their original social status and political power vis-à-vis other Nuevomexicanos; however, in the eyes of many Anglo Americans, they would never fully enter the mainstream of "American" society.

⠭ Blood, Soil, and the Conquest Heritage

The language of blood that helped to codify social relations and civic identities prior to and (to a lesser degree) during the Mexican period also encompassed an array of symbols that spoke of Nuevomexicanos' spiritual devotion. Perhaps no more vivid illustration of that devotion was to be found than in practices of the lay religious society known during the nineteenth century as la Hermandad de Nuestro Padre San Francisco, or los Hermanos Penitentes. In Lenten and Holy Week rituals that resemble medieval penitential traditions, the Penitentes venerated the Passion of Christ through various means: prayer, hymns, procession, cross-bearing, mortification, self-flagellation, and sometimes crucifixion. The last three of these practices induced substantial pain and bleeding and served as physical confirmation of one's piety and *penitencia,* or penance. But it was also the focal point for ecclesiastic consternation and popular Anglo American abhorrence and fascination (as discussed in chapter 4).[92]

Though the society's origins remain unknown, they are believed to date to at least the late eighteenth century and commonly are attributed to the Third Order of Saint Francis. It is perhaps no small coincidence that those obscure origins are commonly associated with the equally obscure naming of the Sangre de Cristo (Blood of Christ) mountains north of Santa Fe that were (and still are) home to many of the chapters (*moradas*). At some point during the eighteenth century, the appellation replaced la Sierra Madre or la Sierra Nevada as common appellations for the mountains.[93] Arguing that New Mexico's penitential roots extend further back in time, some observers have pointed to the "sea of crimson blood" that flowed from soldiers during Juan de Oñate's Holy Week observance in 1598—an event that was chronicled in 1610 by Gaspar Pérez Villagrá. In fact, both the roots and the social function of the Penitentes are the subject of considerable debate.[94]

What is undisputed is that by 1833 the Penitente brotherhood had grown sufficiently in size and visibility that it attracted the attention of visiting Bishop José Laureano Antonio Zubiría y Escalante of Durango. In a pastoral letter read before parishioners, Zubiría condemned penitential practices and called for the brotherhood's dissolution. But his edict—and those of Archbishops Jean Baptiste Lamy (1850–85) and Jean Baptiste Salpointe (1885–94)—went unheeded. Indeed, nearly every effort to rein in the Penitentes during the nineteenth century seemed only to embolden their resolve to survive. By the twentieth century, several of the society's dozens of moradas sought to ensure their autonomy and survival through legal incorporation. Whatever their origins, it is also clear that the Penitentes flourished just as Americans flowed into the region and compelled myriad cultural and economic adaptations by Nuevomexicanos.

The point here is that during the nineteenth century blood itself (the physical substance) evoked strong reactions from all parties who learned of the Penitentes. During the American occupation and annexation of New Mexico, especially, it was one thing to profess one's "Spanish blood" as a marker of social status, but it was wholly another to educe one's blood (and mark the soil with it) in the name of spiritual devotion.

Following the U.S. invasion of New Mexico, the language of blood gained scientific complexity. Although medieval notions of casta were forever abandoned, the concept of limpieza was revived, redefined, and redeployed as Nuevomexicanos tried to explain their racial pedigree amid accusations that they were a "mongrel race" unfit for statehood. Modern allusions to Spanish blood, then, were by and large a response to Anglo American scientific racism.

Michel Foucault writes that modern notions of race date to the ancient veneration and privileging of blood and bloodlines: "The blood relation long remained an important element in the mechanisms of power, its manifestations, and its rituals. For a society in which the systems of alliance, the political form of the sovereign, the differentiation into orders and castes, and the value of descent lines were prominent; for a society in which famine, epidemics, and vio-lence made death imminent, blood constituted one of the funda-mental values."[95] Through the ages, the language of blood survived and evolved, lending itself to an increasingly racialist discourse founded in biology, science, and nation.

Under the terms of the 1848 Treaty of Guadalupe-Hidalgo, all former Mexican citizens, including Pueblo Indians, were to become citizens of the United States if they chose to remain, but this turned out not to be the case for Pueblo Indians. Their status reverted to "wards" of the United States, and their land was treated separately from that of non-Indians. Between 1857 and 1864, Pueblo Indian land "grants," which had been originally conferred by the Spanish Crown during the eighteenth century, were confirmed by Congress. If the Pueblo Indians' lands gained recognition, their civil and political rights did not. Pueblo Indians were denied the right to vote in ter-ritorial elections.

Spanish-speaking New Mexicans, on the other hand, were legally deemed "free whites" with voting rights. Their land claims—treated separately from those of Indians—had to be confirmed by a process initiated in 1856 by the creation of the Office of the Surveyor General, and later, in 1891, by the Court of Private Land Claims. After nearly a half-century, the net result of their struggle for recognition of their land claims was the widespread loss of communal land grants. Legal "equality" for Nuevomexicanos under federal rule was accompanied by appropriation of their lands and socioeconomic displacement—phenomena that have been thoroughly documented by scholars but that lie outside the purview of this study.

If Nuevomexicanos were enumerated in censuses as "white" by their Anglo counterparts, they were certainly not considered equals in social contexts or political realms. Indeed, the popular impression was that they were nonwhite and consequently not capable of or qualified to be full-fledged American citizens. As early as the 1830s, while Anglo Americans began exploiting commercial routes to Santa Fe, Josiah Gregg remarked on racial differences between "Mexicans" and "Americans." He noted that two classes of Mexicans dominated the landscape: the impoverished masses of "*mestizos*, or mixed cre-oles, [who numbered] 59,000," and the elite "white creoles, [at] say 1,000."[96] The latter dominated the former, wrote Gregg, through a system of patronage and conspiracy. He cited the Ortiz mine as an example of the elite's insidious machinations of the system for their economic gain.[97] On the character of both classes, Gregg wrote, "The New Mexicans appear to have inherited much of the cruelty and intolerance of their ancestors, and no small portion of their bigotry and fanaticism. . . . [T]here are but little bounds to their arrogance and vindictiveness."[98]

Throughout the nineteenth century, the racial and moral character of Spanish-speaking New Mexicans would become the focus of debate among Anglo American legislators as well as the reading public. Nuevomexicanos' relations to Anglo Americans centered on the question of whether to incorporate the New Mexico territory into the Union, fulfilling Nuevomexicanos' right to self-government as promised in the 1848 Treaty of Guadalupe-Hidalgo. Soon after the U.S. conquest of the region, both opponents and advocates of statehood turned their attention to clarifying and, in some cases, redefining New Mexicans' ethnic identity and racial genealogy.

From the language of blood that had evolved during Spanish colonial and Mexican times would emerge a new, highly politicized vocabulary that defined Nuevomexicanos as "Spanish" in race, blood, language, and history, and "American" in civic identity and national loyalty. Terms such as "Mexican," "Spanish," "greaser," and "American" would repeatedly be invoked and openly contested in congressional debates over New Mexico's statehood. As scientific and popular notions about race permeated legal, political, and cultural spheres during the late nineteenth century, those deemed to be "nonwhite" or "of mixed blood" were viewed with contempt or suspicion, their civic identities usually proscribed by both racial and gender restrictions. As Ian Haney López and Matthew Frye Jacobson have noted in their respective studies on whiteness, full entry into the U.S. body politic was elusive to nonwhites.[99] Whiteness was a slippery entity, not clearly delineated by the courts or agreed upon by scientists, lawmakers, or *políticos* of the day. The very indeterminacy of whiteness, notes Matthew Frye Jacobson, "rendered it impossible for some to attain."[100] In the quest for full inclusion in the nation's body politic, the challenge for Nuevomexicanos, then, was to establish their whiteness and, with the rise of Mexican immigration in the early years of the twentieth century, to distance themselves from "Mexicans from Mexico." Having regularly been characterized as "mixed-blood Mexicans," this challenge would prove formidable and would move them to boast of their "Spanish" ancestry, dredging up old rhetoric about their "purity of blood" and refashioning their "Spanish" genealogy.[101]

With the rise of tourism, Anglo America's phobias turned to fascination with all things "Indian" and "Spanish." This form of colonization treated Indian and Spanish cultures primarily as commodities. Nuevomexicanos, however, saw in their history something more valuable than touristic appeal. They saw political and social opportunity. In its most benign form, the Spanish ethos appealed to Anglo Americans' touristic sensibilities, inspiring an industry based on cultural difference. But in its most politicized form, the Spanish ethos allowed Nuevomexicanos to lay claim to whiteness as an argument for full inclusion in the nation's body politic.

When Eusebio Chacón arose to address the crowd gathered at the Las Vegas plaza, he was the voice of a new generation of Nuevomexicanos, one evermore conscious of its marginality to the nation. For more than a half-century opponents to New Mexico's statehood founded their positions in the belief that "mixed-blood Mexicans" were unfit to govern themselves. Nuevomexicanos were painfully aware, in the new Anglo-Saxon racial order, the mere perception of mixed blood was sufficient to deny them self-government. Chacón's prescription for his compatriots was to fight for equality, or leave the land:

> People of New Mexico, if your destiny is but to be
> a beast of burden; if you must remain forever in this
> sad tutelage of government which you have had until
> now; if you must never participate in the public
> affairs of this nation, which is yours; if your Anglo-
> American brothers view you with distrust, and they
> begrudge you the minor happiness of governing
> yourselves; it is time to pick up your belongings . . .
> and move to a more hospitable country.[102]

As the following chapters will bear out, self-described "Spanish Americans" neither abandoned their native land nor their aspirations for equality; rather, they fought both for recognition as full-fledged "American" citizens, and for greater control over their "Spanish" culture, history, and language.

Chapter Two

Citizenship in the American Empire

A great many of them have but a very small dash of white blood, others have a pretty considerable dash of the African. No matter what their blood or race is; no matter how or of what that population is made up, they are all our fellow-citizens now—made so by the treaty; and it is too late now to regret the possibility that some of them may be sitting along side of us here before a great while.
—*Rep. Joseph M. Root of Ohio, 1850*[1]

No quiso el Tío Samuel
Admitirnos como estado
Y al Nuevo México fiel
El Congreso ha rechazado

[Uncle Sam did not want
To admit us as a state
And loyal New Mexico
Has been rejected by Congress]
—*Anonymous,* El Nuevo Mexicano, *1898*[2]

⁞⅄ The Mongrel Race

Standing before Congress in January 1848, Senator John C. Calhoun of South Carolina implored his colleagues to exercise restraint. As officials thousands of miles away negotiated the Treaty of Guadalupe Hidalgo, lawmakers in Washington pondered the spoils of the United States' war with Mexico. Calhoun warned his colleagues that the

United States should not annex all or large parts of Mexican territory, for to do so, he claimed, meant admitting Mexicans into the United States, something that would precipitate a collapse of the racial order.

> [W]e have never dreamt of incorporating into our Union any but the Caucasian race—the free white race. To incorporate Mexico would be the first instance of the kind of incorporating an Indian race; for more than half the Mexicans are Indians, and the other is composed chiefly of mixed tribes. I protest against such a union as that! Ours, sirs, is the Government of a white race. The greatest misfortunes of Spanish America are to be traced to the fatal error of placing these colored races on an equality with the white race. That error destroyed the social arrangement which formed the basis of society.[3]

The United States' conquest of Mexico in 1848 did not destroy "the social arrangement" by which white Americans predominated over the "colored races." It did, however, add a new dimension to race relations in the western United States and prompted discussions in the halls of Congress about the Mexicans' racial character and their "fitness" for democracy. Lawmakers in Washington suddenly found themselves contemplating whether and how to "incorporate" more than one hundred thousand Mexican citizens into the nation's body politic, and asking: Were Mexicans "fit" for self-government or statehood?

Some Anglo Americans viewed Mexicans as political subversives or permanent rebels. "Never will the time come," Calhoun admonished, "that these Mexicans will be heartily reconciled to your authority. They have Castilian blood in their veins—the old Gothic, quite equal to the Anglo-Saxon in many respects." But, he continued, they remain too loyal to their Mexican nation to ever become United States citizens. Calhoun posed important questions to his colleagues: If the United States was destined to reign over North America, was it capable of managing millions of mixed-blood Mexican subjects? Was it prepared to "incorporate" them into its citizenry? "Are Mexicans fit for self-government or for governing you?" He asked, "Are you, any of you, willing that your States be governed by . . . a population of about only one million of your blood, and two or three millions of mixed blood, better informed, all the rest pure Indians, a mixed blood equally ignorant and unfit for liberty, impure races, not as good as the Cherokees or Choctaws?"[4] With comments such as these, Calhoun sought to suggest that Mexicans were more "savage" than Indians and, therefore, were incapable of governing themselves or white Americans. Many Anglo Americans shared this view. They perceived Mexicans in general and New Mexicans in particular to be persons of mixed (Spanish and Indian) blood, to have inherited the worst characteristics of both races, and to be "unfit" for U.S. citizenship or for self-government.[5] Not all congressmen, however, agreed. These perceptions—which lasted well into the twentieth century—elicited vocal resistance from many Nuevomexicanos who, like Eusebio Chacón, insisted they possessed "Spanish blood." They did so both to rhetorically uplift their racial pedigree in the eyes of white Americans—and thereby assert their racial equality with Anglo Americans—and to define themselves in their own ethnic terms.

As previously noted, during the last half of the nineteenth century, most of New Mexico's Spanish-speaking population variously referred to themselves in Spanish as Nuevomexicanos, vecinos, mexicanos, neomexicanos, or hispanoamericanos. By the twentieth century, however, many had begun to refer to themselves in English as "Spanish Americans." The transformation from Spanish to English nomenclature, and from "Mexican" to "Spanish" racial referents, reflects a broader transformation in the way Anglo Americans viewed Nuevomexicanos, and in the way "Spanish Americans" viewed themselves (or wished to be viewed). Spanish Americans began to invoke their European racial identity and long history of conquest and colonization to gain acceptance and recognition of their political rights through statehood. Both Anglo and Nuevomexicano statehood proponents made congressional approval of statehood possible by recasting New Mexico's "Mexicans" as "Spanish" in race, culture, history, and language, and "American" in citizenship and national loyalty.

Between 1850 and 1912, the struggle for statehood ebbed and flowed along with other political issues, such as land disputes, public education, and taxes. During these sixty-two years, the statehood campaign became particularly intense during three periods: 1848–50, 1872–76, and 1888–1912. At each of these junctures, the statehood debate illustrated how racial perceptions and relations played a major role in the formation of the Spanish American consciousness.

The United States' conquest of northern Mexico in 1848 reshaped ethnic relations and identities in New Mexico in two significant ways.[6] First, federal and territorial officials reinstated the legal distinction between "Indians" and non-Indians, a distinction that had formed the basis of Spanish colonial society and that been legally abolished in 1821 by the Plan de Iguala. As noted in chapter 1, the sociocultural division between españoles (or vecinos) and their Pueblo Indian neighbors persisted throughout the Mexican period. Under U.S. rule, however, federal and territorial laws formalized that ethnic division by treating Pueblo Indians and their lands as entities separate from non-Indians and their lands.[7] Although, by Article IX of the Treaty of Guadalupe-Hidalgo, Pueblo Indians were given the option of retaining their Mexican citizenship or acquiring U.S. citizenship by default after one year, the political and civic rights of Pueblo Indians were contested for a full century. According to historian Joe Sando, "Not a single Pueblo Indian elected to retain Mexican citizenship."[8] This fact does not mean that they became full U.S. citizens with the same rights and privileges that Nuevomexicanos enjoyed. Rather, when New Mexico became organized into a territory in 1850, its enabling legislation gave only "free white male citizens" (which included Nuevomexicanos) the right to vote.

Three years later, New Mexico's largely Nuevomexicano legislature pointed to the Organic Act of 1850 in deciding an electoral controversy. Having lost a bitterly contested election for a house seat to represent Santa Ana County, Miguel Montoya petitioned for a recount. A house committee determined that 139 Pueblo Indians from Zia and Jemez had "illegally" cast ballots that allowed Montoya's opponent, Jesús Sandoval, to win the election. Those votes were declared void. In ruling for Montoya, the committee referred to the territory's Organic Act, which stated that only "free white male citizens of the United States" were entitled to vote in territorial elections and that Pueblo Indians were not white. Noted the committee report, "[W]ho will say that the Indians are white males?"[9] Sandoval's counsel countered that, according to both the Plan de Iguala and the Treaty of Guadalupe-Hidalgo, Pueblo Indians were fellow "citizens of Mexico" who were later given all the "rights of citizens of the United States." Further, he argued, "A free white male inhabitant has been repeatedly decided to be any person who is not the descendant of an African."[10] The committee's ruling reestablished the political and ethnic division between Indians and non-Indians.

The second way in which U.S. conquest reshaped ethnic relations and identities was by subverting Nuevomexicanos' traditional dominance over local resources and political offices. This subversion was carried out, in part, by denying New Mexicans statehood. Many congressmen initially opposed admitting New Mexico on the grounds that doing so would disrupt the balance of power between free and slave states, while others opposed granting statehood on racial grounds.

Just months after the Treaty of Guadalupe-Hildago was signed, twelve prominent New Mexicans, led by Father José Antonio Martínez of Taos, convened in Santa Fe to discuss New Mexico's future within the Union.[11] The ten Nuevomexicanos and two Anglo Americans petitioned Congress to replace the military government that had been imposed on them in 1846 with a temporary, territorial form of government "until the time shall arrive for admission into the Union."[12] But their petition offended many Southerners. It boldly proclaimed that New Mexicans did not "desire to have domestic slavery within our borders. . . . We desire to be protected by Congress against the introduction of slaves into the Territory."[13] When read before the U.S. Senate on December 13, 1848, this passage reportedly caused "a storm of comment, especially from the pro-slavery senators, who were astounded at what they termed 'the insolence' of the language of the document."[14] Southern leaders had counted on New Mexico as a potential slave state to offset their pending loss of California. Thereafter, southerners entrenched themselves against statehood for New Mexico and impeded any action on the petition for a territorial government, leaving New Mexico's future unclear.

Frustrated by this response, political leaders reconvened in Santa Fe in 1850 and debated whether to adopt a state or a territorial constitution. The latter stood a better chance for passage in Congress, but the former promised greater sovereignty. As they debated, the political climate at home was rapidly changing. A rumor circulated that Texans were preparing to invade New Mexico, as they had done in 1841 and 1843. Fearful that New Mexico would be annexed or parceled out to Texas, convention delegates quickly agreed that statehood would better protect New Mexico's sovereignty. On drafting a state constitution, they submitted it to a popular vote. Voters overwhelmingly approved it, 6,371 to 39. A state government was hastily formed and officials were elected. Lieutenant Governor Manuel Álvarez, acting in Governor Henry Connelly's absence, forwarded the constitution to Congress for approval. But this bid for a state government proved fruitless. Fate interceded. While the document was en route, President Zachary Taylor, a staunch supporter of New Mexico's statehood, contracted cholera and died on July 9.[15]

Following President Taylor's death, New Mexico's principle statehood advocate was Representative Joseph M. Root of Ohio. Despite overwhelming opposition, Root lobbied steadfastly for New Mexico's statehood, insisting that it was clearly mandated by the Treaty of Guadalupe-Hidalgo. However, in a gesture of compromise to statehood opponents, Root offered to grant New Mexico territorial status and admit California as a free state. New Mexicans, he said, were now "a people belonging to the United States" who needed "a clear law" and government. Although her people were "as incongruous a population as it is possible to find on the continent," they merited a territorial government until such time as they could achieve statehood.[16] Their race or "blood mixture" was of little consequence to their ability to govern.[17] William H. Seward of New York was New Mexico's most vocal supporter in the Senate. In a contentious Senate exchange over the fate of the western territories, Seward insisted that New Mexico merited statehood because it possessed more than the required minimum population of at least sixty thousand residents to select a member of Congress.[18] Seward argued that "New Mexico more than fulfills that condition. She has a population of over one-hundred-thousand souls . . . double that of Florida when she was admitted as a state. Sixty-thousand inhabitants were deemed sufficient to entitle the State of Ohio to admission. That same number was required of Michigan, Indiana, Illinois, and Iowa. And New Mexico exceeds it by more than two-thirds."[19] Although New Mexico's actual population was later measured at 61,547 (not including Pueblo Indians) in the 1850 census, the territory did possess a population large enough to meet the requirement for admission to the Union.[20]

Seward further insisted that the population of New Mexico (presumably he was referring to the "Mexican" population) was eminently capable of self-government, despite declarations to the contrary on the part of people such as Calhoun. New Mexicans claimed a long and rich history of colonization that spoke of their fitness for self-government, said Seward.

> They are a mingled population, marked by charac-
> teristics which resulted from the extraordinary
> system of colonization and government maintained
> by Old Spain in her provinces. . . . The Anglo-Saxon
> colonization left the aborigines of this Continent out
> of its sympathy, and almost out of its care. It left them
> barbarous and savage; and they still remain so. . . . On
> the other hand, the peculiar civilization which the
> colonists of Spain carried into her provinces . . . oper-
> ated successfully in winning the Indians to
> Christianity and partial civilization.[21]

That Spaniards were more successful in bringing "Christianity and partial civilization" to the Indians than their "Anglo Saxon" counterparts represented a challenge to the popular "Black Legend," which denounced all Spanish deeds in the Americas as "tyrannical" and "barbarous."[22] Seward implied that, to the contrary, Spain's colonization of the Pueblo Indians in New Mexico was both benevolent and peaceful.

Significantly, Seward's speech made no reference to the period of Mexico's administration of New Mexico (1821–46), a period that was marked by political tumult and confusion. He completely refrained from invoking the term "Mexican," perhaps to avoid stirring up anti-Mexican prejudice. By praising the Spanish colonial past, Seward implied that New Mexico's Indians and Nuevomexicanos heralded from a genteel, colonial society characterized by Christianity and racial order. His allusion to Pueblo Indians as peaceful and sedentary farmers, and to Nuevomexicanos as the descendants of Spanish settlers, suggested that New Mexico's "mingled population" was stable and racially "fit" to govern itself. Between 1850 and 1912, statehood advocates made numerous references to the Spanish colonial past. As we shall see, these allusions contributed to the arousal of a Spanish American ethnic and political consciousness.

Perhaps Seward overemphasized New Mexico's Spanish colonial past. Opponents in the Senate railed against New Mexico's admission on the grounds that her people were too fond of their imperial past, that they secretly aspired to a "kingly Government" founded on monarchical and Catholic principles, not democratic and secular ones. Opponents even found disturbing some fairly innocuous statements in the state constitution and read into them their worst fears. An example was the Nuevomexicanos' expression of belief in the supremacy of a higher spiritual power: "[We, the people of New Mexico,] Acknowledging with grateful hearts the goodness of the Sovereign Ruler of the Universe, and imploring His aid and direction in its accomplishment, do ordain and establish the following Constitution."[23] Many congressmen saw in this statement a plot by New Mexico's Catholic "Mexicans" to insinuate their religious beliefs into government, a scheme that made them patently incapable and unworthy of democratic self-government. To whom did New Mexicans pledge most allegiance, asked one senator, to an unnamed Catholic monarchy, or to the Constitution of the United States?[24]

Compounding New Mexico's woes in Congress was a longstanding boundary dispute between Texas and New Mexico. The former, since declaring its independence in 1836, had claimed half of New Mexico's present-day territory, including all land east of the Rio Grande—some ninety thousand square miles. Seward proposed to grant New Mexico statehood, but to refer the question of its boundaries to the U.S. Supreme Court. His proposal met with swift and fierce opposition by Texans who, in solidarity with fellow southerners, sought to expand the boundaries of slavery and feared New Mexico's admission as a free state. Seward's proposed solution proved fruitless and was rejected 42 to 1, with Seward casting the lone affirmative vote.[25]

Two thousand miles away, leaders in Santa Fe nervously awaited Congress's decision. Little did they know that New Mexico's fate had become enveloped by an issue much larger than the mere wording of their proposed constitution. The sectional controversy over slavery remained the nation's central concern.[26] In September, word finally arrived in Santa Fe from across the Great Plains about the Compromise of 1850: Congress admitted California as a free state and made New Mexico and Utah, and all lands acquired from Mexico in 1848, into territories, without reference to slavery. Texas abandoned its claim on New Mexico and, in return, received handsome compensation.[27] Congress had put the question of statehood to rest for a long spell. In the words of one historian, "the people [of New Mexico] settled down to a new order of things, and nothing was heard of Statehood for several years."[28]

Not until the end of the Civil War was the issue resurrected in public debate. In December 1865, Territorial Governor Richard Connelly revisited the issue in his annual address to the legislative assembly. In contrast to Rep. Root, who fifteen years earlier had praised the Spanish conquest as evidence of Nuevomexicanos' fitness for self-government, Governor Connelly viewed the Spanish colonial past as a period of ineffectual administration. Noting the "retarded" condition of the territory, Connelly lamented that two centuries of "paternal [Spanish] governments" had left New Mexico without "all means of progress in the arts, industry, immigration, [and] schools . . . by which our territorial neighbors have surpassed our condition."[29] While remaining ambiguous as to whether he supported statehood, he simply remarked, "this is a century of progress, and that race or community which decides to stand still amid a fervor of activity . . . will be run over."[30] Within months of Connelly's address, statehood advocates reorganized, and the legislature passed an act calling for a constitutional convention to meet in Santa Fe in 1866. "Apparently," observed one historian, "nothing of a practical nature was accomplished under this act."[31] The same can be said for a similar act of 1870, which produced no visible results. If New Mexicans had reawakened to the issue of self-government following the Civil War, they did not express sufficient resolve to fight for it.

ـ🙂ـ The Santa Fe Ring and the Statehood Struggle, 1872-1876

The 1870s saw the revival of New Mexico's statehood campaign. The issue regained public attention, becoming the subject of sharp debate in newspapers, in the territorial legislature, and in Congress. As before, the politics of race permeated the struggle, though on this occasion the rhetoric and issues differed significantly from those of the antebellum period. Whereas between 1848 and 1850 the issues of slavery and westward expansion had been paramount, between 1872 and 1876 hostility focused on New Mexico's "Mexicans." Such anger, combined with the continued political marginalization of these people, forced Nuevomexicanos and certain Anglos to reflect upon Nuevomexicanos' racial and historical identity. This reflection sowed the seeds of indignation from which a "Spanish American" ethos later would flourish.

The statehood struggle of the 1870s was not initiated by a groundswell of popular sentiment, but rather by the political calculation and promotional efforts of Anglo and Nuevomexicano politicians, lawyers, and ricos, the elite class of landed Nuevomexicanos. Notwithstanding the 1850 and 1872 popular elections for proposed state constitutions, it is difficult to assess what most Nuevomexicanos—in particular the pobres and nonliterate citizens—thought about statehood. From what source did they derive their information and opinions? What was the role of word-of-mouth or traditional political loyalties in forging popular opinion about statehood? These are questions that merit scrutiny but cannot be answered by the documents at hand. The *Congressional Record* and newspaper articles do not capture the voices of los pobres, but they do capture the voices of prominent political forces, such as the Santa Fe Ring.

During the mid-1870s and late-1880s, the Santa Fe Ring—a loose affiliation of Anglo and Nuevomexicano lawyers, políticos, and ricos—was an especially visible proponent of statehood. Its members propagated their views in newspapers throughout the territory, especially in newspapers of the capital, the *Santa Fe New Mexican* and its weekly Spanish-language counterpart, *El Nuevo Mexicano*. What was the Ring's motivation for statehood? What did its members stand to gain from New Mexico's admission into the Union? Ostensibly, statehood was fought on behalf of Nuevomexicanos' right to full participation in national politics, but it was equally a campaign on the part of lawyers, políticos, and ricos to gain greater local control over land, resources, and political offices.

In considering the Ring's motivation for supporting the statehood campaign, it is important to recall that, for the greater part of the nineteenth century, New Mexican society remained largely bifurcated. There were those who possessed education, wealth, land, and/or political power, and those who did not. The vast majority of Nuevomexicanos subsisted on small-scale farms and ranches, and on communal land grants. Pueblo Indians, likewise, farmed and ranched. There were also the ricos, who, according to Ramón A. Gutiérrez, "enjoyed the life of comfortable regional gentry, engaged in mercantile activity, and lived by exploiting their retainers, their poorer kin, and their share-croppers (*partidarios*)."[32] These ricos, along with Anglo merchants, land speculators, lawyers, and territorial officials, stood at the political and economic vanguard of society. Ultimately, the ricos and Anglo Americans stood to reap the benefits of increased trade, industry, in-migration, and statehood. Enormous stretches of disputed land, as well as water rights, hung in the balance. Statehood would mean greater local control over these, and it would create political capital by enabling thousands of political appointments and patronage. But, as in the past, statehood hopes repeatedly would fall victim to the vicissitudes of national politics and the prevailing racial discourse in Congress and throughout the country.

During the first three decades of the territory's existence, Nuevomexicano and Anglo American officials accumulated huge tracts of land through illicit claims and nefarious deals.[33] The Maxwell land grant, located in the northeastern portion of the territory, represents the most notorious example of such corruption. Confirmed by Congress in 1869, the grant encompassed 97,000 acres, or twenty-two leagues. The next year, a group of investors headed by the young Santa Fe lawyer Stephen B. Elkins and a wealthy Colorado mine owner, Jerome B. Chaffee, purchased the grant for $1.35 million. The pair then hired U.S. Deputy Surveyor for New Mexico W. W. Griffin to resurvey the grant. To no one's surprise, Griffin's survey estimated the grant to contain nearly two million acres—some twenty times the number confirmed by Congress. Griffin filed his report with the Department of the Interior, whence it was forwarded to Congress for confirmation.

Had Elkins and Chaffee awaited word from Washington on their claim, the story would have ended there, but they did not. They immediately sold their presumed grant to a London-based company. The company then issued five million dollars worth of stock to support their plans to mine, ranch, farm, and speculate in the land. Meanwhile, company officials appointed Elkins director and local attorney of the company. Elkins's associates—New Mexico Governor William A. Pile, Miguel Antonio Otero, and Judge John S. Watts—were all made vice presidents. These men, along with the territorial attorney and business partner Thomas B. Catron, comprised the core members of the Santa Fe Ring, whose political interests were defended by a vast, mostly Republican, network of local políti-cos. By all appearances, Elkins's and Chaffee's investment had produced a tremendous profit, but in 1871 Secretary of the Interior Columbus Delano ruled invalid Griffin's two-million-acre survey. To Elkins's disbelief, Delano declared the grant to contain only 97,000 acres as originally surveyed. The company was thrown into crisis and later went bankrupt. Eventually, much of the nearly two-million-acre claim was restored, but not without protracted litigation.[34]

The 1871 ruling exemplified the power that the federal government wielded in New Mexico during its territorial period. It was precisely this kind of intervention that Ring members, and Nuevomexicanos throughout northern New Mexico, despised about the federal government. Statehood promised to render more autonomy and local control over such issues. Had the grant been adjudicated by state authorities, it would no doubt have been confirmed in its entirety. But as citizens of a territory, Nuevomexicanos and Anglos alike were at the mercy of disinterested parties in Washington, D.C.[35] It should come as no surprise, then, that Elkins himself set out for Congress to lobby for New Mexico's admission to the Union. The year following the ruling, Elkins ran for and won the office of territorial delegate to Congress. According to historian Howard Roberts Lamar, Elkins "promised his constituents that he would settle all land claims and at the same time secure statehood for New Mexico. . . . Aided by promises, money, pressure, and fraud at the polls, he was elected by a majority of 4,000!"[36] During his four years in Washington, D.C., Elkins was New Mexico's most vocal advocate for admission.

If the Santa Fe Ring stood to profit by statehood, so too did other land agents. They initiated publicity campaigns to attract immigrants and garner their business. Publications began to reach East Coast residents that erroneously announced that New Mexico's admission was imminent. A publication authored by Santa Fe land agent Elias Brevoort illustrates this point.

In the final weeks of 1873, Brevoort scurried about his Santa Fe bureau assembling the most thorough compendium of New Mexico's resources to date. Intended as a promotional brochure for East Coast in-migrants and speculators, Brevoort's *New Mexico: Her Natural Resources and Attractions* urged land investors to act fast, because "[l]ike the sleeping giant, New Mexico has been reposing in the consciousness of her strength and power, to arouse when the time should come, and to assume among the political divisions and powers of the Union, and in the busy world, the position and rank [of state] which the laws of Nature and of Nature's God entitle her."[37] New Mexico, he said, was poised for statehood, and statehood promised further in-migration and higher land values. According to Brevoort, of the territory's

77.5 million acres, only eleven million had been surveyed and settled. Between nine and ten million of these, Brevoort quoted New Mexico's surveyor general as saying, consisted of Spanish and Mexican land grants, grants that would be opened up for private purchase upon their inevitable legal dissolution.[38] Of the remaining unsurveyed lands, as much as one-tenth was arable and capable of sustaining "an extremely large agricultural, pastoral and mining population." "The table plains," Brevoort added, "are inexhaustible in pasturage and in the mountains are treasures of vast stores of mineral wealth."[39] Such claims bordered on the illusory, and clearly were based more on optimism than documentation. In 1874, New Mexico remained "very partially explored and scarcely prospected." "Her" material potential was unknown. Therefore, the mystery surrounding "her resources" raised expectations among speculators and miners, and heightened their sense of adventure and conquest.[40]

Like other land agents, Brevoort favored statehood because of his desire to profit from immigration and land speculation. Brevoort made no effort to hide his disdain for "[t]he Spanish and Mexican race," which had "caused the country to progress scarcely a move in the march of material improvement and wealth beyond what it was in the days of the Spanish vice-royalty in Mexico to which it was once subject."[41] To many whites such as Brevoort, the "march of material improvement" embraced Protestant and decidedly capitalist ethics. Historian David R. Roediger has documented how notions of labor, commerce, and industry had become inextricably bound up in American "whiteness."[42] In a similar vein, Reginald Horsman points out that the United States' "Manifest Destiny" implied the domination of both land and people residing on it. "American Anglo-Saxon" racial ideology was shaped by the shifting demographic landscape of the nineteenth century, especially in the U.S. West, where contact with "Mexicans" forced many "Americans" to reevaluate their own racial identity, and where competition over resources heightened ethnic boundaries.[43] The *Congressional Record,* journals, and newspapers nationwide documented Anglo Americans' growing awareness of Mexicans' presence in the western lands.[44] In the debate over statehood, white "American" identity was articulated in juxtaposition to mixed-blood "Mexican" identity.

Although among some land agents, such as Brevoort, statehood was but a tool for personal financial gain, for other individuals—

Nuevomexicanos and Anglos alike—statehood promised greater sovereignty over New Mexico's borders, which again were being violated. In 1872, Colorado had made clear its intention to annex six northern counties from New Mexico as part of its own statehood campaign. Those six counties promised to give the northern neighbor the additional population needed for statehood. This threat moved Nuevomexicanos to act quickly to defend their lands. In May, Col. José Francisco Chaves presided over a hastily organized constitutional convention in Albuquerque, which many leading Nuevomexicanos attended. The legislature passed a resolution condemning Colorado's proposed annexation and affirming New Mexico's sovereignty. As long as New Mexico remained a territory, declared the resolution, it was subject to periodic raids on its land. At stake, however, was more than just land. Colorado's annexation (carried out in 1876) threatened the very livelihood of "native" New Mexicans. Statehood was seen as the only sure protection from such incursions. "We are impelled to [t]his course by our pride and our independence," the resolution stated, "and to prevent our people, our relations and our interests from becoming separated, divided and made tributary to a neighboring Territory; and we call on the people throughout the whole Territory, as they love their native soil, their homes, their wives and children . . . to vote for our admission into the Union." [45] The resolution's reference to "native soil" marked the beginning of a movement to politicize Nuevomexicanos' identity and historical attachment to their land. Statehood offered protection for traditional Nuevomexicano land and lifeways and thus was a vehicle for what historian Robert J. Rosenbaum has called "the sacred right of self-preservation." [46]

Two weeks later, Antonio Ortiz y Salazar presided over another convention in Santa Fe, which produced a similar resolution calling for statehood and promoting a state constitution. [47] The *New Mexican,* a Republican-owned newspaper and fervent statehood advocate, devoted one and one-half columns to "Reasons Why the People of New Mexico Should Adopt the State Constitution." Among other things, statehood promised New Mexicans the means "[t]o avoid ruin, annexation to other territories, division of our people, our interests, and separation of our relatives; to sustain our pride, our independence, and our history, the oldest in the United States . . . [and] to manage our own affairs and select our own officers." [48]

Whether most Nuevomexicanos agreed with or were convinced by arguments such as these is difficult to determine. The only known gauge of public opinion was the referendum conducted in June 1872 on the adoption of a state constitution. The results of that referendum suggest that citizens of Santa Fe and Albuquerque took a greater interest in the issue than did outlying villagers. This difference likely reflected the influence of the newspapers in shaping opinion in their respective areas of distribution. By contrast, writes one historian, "away from the centers of population the people were apathetic."[49] In several counties, certain precincts failed to participate in the referendum; in other counties, so few votes were cast that it raised the governor's suspicion that the referendum had been subverted. Voters in Santa Fe, who were most likely to have read the pro-statehood editorials of the *New Mexican,* overwhelmingly approved the proposed constitution, 424 to 77. Those living outside the city, in the more remote parts of Santa Fe County, voted against the constitution, 269 to 130.[50] Due to the referendum's low turnout, Governor Giddings dismissed the results, saying the vote was not sufficiently large to represent the will of the people and would therefore be considered invalid by Congress.[51] The statehood movement ended before any petition reached Congress.

Ostensibly, the vote reflected the resolve of the people "to manage our own affairs and select our own officers . . . to make us a happy, intelligent, enterprising and prosperous people."[52] However, the referendum's returns showed that a substantial opposition to the constitution had arisen in the rural communities, though it is not known why this was the case.[53] It is unlikely that opponents objected to the principles of statehood, such as political equality, territorial sovereignty, and democratic representation. And since the constitution made no reference to contentious issues such as public education, taxes, or land grant struggles, voters were not likely motivated by these issues either. Exactly what motivated the rural communities to oppose statehood cannot be deduced from the newspapers, whose pages seldom represented concerns of the countryside. It should be remembered, however, that partisan politics and traditional family loyalties remained very strong during this period, and these may have had a hand in shaping the referendum's results.

Given the nature of partisan politics in New Mexico, it is ironic that, two years later, Republicans and Democrats, Nuevomexicanos and Anglos, would come to an agreement on statehood. In 1874, New Mexico's legislature, also known as *la asamblea,* convened in Santa Fe and unanimously passed a memorial imploring Congress to grant statehood to New Mexico. The memorial argued that New Mexico was fast becoming a prosperous and populous territory, and was deserving of equality with other states in the Union. The six-hundred-word memorial rang in harmony with land agent Brevoort's words. It boasted New Mexico's bright prospects for early investors, and paid homage to the European and Anglo American settlers who had brought with them industry and commerce.

The document's foremost concern seemed to be the portrayal of New Mexico as a territory being "civilized" through American and European in-migration and the development of mines. It boldly, though erroneously, declared that New Mexico's population had grown more than 50 percent in just four years—from 91,000 in 1870 to over 140,000 in 1874.[54] Not counting "hostile Indians," New Mexico's residents were an industrious and civilized people, yeoman farmer types, self-sufficient and democratic. The Pueblos (whose numbers were put at 10,000) were vividly portrayed in this light: "The Pueblos or Village Indians, who, from time immemorial, have been agriculturists . . . [are] among the best citizens of our territory," and they remain "as truly loyal to the government under which they live as any people under the sun."[55]

By portraying the Pueblos as sedentary and peaceful, the memorial distinguished them from the less sedentary Apache and Navajo. In addition to alluding to such a distinction, the memorial portrayed New Mexico as a dynamic territory that was being culturally and demographically transformed by the influx of American and European migrants. It read, "We believe that, outside of the native Mexican population of this Territory, there are at least 40,000 people of American and European descent among us who are permanent residents."[56] Twenty thousand of these were recent migrants, "bringing with them capital and means. . . . This new population is dispersed very generally throughout the Territory, but will be found mostly in the mining-regions, which are fast becoming developed."[57] By associating white immigrants with increased mining activities, the memorial affirmed the idea, popular in Congress, that white Americans and Europeans were the progenitors of "civilization" and "industry." But the memorial must have left plenty of questions in the minds of Congress.

Exactly who comprised those "of American and European descent" and who comprised "the native Mexican population"? Where did the Nuevomexicano elite figure into the racial landscape they had painted? Did the wealthy Nuevomexicanos figure among the forty thousand permanent residents "of American and European descent"? One can only speculate how members of Congress racially classified the memorial's signatories—"Pedro Sanches [*sic*], *Presidente del Senado,*" and "Grego. N. Otero, *Presidente de la Camara*"—or how these individuals classified themselves. Of what race did congressmen perceive "the native Mexican population"? Were they white? Spanish? "Mixed-blood"? "Fit" for democracy? In the coming decades, these were no small questions, and they would figure centrally in debates over New Mexico's statehood.

Much can be gleaned by the way the asamblea packaged and presented Nuevomexicano and Pueblo Indian identities in 1874, that is, by what the asamblea chose to include in or omit from the memorial. Nuevomexicanos presumably numbered ninety thousand, yet the memorial made no mention of their culture or lifeways, as it did for Pueblo Indians, Europeans, and "Americans." What prompted the Spanish-speaking asamblea to avoid any reference to *lo mexicano*—that which was Mexican—in their plea to Congress? Why did it label Nuevomexicanos "the native population" and not simply "Americans"? The asamblea's decision not to elaborate on the racial, cultural, or demographic attributes of Nuevomexicanos suggests that it may have sought to avoid stirring anti-Mexican prejudice among members of Congress. As later evidence suggests, Nuevomexicans contributed to and sometimes undermined Anglo constructions of Nuevomexicano identity. In the decades to come, the statehood debate would center on the racial character of Nuevomexicanos and on their history, education, language, and religion.

When Territorial Delegate Elkins introduced the memorial to Congress in 1874, he read a thirty-three-page speech that highlighted New Mexico's right to statehood, based on the promise—made in the Treaty of Guadalupe Hidalgo—that former Mexican citizens would be eventually "incorporated into the Union of the United States and be admitted, at the proper time (to be judged by the Congress of the United States) to the enjoyment of all the rights of citizens of the United States according to the principles of the Constitution . . . ,"[58] He also repeated the assertion, made in 1850, that New Mexico possessed the requisite population for statehood.[59] Like Brevoort's *New Mexico* publication, Elkins's testimony exaggerated the mineral and natural wealth of the land, but it also gave Congress a brief sketch of New Mexico's history, noting that Santa Fe was "the oldest town in the United States, except for San Augustine, Florida. . . . And her palace, old and unique, but dear to the people, furnishes a home for the present governor, as it has done for his long line of Mexican and Spanish predecessors reaching back nearly three hundred years."[60] Aside from proffering this brief history, Elkins's testimony, like the asamblea's memorial, refrained from discussing the "native Mexican" population, and focused instead on the material progress that New Mexico had witnessed through immigration.

Following Elkins's speech, New Mexico's statehood effort gained broad support in Congress, winning the recommendation of the House Committee on the Territories. Statehood bills passed the House and Senate by a nearly three-to-one margin. The House Committee on the Territories produced a glowing four-page recommendation that highlighted the territory's vast terrain, its bountiful grazing lands, stands of timber, and "minerals of all kinds [which] exist in inexhaustible quantities, especially coal." It further pointed out that seventeen states previously had been awarded statehood while possessing fewer residents than New Mexico.[61] Although the recommendation made no direct reference to the land's "Mexican" population, it did conclude that admission into the Union would induce "Europeans" and "Americans" to migrate to the state, exploit its resources, and manage the affairs of the state. To substantiate this conclusion, the committee produced statistics showing how other territories, once admitted into the Union, had rapidly gained in white population.[62] Despite having passed both the House and Senate, the two statehood enabling bills failed to clear their last obstacle, the reconciliation process. For reasons unknown, the language of the two bills proved elusive to mediation. The second session of the Forty-third Congress adjourned without a compromise, leaving New Mexico a territory as before.

In 1876, under Elkins's command, a reinvigorated statehood campaign swept into Washington, D.C. New Mexico's asamblea issued a new memorial, this one more strident in tone. It chided congressmen for neglecting the territory's earlier plea, and insisted that statehood had been promised under the terms of the Treaty of

Guadalupe-Hidalgo. It also voiced the asamblea's growing contempt for Congress, declaring that "[t]he citizens of New Mexico have noticed with the greatest mortification that their Territory and her claims, based on the high obligations of national treaty, have been disregarded and left without respectable attention or consideration."[63] Nuevomexicanos stood defiant before Congress and demanded that their cause be given greater attention: "the people of New Mexico should be admitted to the enjoyment of all the rights of citizens of the United States, according to the principles of the Constitution; they therefore . . . protest against any further discrimination and distinction against them and in favor of other Territories."[64]

The 1876 statehood bill did go on to win the support of the Committee on the Territories, but this time the bill met with openly racist opposition in Congress—possibly because of the contemptuous tone of New Mexico's latest plea. In a fifteen-page minority report, opponents argued that New Mexico possessed neither the "population, industry, intelligence, [nor the] wealth to entitle this Territory to admission in the Union as a sovereign state."[65] Not only had New Mexico's demographic and economic growth been misrepresented, the minority report argued, but hostile relations between "the native population" and Indians had also drawn a dark cloud over all traces of "American" civilization in the region. New Mexico remained a forsaken territory, savage and undemocratic. Its people's "peculiar character" made it unworthy of self-government. The report further disparaged Nuevomexicanos for their lack of formal education, their deficiency in English, their fervent Catholicism, and most importantly, for their not possessing European or Anglo American ancestry or culture. It painted Nuevomexicanos as mixed-blood "Mexicans" of Spanish and Indian parentage, and possessing only the worst of both races: "Of the native population but few are pure-blood or Castilian, probably not more than fifty or one hundred families in all, the rest being a mixture of Spanish or Mexican and Indian in different degrees. With the decadence of early Spanish power and enterprise on this continent the inhabitants of this isolated region, with few exceptions, continued to sink, till now, for nigh two hundred years, into a condition of ignorance, superstition, and sloth that is unequaled by their Aztec neighbors, the Pueblo Indians."[66]

The minority report reveals the "scientific" racial ideology that had gained popularity in the latter half of the nineteenth century.[67]

According to Reginald Horsman, this ideology viewed racial difference either in biological or environmental terms. Borrowing from the ideas of Charles Darwin and Herbert Spencer, American "Anglo Saxons," writes Horsman, believed that their racial superiority, their "Manifest Destiny," was rooted in racial purity—in not having mixed with the other, nonwhite races. "Miscegenation," they felt, would bring about the contamination of the races and lead to the decline of Anglo Saxon supremacy. As an example, Horsman remarks that American visitors to the Southwest tended to "praise the [racially pure] Pueblo Indians in order to debase the 'mongrel' Mexicans."[68] Throughout the nineteenth century, as a multitude of ideas about race permeated the halls of Congress, each competed for legitimization through science. Phrenology, eugenics, biology, and anthropology served to reaffirm racist theories and inform political debates.

Horsman notes how American "Anglo-Saxon" ideology was the foundation for U.S. foreign policy from the Monroe Doctrine to Theodore Roosevelt's "Big Stick" diplomacy.[69] Yet domestic politics, too, were informed by scientific theories about "the races." Divergent approaches to the "assimilation" of Indians, the preservation or abolition of slavery, the segregation of blacks from whites, or the exclusion of Chinese immigrants turned on the principle that racial difference was broken down through racial mixture, and that the consequence of such mixture was the devolution of the "pure" races. For segregationists, interracial marriage and mixed-blood progeny threatened to break down the United States' Anglo-Saxon reign over society and invited unwanted scrutiny of the existing social order. White supremacy necessitated the social and sexual compartmentalization of the races.

Just as blood had become a signifier for race and culture in medieval Spain and Spanish America, so did it inform nineteenth-century scientific notions of race among Anglo Americans and, later, Spanish Americans. By scientific standards, blood held the key to an individual's racial identity. Thus, testimonials against statehood for New Mexico, such as this one from the minority report of 1876, often imputed Nuevomexicanos on the basis of their "mixed blood" and "inferior" racial stock, their religion, and their class:

> I am told, and I readily believe, that the mass of the
> people once constituted the peon class. These appear

to have more Indian than Spanish blood in their
veins. They are Roman Catholics, retaining yet some
of their Indian superstitions. In secret the fires of
Montezuma are kept burning as brightly and continuously as a century and a half ago.[70]

In the minds of many Anglo Americans, Nuevomexicanos were an
impure race, a "mixed blood" and shifty people. Pueblo Indians, on the
other hand, were thought by some to be of purer blood, noble descendants of the Aztec empire. In appearance, Nuevomexicanos were too
"swarthy" to be purely Castilian, yet too culturally Hispanicized to be
deemed "Indians." Unlike their Pueblo neighbors, Nuevomexicanos
were seen as a people without a clear racial identity or history. Although
the U.S. Census, beginning in 1850, deemed Nuevomexicanos to be
"white" for the purposes of enumeration, members of Congress continued to refer to them as "Mexicans" and not "Americans," suggesting that these terms carried racial connotations.

By the 1870s, Nuevomexicano legislators, as illustrated by their
strength in the asamblea, had entrenched themselves in a regional vari-
ation of American democracy. At the same time, they were under-
standably enraged by the implication that as a "mongrel" race they
remained "unfit" for self-government. Although colonial caste distinctions had been abolished more than fifty years earlier, the "language of blood" had been resurrected by Anglo American legislators.[71]

New Mexico's fate in 1876 also turned on the perception of economic stagnation. While a small sector of the population had begun
to engage in wage labor—as miners, field hands, muleteers, and laun-
dresses—few New Mexicans participated in large-scale industry. The
railway had yet to arrive.[72] Other western territories, however, had
boomed with precious metal mining, nascent agribusiness, small
manufacturing, and related industries, prompting statehood opponents to complain that "There is none of the vitality that marks
Colorado, Montana, and Territories purely of American immigration."[73] New Mexico, like its mixed-blood population, appeared
stagnant and shiftless in the eyes of Congress. It lacked both the material wealth and a large white "American" population thought necessary for statehood.[74]

In the waning days of the Forty-fourth Congress, Colorado and
New Mexico briefly joined forces in their statehood bid, but New

Mexico's detractors ultimately managed to drive a wedge between them by introducing separate statehood bills for the territories. As Congress was preparing to adjourn, Colorado's Republican supporters managed to wrest crucial last-minute crossovers among southern Democrats; its bill passed handily, making that territory the nation's "Centennial State." However, New Mexico's bill fell seven votes short of the required two-thirds majority.[75] New Mexico's defeat was likely sealed by Elkins himself, who wandered into the House chamber in the middle of a "bloody shirt" speech, in which a northern Republican was deriding southern Democrats for their Civil War legacy. Without having heard a word of the oratory, Elkins joined others in congratulating the speechmaker by shaking his hand. Southerners looked on in horror. Historian Robert Larson believes that the famous "Elkins handshake" led statehood supporters from Alabama and Georgia to reverse their support.[76] With a simple gesture, New Mexico was swept into the politics of Reconstruction, just as it had been swept into the politics of slavery and westward expansion.[77]

By 1876, racial politics and perceptions—in addition to the territory's perceived material development or population size—dictated New Mexico's fate. Though the Bureau of the Census enumerated Nuevomexicanos as "white," both supporters and detractors of statehood operated on the assumption that Nuevomexicanos and Anglo Americans personified two discrete races and cultures. This assumption shaped local, as well as national, politics. In Santa Fe, the capital's leading English-language newspaper, the *New Mexican,* had since its founding in the 1850s employed the terms "Mexican" and "American" when referring to Nuevomexicanos and Anglo Americans, respectively. Similarly, Spanish-language newspapers, such as *El Nuevo Mexicano* and *El Independiente,* used the terms "mexicano" and "americano." Thus the ethnic boundary between the two groups seems to have been mutually agreed upon, which is to say that each group recognized the other as ethnically "different." This recognition does not mean, however, that the terms conjured up the same meanings for each group.

Although many Anglo Americans viewed all "Mexicans" as a "mixed-blood" race with loyalty to Mexico, others viewed them as fellow U.S. citizens. Many of Santa Fe's Anglo American and European immigrants engaged Nuevomexicanos in trade, married into their families, and established common political agendas, especially within the Republican party. Nuevomexicanos themselves, meanwhile, remained divided by class, education, language abilities, and family allegiances. From the 1880s to 1900, these divisions created internal obstacles to statehood, as some Nuevomexicanos defied their Republican leaders' call for public education, viewing it as a threat to their Catholic schools and beliefs. Nevertheless, Nuevomexicanos' continued marginalization from national politics—underscored by racist rhetoric—reinforced a common ethnic sensibility that centered on their "Spanish" history and identity, and on their "American" citizenship and national loyalty. By the twentieth century, as internal dissension abated, the statehood struggle came to embody Nuevomexicanos' desire to become full members of the nation-state.

The minority report of 1876 invoked racial slanders to deny Nuevomexicanos full U.S. citizenship, establishing race as a central issue in the debate over New Mexico's statehood. Thereafter, Nuevomexicanos felt compelled to defend their racial "fitness" for self-government. Their most vocal leaders began proclaiming that, as "pure-blood" descendants of the Spanish conquistadores, Nuevomexicanos were both racially and culturally fit to govern themselves. This counterargument became particularly pronounced during the third phase of New Mexico's statehood struggle, from 1888 to 1912.

⠌ Becoming Spanish American, 1888–1912

For the better part of the 1880s, New Mexico's statehood effort was at a standstill. The asamblea's support for statehood had evaporated because of intense partisan politics. As a consequence, New Mexico's congressional delegates during this period—Trinidad Romero, Mariano Otero, Tranquilino Luna, and F. A. Manzanares—did not bother to lobby for New Mexico's admission into the Union.[78] Though the territory's population grew rapidly with the advent of the railway in 1880, ethnic and political factions began to form over land disputes, taxation, and public education. There was a growing concern among Nuevomexicanos that statehood could precipitate an "invasion" of Anglo American lawyers, corrupt officials, and land speculators who would attempt to displace Nuevomexicanos from their lands. The territory's newspapers made almost no reference to the statehood issue during this period, suggesting that public officials (the Santa Fe Ring in particular) did not follow through with their 1870s campaign to raise popular support for the issue. Nevertheless, Congress and newspapers nationwide did discuss New Mexico's prospects as a future state.

In 1882, for example, Congress debated statehood but took no favorable action. That same year, a Trinidad, Colorado, resident wrote the *New York Times* that New Mexico's admission would be "simply detestable" because "about two-thirds of the population of the Territory is of the mongrel breed known as Mexicans—a mixture of the Apache, negro, Navajo, white horse-thief, Pueblo Indian, and old-time frontiersman with the original Mexican stock."[79] According to this individual, Nuevomexicanos were racially mixed and, therefore, unfit to govern themselves and Anglos. On reading this, New Mexico's chief justice, LeBaron Bradford Prince, responded with indignation: "His suggestion of a mixture of "negro" blood in the general population is especially unfortunate, as the census of 1870 showed that even as late a date as that there were but 127 persons of African descent in the whole Territory. . . . While some of the Pueblo villages are quite near Spanish towns, yet no marriage or similar connections take place between the races; they are as separate in such respects as if a Chinese wall ran between."[80]

Prince's response is significant for two reasons. First, like Juan Bautista Pino's 1812 report to the Spanish Cortes (discussed in chapter 1), it minimized the extent of African "blood" in New Mexico, as if to eliminate the "darkest" and most "inferior" racial element from the population. Second, it incorrectly argued that racial mixture between the "Spanish" and "Indian" races had never occurred, and that the population was therefore of "pure" Spanish or "pure" Indian blood. This biracial depiction of New Mexico's society would become an essential referent in the making of a Spanish American consciousness. That consciousness would be premised on Nuevomexicanos' racial, cultural, and linguistic distinctiveness and "difference" from both Anglo Americans and Pueblo Indians. Since "the native people of New Mexico" possessed "Spanish" blood, wrote Prince, they necessarily descended from the first Spanish settlers and had inherited their traits: "A more courteous, hospitable, and chivalric social element does not exist in the land. They are fit representatives of the land of the Cid, and successors of the historic discoverers and conquerors of the soil."[81] Implicit throughout Prince's defense, of course, is that these Spanish Americans bore little resemblance to their "mixed blood" counterparts from Mexico. Like many of his contemporaries, Prince tacitly accepted the assumption that racial mixture was undesirable because it made a people unfit for self-government.[82]

Moreover, Prince felt that Nuevomexicanas (that is, women), whom the Colorado author of the *Times* article had derided as prostitutes, embodied authentic "Spanish" traits. Defending the "virtue of our countrywomen" against the author's "vile" accusation, Prince declared: "No more high-bred, noble, and pure-minded women are to be seen on earth than among the Spaniards of New Mexico. They are brought up with a care similar to that seen in Europe, and which seems almost too strict to us who are accustomed to the freedom of girl life in general in the United States."[83] Nuevomexicanas, according to Prince, embodied the purity of their race—purity of blood, culture, and character. On the basis of these virtues, he argued, their sons were most capable of self-government.[84]

During the 1880s, Prince earned a reputation among Anglo Americans as New Mexico's most ardent statehood supporter and tourist booster. Later, some would refer to him as "the Father of Statehood."[85] As an avid Republican, Prince was also associated with the Santa Fe Ring. In 1910, congressional approval of New Mexico's enabling act was made possible, in part, because of Prince's lobbying over the course of three decades. He served the statehood cause in several capacities—as territorial chief justice (1879–82), territorial governor (1889–93), and president of the Historical Society of New Mexico (1882–1922). As chapters 3 and 4 will attest, Prince helped to reshape the way Anglo Americans perceived Nuevomexicanos (and the way Nuevomexicanos ultimately viewed themselves) by promoting an idealized, biracial (Spanish and Indian) image of New Mexico's society and history. This Spanish colonial image served to attract Anglo American immigrants and tourists to the territory, and rendered a new and romantic understanding of Nuevomexicanos' "Spanish American" identity, history, and culture. But the impression of New Mexico that prevailed in the 1880s was one of backwardness and racial mixture.

This impression was evident in 1888 when the House of Representatives revisited the statehood question. A minority report from the Committee on the Territories opined that New Mexico should not be granted statehood because "the inhabitants, with the exception of a few Americans residing in the place, are ignorant and degraded. The place [Santa Fe] bears an evil reputation as one of the most reckless and miserable towns on the globe."[86] The minority report quoted numerous "authorities" on New Mexico, including one who had written: "[Santa Fe's] history is one long continued strife between the cruel and hated Spaniards and the native Pueblos."[87] The "Black Legend" was still indelibly imprinted upon the minority's historical imagination, leading opponents to ask, "Is it not apparent that the people of New Mexico are not yet prepared for intelligent, honest and capable management of State government?"[88] The minority report quoted William Hart Davis, U.S. attorney in New Mexico during the 1850s, as saying: "The great mass of people are dark, a mixture, and only a few can legitimately claim to be pure-blood Spaniards. As long as there is intermarriage there is no hope of improving the color of the people."[89] Opponents once again proved successful in their efforts. New Mexico was eliminated from an omnibus bill that granted statehood to Montana, Washington, North Dakota, and South Dakota.

The following year, Prince was appointed territorial governor. From 1889 to 1893, Prince collaborated with Antonio Joseph, territorial representative in Congress, to lobby for three statehood bills; in 1895, Joseph backed a fourth bill. Yet all four were defeated for essentially two reasons: first, there was a growing sense in Congress that residents were divided over statehood; and second, New Mexico's "Mexicans" were still viewed by some observers as incapable of self-government.

The first reason had merit to it. Congressional opponents argued that New Mexicans themselves were not in agreement on the issue, that there was insufficient popular resolve for self-government. And it was true, the territory was becoming deeply divided over statehood.[90] Democrats, overwhelmingly Anglo and oriented toward the interests of southern ranchers and small businesses, feared statehood would bring about a demise in their political power, unless accompanied by a provision requiring English to be used in the courts, schools, and polling booths. Moreover, merchants worried that the new state government would demand a sales tax, and ranchers feared the state would impose restrictions on grazing in the public domain. Without addressing these latter concerns, Republicans, who enjoyed overwhelming support among Nuevomexicanos, objected to any English-only provision. They countered that statehood would precipitate European and Anglo American immigration, and thus would stimulate a natural evolution from Spanish to English usage in all public spheres.

In place of a language provision, Republicans proposed improvements in secular education to teach Nuevomexicanos English, something that the Catholic church loudly opposed. Viewing secular education as a threat to their parochial schools and religious influence, church officials implored Nuevomexicano parishioners to oppose any state constitution that would mandate public education. And Nuevomexicanos complied. In 1890, many of them joined Democrats in voting down a state constitution, 16,180 to 7,493.[91] It should be noted that in Santa Fe County the vote was much closer: 1,068 for and 1,549 against, whereas in areas of higher Democratic representation, such as San Miguel County, the vote was overwhelmingly against by a ratio of 4 to 1. Over the next five years, the 1890 vote would serve to reaffirm the minority's impression that Nuevomexicanos simply were not ready for statehood.

The second argument against statehood was strictly a racial one. The opposition portrayed Nuevomexicanos as resistant to "progress" and education. In Washington, D.C., and nationwide, opponents continued to lash out against Nuevomexicanos, calling them "grossly illiterate, superstitious, and morally decadent."[92] In 1893 the *Chicago Tribune* editorialized that New Mexicans were "not American, but 'Greaser,' persons ignorant of our laws, manners, customs, language, and institutions." It noted that New Mexico would do well to seek joint unity with the Arizona territory, which boasted sixty thousand white Americans and only ten to fifteen thousand Indians, mestizos, or Mexicans.[93] The opposition repeatedly defined the issue of statehood around national and racial identity, education, language, and religion, a tactic that put advocates, especially Nuevomexicanos, on the defensive. One ally in Congress, New Jersey Democrat William McAdoo, lamented that the issue had become enveloped in what he euphemistically called "misrepresentation." "The Spanish Americans of New Mexico," McAdoo responded, "are Americans by birth, sympathy, and education." He pointed out that New Mexico had risked more soldiers for the Union cause than many existing states.[94]

Nuevomexicanos, for their part, were not silent in the face of racist attacks. In 1889, *Senador* Casmiro Barela eloquently urged support for statehood and denounced its opponents:

> I know that the enemies of New Mexico's admis-
> sion claim that its native population still are not
> qualified to assume the burden, rights, and obliga-
> tions of citizenship. They charge that the Mexican
> population is ignorant and can be easily manipulated
> by talented but desperate American adventurers who
> have infested the Territory, and who seek to utilize
> the Mexican population as instruments in their cor-
> rupt plans. I reject that accusation with disdain. . . .
> Since 1848, the Mexican population has advanced in
> education, in independence, in mental vigor, and in
> firm loyalty to the American Government.[95]

Barela's speech, later published in the Spanish-language newspaper
La Voz del Pueblo, elaborated the material and intellectual developments that proved New Mexico was ready for statehood. He cited
its two thousand miles of railway; its mines, machinery, and agricultural lands; and, most importantly, its improvements in education: "I don't deny that the rate of illiteracy among the native
population was high when New Mexico first became part of the
American dominion, but this is changing rapidly. Official reports
show that rate has been reduced by 20 percent over the last five
years."[96] With regard to the charge that Nuevomexicanos were
incapable of self-government because "four-fifths of the population
are peon Aztec Indians," Barela responded: "When I speak of the
character of the population, I find myself . . . resenting the many
insults that have been leveled by its enemies. . . . The greater part of
the native Mexicans are not as aggressive and volatile as their Anglo-
Saxon brothers."[97]

Another prominent Nuevomexicano, José D. Sena, a Santa Fe delegate to the constitutional convention, wrote: "It is an insult to the
descendants of Hidalgo, Morelos, and Iturbide when the opponents
of statehood say, 'we' are not fit to govern ourselves."[98] Sena apparently referred to these Mexican heroes of the Revolution to illustrate that Nuevomexicanos possessed republican sentiments, not
monarchical ones. Antonio Joseph, who was of Nuevomexicano and
Anglo parentage, unequivocally expressed such views:

> It is not by blood or language that one measures the
> devotion of New Mexico's people to the United
> States and its institutions. For these are the descen-
> dants of the daring discoverers who abandoned the
> monarchical institutions of Spain and moved to the
> New World . . . to break away from foreign domina-
> tion. The devotion to republican institutions on the
> part of the descendants of Spain and Mexico is no less
> than that of the heroes of the [Mexican] revolution.[99]

According to Joseph, whether or not Nuevomexicanos possessed
"mixed blood" or spoke only Spanish, they possessed a heritage of
conquest, courage, and republican sentiment dating to the colonial
period. By referring to them as "descendants of the daring discoverers," Joseph implied that Nuevomexicanos were ethnically, if not
racially, "Spanish."

Some Anglo American opponents of statehood feared that, once
New Mexico was in the Union, Nuevomexicanos would conspire
against them and exclude them from political office. In 1893, the
Nuevomexicano newspaper *La Voz del Pueblo* responded to an accusation that New Mexico's Nuevomexicanos sought statehood as a
means of placing their own people in positions of power. Calling
these accusations "political strategies," an editorial countered,
"Whatever their nationality, New Mexicans will vote for the most
deserving candidate. The question of race never has come between
New Mexicans, for they are too divided to unite on the question of
race."[100] To be certain, Nuevomexicanos did not represent a mono-
lithic political entity, despite the fact that they overwhelmingly supported the Republican party in territorial elections. As noted,
whatever ethnic solidarity they felt belied divisions based on family
allegiances and local issues.

With the growth of Spanish-language periodicals in the 1890s,
such divisions became less pronounced. Newspapers such as *La Voz
del Pueblo,* Albuquerque's *El Nuevo Mundo,* and Santa Fe's *El Nuevo
Mexicano* increasingly advocated admission to the Union as a remedy
for Nuevomexicanos' continued political marginalization. Perhaps
due to their influence, a general consensus in favor of statehood
emerged among Nuevomexicanos. Editorials regularly appeared that
defended the patriotism of "those in whose veins runs the blood of

Cortez, Pizarro, and Alvarado."[101] Like their ancestors, and like other Americans, Nuevomexicanos valued patriotism and human dignity more than their own lives, stated the editorial. They would remain unquestionably loyal to the United States.

Ignoring Nuevomexicanos' growing consensus on admission to the Union, congressional opposition managed to squelch New Mexico's statehood efforts on five occasions between 1888 and 1895 by invoking overtly racist arguments. Ironically, during this period, a principal obstacle to statehood—the lack of public education—was overcome. In 1889, the territorial legislature—in spite of the Catholic church's opposition—established public education on primary, secondary, and postsecondary levels, including land grant universities and normal schools. By 1890, New Mexico boasted 342 public schools, 143 of which taught exclusively in the English language and 106 in the Spanish language; 93 were bilingual. In addition, there were numerous private Catholic schools. Despite improvements in education, congressmen continued their opposition, thwarting every move toward admission between 1888 and 1895.

The 1890s were a key decade in the making of Spanish American identity. Anglo immigration and tourism (discussed in chapter 3) increased significantly. The use of English language in public realms grew, as did the number of English- and Spanish-language newspapers. A larger proportion of Nuevomexicanos was becoming bilingual and therefore skilled in maneuvering between Anglo American and Nuevomexicano political and cultural arenas. Literacy rates were improving. Nuevomexicanos now gained access to news from Spain, Mexico, and the rest of Latin America in newspapers such as *La Voz del Pueblo,* a Democratic and Las Vegas–based periodical. In 1893, *El Boletín Popular* reported on a meeting of "la Prensa Asociada Hispano-Americana," which represented some "64 *publicaciones hispano-americanas*" published in the United States.[102] By that year, the five largest Spanish-language newspapers of northern New Mexico—*El Nuevo Mexicano, La Voz del Pueblo, El Boletín Popular, El Independiente,* and *El Nuevo Mundo*—had begun to print stories favorable to statehood and critical of those who disparaged Nuevomexicanos.[103]

It is difficult to assess whether these newspapers promoted a sense of spiritual kinship with Latin America or Spain, but they clearly viewed statehood as a vehicle for ethnic solidarity. This solidarity expressed itself in pro-statehood articles advocating Nuevomexicano pride in their "Spanish" language, culture, and history, as well as in their "American" national loyalties. Changes in ethnic nomenclature evinced a growing "Spanish" consciousness. With increasing frequency, newspapers employed the term "hispano-americano"— which literally translates "Hispanic-American," but which was rendered loosely as "Spanish American"—in place of "mexicano." As historian Adrián Herminio Bustamante notes, "By the end of the 1890s the term *hispano-americano* becomes more prevalent" in newspapers. "*Hispano-americano* was a strategic term to use vis-à-vis the Anglo Americans."[104] The term "hispano-americano" underscored a rise in Nuevomexicanos'"Spanish" ethnic sensibility and "American" national allegiance. At the same time, it relieved Nuevomexicanos of the "Mexican" label that Anglo Americans had used to disparage them. Thus the term "hispano-americano" conveyed a growing "Spanish American" consciousness. Phillip B. Gonzales, who has studied this phenomenon, contends that "all ethnic identification is variable, in which case the meaning of Spanish identity is found to lie in the social and historical circumstances in which it is expressed."[105] In the context of their continued exclusion from national politics, and in light of the racist justifications for their exclusion, Nuevomexicanos empowered themselves by redefining their identity in new ethnic, historical, and racial terms. This is not to suggest, however, that there was not a clearly commercial, tourist component to the "Spanish" ethos that began to flourish in the 1890s, for the Santa Fe railway and the New Mexico Bureau of Immigration were key to the promotion of a biracial ("Spanish colonial" and "Indian") image of New Mexico's native communities.

In some instances, the term "hispano-americano" might seem to possess transnational implications, broadly referring to "Spanish Americans" of any Latin American country, but in northern New Mexico it possessed a particular meaning and rhetorical function in the context of New Mexico's struggle for statehood. That function was, in part, to define a group of people with a shared history in terms that were intelligible to those in power and that met the established criteria (whiteness) for admission into the body politic. So much was at stake. Recall that statehood promised Nuevomexicanos national political participation and local control over resources and political offices. As employed in newspapers in northern New Mexico, the terms "hispano" (in Spanish) or "Spanish" (in English) were subtle forms of resistance to associations with Mexico or Mexican immigrants. As *Spanish* Americans, Nuevomexicanos possessed a readily understood racial identity, a documented historical lineage, and a claim to the land that dated to the very "conquest" of New Mexico, beginning in the sixteenth century. In a rhetorical sense, then, this term restored their presumed "Spanish blood" and, by implication, rendered them racially "fit" for—and deserving of—self-government and "American" civic rights and responsibilities. In essence, Nuevomexicanos argued that full citizenship and self-government were their birthright.

This was the case in 1893, when Antonio Joseph issued yet another plea for statehood and lamented that "[t]he result has always been the same. . . . They [members of Congress] have denied us statehood because . . . some of those individuals cannot see beyond the ends of the noses, and they have been and remain against the *hispano-americanos,* the legitimate owners of this land."[106] This statement draws a relationship among hispano-americano identity, resistance to racial discrimination, the denial of statehood, and ownership of the land. Whether or not a Nuevomexicano actually owned land, he or she often claimed a legacy of occupation dating to the Spanish conquest and, consequently, direct descent from the conquistadores who had conquered and settled the land.

By the turn of the century, Nuevomexicanos began to employ a familiar racial rhetoric based on consanguinity, referring to their "blood," or lineage, as evidence of their European racial heritage. The 1901 Las Vegas protest, discussed in chapter 1, merits further consideration in this regard. As previously mentioned, Eusebio Chacón's protest of Nellie Snyder's racist editorial embodied a growing "Spanish American" consciousness that was bound up in notions of "Spanish" race, history, language, and culture and "American" national loyalties.[107] Chacón's oratory went on to discuss how Snyder's racist rhetoric was the same that Congress used to deny New Mexico statehood. "The government, which boasts so much nowadays about educating Cubans, Puerto Ricans and Filipinos," Chacón noted, "has done nothing to spread education among us. The few educational institutions which there are among us are the fruits of our own labor. . . . We have patiently awaited the hour of our redemption; but that redemption is not borne, for sure, by those who insult our homes and our beliefs. We return today, with the zeal of those who know no other homeland or banner than the American, to petition, perhaps for the twentieth time, that overly desired admission to the sovereignty of Statehood."[108]

Chacón articulates a keen awareness of the broader national and international context within which Nuevomexicanos struggled for self-government. If many Americans felt it was the United States' "White Man's Burden" to liberate Spain's former colonies in the Caribbean and the Philippines, was it not also its obligation to liberate Nuevomexicanos from their colonial relationship to the federal government? The continued denial of statehood was particularly poignant given the intense scrutiny that Nuevomexicanos (men) received during the Spanish-American War.

Many Americans apparently remained unconvinced of Nuevomexicanos' loyalty to the United States. According to historian Anselmo F. Arellano, "rumors began to circulate throughout New Mexico about their disloyalty and lack of patriotism. . . . Much of the criticism centered on the opinion that *Nuevomexicanos* did not want to fight against their mother country Spain."[109] A Silver City newspaper spoke of the "Spanish Americans'. . . link . . . with the language which has prompted an allegiance with their Spanish ancestors."[110] Such accusations moved one Nuevomexicano to publish the following poem in *El Nuevo Mexicano:*

Muchas son las opiniones	[Many are the opinions
En contra del pueblo hispano,	Against the *pueblo hispano,*
Y le acusan de triador	And they accuse them of betraying
Al gobierno americano	The American government.
Haciendo un experimento,	Making an experiment,
Quedarán desengañados,	They will be disillusioned,
Que nuestros bravos nativos	Our brave native men
No rehusan ser soldados,	Do not refuse to be soldiers.
No importa lo que se diga	It matters not what is said
Y difame de su fama,	Or how they defame them
Per pelearán gustosos	As they will gladly fight
Por el águilar americano,	For the American eagle.
A nuestro pueblo nativo	They accuse our *pueblo hispano*
Le acusan de ser canalla,	Of being rabble
Pero no ha demostrado serlo,	But they have not proven to be so

En el campo de batalla . . .	On the battlefield.
Como buenos compatriotas	Like good countrymen
Y fieles americanos,	And faithful Americans
Libraremos de ese yugo	We will free from that yoke
A los humildes cubanos . . .	The humble Cubans.][III]

As this text (and other such newspaper contributions) suggests, at issue was not merely Nuevomexicanos fealty, but their very "manhood" and, thus, their qualifications for suffrage and full citizenship.[112]

Although the authorship of this and other editorials in Spanish-language newspapers often went unrecorded, it is important to acknowledge that formal education was the source of a significant divide among Nuevomexicanos. Usually, only the voices of the educated made print in local newspapers. Chacón is representative of the Nuevomexicano literati. An articulate man, he had been educated at the University of Notre Dame in Indiana. As a lawyer, author, translator, and acknowledged intellectual, he can be considered among the "elite" Nuevomexicanos who possessed education and who claimed to speak on behalf of a constituency. But to what extent did literate Nuevomexicanos like Chacón vocalize a popular identity? How pervasive was the "Spanish" sensibility among those who read the newspapers, and those who could not read them? Conversely, to what extent did the literate propagate their own particular notions of identity? Was Spanish American identity mostly an elitist invention?

These questions merit consideration, yet they are difficult to answer with much precision.[113] Doris L. Meyer, in her thickly researched study of Spanish-language newspapers of the late-nineteenth and early-twentieth centuries, reminds us that "[d]iscourses of cultural identity are always plurivocal" and that hearing Nuevomexicano voices in texts "demands an ear for multiple modes of articulation and an ability to distinguish among diverse tonalities. Witnesses of the past—especially those relegated to silence by virtue of their class, gender, race, or economic condition—rarely left behind evidence of their 'take' on history."[114] Indeed, nonliterate or semiliterate Nuevomexicanos left few textual records. Existing in somewhat greater number are the oral texts left behind in the form of unrecorded poems, songs, and folklore—subjects that gained the attention of linguist Aurelio Macedonio Espinosa at the turn of the century. As chapter 5 points out, his studies of New Mexico folklore emphasized similarities with the folklore

of Spain and archaisms that date to the colonial era.[115] Though
Espinosa's study of Nuevomexicano oral traditions has been widely
contested, his assertion that Nuevomexicanos possessed a deep-rooted
Spanish ethnic sensibility that was closely linked to a "native" or pioneer ethos seems to confirm the record left by literate and, especially,
bilingual officials who occupied the middling ranks of society: court
translators, postmen, merchants, and the like.

Evidence of Nuevomexicanos' burgeoning Spanish American
consciousness—and of Anglo Americans' growing perception of
them as "Spanish"—can be found in the transcripts of congressional
statehood hearings. In 1902, a delegation representing a subcommittee of the Committee on the Territories sought to ascertain whether
Arizona, Oklahoma, the Indian Territory, and New Mexico merited
statehood. The delegation visited various locations in New Mexico
and conducted hearings involving Nuevomexicanos and Anglo
Americans. Although some of these hearings involved individuals
who spoke only Spanish, several involved bilingual Nuevomexicanos
who were educators, court translators, or census takers, and who
responded in English. To assess whether Nuevomexicanos were adequately prepared for or deserving of self-government, the delegation
inquired into their ability to speak English and their racial identity.
The following excerpts are revealing:

> Castañeda Hotel, East Las Vegas, N. Mex., Wednesday,
> November 12, 1902, 2 o'clock p.m. The committee
> began the hearing of testi- [sic] at the above-named
> place on the above date.
>
> Nepomuceno Segura, first having been duly sworn,
> testified as follows:
>
> > Q. How long have you lived in the Territory?
> > A. I have lived all my life in the Territory.
> >
> > Q. How old are you?
> > A. I was born in 1853, at Santa Fe, N. Mex.
> >
> > Q. Are you the court interpreter here?
> > A. I am; yes, sir.

Q. The court interpreter is appointed by the judge of the court?

A. Yes, sir.

Q. Will you describe to the committees the duties—the nature of your duties in that office?

A. Yes, sir. The nature of my duties are to interpret from English into Spanish all evidence given before the court. There are very many Spanish-speaking people that come before the court as defendants and witnesses, and I have to interpret both ways—from the Spanish into the English and from the English into the Spanish; also the arguments of counsel, both into English and Spanish. That is the amount of the duties of a court interpreter.

Q. But in the majority of the cases in which your services are required—what is the nature of the majority of the cases in which your services are required?

A. Well, the majority of them are criminal cases, because I act as interpreter both for the United States court and for the Territorial courts; you understand they are both separate courts, of course.

Q. The majority of the cases under the Edmunds law has been due to the influx of the Mormon population?

A. No, I do not believe so. . . . Generally, it comes from the lower strata of our people (and when I say "our people" I mean the Mexican people) that are brought before the court under the law.

Q. Now, will you take up these counties in their turn and give your estimate as to the proportions of the population, native and foreign, and the kind of cases that predominate in each county?

A. I will take San Miguel, which is the largest, I think, in New Mexico. We have that proportion of people here. Now, having that proportion of people here—of Mexican people here—foreign element you would call it—the Mexican element, so called, won't come up to half of the criminal proportion in the courts.[116]

This excerpt of Nepomuceno Segura's testimony is typical of the dozens of Nuevomexicano testimonies during the 1902 hearings. Most of those who testified invoked the term "Mexican" in referring to themselves and their "people." They established that "Mexicans" were the predominant component of the population, and that "Americans" comprised the minority, both demographically and linguistically. Sometimes, "Mexican" and "American" were used as euphemisms for "foreign" and "native"; however, the opposite association was most common. Nuevomexicanos were regularly asked if they were "natives" of the territory.[117]

Similarly, although "Mexican" was the most common ethnic term employed, several Nuevomexicanos and some Anglo Americans referred to Nuevomexicanos as "Spanish" or "Spaniards." For example, there is the testimony of census taker Pablo Jaramillo of the Las Vegas precinct, who never uttered the word "Mexican," even when prompted by the senators:

Q. What proportion [of your precinct] were Mexicans?
A. More than half of them.

Q. Do you speak Spanish?
A. Yes, sir; I am a Spaniard.

Q. And in taking the census you used both languages, did you?
A. Yes, sir; where there were Spanish people I used Spanish, and where there were American people I used English.

Q. Are you a native of the territory?
A. Yes, sir.[118]

Jaramillo's refusal to use the term "Mexican" and his invocation of his "Spanish" identity reveal how some Nuevomexicanos had begun to distinguish themselves from Mexican nationals, as if to vanquish Anglo impressions of them as foreigners or of mixed blood. No Nuevomexicanos objected outright to the use of the word "Mexican," but a number of witnesses did describe their people as "Spanish," especially in association with language usage. Census taker José Lino Rivera, for example, claimed to use the "Spanish [language] with the Spanish people."[119]

Non-Nuevomexicanos, or so-called "American" witnesses, similarly described Nuevomexicanos as "Mexicans" or "natives." Justice of the Peace H. S. Wooster, a New York native, summed up his impression of the racial composition of New Mexico thusly:

> Q. The population over there [Las Vegas] is, as we all understand, principally Spanish?
> A. Chiefly Mexican. By that we distinguish the Spanish-speaking people from the others; there is some Spanish and some Indians, and a mixture of people.
>
> Q. Are most of these people who live out in the country away from the town Mexicans, as that term is used down here?
> A. Yes, sir.
>
> Q. And they speak what language?
> A. They speak the Spanish language, or try to; but I understand that it is not pure Castilian; it is a sort of a jargon of their own.[120]

The senator's phrasing—"Mexican . . . as that term is used down here"—hints at his awareness of the complexity of ethnic nomenclature in northern New Mexico. At the turn of the century, among both Nuevomexicanos and Anglo Americans, "Mexican" and "Spanish" labels were often interchanged to refer to Spanish-speaking, often bilingual, natives of New Mexico. Locally, the term "Mexican" did not have overt nationalist overtones or refer to citizens of Mexico, as many congressmen apparently believed. By either designation, Nuevomexicanos defined themselves in opposition to the objectified "Indian" and so-called "American." However, with increasing frequency statehood proponents characterized Nuevomexicanos as "Spanish" and not "Mexican."

Appearing before the Committee on Territories in 1903, Prince insisted that New Mexico's "Mexicans," as he referred to them, were "Americans of Spanish descent." The mayor of Santa Fe, appearing before that same body, concurred, stating, "Real Mexicans in our town are about as rare as they are in the city of Washington."[121] As the groundswell for statehood intensified, leaders of the movement tried to vanquish all "Mexican" impressions of these "Spanish" Americans. This was a formidable proposition, however. Congress refused to act on the statehood issue as long as Arizona representatives rejected jointure with New Mexico. As one Arizona resident put it, "Shall we join the Mexican greasers to Arizona and let them control it?"[122]

Popular support for statehood in New Mexico prompted intense lobbying efforts in Washington, D.C. On six occasions between 1901 and 1910, New Mexico leaders appeared before Congress pleading for statehood. Their receptions were mixed. But despite repeated setbacks, they maintained an appearance of optimism. Prince continued to boast of New Mexico's resources and vast improvements in public education, while continually having to defend the use of Spanish in public documents, the courts' use of interpreters, and Nuevomexicanos' English competency and patriotism. As for patriotism, observed Prince during a 1903 congressional hearing, "no less than 1,089 volunteers" had enlisted for the Spanish American War, and some five hundred "Rough Riders" had valiantly marched up San Juan Hill with Roosevelt. These were no ordinary "Mexicans" from "Old Mexico," Prince explained. "I have used the term 'Mexican,' and 'American,' as they are commonly used there, the former to represent an American of Spanish descent and the latter of English descent."[123] When asked if statehood might "induce Mexicans to come in from old Mexico," Prince snapped, "Not one, probably. They never have come. Mexicans are as scarce in New Mexico as Alaskans; I have never seen over four or five in the twenty-four years I have lived there."[124]

Four days later, Ishmael Sparks, mayor of Santa Fe, sat before the same body and reaffirmed the distinction between New Mexico's "Mexicans" and "Mexicans from Old Mexico":

Mr. Lloyd. What is the relative population of the Americans and Mexicans in the city of Santa Fe?

Mr. Sparks. There is probably a small majority of Mexicans in the city of Santa Fe.

Mr. Lloyd. What do you mean by "Mexicans?"

Mr. Sparks. The native-born people, of Spanish descent.

Mr. Lloyd. Simply of Spanish descent? You do not mean by that, though, they were born in Mexico?

Mr. Sparks. Oh, no.

Mr. Lloyd. What per cent of the population that you call "Mexican" were born in Mexico?

Mr. Sparks. I will put that very low. Real Mexicans in our town are about as rare as they are in the city of Washington.[125]

As the groundswell for statehood intensified, leaders of the movement tried to vanquish all "Mexican" traits from the population, underscoring the Nuevomexicanos' "Spanish" legacy. Notwithstanding such claims, many congressmen and Arizona residents remained unconvinced that Nuevomexicanos were truly "Spanish," and were not willing to accept them as full "Americans." Moreover, Anglo Americans worried that Nuevomexicanos, if elected to state positions, would collude to diminish their political power or cultural importance. One immigration brochure tried to put to rest this fear: "The Mexican population is not dominant, although it is sufficient to give a decided color to the prevalent impression. With the influx of immigrants from the eastern states, bringing with them the education and culture of their surroundings, the influence of the Mexican and his out-of-date customs will become less and less."[126]

Having been rebuffed in 1903, New Mexico's delegation believed that statehood could only be brought about if Arizona and New Mexico were admitted jointly. It called upon Arizona to support the effort. But, as before, Arizona leaders protested such an "amalgamation" because they feared "being dominated by people whom we do

not believe should be mixed up with us at all."[127] New Mexico's delegation then worked to convince Congress that "jointure"—as many
referred to the joint admission idea—was not only feasible but desirable, since it would ensure a large English-speaking population and
Anglo American majority. The delegation even agreed to call the
prospective state "Arizona," as opposed to some of the alternative names
proposed, such as "Montezuma" or "New Mexico." In a 1905 address
to Congress, President Theodore Roosevelt called for joint admission
of Arizona and New Mexico, ostensibly to repay New Mexicans for
their exemplary participation in the Spanish American War.

The following year, against protestations from both Arizona and
some New Mexico officials, Congress complied with Roosevelt's
request and passed a joint statehood bill, which Roosevelt readily
signed. The measure, however, contained a major proviso: each territory had to hold an election to approve of joint statehood. On
learning that the new state would be called Arizona, many New
Mexicans expressed dismay at losing their territory's historic name,
and opposed the measure. Additional internal dissension came from
prominent county bosses, such as Thomas Catron of Santa Fe, who
warned that Arizona's growing population of Anglos would eventually dominate state politics and probably attempt to disenfranchise
Nuevomexicanos with an English literacy requirement at the polls.
Most New Mexicans desired separate statehood, observed Prince,
but they nevertheless preferred "any kind of statehood to none at
all."[128] Despite such opposition, voters approved joint statehood,
26,195 to 14,735. Most voters seemed to have agreed with Lebaron
Bradford Prince, a late convert to joint admission.

Opposition outside New Mexico, however, proved insurmount-
able. Some newspapers, such as the *Boston Transcript* and the *Pittsburgh
Times,* continued to emphasize the widespread use of Spanish as the
territory's main liability and, according to historian Robert Larson, still
referred to Nuevomexicanos as "a mongrel population too ignorant
and lazy to assume the privileges of full citizenship." Not unexpect-
edly, Arizonans thoroughly rejected jointure, 16,265 to 3,141, thereby
nullifying the enabling act. "New Mexico's predominantly Spanish-
speaking population and Arizona's Anglo majority," surmises Larson,
"seemed to many an incompatible combination."[129]

In 1909, Roosevelt made a last-ditch effort to bring about statehood. This time he abandoned the idea of joining the territories, and

sought for them separate statehood enabling acts. Unfortunately, those bills did not survive the Committee on the Territories, headed by statehood foe Senator Alfred Beveridge of Indiana, who unleashed damaging charges of scandal and corruption among New Mexico's territorial leaders. The following year, President William Howard Taft, eager to resolve the persistent issue, urged the Sixty-first Congress to act swiftly. It passed bills authorizing separate statehood and referred them to the Committee on the Territories, where Beveridge, viewing the growing support for the bills, relinquished his opposition to them.

Sixty years after New Mexico's quest began, President Taft signed the enabling legislation admitting Arizona and New Mexico as separate states on June 20, 1910.[130] Their formal entry into the Union came two years later, despite numerous last-minute challenges on the part of some congressional democrats—who protested specific provisions of the constitution dealing with recall procedures. On January 6, 1912, after constitutions had been drafted and approved by both Congress and the president, New Mexico became the first—and, so far, only—state to possess two official languages—English and Spanish. Its constitution mandated that all public documents be printed in both languages, that English proficiency not be a prerequisite for holding office or jury duty (translators would be provided), and that "children of Spanish descent" be guaranteed an education in their native language.[131]

Despite New Mexico's admission into the Union, some Anglo Americans remained skeptical about Nuevomexicanos' capacity to govern themselves and continued to deride them as "a race speaking an alien language" and a people not possessing the "best blood on the American continent."[132] Such perceptions had earlier prodded Nuevomexicanos to redefine themselves as "Spanish" in ethnic origin and "American" in nationality, an effort, as we shall see, that persisted and permeated many aspects of life following statehood.

Figures 3 and 4. These early photos of the Matachines dance and procession were likely taken in Monticello, New Mexico, circa 1893. Still
performed in Nuevomexicano and Pueblo Indian communities, as
well as in parts of Texas and Mexico, the dance is imbued with symbolism and local meaning. For many Nuevomexicanos, the dance is
an expression of their Catholic devotion and a marker of their historical link to the Spanish colonial settlement of New Mexico. Schmidt
Collection, Center for Southwest Research, General Library,
University of New Mexico.

Figure 5. At the annual Fiesta de San Lorenzo in the late-1960s, the Bernalillo Matachines procession pauses as dancers pay respects to two images of the town's patron saint. Courtesy of the Sandoval County Historical Society.

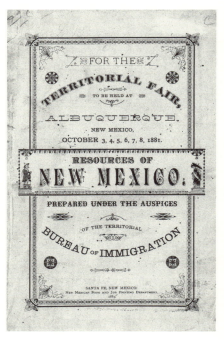

Figure 6. From its founding in 1880 through the achievement of statehood in 1912, New Mexico's Bureau of Immigration published hundreds of brochures advertising the land and its resources to prospective immigrants. Courtesy of the Lilly Library, Indiana University, Bloomington, Indiana.

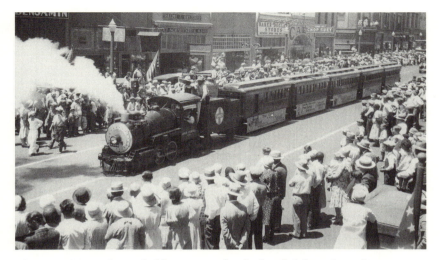

Figure 7. More than a half-century after its local debut, the railway was remembered in Albuquerque's Jubilee Parade for having brought New Mexico into the "modern era" of immigration, commerce and tourism. Cobb Memorial Collection, Center for Southwest Research, General Library, University of New Mexico.

Figure 8. German immigrant Nathan Bibo opened a store in 1871 that later became the Bernalillo Mercantile. Shown here in the 1920s, "the Merc" became a hub of commerce and social interaction between Nuevomexicanos, Pueblo Indians, immigrants and "Anglos." Courtesy of the Sandoval County Historical Society.

Figure 9. Anglo and Nuevomexicano workers pose together before a U.S. flag in this undated photograph, believed taken between 1917 and 1924. Schmidt Collection, Center for Southwest Research, General Library, University of New Mexico.

Figure 10. The Penitentes' Holy Week observances became the object of Anglo American fascination as well as disdain during the late-nineteenth century. This engraving appeared in an 1885 article in *Harper's* that described Nuevomexicanos as fanatical, lazy, and superstitious. Four years later, Charles Fletcher Lummis published illicit photos of the Penitentes and described them in similar terms. Source: *Harper's New Monthly Magazine* 70 (May 1885), p. 833.

Figure 11. Incensed by charges that "a portion of our population" sympathized with Spain during the Spanish-American War, prominent Nuevomexicanos and Anglos organized a *junta pública* at the Santa Fe Courthouse on 26 April 1898. Speeches were delivered in English and Spanish to denounce the "enemies of our people" who had spread "false" and "calumnious" rumors in the press and at the plaza. Courtesy of the New Mexico State Records Center and Archives. L. Bradford Prince Papers.

CUBA LIBRE!

Habiendo venido al conocimiento de los abajo firmados que los enemigos del Territorio de Nuevo Mejico y su pueblo han calumniado nuestro Territorio y su pueblo, falsa y maliciosamente, mandando informes fuera del Territorio al efecto que una porcion de nuestra gente simpatiza con Espana en la presente guerra:

Por lo tanto una junta publica sera tenida en la Casa de Corte el

MARTES, 26 DE ABRIL 1898

A LAS 7:30 DE LA TARDE,

Con el fin de tomar pasos para desmentir dichos falsos informes y calumnias. Varios oradores se dirigiran a la junta ambos en Ingles y Espanol.

Antonio Ortiz y Salazar.   Candelario Martinez,
Atanasio Romero,   Epifanio Vigil,
Thomas B. Catron,   Luciano Baca,
A. L. Morrison,   H. L. Ortiz,
Max. Frost,   J. D. Sena,
B. M. Read,   Benigno Muniz.
Chas. A. Spiess.

Figure 12. Albuquerque welcomes President Theodore Roosevelt during his 1904 presidential campaign stop. Many New Mexicans pinned their hopes for statehood on the president's fortunes. But even his political might could hardly sway the skeptical senator from Indiana, Albert J. Beveridge. Cobb Memorial Collection, Center for Southwest Research, General Library, University of New Mexico.

Figure 13. These children are identified as "Students of the Mexican Department" of the Albuquerque Academy, circa 1886. Cobb Memorial Collection, Center for Southwest Research, General Library, University of New Mexico.

Figure 14. Women of the Albuquerque Relief Corps crusaded to promote good nutrition, hygiene and patriotism at clinics such as this one, circa 1918. Cobb Memorial Collection, Center for Southwest Research, General Library, University of New Mexico.

Figure 15. In 1943, an agent for the Farm Security Administration noted that "Mrs. Maclovia López can read and write English well; she also keeps the family books in the evenings and helps the children with their homework." In the homes and in the schools, women were often viewed as conduits of culture and language as officials sought to "Americanize" Spanish-speaking children. Photo by John Collier for the Farm Security Administration. Courtesy of the Center for Southwest Research, General Library, University of New Mexico.

Figure 16. A boy reads in a one-room school in the mountain village of Ojo Sarco. "Most of the teaching is in Spanish, the language spoken in the children's homes," notes the Farm Security Agent, "and as a result they rarely speak English fluently." Photo by John Collier for the Farm Security Administration. Courtesy of the Center for Southwest Research, General Library, University of New Mexico.

Figure 17. Woman sitting with portraits. Peñasco, New Mexico, January, 1943.
Photo by John Collier for the Farm Security Administration. Courtesy of the
Center for Southwest Research, General Library, University of New Mexico.

Figure 18. When she was not advocating "the bilingual
method" of instruction in the public schools or the
preservation of traditional Spanish colonial arts, educator
Adelina Otero-Warren was involved in public commemorations of the Spanish past. Here, she is dressed as
a Spanish *doña* during the Santa Fe Fiesta of 1930.
Source: *Survey Graphic* 66, no. 3 (1931).

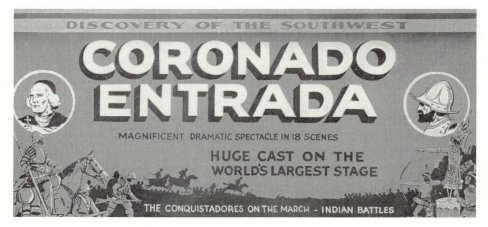

Figure 19. The 1940 Coronado Cuarto Centennial was conceived as a statewide celebration of Francisco Vázquez de Coronado's trek through New Mexico. More than 125 events were planned at venues large and small. This elaborate spectacle, staged in a football stadium, drew thousands of spectators; but few of the expected six million tourists showed up for the events. Coronado Cuarto Centennial Commission Collection, Center for Southwest Research, General Library, University of New Mexico.

Figure 20. Few schoolchildren could forget their drama class of 1940. Teachers were encouraged to develop teaching plans that involved some component of Spanish colonial history and folk culture. Coronado Cuarto Centennial Commission Collection, Center for Southwest Research, General Library, University of New Mexico.

Figure 21. The marketing of "the Land of Enchantment" in this 1939 tourist brochure relied on a panoply of racial stereotypes and symbols that appealed to Anglo American tourists, but bore little relation to historical and contemporary realities. Manuscript Collection 115, Center for Southwest Research, General Library, University of New Mexico.

Figure 22. Reenactments of Coronado's *entrada* into New Mexico periodically
were incorporated into festivities that honored local patron saints. Such was
the case in 1976, when Warren (Joe) Nieto (the author's uncle) depicted the
conquistador during the *fiesta de San Lorenzo* in Bernalillo. Private collection.

Chapter Three

Montezuma and the Iron Steed

Nuevo Méjico, ¿hasta cuándo
se verán tus desconsuelos,
el extranjero mamando
y tus hijos por los suelos?

[New Mexico, How long before
they see your suffering,
the foreigner suckling
and your children on the floor?]
　　　　　—*Félix Martínez, circa 1910*[1]

Hundreds of Anglo-American citizens still live today
who have entered our land poor, discouraged,
hungry, and even ragged; we, inspired by the generosity that has been ours in New Mexico, extended
them a cordial welcome, offering them the best place
that our humble homes had. . . . But now in turn,
many of them have cloaked themselves in the black-
est ingratitude, recognizing us as inferior beings, as
citizens useless to our government.
　　　　　—*Anonymous,* La Voz del Pueblo, *1897*[2]

La Entrada

On the eve before the Fourth of July in 1879, the sleepy plaza of Las
Vegas came alive with patriotic fervor. Rockets and fireworks lit up
the night sky. Around midnight, gunshots rang out from every part
of town. Jubilant citizens partied through the night and into the

dawn, when a thunderous canon announced the coming of the new day. This was a momentous occasion for all New Mexicans, not solely because it marked American independence, but because on this day the locomotive was scheduled to make its debut. The railway was going to bring about a new era, the newspapers professed, one marked by prosperity and progress.[3]

At eleven o'clock that morning children and their parents lined the tracks in anticipation of their first glimpse of the fabled "Iron Steed." In the distance they heard its mighty whistle bellow. Then there was a long silence. Finally, after much waiting, lumbering down the rails came, not a locomotive, but several steel railcars spilling over with workers and townsfolk. To the great disappointment of the multitude, the engine did not arrive for two more days. And even then, no important officials paid visits or delivered eloquent speeches as expected. The inauguration of the railway proved anticlimactic. Yet it came to symbolize the dashed hopes that many Nuevomexicanos experienced in the decades that followed. Though the railway brought New Mexico into the modern world, it delivered few of the benefits local leaders had promised.

When the locomotive reached Santa Fe on February 9, 1880, its debut was met with far more pomp and ceremony. "What a strange event this is to-day," declared Chief Justice LeBaron Bradford Prince, a recent arrival to the territory, "The railroad which is the type of modern progress, coming to the most ancient capital on American soil! . . . And what may we expect of the union which is now to come of two almost distinct civilizations[?] Here is the historic race of old Spain, full of the spirit of chivalry[,] of hospitality, and generosity, preserved through more than two centuries. . . . And coming now is all the enterprise and energy, the determination and perseverance, the aspiration and the ambition of the American character."[4] Prince viewed the coming of the railway as the courier of "American" civilization in this former "Spanish" colony. If the best of these two "elements" could be preserved by their "mingling," he said, New Mexico would possess a population "such as the world has never seen equaled before." The two people would be united in national and civic spirit, and together they would strive for statehood, commerce, and prosperity. Racial divisions and labels, he said, promised to disappear forever: "We realize now the unity of our whole people as we have not in the past. Shall we not then, to-day, determine forever to drop the use of the terms 'American' and 'Mexican' as heretofore too much employed as words of division among those who are all equally American citizens."[5] Although "Americans" and "Mexicans" (whom he soon referred to as "Spanish Americans") possess distinct historical and racial roots, declared Prince, they profess a single national identity and a common desire to prosper through commerce and industry.

Taking the podium after Prince, Mayor José D. Sena completely concurred, proclaiming in Spanish that the railway would bring "all the advantages of civilization and progress."[6] For many Nuevomexicanos—and especially for those of means and influence like Sena—the iron steed represented a harbinger of material advancement. It promised increased trade, immigration, a boom in real estate, and the territory's further incorporation into the nation's economy. And in these respects it at least partially delivered. But any "advantages" wrought by the railway were accompanied by much more sobering consequences: the gradual erosion of Nuevomexicano political power and continued impoverishment among the vast majority of Nuevomexicanos.

The occasion was indeed momentous. But contrary to Prince's exaltation, the railway did not bring about the full integration of "Americans" and "Mexicans." Nor did it render the kind of prosperity Nuevomexicanos like Sena had envisioned, though certainly an echelon of commercial and real estate interests profited from the railway. Most disappointing to Anglos and Nuevomexicanos alike, the advent of the iron steed failed to result in New Mexico's swift admission into the Union. Instead, it inaugurated an era on the upper Rio Grande that was characterized by the neat delineation of "Spanish" and "Indian" racial tropes, the primary function of which was to attract white tourists and prospective immigrants to the region.[7]

The process of bifurcation had several consequences. First, it dispelled the pervasive fear among Easterners that New Mexico was a land teeming with savage Indians, mongrel Mexicans, illiterates, and idol worshippers. The New Mexico of booster literature was, instead, a land of two enduring civilizations—one indigenous, the other European—that had withstood the ravages of time and nomadic Indian depredations. Second, racial bifurcation sanitized the untidy social landscape, in essence eradicating from the Anglo imagination the legacy of what became termed "miscegenation" and bringing into sharper focus the Spanish-Indian racial boundary. Finally, because the process of bifurcation focused on racial lines rather than class lines, it rendered an illusion of conquistadorial grandeur that belied the dire reality of a highly stratified Nuevomexicano society marked by peonage, poverty, undereducation, dispossession, and migratory wage labor.[8]

Two booster institutions that were instrumental in broadcasting the new and improved biracial New Mexico were the Bureau of Immigration and the Santa Fe Railway.[9] As a web of iron rails enveloped western lands, it drew New Mexico further into the nation's political economy, transforming it demographically but never really yielding the material benefits nor population growth politicians had promised. True, the railway aided commerce, tourism, immigration, and, ultimately, the statehood cause, but it never wrought the profusion of industry and white settlement realized in California or Colorado. And although Anglo intrusion measurably weakened Nuevomexicano political strength, it never entirely vanquished it as it had Californio power. In fact, the economics of tourism in New Mexico was premised in part on the urgency of witnessing the last vestiges of "the dying race" (Indians) and the sons of the conquistadors. To a significant degree, ethnic tourism necessitated their survival, if also their containment. What set New Mexico apart from other tourist destinations in the Southwest were its thriving village traditions and its native peoples, upon whom boosters based their racial tropes. Together, these were the object of Anglo enchantment.

The railway company's and the immigration bureau's clever marketing of New Mexico as the preindustrial "playground of the Southwest" and "the land of sunshine" fostered a new and romantic vision of social relations that was, in its essence, a Spanish colonial motif. This motif celebrated the chivalric Spanish conquistador and the noble Pueblo Indian convert.[10] The emergence of the Spanish colonial motif in the latter years of the nineteenth century, during the nation's imperial expansion into other "nonwhite" lands in the Pacific and the Caribbean, raises an imperative question: To what extent did this biracial motif respond to local political and social exigencies—such as contests over tourist resources, land allocation, and political affiliations—as well as to the white nation's need to clarify and, through tourism, pacify the racial terrain of this territory?

Some answers are to be found in the images and texts that people left behind—in their postcards, newspapers, and booster pamphlets.

These reveal how New Mexico's Spanish past was propagated, contested, and disseminated to Anglo American tourists and migrants.[11] And they are poignant testimony to the way two institutions marketed "ethnic" peoples, and the way those peoples responded to the commodification of their history and culture.

∴ The Promise of the Locomotive, 1850-1880

In 1880, pageantry awaited the first train at each major town along the Rio Grande, as the railway charged southward to link up with the Southern Pacific in El Paso, thus forming the southern transcontinental railroad in June 1881.[12] Local officials in Albuquerque were jubilant. Their fledgling town, having endured two centuries in the shadow of Santa Fe—the religious, political, economic, and military outpost of New Spain's northern frontier—was about to emerge as New Mexico's new hub of commercial traffic.[13] Speechmakers trumpeted its arrival, declaring that progress and industry would redeem their city and the region as a whole. Judge William Hazeldine, fervent statehood advocate and eventual Bureau of Immigration official, announced that the "new civilization of the east is brought into contact with the ancient civilization of New Mexico. Today the bell of the locomotive tolls the death knoll of old foggyism [sic], superstition, ignorance, and proclaims in clairion [sic] notes that henceforth knowledge, education, advancement and progress shall be the right of our people." New Mexico would "no longer be known as *Terra Incognita*." In fact, New Mexico would remain precisely that throughout the 1880s. But by the twentieth century, New Mexico would become known by an ever larger segment of well-read Americans and railbound tourists, thanks in part to railway and government-sponsored propaganda.[14]

Boosters throughout the territory heralded the transforming potential of the railway. The railroad promised to bring institutions of commerce, education, and industry, institutions that embodied "American" values, language, culture, and identity. For many, it marked a major achievement in the United States' domestication of a land that, since its annexation from Mexico in 1846, had languished at the periphery of the U.S. political economy. For three decades, "progress"-minded New Mexicans looked on in envy as other western entities, especially California and Colorado, realized massive Anglo American and European immigration, coupled with economic expansion and statehood. Commercial trade along the Santa Fe Trail—between Saint Louis, Santa Fe, and all points south into Mexico—had wrought much freight traffic but little permanent immigration or development. New Mexico's land was largely unsettled, its resources unexploited, its communities lacking industry. For these reasons, or so some officials believed, statehood had eluded the territory.

The largest Spanish-language newspaper of Santa Fe, *El Nuevo Mejicano* (later spelled *Nuevo Mexicano*), lamented that New Mexico, "during two centuries of mental and material paralyzation, has not progressed.... Now that the impenetrable barriers to civilization are fallen—those [barriers] which condemned to a slow death the arts and industries we inherited from our ancestors—we will soon see New Mexico completely transfigured and made into a new being." That transfiguration would allow New Mexico to "compete with any state in the Union" in material wealth, such as "industry, agriculture, mining and pastoral production."[15]

According to newspapers and public officials, untold deposits of coal and silver were rumored to run through these mountains. Bountiful farmlands and pastures awaited pioneers. On fertile lands graced by sunshine and mild weather, wrote Santa Fe land agent Elias Brevoort in 1874, "thousands of families could obtain happy homes."[16] And the railroad would make this possible. For land speculators, the railroad held the key to immigration and empire. Not only would it facilitate the movement of people and products, reducing the arduous thirty-day trip from Saint Louis to Santa Fe to forty hours, but the railroad would increase access to, the demand for, and the value of land.[17] Those who invested in this terrain were certain to reap great rewards, Brevoort exhorted, if they acted quickly, before New Mexico's material development. Land speculation, naturally, meant more business and profit for land agents.

Brevoort's *New Mexico, Her Natural Resources and Attractions* was one of a number of private booster publications that appeared prior to the coming of the railway. Subtitled *Being a Collection of Facts, Mainly Concerning Her Geography, Climate, Population, Schools, Mines and Minerals, Agricultural and Pastoral Capacities, Prospective Railroads, Public Lands, and Spanish Land Grants,* the publication extolled the pristine virtues of this country, namely, its fertile land, sunshine, and water.[18] According to Brevoort, these resources awaited exploitation and conquest. The fact that New Mexico had yet to be conquered caused him to lament that "[h]itherto we have had almost absolutely no institutions of learning, no statesmen, no public spirit, no boards of immigration, no colonies, no railroads."[19] Over the next three decades, each of these deficits would be remedied.

Brevoort's publication was preceded by a handful of others that offered up similar exhortations. Dr. William H. McKee's twelve-page pamphlet of 1866 gave a meticulous description of New Mexico's mining operations, proclaiming that "There can be no safer investment than in the stocks of the bullion banks of the Rocky Mountains."[20] The following year, New Mexico's congressional delegate, Charles P. Clever, claimed he was "so often written to and questioned about New Mexico" that he felt compelled to write a forty-seven-page booklet on its natural resources, especially precious metal mines.[21] Publications appeared promoting more than just mines. In 1873, Samuel Woodworth Cozzens published a fictional account of his travels through southern New Mexico and Arizona, titled *The Marvelous Country,* illustrated with fantastic engravings of warlike Apaches and Mexicans.[22] Some pamphlets even reached Europe, such as the French-language brochure of 1874 that described the prospects for "the colonization of Colorado and New Mexico." In ten years, it predicted, Colorado and New Mexico should have a population of 2.4 million, annual production of $600 million, and four thousand miles of railroad.[23] Though these predictions proved wildly inaccurate, they nevertheless did heighten expectations among speculators and would-be settlers.

Until the arrival of the railway, New Mexico's population grew only sporadically and was dominated by Nuevomexicanos until the first decade of the twentieth century, when Anglo Americans eclipsed them in number and power. Of the roughly 60,000 residents of the northern counties of New Mexico in 1850, 90.9 percent were Nuevomexicanos (that is, possessed Spanish given names or surnames, were born in the territory, and were designated racially "white"). Five percent were Native Americans ("Pueblo Indians" and "Nomad Indians") and 0.6 percent were Mexicans born in Mexico (as defined by boundaries set in the Treaty of Guadalupe-Hidalgo). Just under 1,600, or 2.6 percent, were Anglo Americans and European immigrants, most of whom had settled in towns such as Santa Fe and Las Vegas. By 1860, the population grew to nearly 94,000, but then declined to less than 92,000 ten years later, due to a combination of out-migration and the partitioning of New Mexico in 1862 to form the Arizona Territory.[24] Consequently, the number of those born in New Mexico declined from 84,487 to 83,175 during the 1860s.

Concerned about this apparent stagnation, land agents, boosters, and statehood advocates looked to the railway as the catalyst for population growth.[25] But their optimism belied the sad fact that westbound migrants generally saw New Mexico as little more than a way station en route to California. A relatively forsaken destination in the years before the railway, New Mexico trailed every western state and territory in drawing European and Anglo migrants into its borders. Between 1870 and 1880, Judge Hazeldine's "promised land" lost 8,000 more white Americans than it gained. In other words, U.S.-born white residents of the territory had migrated to neighboring lands in greater numbers than they arrived. Among those outbound migrants were some Nuevomexicano families (whom the census enumerated as "white") that had pushed north into southern Colorado, adding to an already significant presence there; others were Americans who, drawn to jobs in other lands, left the impoverished territory of New Mexico. The 1880 federal census found 12,600 New Mexico–born whites residing outside the territory, of whom 9,500 appeared in Colorado, 1,100 in Arizona, 500 in Texas, and 300 in California.[26] In material terms, these lands prospered through their labor-intensive industries: mining, railroads, surplus farming, and small manufacturing.

Richard L. Nostrand attributes the exodus of Nuevomexicanos to their dwindling traditional land bases and to failed legal battles to confirm their lands or protect them from encroachment. Unable to ranch or farm as freely as before, Nuevomexicano males sought wage-paying jobs in adjacent states—as field hands, railroad workers, and freighters—to supplement or replace their declining village lifeways. "For some," writes Nostrand, "a willingness to take Anglo jobs became a necessity." But for others, it was an affirmative choice prompted by "the arrival of more Anglo jobs" to neighboring states: "To work for an Anglo seasonally, despite the hardships of leaving the family, was simply more remunerative than to work in the village all year."[27] Seasonal migration was a strategy for survival. As poorer Nuevomexicano families became indebted to merchants and landed ricos, seasonal migration afforded a multisource income, a flexible division of labor, the preservation of a communal lifeway, and an outlet for individual enterprise. In seasonal migration, writes Sarah Deutsch, Nuevomexicanos "beheld a new mode of expansion, one that allowed increased density on the land, and one that kept them from poverty without requiring either a permanent departure from their own culture or a permanent entry into Anglo culture."[28] Nuevomexicano villagers took little notice of the political boundaries separating New Mexico from Colorado, Texas, and Arizona. Familial networks traversed these without care.

Among those who migrated to New Mexico, foreign-born whites usually stayed for the long haul. Their arrival resulted in a net inmigration of about three thousand during the 1870s. Nearly one migrant in two was born in Mexico and settled primarily in the southern half of the territory. Europeans numbered far fewer than Mexicans. Most of them came from Ireland, Germany, or England.[29] U.S.-born newcomers accounted for the remainder—about one migrant in three. They typically arrived from New York, Pennsylvania, Missouri, or Texas (table 3.1).[30] But foreigners comprised a rather small share of New Mexico's population, and never exceeded 7.3 percent between 1860 and 1910 (graph 3.1).[31] Similarly, nonwhite movement to New Mexico, composed mainly of Chinese immigrants and African Americans, resulted in a net gain but remained small vis-à-vis the total population.[32]

Among westbound white sojourners between 1850 and 1880, migration meant something life-changing. The distances involved and

Table 3.1

U.S.-Born Migrants to New Mexico by State of Birth 1850–1910

1850	1860	1870	1880	1890	1900	1910
NY 673	NY 400	NY 415	TX 1,015	TX 4,835	TX 8,724	TX 30,506
PA 97	PA 215	PA 292	MO 866	MO 2,326	MO 3,458	MO 11,605
MO 93	MO 171	TX 282	OH 820	IL 1,804	CO 2,721	IL 7,607
n/a	n/a	n/a	PA 685	NY 1,610	IL 2,531	OK 7,348
n/a	n/a	n/a	NY 665	OH 1,604	KS 2,053	KS 6,281
n/a	n/a	n/a	n/a	PA 1,518	OH 1,768	IN 4,764

Sources: Bureau of the Census, *U.S. Census of Population, 1850–1910*; Richard R. Greer, "Origins of the Foreign-Born Population of New Mexico during the Territorial Period," *New Mexico Historical Review* 17, no 4 (October 1941): 281–87.

Graph 3.1

Population of New Mexico, 1850–1910

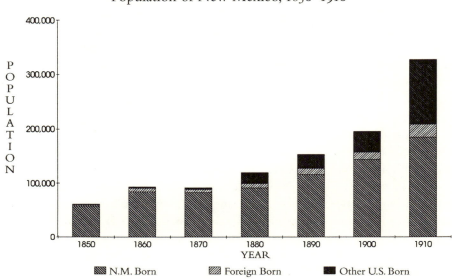

Sources: Bureau of the Census, *U.S. Census of Population, 1850–1910;* Richard R.
  Greer, "Origins of the Foreign-Born Population of New Mexico during the
  Territorial Period," *New Mexico Historical Review* 17, no. 4 (October 1941):
  281–87.

the absence of rail transport made return migration difficult. Many of
these migrants learned Spanish and/or Indian languages and became
successful traders, merchants, ranchers, or farmers. They often adapted
to their surroundings by marrying into a Nuevomexicano community, or by settling into one of the small, far-flung Spanish-speaking
villages of the north.[33] For many migrants, New Mexico was the last
stop on a tortuous journey from the eastern seaboard through conduit cities such as Saint Louis and Chicago. For others, it was safe haven
on the dangerous trek to California. And for the less fortunate, like
the German-born William Kronig, New Mexico offered little more
than refuge from indigence and a chance at redemption.

Stranded in Santa Fe, penniless and desperate for a hot meal,
Kronig barely survived the spring of 1849. Halfway to California's
gilded streams, he arrived in Santa Fe only to discover that a money
order he had purchased in Independence, Missouri, proved unre-
deemable. The merchant who sold Kronig the money order had since

died. When his assets were liquidated, Kronig's life savings were instantly reduced to a worthless piece of paper. Desperate, Kronig sold his last possessions—a feeble horse and a stash of tobacco—and joined the U.S. Army in its campaigns against the Plains Indians. Five years later, we find him in southern Colorado. Gifted with languages, Kronig had become a prosperous trader among the Nuevomexicanos, Cheyenne, Arapaho, Comanche, and Sioux. By 1857, his profits had enabled him to purchase six hundred acres near the New Mexico village of Watrous on the Santa Fe Trail. There Kronig married, raised a family, ranched, and mined. Later, he would serve as Mora County's commissioner to the Bureau of Immigration, advising fellow immigrants as to the lay of the land and its mineral riches. And it was there, in Watrous, that William Kronig would live out his days.[34] Kronig exemplifies the multiple ways in which white migrants, especially European migrants whose first language was other than English, adapted to the circumstances in which they found themselves.

European migrants were generally more adaptive to their environs than their Anglo American counterparts, who often sought to impose on native western communities Anglo Saxon values and codes of behavior.[35] As Anglo Americans encroached from the east, they brought with them distinct notions of God, property, industry, and capital, as well as fixed ideas about race.[36] In New Mexico, as throughout the Southwest, Anglo Americans sought to refashion the culture of their adopted hometowns to suit their Protestant values, material tastes, and prejudices. But in New Mexico, in contrast to California, Arizona, and Texas, Anglo Americans did not numerically eclipse Nuevomexicanos and Native Americans until 1910.

The coming of the railway portended a dramatic rise in the number of migrants from Texas and the Midwest. And to a large extent, it delivered. The volume of Texans between 1870 and 1910 jumped from 1,015 to 30,506. Those from Missouri increased from 866 to 11,605. Illinois, Oklahoma, Kansas, and Indiana replaced New York and Pennsylvania as the largest contributors to New Mexico's population between 1870 and 1910. The railway enabled thousands of transplants to make the journey faster and cheaper than ever before (table 3.2).[37]

Nineteenth-century thinkers believed that migrants brought with them certain enterprising values that allowed civilization to vanquish savagery and prosperity to take root in the western territories. Some scholars argue, to the contrary, that prosperity attracted

Table 3.2

New Mexico Population by Place of Birth, 1850–1910

		Born in NM		Born Outside NM		U.S.	Foreign
Year	Total	No.	%	No.	%	Born	Born
1850	61,547	58,421	95.0	3,126	5.0	1,063	2,063
1860	93,516	84,487	90.0	9,029	10.0	2,306	6,723
1870	91,874	83,175	91.0	8,699	9.0	3,079	5,620
1880	119,565	91,575	76.6	27,990	23.4	19,939	8,051
1890	153,593	116,254	76.7	37,339	23.3	26,080	11,259
1900	195,310	143,881	74.7	51,429	25.3	37,804	13,625
1910	327,301	184,749	57.4	142,552	42.6	119,406	23,146

Sources: Bureau of the Census, *U.S. Census of Population, 1850–1910;* Richard R.
Greer, "Origins of the Foreign-Born Population of New Mexico during the
Territorial Period," *New Mexico Historical Review* 17, no. 4 (October 1941):
281–87.

migrants like a magnet and that economic growth induces, and later results from, migration. Other scholars, such as Nostrand, have explained migration as a function of "push" and "pull" factors. They cite the repelling force of poverty and economic displacement in one's place of origin, and the distant lure of jobs or a higher standard of living. Still others see "chain migration" and "return migration" as self-sustaining patterns that function in conjunction with culture, family, and economic incentives.[38] Whatever the precise mechanics of migration, suffice it to say that New Mexico did not receive the same volume of immigrants as other western lands, and this fact confirmed the popular impression that New Mexico was a land lacking prosperity, industry, progress.

The climate of anti-Mexican sentiment in Congress, combined with sluggish "American" migration to New Mexico, did not bode well for self-government. The territory continued to lack a sufficiently large Anglo American population to gain bipartisan support for its statehood bid. Opponents seized on this fact in their unyielding attacks and continued to characterize Nuevomexicanos as lacking industry, intelligence, and enterprise. Even certain proponents of statehood subscribed to the notion that "the Spanish and Mexican race has caused the country to progress scarcely a move in the march of material improvement and wealth."[39] To counter this impression, New Mexico's leaders explored ways to stimulate Anglo American and European immigration, viewing it as beneficial to the statehood cause.

Indeed, throughout the western territories, Anglo American immigration and exploitation of the land's resources were viewed as essential to gaining admission to the Union. It is not surprising, therefore, that in petitioning for statehood, New Mexico's asamblea would overestimate the number of European and Anglo American residents in the territory in 1874 and 1876. Members of the asamblea felt compelled to paint New Mexico as a rapidly industrializing frontier, whose mines and agriculture promised extraordinary riches.[40] But a skeptical Congress steadfastly rejected such claims. New Mexico would need a much larger Anglo American population if it wished to become a state.[41]

Despite numerous setbacks in the 1870s, officials in Santa Fe beamed with optimism on the railway's arrival in 1880. In the previous two years, Chinese, Mexican, and Irish workers had spiked more than one thousand miles of railway across the territory, linking New Mexico to populations and markets on either coast. Newspapers announced that "the coming of the iron steed" foretold great things for the people and the territory, including increased immigration, commerce, better communication, and, ultimately, statehood. More precisely, the advent of the railway meant that: (1) by federal mandate, the lands adjoining the rails were about to be surveyed and offered for sale; (2) land in towns stationed in its path would accrue value through subdivision and an increased demand brought about by immigration; (3) timber, mines, and trade centers would be better accessed and exploited, and their products more efficiently transported to national markets; and (4) New Mexico would attract much-needed capital to exploit these resources.[42]

The *Weekly New Mexican* acknowledged the relationship among the railway, land speculation, and immigration, stating, "We have many citizens who are owners of thousands of acres of land—possessing large grants—the resources of which would yield to the holders hundreds of thousands of dollars if settled and developed. Why, then, do not our land grant men move to adopt measures to show to the railroad companies and others the value of our lands and the resources of our Territory, so that they can be increased in value by their development[?]"[43] It was clear to statehood advocates, land agents, and políticos alike that, with the advent of rail transport, New Mexico stood on the precipice of change. As Prince suggested, the coming of the railway did, in fact, bring about the "mingling" of peoples and cultures. But few could have imagined that the railroad would permanently reshape social relations in New Mexico by diminishing Nuevomexicano dominance and power, and by commodifying "Spanish colonial" and, to a much greater degree, "Indian" cultures.

Most Nuevomexicanos were quite upbeat about the future, though not all possessed the exuberance voiced by Sena or Prince. Some even expressed reticence or outright hostility. In 1872, running on a traditionalist platform that opposed the railway and further immigration, the influential político Francisco Perea declared, "We don't need you damned Yankees in the country. . . . We can't compete with you, you will drive us all out, and we shall have no home left us." Eight years later, discontented Nuevomexicanos attacked railway construction workers at a place called Cow Creek Hill, though the incident appears to have developed less out of resentment of the railway's intrusion than out of racial tension that exploded during a social dance.[44] The Las Vegas–based *Revista Católica* worried that the railway would open the door to land-hungry immigrants who might try "to obtain possession of the best lands of the Territory." It cautioned Nuevomexicanos to "obtain clear title to your lands" before the impending onslaught of Anglo immigrants.[45]

Generally speaking, however, opposition to things "modern" was muted, and enthusiasm prevailed. Most Nuevomexicanos recognized that the railway would hasten immigration and fuel tourism, but few could have predicted its impact on their culture, or on relations with their Anglo American and Pueblo Indian neighbors.

ϟ The Bureau of Immigration, 1880–1912

Six days after the railway reached Santa Fe, New Mexico's legislature passed a bill authorizing the creation of the Bureau of Immigration. In doing so, leaders acknowledged the need for an organized campaign to draw more Anglo American migrants to the territory. But as immigration bureaus go, New Mexico's was slow to organize, and, by the time it did, it was faced with stiff competition from bureaus in other territories and states.[46] The *Weekly New Mexican* implored the bureau to act quickly. While territories such as Kansas, Colorado, and Arizona offered generous inducements for railway expansion and had disseminated pamphlets to eastern states, New Mexico's bureau had done "comparatively nothing."[47] However just days after that pronouncement, twelve governor-appointed commissioners convened in Santa Fe and elected the bureau's first president, Chief Justice LeBaron Bradford Prince.[48]

From the arrival of the railway in 1880 to the achievement of statehood in 1912, the Bureau of Immigration was New Mexico's leading booster organization. It guiding mission was to "prepare and disseminate accurate information as to the soil, climate, minerals, resources, production and business of New Mexico, with special reference to its opportunities for development, and the inducements and advantages which it presents to desirable immigration and for the investment of capital."[49] In practice, however, the bureau was a vigorous promoter of statehood. It sought to increase both immigration and tourism as a means of transforming New Mexico's racial demography, thereby vanquishing the popular perception that New Mexico was a territory lacking Anglo American civilization.

The Bureau of Immigration disseminated over five hundred thousand pamphlets, brochures, and newsletters announcing the territory's material wealth, healthy climate, and exotic cultures. By the twentieth century, it had succeeded in creating among Anglo Americans outside New Mexico a popular image of Pueblo Indians as docile, sedentary, and semicivilized, and Nuevomexicano villagers as descendants of the conquistadores. This biracial impression was at complete variance with the image that dominated in the outside world during the nineteenth century: that Indians were "savages" and Nuevomexicanos were "greasers." In the same way that the statehood debate in Congress reshaped racial perceptions and ethnic identities, so did the booster publications alter the way that Anglo Americans perceived Pueblo Indians and Nuevomexicanos.

Their new-and-improved images can be found in the bureau's many publications, which carefully marketed Indian and Spanish identities to make the territory more alluring to tourists and migrants. Bureau pamphlets (as well as railway company brochures) put to rest any fears that New Mexico ran wild with hostile Indians and cruel, swarthy Mexicans; they described the land as a meeting ground, wherein peace-loving Pueblo Indians and noble Spaniards had coexisted for nearly three centuries. This image, of course, spoke volumes about Anglo American fantasies and desires. It catered to American tourists' search for the primitive while assuaging their concerns for their safety. Implicit (and sometimes quite explicit) in the bureau's brochures was a kind of celebration of American progress and industry, which made the backward ways of native peoples in New Mexico all the more distinctive and exotic.

A recurring subtext of tourist propaganda depicted New Mexico as a three-tiered society wherein Indians possessed the most pristine and least developed civilization, Nuevomexicanos had conserved medieval traditions and chivalry, and Americans were the bearers of industry, science, or progress. Most Americans latched onto the Indian image and showed much less interest in the Spanish heritage of the region.

Very early in the bureau's existence, its visionaries had come to comprehend tourism—the temporary visitation of New Mexico's places and peoples—as a profitable industry unto itself. Tourists, like migrants, had material needs. They were consumers, with an appetite for ethnic cultures. The railway allowed individuals—at least those who could afford a ticket—the freedom of travel, and it initiated an era of migration and leisure travel that grew steadily into the twentieth century. New Mexico's Bureau of Immigration merely sought to capture as much westward traffic as possible, hoping to persuade visitors to plant themselves and buy land in the territory. One 1883 Las Vegas Hot Springs brochure summarized this new recreation, saying, "Among the principal objects of tourist travel are health, rest, [and] recreation . . . but the chief aim of the tourist is to see something new, interesting and instructive."[50] Rendering New Mexico's landscape "enchanting" and peoples "exotic" would become an enduring occupation of the bureau. Tourism not only offered the prospective migrant a chance to experience New Mexico's enchantment as a prelude to settlement, but also represented an increasingly popular and profitable form of rail business. Railway companies initiated their own booster campaigns to increase tourism, sometimes in collaboration with the bureau.[51]

Ethnic cultures, by themselves, were not the main selling point between 1880 and 1912; rather, the richness of the land and salubrious weather were New Mexico's foremost commodities. In its first five years, the Bureau of Immigration circulated over one hundred thousand publications to prospective settlers.[52] Most of these echoed themes found in Brevoort's *New Mexico*. They emphasized the territory's natural resources, opportunities for wealth, and excellent climate. "Rich mines can be found in almost every direction," touted one bureau publication; "our mountains contain illimitable treasures, in the shape of lead, iron, copper, silver, mica, and gold." "Large tracts of good-sized pine trees," declared another, "and an abundance of wood for charcoal; gypsum, marble, flagging and building stone . . . are quite general through the county."[53] Although land and natural resources were showcase items for such propaganda, New Mexico's climate increasingly became a selling point unto itself. The area's dry and mild weather had long been recognized as the finest in the nation for respiratory ailments, especially tuberculosis, the country's leading killer in the nineteenth century.[54] While in New England tuberculosis was claiming one life of every four, in New Mexico it claimed only one in thirty-three, the lowest rate in the nation. Publications frequently cited medical opinions as to the rapid recovery among tuberculosis patients. One Lew Kennon, a Santa Fe doctor, testified that "even when the lungs were irreparably diseased, very much benefit has resulted. Invalids have come here with their system falling into tubercular ruin, and their lives have been astonishingly prolonged by the dry, bracing atmosphere. I have never known a case of bronchitis brought here that was not vastly improved or altogether cured."[55] Absent a medicinal cure, tuberculosis patients sought out the dry climate of the West in greater numbers as the railways made transportation easier. "Lungers," as they were sometimes called, flocked to New Mexico's sanatoria and mineral hot springs by the hundreds from as far away as France. By 1912, New Mexico boasted twenty-three sanatoria; eight so-called "health homes," ranches, and camps; and more than a dozen mineral springs and spas.[56] Pamphlets declared New Mexico "a National Sanitarium."[57]

In addition to publishing propaganda, bureau agents traveled to expositions and conventions throughout New Mexico and the nation, showcasing the territory's products and distributing pamphlets. In 1881, for example, agents helped to organize the First Annual Territorial Fair in Albuquerque, where the bureau distributed a sixty-six-page booklet entitled *Resources of New Mexico*.[58] Bureau representatives also attended the 1893 Columbian Exposition in Chicago. In the 1890s, with passage subsidized by various railways, bureau agents showcased New Mexico's agricultural produce and precious minerals at conventions in Nebraska and Tennessee, where they handed out more than 125,000 pamphlets. Prince himself traveled extensively on behalf of the bureau and on behalf of the territory's campaign for statehood. In 1881, he chaired a Trans-Mississippi Commercial Congress in Houston, where he authored a resolution urging the federal government to approve statehood for New Mexico. And in 1904 Prince represented the bureau at the Louisiana Purchase Exposition in St. Louis.[59]

Although the bureau's principal purpose at these conferences was to exhibit New Mexico's agricultural and mineral wealth, its secondary purpose was to disseminate brochures that depicted New Mexico as a rapidly industrializing territory that was ripe for investment and settlement. Between 1880 and 1885, William Gillette Ritch (who presided over the bureau from 1883 to 1885) authored a series of publications, with titles such as *Illustrated New Mexico: Historical and Industrial* (which went through five editions) and *Santa Fé: Ancient and Modern, Including Its Resources and Industries*. "The Territory of New Mexico," wrote Ritch in the former work, "is anomalous, in that it is the seat of the antipodes of civilizations upon the continent." In this land, "modern energy, enterprise and prosperity, with the coming of steam transportation . . . has here peaceably met, face to face, mediaeval conservatism, and the crooked stick plows and industrial methods of the Ptolemies." According to Ritch, New Mexico was the meeting ground for the modern Americans, the descendants of "the old Latin civilization" and the "native [Pueblo Indian] races."[60] It was precisely this convergence that made New Mexico unique in all of the United States, he claimed. Here, Anglo Americans could witness and, indeed, participate in the modernization of the two preindustrial races, the Spanish and the Indian. Here, enterprising "Americans" could build stately homes next to ancient Indian adobes.

The juxtaposition of the modern with the ancient or medieval characterized a large number of the bureau's publications between 1880 and 1912. Rather than depicting Pueblo Indians and Spaniards as savages or barbarians, Ritch cast them as two distinct layers of civilization that were about to be covered over by modern, industrial, American civilization. New Mexico's history, therefore, was characterized by three strata of civilization—the Pueblo, the Spanish, and the American.

Ritch praised Pueblo Indians as the heirs of the original strata of civilization in North America. "Pre-Columbian inhabitants of New Mexico," he said, "possessed many of the characteristics, environments and habits of civilization. These people resided in permanent homes, in houses sometimes three and four stories in height."[61] Ritch distinguished Pueblo Indians from what he called the "wild tribes" that raided their neatly constructed villages. Pueblo Indians possessed racial roots that dated at least as far back as the Teutons: "There was a people here with arts and sciences and culture, gray with antiquity, when our forefathers were barbarians in the woods of Germany."[62] Santa Fe, Ritch insisted, was the very birthplace of the great Aztec Empire. Between 1880 and 1885, virtually all of the bureau's publications alluded to Ritch's Montezuma Legend, and to Santa Fe as the birthplace of Aztec civilization.

In 1885, Ritch went so far as to change the name of his most popular publication from *Illustrated New Mexico* to *Aztlán: The History, Resources and Attractions of New Mexico*.[63] Besides embellishing the material and climatic wonders of New Mexico, Ritch recounted the then-famous Montezuma Legend, which gained notoriety in the 1870s and 1880s. It fixed the birthplace of Montezuma I, founder of Tenochtitlán, or contemporary Mexico City, in the city of Santa Fe or nearby Pecos Pueblo. As recounted by Ritch, Montezuma I was said to have been born into poverty in the vicinity of Santa Fe. Endowed with a magical rattle, he blessed hunters with special powers, garnering for himself status and fame, and eventually power as the monarch of the Pueblo people. One day, as prophesied by the Great Spirit, an eagle appeared before Montezuma. On mounting it, he flew off into the horizon, trailed by a procession of followers. In AD 1325, after stopping several times and establishing many settlements, Montezuma arrived at Lake Tenochtitlán, the promised destination, and here founded the great Aztec civilization that later was defeated by the Spaniard Hernán Cortes.[64]

Ramón A. Gutiérrez has commented on what he calls "the political uses of Indian mythology" in the bureau's early publications. The growing popularity of the Montezuma Legend, he writes, mirrored a rising interest among Americans in evolutionary theory.[65] During the 1870s, notes Gutiérrez, anthropologists, led by Lewis H. Morgan, had begun to "supplant romantic representations of the Indians as Noble Savages, and instead to place Indians at the bottom of an evolutionary scale that led up toward European cultural dominance and superior-ity."[66] By relegating the Pueblos to the bottom of three layers of civ-ilization, Anglo Americans were, in fact, celebrating the triumph of modernity and progress. As a civilized people, Pueblo Indians were suddenly disarmed and docile. The Montezuma Legend also had commercial utility as well. The railway was quick to see the value of Indian mythology in promoting travel. In 1882, Miguel Antonio Otero—former territorial delegate to Congress and acting vice pres-ident of the Santa Fe Railway—alluded to the railroad as the reincar-nation of Montezuma.[67] Standing before a crowd of dignitaries and tourists, Otero inaugurated the fashionable Montezuma Hotel in Las Vegas, proclaiming:

> The [nearby] Pecos Indians . . . implicitly believed that their mighty ill-fated emperor, the glorious Montezuma, disappeared from view amid the clouds of their native mountains, that he promised to return . . . [and] that he would come in glory from the east. . . . The last remnant of the faithful old tribe has disappeared . . . but we who fill their places, have lived to see the return of the mighty chieftain. . . . [T]onight we hail his coming in the new and splen-did halls of the Montezuma![68]

What made Pecos culture so alluring to some Nuevomexicanos like Otero—as opposed to tourists—was its very demise. The disap-pearance of the Pecos Indians announced the coming of the Iron Steed, and with it, all the signs of modernity and American progress. The unspoken subtext, of course, was that Nuevomexicanos as well as Anglos had "filled their places" and "lived to see the return" of Montezuma in his modern form.

Indian mythology also made valuable those artifacts now deemed to be "authentic" Indian wares. It made them leisure commodities to be bought and sold as testimony to the inevitability of American progress and Indian demise. During the 1880s and 1890s, anthropol-ogists were particularly effective at enhancing the commercial value of Indian relics and handmade goods by promoting the false notion that all Indians represented the last of a dying race. Although Native American populations nationwide were indeed diminishing at an astonishing rate during the third quarter of the nineteenth century—especially where Anglo American presence was most notable, as in California—Pueblo Indian numbers were beginning to rebound.[69] According to Ritch, this was because Pueblo Indians possessed a more enduring and vibrant culture than other "savage" tribes. To add scientific weight to such assertions, Ritch invoked the names of two anthropologist friends, Frank Cushing and Adolph Bandelier. Cushing worked at Zuni from 1879 to 1884, and Bandelier lived in Santo Domingo and Cochiti in 1881. Ritch turned to them for "authoritative" reports on the progress of excavations and Pueblo history. They served, effectively, as agents of cultural interpretation.[70] Bureau publications often digressed into a rambling hodgepodge of names, dates, and sites; nevertheless, their authority was revered. Bandelier, for whom a national monument of Indian ruins near Los Alamos would later be named, became a favorite in Santa Fe circles. In one 1885 publication, Ritch praised Bandelier, declaring, "His labor in the Santa Fe group has been particularly indefatigable, and one of love. [He works] single and alone, many times penetrating inhospitable regions, beset with hostile Indians, and gathering both by observation and collections from the remains and monuments of the past."[71] Praised among Anglos, he was merely tolerated at Cochiti.[72]

    As cultural interpreters, Bandelier and Cushing served the forces of American colonization. Through them, the bureau was able to lend an air of authenticity to its fabulous textual (and visual) depictions of Pueblo Indians. These anthropologists consolidated what Dean MacCannell calls their "intellectual empire."[73] MacCannell and others have written a good deal about how anthropology and tourism operate as modern-day forms of colonization and imperialism. "Tourists are purveyors of modern values the world over," says MacCannell, "and so are social scientists. And modern tourists share with social scientists their curiosity about primitive peoples, poor peoples and ethnic and other minorities."[74] James Clifford argues that tourists and anthropologists, in seeking out the "primitive" or "tribal," the "traditional" or "authentic," are in fact defining modernity by opposition.[75] The juxtaposition of the modern and the preindustrial is what made New Mexico so enchanting to the rail traveler as well as to the migrant. One 1893 publication made this clear: "The aspect of the country, the homes, the manners, and customs of native people; the Indian civilization, long antedating the advent of Columbus . . .

all these reached in a few miles or a few hours, from the unsurpassed comforts of civilized life, is what Las Vegas offers to the traveler seeking her gates for pleasure."[76]

The railway, like the anthropologist, was an interloper, a noisy intrusion in the pristine landscape. It symbolized modernity, industry, efficiency. Yet, ironically, the Santa Fe Railway would find itself in bankruptcy in 1893, the year Frederick Jackson Turner declared the "frontier" three years "closed." Turner's conceptualization of westward expansion would have benefited from New Mexico's example. Had he traveled to the territory, he would have witnessed how the meeting ground between "civilization" and "savagery"—or better, the "modern" and the "preindustrial"—was still very much intact. If the railway was a sign of modernity, it is not surprising that the railway companies would embark on a campaign to promote passenger travel by invoking all the artifacts and images of the "dying" Indian race. A 1904 publication put out by the Rock Island Railway portrayed the Pueblos as the last of an ancient race, whose stone and adobe houses stood as testimony to their persistence.

> For the tourist with an eye to the ancient and the curios and a mind for the mysterious, New Mexico affords peculiar and inexhaustible attractions. Well has it been called the land of Sunshine and of Mystery. Here are the monuments of a past race— pyramids—not the tombs of buried kings, but the one-time habitations of a people co-existent with the builders of Nineveh. . . . The Pueblo and Zuni Indians are what remain of the race that left its impress on this part of the world. . . . In the region of Santa Fe and Albuquerque are numerous pueblos with populations ranging from 100 to 2,000 souls, living much as their ancestors did when Coronado first came and saw and—was disappointed.[77]

By simply boarding a Rock Island or Santa Fe train, one could be transported back in time to the preindustrial days and purchase the remnants of ancients, such as pottery and figurines.

Few individuals were as effective at marketing Indian images and artifacts as the hotel operator and entrepreneur Fred Harvey. Harvey's empire consisted of a network of hotels that dotted the Santa Fe rails between Missouri and California, and offered museum-like showrooms of Indian artifacts for sale. In 1902 Harvey constructed the Alvarado Hotel in Albuquerque, where travelers could marvel at Indian, and later "Spanish," commodities. On disembarking the train, visitors would find themselves face-to-face with "real Indians" selling their wares. From the train platform, travelers were ushered into a sort of workshop where Indians were seen weaving and crafting in diligent silence. Then it was on to the display room for purchases of "authentic" handmade rugs, pottery, paintings. Marta Weigle describes the Alvarado Hotel experience as a "world's fair," a display of ethnic culture ordered in such a way as to cater to middle-class sensibilities. Indian artifacts were best appreciated when tourists could spy upon the working artisans within the safe and palatable atmosphere, and within walking distance of modern-day accommodations.[78]

In 1900, the Santa Fe Railway began its own campaign to exploit things Indian.[79] It hired an Indian enthusiast named William Haskell Simpson to advertise "the people's kind of railroad" in order to make it seem more user-friendly.[80] Simpson was the first to devise an effective marketing strategy based upon artists' renditions of Indians, or what they conceived Indians to be. In 1906 he commissioned a team of artists, including William Leigh, the so-called "Sagebrush Rembrandt," and other artists in Santa Fe and Taos, to produce an annual calendar for the company, featuring "the Santa Fe Indian." According to T. C. McLuhan, "This Indian possessed an aura of glamour. An intangibility. An ineffable essence. . . . The Santa Fe Indian represented a prototype of preindustrial society."[81] By invoking wistful images of Native Americans, the railway sought to capitalize on the tantalizing contrast between "primitive" Indian culture and "modern" American culture. This contrast was key to promoting tourism as a means of comprehending and experiencing the preindustrial past; moreover, it inculcated among Anglo Americans an appreciation for their own role in the evolution of the frontier from its original "savage" condition to its present "civilized" state.[82]

In New Mexico, however, this evolution was initiated not by Anglo American pioneers, but by Spanish conquistadores, a point made with increasing frequency in bureau publications toward the end of the nineteenth century. Only in New Mexico, boasted the bureau, could tourists witness the confluence of three distinct living peoples who exemplified three historical epochs and strata of civilizations: Pueblo Indians personified the earliest epoch and lowest stratum, Nuevomexicanos the middle, and Anglo Americans the superior.

Toward the end of the nineteenth century, bureau publications began to emphasize New Mexico's Spanish colonial past and to make fewer references to the Pueblo Indians' Montezuma Legend. This is not to say that the Montezuma Legend ceased to be popular among tourists and the English-reading public, for in 1889 New Mexico writer Susan Wallace observed that "the Montezuma myth is so interwoven with the past and future of the Indians that every allusion to their history and religion must of necessity contain the revered name."[83] Moreover, between 1888 and 1906, Congress repeatedly considered admitting New Mexico into the Union as the "State of Montezuma."[84] Although the new name garnered widespread appeal among eastern congressmen, many New Mexicans vehemently protested it. Among the protestors was the *New Mexican,* though it did so reluctantly: "It is a big sacrifice to surrender a name that has been hallowed by deeds of valor and thrilling events of almost four centuries," editorialized the *New Mexican,* "but New Mexico is willing to pay the price."[85] By the turn of the century, the Montezuma Legend had gained a following throughout the country, but in New Mexico there had emerged a greater appreciation of Spanish history, civilization, and culture.

The bureau's early publications made scant reference to the Spanish colonial period. Ritch's "Historical Sketch" of New Mexico, a treatise on the progression from Montezuma to the Iron Steed, appeared in several booklets and brochures during the 1880s. It emphasized the passive, civilized nature of Pueblo Indians, and it decried the Spaniards' persistent abuses of them. Two centuries of Spanish settlement of New Mexico were described as relatively unimportant: "There is but a trifle of definite or important knowledge, except in relation to the oppressions and revolts" of the Pueblo Indians.[86] The period of Spanish domination saw little material progress in the isolated region. However, during the nineteenth century, wrote Ritch, "Items historical … accumulate with accelerating progression."[87]

Spanish colonization had brought little change to New Mexico, according to many observers in the 1880s. "Here is a country known to civilized man for three hundred years," wrote traveler Noble

L[ovely] Prentis in 1882, yet during that period, Spaniards had not "produced an invention, nor wrote or printed a book, nor had any commerce save that of wagon caravan; now in the space of two years [the territory is] filled with railroads, telegraphs, telephones, iron bridges and daily papers."[88] Spanish descendants offered little more than misery or forced Christian conversion to Native Americans, whereas Anglo Americans would bring progress. One rail traveler commented that "[t]his railroad, built by the lineal descendants of those very Puritan exiles, is the sign and symbol of the future. The Spaniard brought ruin; the descendants of the Englishman of the Seventeenth century will bring restoration. The Indians cannot come back; the fire of Montezuma which they are said to have kept burning amid the ruins of Pecos has gone out forever; but as we passed we saw that the Mexican farmer had discarded the wooden plow, and was turning over the soil with the bright [plow]share of the American."[89] The debasement of Spanish colonial and Mexican history, then, gave Anglo Americans a sense of superiority with respect to present-day Nuevomexicanos.

In 1883, Albert R. Greene, a Kansas City journalist, speaking before his colleagues at the Montezuma Hotel, noted that "the country is [now] accessible by palace cars and the adjuncts of civilization." Greene referred to Santa Fe as "the Damascus of America," noting that "At present the whites comprise but twenty per cent of its population, but it is Americanizing very rapidly, and has daily newspapers, gas, water works, street cars, and modern hotels."[90] In Greene's eyes, New Mexico's Nuevomexicanos were nonwhite and were the product of mestizaje, or racial mixture. From the union of "Spaniards" and "Pueblo maidens," he wrote, "sprang the Mexican race, a race that represents in the phases of its people all the ingredients of its origin—Spaniard, Moor, Indian—Mexican. There are a few families in which Castilian predominates, but the great majority are scarcely fairer than their aboriginal neighbors."[91] As this quotation illustrates, one means of invoking Anglo American racial superiority was by disparaging Nuevomexicanos as mixed-bloods and lacking in virtues of industry or sexual restraint.

While some privately published brochures, such as those described above, disseminated a negative image of Nuevomexicanos during the 1880s and 1890s, Bureau of Immigration brochures made little mention of Nuevomexicanos' history or racial origins. Some brochures claimed simply to remedy "misrepresentations" about the territory and its people. One Spanish-language bureau article said that New Mexico's "citizens now understand that the clouds of error and falsehood regarding this country are disappearing, and the light of truth . . . shall show New Mexico as it really is, full of resources, honesty, and patriotism." In order to bring immigration to New Mexico, continued the article, the bureau desired the "cooperation of all, be they Republican or Democrat, Spanish or American, rich or poor."[92]

Despite the bureau's efforts, East Coast readers were deluged with privately published propaganda that projected a negative image of Nuevomexicanos based on their mixed blood. Others depicted Nuevomexicanos as a race improving over time. A 1891 tourist book, authored by Horatio O. Ladd, noted that "[t]he population, in 1846, was about 45,000, a few of whom were Spaniards. The rest were mestizos, partly Spanish and Indian by birth. In character they were generally indolent, and the men, sunk in ignorance and vice, were utterly unfit for self-government, while the women were affectionate, sympathetic with suffering, and rather attractive in personal appearance."[93] However, by the 1880s, writes Ladd, "the native New Mexican" came to appreciate the "increasing demand for knowledge," and the residents established public schools. The population was "greatly changed in its character." A good number of Nuevomexicanos had "spent their blood and treasure" to defend the Union in the Civil War.[94] Ladd advocated New Mexico's admission into the Union, saying that "her rejection" in Congress was due to "a prejudice which early gained strength against her among the people of the North." In order to achieve statehood, he continued, New Mexico needed to attract one hundred thousand "intelligent immigrants" and establish a public education system.[95]

As Ladd's work points out, not all booster publications of the 1880s and 1890s simply disparaged Nuevomexicanos or their history. During this period there existed a small but growing movement dedicated to appreciating Spain's colonization and missionization of Native Americans in the West. This movement was partly inspired by Helen Hunt Jackson's 1884 novel *Ramona*. Set in the Mexican period, *Ramona* is the story of a Hispanicized mixed-blood (Irish-Indian) maiden who falls in love with Alessandro, a handsome Temecula Indian. Adopted as a child, Ramona forsook her Castilian lifestyle on a California *rancho* and eloped with her lover. Having abandoned the estate, they were doomed to starvation and death at the hands of Anglo American pioneers.[96] *Ramona* did not embrace the "noble savage" ideal. Rather, it lamented the decline of an idealized, biracial, missionary period, a period marked by two racial archetypes: the benevolent Spanish civilizer and his loyal Indian convert.

In the next chapter we will explore how the popular celebration of these archetypes had its roots in the romantic writings of such authors as Helen Hunt Jackson and Charles Fletcher Lummis. Suffice it to say, however, that during the 1880s and 1890s, a general antipathy toward things Mexican or Spanish still prevailed among most Anglo Americans. Bureau publications, therefore, sought to do two things: dispel racial prejudice, or Hispanophobia, by romanticizing the colonial past, and show Nuevomexicanos to be the descendants of the conquistadores.[97] Although these objectives were not explicitly stated, they were evident in publications dating to the 1890s.

Increasingly, the bureau viewed Spanish colonial history as part of the historical progress of civilization from a precontact indigenous era to the coming of the railway. According to one 1890 brochure, the distant past and present were equally romantic and worthy of appreciation:

> In Santa Fe is the oldest Christian church within the limits of the United States, consecrated to God before the founding of Jamestown or the landing of the Pilgrims at Plymouth....The narrow tortuous streets, the adobe houses, the Mexican inhabitants composing three-fourths of the population, their characteristic dress—all bespeak a time later than that of the Indian domination. But these, too, are old and have an interest for the last comers all their own. Side by side with them are the busy restless Americans of today, injecting their energy into the civilization of the past, and gradually molding it in accordance with their ideas of development and progress.[98]

As the above passage suggests, the 1890s saw a gradual shift in the way that Nuevomexicanos were portrayed in bureau documents. Two phenomena marked the period from 1890 to 1912. First, the

Spanish colonial past gained greater attention and appreciation in bureau documents. And second, present-day Nuevomexicanos were said to be progressive, not stagnant, and to be in the process of being "Americanized." Moreover, their national loyalty was a badge of honor. One 1890s bureau text assured readers that "New Mexicans sealed their faith in universal liberty with their blood.... [T]he Native New Mexican, who blazed the path of freedom, watered it with his blood, fought heroically for the vital interests of his government, has been restrained in a state of pupilage for half a century. The story of the peculiar and unique devotion of the New Mexican of Spanish descent to the American flag is a theme of eloquence."[99]

An 1894 bureau publication, authored by bureau secretary Max Frost, sought to dispel the "epigrammatic slanders" that had "detracted from [New Mexico's] good reputation." Referring to the failing struggle for statehood, Frost wrote that "Although some of these utterances were on the floor of Congress, their reading would hardly make polite literature to-day. The New Mexicans of Spanish descent are among the most honest people in the world. They have not to be sued for a debt, but will pay it to the last cent either in money or service. The task of portraying in straightforward, unexaggerated language the facts about this unknown land is very difficult."[100] According to Frost, the same prejudices that kept New Mexico from becoming a state were keeping immigrants from moving into the territory. He sought to recast New Mexico as "an unknown land of wonderful resources." "Its history is romantic," he said, "and its thousand valleys offer a multitude of opportunities to the industrious."[101]

From 1890 to 1906, Frost served as secretary of the bureau. Simultaneously, he served as editor of the *New Mexican,* whose presses generated bureau publications. More than any of his predecessors, Frost challenged the negative impressions that many easterners held of New Mexico's Nuevomexicanos.[102] In the bureau literature that he edited, Frost projected Nuevomexicanos to be "of Spanish descent," of upstanding moral and racial character, and loyal American citizens. Like Charles Lummis, whose writings on Spanish and Indian cultures captured the imagination of Anglo Americans from the 1890s to the 1920s, Frost made Spanish colonial history a thrilling component in bureau texts. To borrow from historian John R. Chávez, Frost "glorified the Spanish conquistadores and ... opened the way for the thorough romantic Hispanization of the people, culture, and history of New Mexico."[103] Implicit in "Hispanization" is a reconceptualization of living Nuevomexicanos as Spanish and distinctly not Mexican nor mixed-bloods.[104]

Subsequent bureau publications continued to underscore the European presence in New Mexico and the many trials that the Spanish colonizers endured in their triumph over the land and over Native Americans: "The thrilling and romantic incidents composing its history; the protracted and bloody struggles with hordes of savage Indians; the recapture and pillage by hostile Pueblos in 1680; the general massacre of missionaries . . . the reconquest by Diego de Vargas twelve years later . . . afford the material for an epic poem of deep interest."[105] Gone from this 1906 publication are all references to the Montezuma Legend or to Santa Fe as the birthplace of Aztec civilization; a distinctly Spanish, *colonial* discourse had replaced them.[106]

In another brochure, the pre-Columbian presence of Pueblo Indians in Santa Fe is merely implied, not explicitly stated as Ritch had done during the 1880s. Pueblo Indian civilization had, effectively, been written out of the record. The Montezuma Legend had been replaced by a distinctly Spanish colonial discourse that emphasized European conquest and settlement: "Tradition speaks of two prosperous Indian pueblos upon the site of the City of Santa Fe, prior to the coming of the Spanish Conquistadores, over 350 years ago, and it is within the confines of Santa Fe County that the first permanent white settlements in the United States were made."[107] Under the direction of Max Frost, the bureau invoked the history of the Spanish conquest and changed the way Anglo Americans viewed New Mexico's "Mexicans."

The transformation of racial identities in bureau publications between 1894 and 1906 mirrored the transformation that was taking place in the congressional debate over New Mexico's statehood, discussed in the previous chapter. No longer mixed-bloods, the descendants of the conquistadores possessed a clear racial lineage and identity, one that complemented the nation's imperialist discourse at the turn of the century. It was also one that rationalized the Republican claim that Nuevomexicanos were indeed fit for self-government and were truly American citizens. Even the most overt racists conceded that northern New Mexicans possessed a purer lineage than those of the southern part of the territory. In 1898, "ranchwoman"

Edith M. Nicholl surmised that "[t]here is distinct evidence of caste among them, and I am assured that the further one travels from the border, the more marked becomes the improvement in the race."[108]

In addition to disparaging Nuevomexicanos because of their alleged race, Anglo Americans sometimes suspected them of disloyalty to the United States. During the Spanish American War, as rumors abounded that Nuevomexicanos were "sympathizing with the cause of Spain," Max Frost retorted that "[t]he native people of New Mexico have repeatedly proved their loyalty to the American flag and their patriotism is unquestioned."[109] Two years later, the *New Mexican* advocated abolishing the term "Mexican" to describe "the original Caucasian settlers" (that is, Nuevomexicanos) of New Mexico. "There is some difference in race and blood between the descendants of the Spanish settlers of New Mexico and the later immigrants who represent scattered nationalities from Europe, Asia and Africa, but if anybody is entitled to the appellation American," it was the descendants of the original Spanish settlers. All New Mexicans, declared the editorial, were now Americans by virtue of their education and citizenship: "Now that statehood is almost assured ... the public schools are teaching the rising generation without distinction of nationality."[110]

Some railway brochures eliminated all "Mexican" traits from the population by implying that Nuevomexicanos were destined, like the Indian, to assimilate into or disappear amid a growing Anglo American population. One 1904 Rio Grande Railway publication read:

> The Mexican population is not dominant, although it is sufficient to give a decided color to the prevalent impression. The Catholic church is the original church of the southwest—it is the church to which the Indian population as well as those of Spanish origin adhere.... With the influx of immigrants from the eastern states, bringing with them the education and culture of their surroundings, the influence of the Mexican and his out-of-date customs will become less and less. ... New Mexico's social conditions differ in no way from those of any other well-ordered American community.[111]

If the "Mexican" seemed to be disappearing, his history was being elevated to great heights. The pamphlet continued: "The history of Santa Fe is the history of the Great Southwest from the invasion of Coronado in 1541 to the industrial invasion which began with the first railroad in 1880."[112]

Railways also capitalized on the Spanish colonial motif. Fred Harvey and the Santa Fe Railway began designing hotels in the California Mission style and dedicating them to conquistadores.[113] Recall, for example, that Fred Harvey's hotel in Albuquerque bore the name of Coronado's lieutenant, Hernando de Alvarado.[114] "Having mastered an effective method of merchandising the Indians," writes Marta Weigle, "the Harvey Company now faced the challenge of incorporating Spanish colonial culture into their marketable version of the Southwest."[115] Neither tourists nor Congress were fully convinced that Nuevomexicanos were "Spanish," nor were they willing to accept them as "American." In the eyes of many, they remained simply mixed-bloods and "Mexican." Indian artifacts continued to be the most popular ethnic commodities of northern New Mexico. Indian fiestas were advertised in railway brochures.[116] Among easterners, the objectified Indian was perhaps a more familiar racial referent than the Mexican or "Spanish American." Nevertheless, by the twentieth century, bureau publications began to invoke both Spanish and Indian images in their publications, saying, "Tourists are welcomed. New Mexico . . . is the land of the Cliff Dwellers; of the Pueblo Indians; of the Indian dances; of the Conquistadores; of towns and buildings older than the oldest historic monuments of any other part of the United States."[117]

⚓ The Impact of Tourism and Immigration, 1890–1912

The precise number of tourists and migrants who were lured by the bureau's booster propaganda is impossible to gauge. However, evidence of its impact is suggested by the significant rise in bureau correspondence between 1889 and 1902 (table 3.3). By the turn of the century, inquiries about the territory were arriving in record numbers from all parts of the United States, Europe, and Latin America. According to bureau reports, letters written on behalf of whole groups of eager migrants asked about the availability of farmland, irrigation, mining, and weather conditions.[118] The bureau tried to

Table 3.3

Volume of Letters Received by the Bureau of Immigration, 1889–1902

1889–1890	1,400
1897–1898	1,010
1899–1900	2,200
1901–1902	6,000

Source: Herbert H. Lang, "The New Mexico Bureau of Immigration, 1880-1912," *New Mexico Historical Review* 51 (1976): 193–214.

answer each inquiry, but struggled to keep pace with the volume. Frost complained that he lacked the staff to answer all of them. In 1897 and 1898, over a thousand letters reached the bureau. Of these, 436 were recorded as "general in nature"; 252 asked about agricultural programs and irrigation; 198 concerned mining; and 124 concerned the climate. During the next biennium, more than six thousand letters deluged the bureau's office.[119] It remains unknown whether these inquiries were in response to the bureau's publicity campaign, or how many of the correspondents ever actually settled in New Mexico. What is certain is that the population grew dramatically between 1890 and 1910, and much of that increase was due to in-migration.

Although New Mexico saw a minor net out-migration of one thousand white Americans during the 1890s, it realized spectacular growth during the first decade of the twentieth century, during which sixty thousand more persons settled in New Mexico than left the territory (table 3.4). Less dramatic, though equally interesting, was the net migration of foreign-born whites, which grew from four thousand to twelve thousand for the same respective decades (table 3.5).

Corresponding with a rise in net migration, decennial censuses indicate that New Mexico's total population nearly tripled between 1880 and 1910, from nearly 120,000 to 327,000 (see table 3.2). In the first ten years of the twentieth century, white Americans flooded New Mexico three times as fast as during the previous decade. Of the total population, U.S.-born migrants numbered 20,000 in 1880, 26,000 in 1890, 38,000 in 1900, and 120,000 in 1910. The foreign-born population made less remarkable, though still significant, growth, from 14,000 in 1900 to 23,000 in 1910. New Mexico's phenomenal rise in

Table 3.4

Net Migration of the U.S.-Born White Population in Western
Territories and States (in thousands)

States and Territories	1870–1880	1880–1890	1890–1900	1900–1910
Colorado	95	115	45	122
California	72	125	117	465
Oregon	30	65	34	146
Washington	25	150	69	349
Arizona	13	8	18	29
Idaho	10	29	38	95
Montana	9	45	46	59
Wyoming	6	22	12	22
Nevada	2	–13	–5	23
Utah	2	4	–1	4
New Mexico	–8	4	–1	60

Source: Adapted from Hope T. Eldridge and Dorothy Swaine Thomas,
*Demographic Analyses and Interrelations, vol. 3 of Population Redistribution
and Economic Growth in the United States, 1870–1950*, ed. Simon Kuznets
and Dorothy Swaine Thomas (Philadelphia: American Philosophical
Society, 1957), table A1.17, 257.

in-migration was unmatched by that of California or Colorado
during the first decade of the century; however, New Mexico still
possessed a small total population by comparison.

These statistics beg the question: Did the Bureau of Immigration
prompt greater immigration to New Mexico? Bureau officials certainly believed so. Their biennial reports tried to attribute the rise in
immigration to their booster campaign, saying, "owing to the efforts
of the Bureau, more capitalists, healthseekers, tourists and home-
seekers have come to New Mexico during the year 1901 and 1902
than ever before in its history."[120] However, one scholar dismisses such
a relationship, saying, "It is unlikely that the Bureau of Immigration
was responsible for bringing to New Mexico many people who
would not have gone West anyway."[121] As officials in 1880 had predicted, the railroad, indeed, had ushered in an age of expansion,
marked by commerce, industry, and immigration; however, the real
effect of the bureau may never be known. Nevertheless, much can
be said about the social impact of migration to New Mexico.[122]

Table 3.5

Net Migration of the Foreign-Born White Population in Western Territories and States (in thousands)

States and Territories	1870–1880	1880–1890	1890–1900	1900–1910
California	77	11	79	271
Colorado	33	48	20	52
Utah	18	17	12	23
Oregon	14	30	14	60
Arizona	9	5	7	28
Washington	8	75	28	156
Nevada	6	-6	-1	11
Montana	4	32	27	37
Idaho	3	10	9	23
New Mexico	3	4	4	12
Wyoming	2	10	4	13

Source: Adapted from Hope T. Eldridge and Dorothy Swaine Thomas, *Demographic Analyses and Interrelations, vol. 3 of Population Redistribution and Economic Growth in the United States, 1870–1950,* ed. Simon Kuznets and Dorothy Swaine Thomas (Philadelphia: American Philosophical Society, 1957), table A1.14, 254.

By the end of the nineteenth century, Nuevomexicanos had begun to take note of the rapid increase in the Anglo American population. They had also begun to voice a consciousness about their relation to Anglo Americans, and sought to borrow from them the tools of education, commerce, and technology as a means of material advancement. As Spanish-language newspapers proliferated during the 1890s, they disseminated familiar messages in the form of editorials, urging their readers to take advantage of education and commerce as means of advancement. "We are living next to the American, who due to circumstances is our brother, because we are protected by the same flag. Let's take then from him the knowledge which he has that is superior to ours and let's profit from it."[123]

Not all Nuevomexicano newspapers greeted the advent of Anglo Americans with the same enthusiasm. Many objected to the various aspersions cast on them by East Coast travel writers and recent migrants. During its first few months of circulation in 1897, Albuquerque's *El Nuevo Mundo* filled its front pages with observations on "The Past and Present of New Mexico." These articles decried the racist and arrogant travel accounts that had appeared in New York and Chicago journals. Tourists and tourist writers, said *El Nuevo Mundo,* simply did not understand Spanish and Indian peoples.

> If the tuberculars who come to seek health in the benign quality of our climate and pure breezes of our mountains had judgment, if the intelligent tourists who, from the window of a Pullman running at 60 miles per hour, perform the miracle of studying our people and their customs . . . the eastern press would neither fill their pages with unbelievable tales, nor . . . criticize [our] culture. . . . From the descriptions of these tourists, we are considered more barbarous than the ancient redskins found in this country by the Breton conquistadores, and it is a miracle that they do not consider us cannibals.[124]

By the close of the nineteenth century, Nuevomexicano newspapers had begun to voice a growing awareness of the way that tourism and tourist publications had shaped racial impressions and relations in New Mexico. Nuevomexicanos resented being depicted as "dirty, ignorant, unattractive." *El Nuevo Mundo* editorialized that Nuevomexicanos "have never lived like the Anglos, in pigsties located in the barrios of New York."[125]

According to *El Nuevo Mundo,* Anglo tourists simply lacked awareness of Nuevomexicanos' glorious history of conquest: "If these train-bound passengers would like to take the trouble to study even a little of the history of these regions, they would understand that the brave colonizer . . . devoted half his time to survival, and the other half to waging campaigns against the indomitable Apache and bloody Navajo."[126] Anglo Americans' ignorance appeared to be at the heart of their racist sentiment, insisted the article.

El Nuevo Mundo was not an anti-American journal. Rather, it celebrated "American progress" and education, but believed that, in spite of significant changes brought about in the recent years, "for our race, there has been no improvement whatsoever. . . . American progress has hardly benefited our popular masses, and it is urgent that the government pay attention to this."[127] Education—for Anglo Americans and

Nuevomexicanos—was the sole means by which ignorance, prejudice, and underdevelopment could be defeated, the article continued.

Another Spanish-language newspaper, *La Voz del Pueblo,* took note of Anglo American racist impressions. In that same year, 1897, it issued a plea for statehood and blamed the "ignorant" tourists and Congress for New Mexico's continued impoverishment.

> Hundreds of Anglo-American citizens still live today who have entered our land poor, discouraged, hungry, and even ragged; we, inspired by the generosity that has been ours in New Mexico, extended them a cordial welcome, offering them the best place that our humble homes had. . . . But now in turn, many of them have cloaked themselves in the blackest ingratitude, recognizing us as inferior beings, as citizens useless to our government. . . . They possess the view that money is God, is government, and that we do not possess this God. [128]

Again, "American progress" had eluded Nuevomexicanos. *La Voz del Pueblo* insisted that Anglo Americans had intentionally excluded Nuevomexicanos from the means of progress: "Now, if they insist on scorning us, on looking at us only with greedy eyes, on recognizing us only as good subjects for exploitation, we will remind them without mental reservation that we still possess a heritage of gentility. . . . [For] there are many other virtues that are worth more than money." [129] According to this article, Nuevomexicanos possessed a long heritage of "nobility," which, in spite of their poverty, gave them pride and legitimized their claim to statehood and equal treatment by Anglo American tourists and Congress.

By the beginning of the twentieth century, Nuevomexicanos' claim to legitimacy and statehood was premised on their history and their legacy of settlement and conquest. Recall the eloquent discourse of Eusebio Chacón, who, in 1901, declared:

> This is not the first time that the people of New Mexico grow pale from attacks which are gratuitous as well as unjustified. . . . [T]he fact remains . . . that since our forefathers came from Spain, we have lived

on this soil, claiming it through our labors and pop-
ulating it with our progeny. . . . And this seems to be
our crime . . . having come to populate the New
World. . . . But times have changed. . . . Today the
train crosses bellowing and speeding. The entire face
of the Territory has changed, but our fortune . . . has
not changed much.[130]

The above quotations demonstrate that a "Spanish American," or
"*hispano-americano*," consciousness had begun to emerge in New
Mexican newspapers by the turn of the century. To a large degree,
this consciousness was born in a sense of alienation from the Anglo
American political economy. It was articulated within a colonial, historical discourse that served both touristic and political ends, and it
functioned in opposition to Anglo American racist impressions of
"native New Mexicans." Implicit in this consciousness, and sometimes explicit, was the idea that Nuevomexicanos were a "race" apart
from both Pueblo Indians and "savage" nomadic tribes. The notion
of lineal descent from conquistadores, historical attachment to the
land, and Nuevomexicanos' growing pride in their own history mirrored the discourse that had begun to mark tourist literature disseminated by the bureau. History, therefore, had multiple uses as New
Mexico inched toward statehood. It was a means of establishing prior
land occupation as immigrants and settlers flowed into the territory,
and it rendered a disarming and commercially appealing image of
Nuevomexicanos. Perhaps most important, the mantra of Spanish
descendancy was an effective means of "whitening" Nuevomexicanos
in the minds of outside observers, a point we shall explore in chapters to come.

By 1910, the bureau had become an outspoken vehicle for statehood, but its campaign hinged on the notion that Spanish Americans
were becoming integrated into the mainstream of English-speaking
America. It published a leaflet entitled *Why New Mexico Is Entitled
to Statehood*. "Our people are industrious, progressive Americans," it
stated. "Within five years there will not be a native born citizen of
New Mexico twenty-one years of age who cannot speak the English
language."[131] Another brochure touted Santa Fe's seventeen thousand residents, saying that "Fully three-fourths of these inhabitants
speak the Spanish language, but many of these can speak, or at least

understand, English. They are peaceable, conservative and hospitable, and to a certain degree independent." [132]

In the years leading to New Mexico's statehood, Santa Fe was alive with cultural activity. The Historical Society, a longtime conservator of Spanish and Indian artifacts, had gained widespread visibility throughout the region. In 1907, anthropologist Edgar Hewett was named to head Santa Fe's newly founded School of American Archaeology, which would become a leading anthropological institution of the Southwest. In 1909, the legislature established the Museum of New Mexico to showcase the finest pieces of "Indian Art" and pottery. That same year, Hewett supervised the remodeling of the Governor's Palace and rendered it in "Spanish-Pueblo" style, later to become "Santa Fe style." [133] New Mexico would enter statehood equipped with all the trappings of Anglo American civilization. Among immigrants, tourists, and academics alike, it was the absence of industry and the abundance of "ethnicity" that would reaffirm modernity in New Mexico.

On the eve of statehood, New Mexico was astir with "*grandes conmociones,*" declared educator Aurora Lucero. After over sixty years of patient waiting, she said, New Mexico was shedding the rags of territorial status for the splendid suit of statehood.

> From the time that Fray Marcos de Niza and Captain Coronado traveled up the Rio Grande . . . to Santa Fe, to the United States' submission of the last savage Indians in Arizona and New Mexico, the ancient people of this new state, who are nothing but the descendants of the *conquistadores* that braved the mysterious seas . . . have gallantly fought for the preservation of their homes. . . . Today, the descendants of the *conquistadores* of this soil, here since the fifteenth century, are obliged in the new order of things to fight for something more important than life itself: the prestige of their race. [134]

By the time New Mexico had gained statehood, Nuevomexicanas and Nuevomexicanos had grown tired of battling the racial arguments used to deny them equal representation in Congress and a state government. In their quest to be viewed as "fit" for statehood (that is, as racially white), the Bureau of Immigration proved most helpful. Its publications effectively broadcast their "Spanish" heritage in a way that gained them a modicum of respect and admiration. For many Nuevomexicanos, the bureau's publications had redeemed their past and thus emboldened their own sense of Hispanidad. For Hispanophiles and Indian enthusiasts, the "Land of Enchantment" had become a playground for their historical imagination. One tourist brochure proclaimed, "The first pages of the history of New Mexico have scarcely been turned, and already it is regarded as a 'wonder book.'"[135] However, many Nuevomexicanos were already painfully aware that "enchantment" had not come without a price.

Chapter Four

Longing and the White Legend

When Spain can laugh at its provincial detractors, and say: "Evidently you don't know the history of Spain nor of your own country," then Spaniards of every class can feel that their national history has nothing to apologise [*sic*] for more than the history of every other nation—at least so far as the history of discovery and conquest and colonization go—and it seems to me obvious that an entirely different national spirit will begin to crystallize. If in such a *renacimiento* anything I have done or can do shall have any effect, God knows it would be the greatest reward I could conceive of in this life or the next.
—*Charles Fletcher Lummis to Arturo Cuyás*[1]

When Spain's hegemony over the southern rim of North America ended in 1821, its long tenure left an enduring legacy that extended beyond the tangible transformation of people and places. More abstractly, Spain's legacy also lingered in American historical memory, where it took on a life of its own.
—*David J. Weber,*
The Spanish Frontier of North America[2]

⠸⠿ Hispanophilia

In 1893, Charles Fletcher Lummis authored *The Spanish Pioneers,* a dreamy 292-page tale of Spain's conquest of the Americas. He wrote the work to publicize the "humane and progressive spirit" with which Spain had subdued, then civilized, "the aborigines" of the New World.[3] And publicize that spirit he did. So widely read was the book that during his lifetime it saw twelve editions and garnered tributes from readers throughout North America. In 1916, when translated into Spanish by the renowned philologist Arturo Cuyás, the book earned Lummis a corresponding membership in Spain's Real Academia de la Historia, as well as knighthood in the distinguished Orden de Isabel la Católica.[4]

Like the original English-language version, *Los exploradores españoles del siglo XVI: Vindicación de la acción colonizadora española en América* was, as the title suggests, a vindication of Spain's colonial deeds. It repudiated the Black Legend, propagated mainly by England and pervasive in the English-speaking world, which held that Spanish exploits in the New World were particularly atrocious when compared to those of other colonial powers. In a letter to Cuyás, Lummis explained that his book had helped to "break down the foolish race-prejudice" in the United States, and that "its publication in Spain might also be helpful to a better understanding between the two countries; and that Spain might feel that ALL American Historians are not bigoted."[5] In fact, by the 1910s a good number of American historians, as well as a broad section of the reading public, had become enamored of Spain's past. Lummis stood at the forefront of a Hispanophilic movement that celebrated four centuries of Spain's presence in the Western Hemisphere. Its creators painted refreshing pictures of the colonial past: they glorified the virile conquistador and the selfless missionary who had defied all hardship to spread Christianity among *los índios bárbaros,* and they penned epic accounts and wistful sketches of "Mother Spain's" imperial grandeur—all in the name of setting straight the historical record.[6]

Hispanophiles were often engrossed in antiquarian detail; no peculiarity seemed too small to mention, no act of kindness insignificant, and few bad deeds were thought deplorable. In fact, Spain's wrongdoings were a relative matter, contended Lummis. "There was incomparably less cruelty suffered by the Indians who opposed the Spaniards," he wrote, "than by those who lay in the path of any other European colonizers. The Spanish did not obliterate *any* aboriginal nation,—as our ancestors obliterated scores,—but followed the first necessary bloody lesson with humane education and care."[7] Hispanophiles frequently judged Spain's transgressions as necessary to the welfare of native peoples. Such assessments dramatically transformed the English-reading public's historical imagination. They consigned to oblivion Black Legend chronicles of carnage, mayhem, miscegenation, and decadence, and replaced them with melancholy tales of dutiful missionaries bringing faith and reason to the Indians, and of knights in armor exploring the farthest reaches of humanity.

The idealized Spanish past was something alluring. It afforded East Coast readers a nostalgic escape to an age unspoiled by industry or urban blight. For recent arrivals to California or New Mexico, it lent a charming air to the concept of living in the Southwest, while helping white transplants make sense of their newfound and complex racial environs. The Spanish colonial motif, which proved so effective in marketing the region to migrants and tourists, was essentially the same motif that characterized Hispanophilia. As romantic histories such as *The Spanish Pioneers* gained a following, they reshaped the way the English-reading public both imagined the region's past and perceived "Indians" and "Mexicans" in their midst. They also provided an outlet for political and social commentary on issues such as "Indian reform" or New Mexico's statehood quest.

Hispanophilia was born of a desire to return to a simpler way of life that, in fact, had never been all that simple. It was a yearning to experience either through text or through tourism an age of adventure that was far removed from the present-day ills of industrial society. Hispanophilia was more than just the manifestation of nostalgia. It was an ideology. Its adherents believed that Spain's past embodied virtues such as idealism, sacrifice for the greater good, generosity, piety, gentility, "manliness," and benevolence toward "inferior" (that is, Native American) peoples. These seemed destined for the dustbin of history, victims of Anglo American materialism, technology, pragmatism, and individualism.[8]

The idealization of all things Spanish, it should be noted, did not of necessity translate into an abiding affection for all persons of "Spanish" descent. Relations between Hispanophiles and the people whose heritage they admired were sometimes marked by a considerable degree of suspicion, ambivalence, or even hostility. Lacking any direct claim to a Spanish heritage themselves, Anglo American Hispanophiles appropriated native knowledge to suit their own ambitions and desires. Hispanophiles were, as the 1925 Talleres Calpe *Diccionario de la Lengua Española* described them, not Spanish themselves, but were "foreign devotee[s] of Spanish culture, history and customs."[9] Many were adept in the Spanish language and were collectors of Spanish colonial relics or manuscripts. Some had become enamored of the Spanish heritage after spending time among native Spanish-speakers. And despite forming and maintaining some close friendships with Nuevomexicanos, Hispanophiles were more often removed from the quotidian events and experiences of Nuevomexicano villagers. Thus they relied heavily on their native contacts and exploited them for the cultural knowledge that would serve as the basis for their presumed expertise. To be certain, well-educated and well-heeled Nuevomexicanos had a hand in the making of Hispanophilia. To the extent that they brokered their knowledge and served as intermediaries between Anglo and Nuevomexicano villagers—as arbiters of "authenticity" and experts on "folk culture"—they gained in both social status and in influence.

The impact of the Hispanophilic movement on Nuevomexicanos' sense of their own past was considerable. Hispanophilia afforded Nuevomexicanos an acceptable means of defining their historical identity in a language that catered to Anglo Americans' fantasies about the past. Hispanophilia was indeed the underpinning of the "fantasy heritage" that Carey McWilliams described in his landmark book *North from Mexico* in 1949, the product of the Anglo tourist's desires and historical imagination, and it could not have been created or embellished without a degree of collaboration, or cooperation, on the part of "natives." Yet it was no less a tool that Nuevomexicanos plied to rhetorically reclaim a means of control over their declining political fortunes, land base, and language.

This chapter will focus on two leading Anglo authors of the Spanish heritage in New Mexico: Charles Fletcher Lummis and Lebaron Bradford Prince. From the 1880s and into the 1920s, the two labored passionately though separately—and sometimes in direct competition—to popularize various aspects of Spanish colonial history. In this endeavor, both were by and large successful, but their achievements were distinct. Lummis authored ten books and dozens of articles exoticizing the distinctive cultures of the Southwest; he cultivated a vast network of social contacts; and he consciously sought visibility not merely for his message, but for his persona. Hispanophilia was, for Lummis, a vocation as much as it was a vehicle for self-pro-motion. Both nationally and abroad he was known as the tempera-mental "lion" whose editorials roared a love of Native American tradition and Spanish chivalry. Lummis was a consummate celebrity who entertained Spanish nobles and traveled with President Theodore Roosevelt, a classmate from Harvard. Prince, on the other hand, cut a rather provincial figure. Best known not for his historical writing but for his political career, Prince was a Republican stalwart and former jurist who served a term as governor of New Mexico (1889–93) and who championed the statehood cause. Though he lacked Lummis's charisma and literary stature, Prince proved more successful in engaging local Anglos and Nuevomexicanos in their "recovery" of New Mexico's Spanish legacy, as president of the Historical Society of New Mexico from 1883 until his death in 1922.

Hispanophiles both, Lummis and Prince became bitter rivals. Lummis once cursed "old Bullfrog" Prince as "slab-sided, splay-footed, with an eye of the basilisk and the breath of pestilence."[10] Despite his antipathy toward Prince, Lummis clearly shared Prince's conviction that Spain's legacy had been maligned. In their writings, both sought to dispense with the Black Legend and replace it with a more "truthful" account of history, which can only be called the White Legend.

:人 The White Legend

The notion that Spain had endowed the New World with religion and civilization was hardly new to Spaniards themselves. It was a cen-tral narrative in the nation's identity; religion and conquest were twin wellsprings of Spanishness, or hispanidad. To Spain's emissary-schol-ars seeking to redeem the nation's honor following the humiliating loss of its colonies in 1898, the munificent White Legend was simply Spain's "true history" in the Americas. But to transplanted New Englanders schooled in textbook renderings of Spanish treachery, greed, heathenism, and barbarity, it was an invigorating new way to comprehend the history of the Southwest. Popular histories such as *The Spanish Pioneers* were both a vehicle for exploration and an affirmation of the very idea of discovery. By turning the Black Legend on its head, Hispanophiles effectively reconfigured Anglo American memory. Writing in the spirit of a new age—of strident expansionism and progress—each rendered a vivid and dynamic vision of "Spanish America." And together, they breathed new life into a subject that, like the moldering empire itself, previously had only reminded the world of Spain's decadence.

The Black Legend that sustained a popular contempt for Spanish history and culture was bequeathed to North Americans by England. On a purely political level, the Black Legend was a rhetorical tool that the British had plied to assert a moral advantage over their colonial rivals, the Spaniards. Following independence, Americans generally followed suit. David J. Weber writes that, in their initial dealings with Spaniards from the Floridas to the California, Americans frequently viewed Spaniards as "unusually cruel, avaricious, treacherous, fanatical, superstitious, cowardly, corrupt, decadent, indolent, and authoritarian."[11] These pejoratives constituted the basic features of the Black Legend, and they captured the moral deficiencies that presumably brought about the collapse of Spain's once-enviable empire. The individual who, rather ironically, is associated with the origins of the Black Legend was none other than Fray Bartolomé de Las Casas, Spain's first Protector de Indios (appointed in 1516), whose treatises on Spain's abuses of the Indians spawned centuries of global condemnation.[12]

We must bear in mind that the Black Legend, though prevalent in the United States, was not uniformly subscribed to. Even as early as 1822, some individuals looked fondly on Spain's colonial past, or at least its people. Take, for example, Governor William P. DuVal of Florida, who in 1822 informed President James Monroe that "the Spanish inhabitants of this country are the *best* even among the most quiet and orderly of our own citizens."[13] Recall also Senator William H. Seward, who, in his 1850 contention that New Mexico deserved statehood, touted Spain's achievements in "Christianizing" native peoples of the New World.[14] Such pronouncements, though hardly common in the literature of the period, suggest that Hispanophobia had not infected the hearts and minds of all Americans. In fact, by the 1870s, as the United States committed its own atrocities against Native peoples in the name of Manifest Destiny, Spain's treatment of Native peoples was beginning to seem relatively civilized. The White Legend, then, gave critics of U.S. removal policies a prescription for how the government might better solve its "Indian problem." It was in the context of U.S. expansion and industrialization that critics seized upon the Spanish colonial pastoral—the White Legend—to wax nostalgic about preindustrial social relations. Popular novels, history texts, travel journals, and tourist brochures began to make known Spanish history from Florida to California, but as a cultural movement Hispanophilia was most pronounced in "the Spanish Southwest." There one could witness firsthand the last vestiges of Indian tradition and Spanish chivalry.

The White Legend was, of course, a powerful racial trope that downplayed mestizaje and venerated institutions that, in theory though seldom in practice, regulated race relations, such as the church, the presidio, and the rancho. Readers of popular literature would come to know the colonial frontier as a kind of biracial paradise wherein enterprising Spaniards carved out frontier communities among the "savages" and undertook to teach them the "blessings" of civilization and Christianity. This imagined pastoral replicated all the virtues of plantation society whose demise even some Yankees had come to lament.

The White Legend was the narrative template for such popular writings as Helen Hunt Jackson's 1884 novel *Ramona,* which rivaled Harriet Beecher Stowe's *Uncle Tom's Cabin* as one of the best-selling books of the nineteenth century.[15] *Ramona* mourned the passing of California's Spanish colonial era that, in Jackson's view, represented the Golden Age of the Southwest. It was an era during which two discrete races—one Spanish, the other Indian—had thrived in relative harmony following a harrowing yet brief conflagration between the two, known as "the conquest." The inevitable demise of the two symbols of that period, the mission and the rancho, at the hands of land-hungry Anglo Saxons, signaled the beginning of the end for the California Indians, according to Jackson. A political activist who two years earlier had penned *A Century of Dishonor* to publicize the plight of Native Americans nationwide, Jackson wrote *Ramona* to illustrate one main point: Native Americans were better off under the Spanish mission system than under the Anglo-American regime.[16] When not campaigning to exterminate or dispossess Indians, insisted Jackson, the American government simply neglected their educational, health, and spiritual needs and allowed them to sink into squalor.

Today we might wish to label Jackson's work "Hispanophilic" for its romanticization of ranchos and missions, but in Jackson's day her writings were understood as a kind of treatise on Indian reform.

Following Jackson's lead, reformers responded to the government's extermination and removal policies with a program, based on their paternalistic benevolence, that called for the protection of Indian lands and the gradual "assimilation" of Native peoples into white society. They advocated more reservations and the creation of boarding schools; they viewed boarding schools as modern-day missions that could teach Indians the skills they needed to survive in the white world.

Latter-day Indian reformers, such as Lummis, took Jackson's ideas one step further. They envisioned the preservation or even the recovery of Indian land and culture, and contended that, without a concerted preservation effort, Native Americans (as individuals) might survive, but their communities and lifeways would be lost forever—to the great detriment of Native peoples and white society. The preservation movement that Lummis spearheaded was premised on the idea that both Native Americans' "primitive" cultures and Spain's "chivalric" past held important lessons for "modern" Americans. Literature and tourism would be the method of instruction. Given Jackson's original "assimilationist" intention in writing *Ramona,* it is somewhat ironic that, three decades after its publication, her pastoral narrative helped to spawn a Mission Revival in architecture and city planning, known mostly for its preservationist impulse and its "Spanish" inspiration. But Hispanophiles were, after all, kindred spirits of latter-day Indian reformers.

Like Indian preservationists, Hispanophiles felt that the last remnants of Spain's conquest should be preserved for the enjoyment of westward migrants and tourists, and not simply allowed to disappear. To that end, the White Legend was an effective tool. It was a kind of eye-catching and reassuring billboard that welcomed Anglo Americans to—as New Mexico's license plates remind us—"The Land of Enchantment."

🚶 The Nostalgic Lion

In the fall of 1884, Lummis set out on foot from Chillicothe, Ohio, in search of the American West. His five-month trek took him through Santa Fe and its outlying villages, where he studied their inhabitants with awe and curiosity. After taking copious notes about the locals and their manners, Lummis published them as travel letters in the *Los Angeles Times* and the *Chillicothe Leader.* Thus began the career of the nation's premier Hispanophile. During his lifetime, Lummis authored 30 monographs and 275 articles—as well as dozens of editorial columns—most of which discussed some facet of the history or cultures of the Southwest.

In 1892 his travel letters were published as a memoir titled *Tramp across the Continent*. This publication inaugurated a fifteen-year period of intense productivity, during which Lummis wrote about such wide-ranging topics as Pueblo Indian pottery and contemporary Mexican politics.[17] Of the two-dozen letters that appeared in the *Chillicothe Leader,* seven pertained specifically to New Mexico. They captivated his audience with tales of danger and images of savagery, but they also exposed his readers to romantic and lasting impressions of genteel Nuevomexicanos and docile Pueblo Indians.

On arriving in Santa Fe in November 1884, Lummis marveled at its quaint architecture, which he deemed "as handsome to me as the New Jerusalem."[18] An "ancient metropolis," Santa Fe was "one of the most interesting places on the continent, and certainly the most unique."[19] Its rustic mud houses belied a three-hundred-year history that deserved to be told. Lummis seemed particularly impressed with the people he encountered, who seemed kind and generous, and possessed what Lummis believed were the features of a virile race. On reaching San Ildefonso Pueblo, he proclaimed its inhabitants "the best looking Indians I ever saw. They are tall, but well built and sturdy. They have light, copper complexions, and good features."[20] Lummis's letters disseminated an image of Pueblo Indians not only as robust laborers, but also as morally superior people. "I do not believe there is a christian [*sic*] American community in the world," he remarked, "which can approach in morality one of these little towns of adobe." Although the Indians had retained many of their religious traditions, they had also managed to grasp the fundamental tenets of Christianity, especially generosity, honesty, and respect for their neighbors. "The Pueblos are sharp but honest traders," Lummis noted, and they are "hospitable far beyond the average white man."[21]

Lummis also praised the Nuevomexicanos whom he met on his New Mexico travels, finding them to possess similar traits of kindness and hospitality: "[W]hite folks . . . are in the minority," he noted in a letter to the *Leader* dated 25 November 1884. "But I find the 'Greasers' not half bad people."[22] The term "greaser" appeared only once in Lummis's 1884 letters and just one more time in his later

writings as an admonition to his readers that the word was "a nomenclature which it is not wise to practise as one proceeds south ... and
which anyway is born of an unbred boorishness of which no
Mexican could ever be guilty."[23] In contrast to Anglo Americans,
Lummis explained, "Mexicans" exhibited good manners and generosity toward strangers:"There is only one sociable thing about the
white folks, they will share your last dollar with you. A Mexican, on
the other hand, will 'divvy' his only tortilla and his one blanket with
any stranger, and never take a cent."[24] One such exemplary Nuevomexicano, observed Lummis, was U.S. Indian agent Pedro Sánchez,
"a very refined and courteous Mexican. Unlike the average Indian
Agent, whose highest use for the red man is to skin him alive, the
Don is very plainly putting his whole energy and attention to such
honest endeavor as is doing vast good.""Don Pedro" had undertaken
the noble task of trying to bring education to the Pueblo Indians,
despite resistance from within his own agency.[25]

While expressing admiration for New Mexico's "Mexicans,"
Lummis at first had only contempt for their ancestors. In a letter dated
1 December 1884, he described the early settlers as "old Spaniards"
who had "kept the Pueblos down in regular slave fashion."[26] His contempt did not last long. One month later, while visiting the San
Mateo ranch of sixty-five-year-old Manuel Chaves, with whom
Lummis had "many interesting talks," he described the elderly man
as "one of the pioneers" of New Mexico who had survived "countless bloody encounters with the savage Apaches, Navajos, and Utes."
A biography of Chaves, he observed, would "read like a romance
[novel]."[27] One can only speculate about the stories Chaves might
have related to him, but Lummis's later writings hint that Chaves and
his son Amado conveyed tales of the colonial period that may well
have prompted Lummis to rethink his view of the Spanish conquest.
Whatever negative impressions he might have held about the conquistadores never resurfaced following his 1885 visit to San Mateo.
In mid-January of that year, he left New Mexico for California.

Lummis's first impressions of New Mexico would not be his last.
Three years after arriving in Los Angeles, where he worked as city
editor for the *Los Angeles Times,* he suffered a stroke and returned to
New Mexico to convalesce. From 1888 until his departure in 1892,
Lummis forged relationships that would endure for decades. Foremost
among them were those with the Chaves family of San Mateo and

the Abeita family of Isleta Pueblo. Through contact with them, he became fluent in Spanish and familiar with Nuevomexicano and Indian folklore and history.

For several months in 1888, Lummis stayed at the home of Amado Chaves, who, four years earlier, had been elected speaker of New Mexico's House of Representatives, and in 1891 would be named by Governor Prince as New Mexico's first superintendent of public education.[28] Lummis's return to San Mateo marked the beginning of his deep interest in Spanish colonial history. There he likely heard "Don Amado" tell stories of his "Spanish" ancestors, for Chaves was descended from a long line of illustrious Spaniards. His lineage could be traced to the seventeenth-century Spaniard Fernando Durán de Chaves, who, as historian Ralph Emerson Twitchell noted in 1917, "was a colonel in the Spanish army and was a knight of the Order of Santiago. The Chaves family is one of the oldest in this country and for centuries has figured prominently in the history of Spain."[29] Little is known of what transpired between Lummis and Chaves, except that by the end of his convalescence, the two had cultivated what would be a lifelong friendship.

With the exception of Lummis's relationship with Chaves, his correspondence and papers leave little clue as to lasting friendships with other Nuevomexicanos. Lummis's most notable (and very public) exchange with them occurred shortly after he arrived to convalesce, when he set out to photograph the Holy Week Penitentes procession at San Mateo. Accompanied by Chaves, he captured the brotherhood performing sacred rituals involving self-flagellation and crucifixion. When the brotherhood learned that Lummis had published those photos in *Scribner's Magazine,* they charged him with violating their code of secrecy and ran him out of town, promising to seek revenge. Among these particular Nuevomexicanos Lummis had the reputation of being an opportunist who had abused their trust and was exploiting their culture to promote his writing career. Lummis retreated to Isleta Pueblo in the summer of 1888 where, the following February, he was shot and wounded outside his rented adobe home. Chaves rushed to his friend's bedside and tried to console him. Although the perpetrators escaped, it was widely believed that they had acted on behalf of the San Mateo Penitentes.[30]

Despite the incident, Lummis remained for three and one-half years at Isleta Pueblo, where he befriended individuals who provided him with enough folklore material to publish in 1894 a 257-page collection entitled *The Man Who Married the Moon and Other Pueblo Indian Folk-Stories.* In this work Lummis, like many of his "progressive" contemporaries, exhibited an attitude of paternalistic benevolence. The Indians of Isleta, he noted, possessed many admirable qualities, such as respect for their elders and a strong work ethic, yet "with all this progress and civilization, despite their mental and physical acuteness and their excellent moral qualities, the Tée-wahn [Isleta Indians] are in some things but overgrown children."[31] If Isleta Indians were but children in Lummis's mind, he was their Anglo American father. As an interpreter and promoter of their folklore, he positioned himself between them and his English-reading audience, and used their cultural or religious traditions—often shared in confidence—for his professional gain, much as he had done at San Mateo. Some three decades after Lummis published *The Man Who Married the Moon,* Isleta tribal officers declared his "folk-stories" fraudulent and reprimanded his alleged informant, Pablo Abeita.[32]

One painful example of Lummis's paternalism—though lacking any benevolence—transpired in 1905. That spring, Lummis employed Felipe Abeita, a boy from Isleta Pueblo, to do sundry chores at "El Alisal," Lummis's California home. Though details of the agreement remain unknown, the boy apparently was sent by his father, Jose Felipe Abeita, to work for a period of "at least two years," during which time Lummis was to send Mr. Abeita his son's wages of eleven dollars per month. In June, just months after young Felipe arrived in California, Lummis was behind in his payments. Mr. Abeita wrote Lummis inquiring about Felipe's well-being and the overdue wages. Heavy rains had wreaked havoc on Isleta, Mr. Abeita explained, and the family desperately needed the money to make ends meet. Three months later, Lummis finally replied. "Every day I had hoped to be able to send you some money," he explained, "but the year has been especially hard."[33] Lummis enclosed a check for twenty-five dollars and promised to send the remainder "another month." The following spring, after expressing concern for Felipe's well-being, Mr. Abeita abruptly instructed Lummis to send his son home "at once."[34] There is no record to indicate whether Felipe's back wages were paid, or what antipathy this incident generated between Lummis and the families of Isleta generally. But the story does suggest that Lummis was not above exploiting his Isleta contacts for their labor, as well as for their cultural knowledge.

Following his return to Los Angeles in 1892, Lummis continued
to write about New Mexico's residents, drawing largely on the vast
array of ethnographic and historical notes he had amassed during his
four-year residency. From 1892 to 1905, he produced ten books on
the Southwest, of which *Tramp across the Continent* (1892) and *The
Spanish Pioneers* (1893) became the most popular, especially on the
East Coast, and attracted glowing reviews in the *New York Evening Post
Literary Review, New York World, Boston Transcript, Pittsburgh Monthly
Bulletin,* and *New York Times,* among others.

Tramp across the Continent recounted Lummis's trek from Ohio to
California. Based on his 1884–85 travel letters, this memoir elaborated on his first impressions of the Southwest and helped to shape
his readers' views of the region and its peoples. The book described
New Mexico as safe, enchanting, and hospitable to Anglo American
tourists, whom he urged to reconsider their long-standing racial prejudices against "Mexicans" and "Pueblos." For too long, he stated, the
people of New Mexico and their history had been ignored or unreasonably judged by unknowing and prejudiced Americans. Historians
had done New Mexico and its inhabitants a disservice by perpetu-
ating a false impression of Spanish-speaking peoples and their past.

> There is . . . [a] dense popular ignorance as to the
> Spanish doings in the beginning of the New World,
> particularly in the beginning of the United States. Our
> partisan histories . . . do not seem to realize the prece-
> dence of Spain, nor the fact that she made in America
> a record of heroism, of unparalleled exploration and
> colonization never approached by any other nation
> anywhere. Long before the Saxon had raised so much
> as a hut in the New World . . . the Spanish pioneers
> had explored America from Kansas to Cape Horn.[35]

New Mexico's history, Lummis continued, was not marked by Spanish
atrocities against Indians, as many Americans had been led to believe,
but by the noble deeds of "hero-missionaries" who braved great obstacles to bring Christianity and civilization to the Indians of the
Southwest. This view contrasted sharply with a Lummis letter in 1884
in which he stated that the Spaniards had "bull-dozed the [Pueblo
Indian] majority" and "kept them in regular slave fashion."[36] Now

Lummis held that "the Spanish never enslaved the Pueblos, and were, on the contrary, the most humane neighbors the American Indian ever had."[37] He acknowledged and apologized for his earlier views. "I had very ignorant and silly notions in those days about Mexicans, as most of us are taught by superficial travellers who do not know one of the kindliest races in the world."[38] Lummis directly challenged the popular assumption that English and Anglo American settlers were somehow less cruel to Native Americans than were Spanish conquerors. "We talk of the cruelty of the Spanish conquests; but they were far less cruel than the Saxon ones. The Spanish never exterminated. He conquered the aborigine and then converted and educated him, and preserved him with scholarship, humanity, and zeal."[39] Here Lummis reflected the views of such other popular writers of the day as Hubert Howe Bancroft and Helen Hunt Jackson. Unlike Lummis, they focused primarily on colonial California, but their glowing assessments of the Spanish conquest resonated with those of Lummis. Wrote Bancroft in his 1888 *California Pastoral:* "Never before or since was there a spot in America where life was a long happy holiday, where there was less labor, less care or trouble."[40] As already mentioned, Jackson captivated East Coast readers with romantic depictions of California's biracial (Spanish and Indian) mission society.[41]

Historian John R. Chávez observes that Bancroft and Jackson romanticized Spanish California just as it was being destroyed. "As Anglo settlement of California increased," writes Chávez in *The Lost Land,* "the earlier Anglo conception of the state changed; by the 1880s California was no longer the wilderness frontier of the Gold Rush, but a booming agricultural wonderland."[42] Historian David J. Weber has made a similar observation about the East and finds in its despoliation the causes for the romanticization of the West. East Coast Americans, repulsed by "excessive commercialism, materialism, vulgarity, and rootlessness," looked to places like New Mexico and California "for pastoral values that they imagined had existed in a simpler agrarian America."[43]

Perhaps more illustrative of Lummis's Hispanophilia and considerably more popular than *Tramp across the Continent* was his *The Spanish Pioneers.* Its importance lies not in its impact on Mexican Americans' self-perception or identification—for there is scant evidence of that—but rather in its widespread circulation and its popularization of the White Legend.

The book began by reiterating Lummis's insistence that certain unnamed history texts had misled Anglo Americans into believing that Spaniards were villainous, treacherous, and inept conquerors. His purpose, he explained, was "to help young Americans to a general grasp of the truths upon which coming histories will be based."[44] Among those truths, he declared, was that "the Spanish pioneering of the Americas was the largest and longest and most marvelous feat of manhood in all history."[45] "The Spanish were not only the first conquerors of the New World, and its first colonizers, but also its first civilizers. They built the first cities, opened the first churches, schools, and universities; brought the first printing-presses, made the first books; wrote the first dictionaries, histories, and geographies, and brought the first missionaries."[46]

These deeds exemplified the "humane and progressive spirit" of Spain's pioneers, who "never robbed the brown first Americans of their homes" as Anglo Americans had done in their westward conquests, but instead "protected and secured" their lands for them by "special laws."[47] New Mexico's missionaries, in particular, exemplified Spain's kindhearted paternalism and warranted an entire chapter devoted to their achievements. Emerging throughout the narrative are two distinct racial and cultural archetypes: the benevolent, gallant Spaniard and the loyal, obedient Indian convert. Ramón A. Gutiérrez writes that by exploiting themes of discovery, conquest, and the "civilization" of savage lands and peoples, Lummis had "tapped into [a] national preoccupation with virility" in the latter decades of the nineteenth century.[48]

Lummis's preeminent achievement was to establish an acceptable master narrative for other Hispanophiles, for tourists, and for Nuevomexicanos, who themselves would elaborate on it. As literary scholar Genaro M. Padilla has noted, "Lummis authorized and instituted a language that has reverberated in other travel narratives, magazine articles, scholarly studies, poetry, novels, and theater of the region."[49] In fact, Lummis himself over the next twelve years authored dozens of books and hundreds of articles reinforcing the message of his *Spanish Pioneers.* Despite becoming, in Lawrence Clark Powell's words, "the greatest booster the Southwest has ever known," Lummis had little to do with the promotion of history within New Mexico itself. That task fell to a local resident, Lebaron Bradford Prince.

ਪੌ Lebaron Bradford Prince

In 1883, Lebaron Bradford Prince published *Historical Sketches of New Mexico,* a book that established him as one of the territory's leading historians and proponents of the White Legend and of Hispanophilia more broadly. Over his lifetime, Prince reinforced this reputation by writing several more books and lecturing widely. In contrast to Lummis, Prince's impact on historical and racial perceptions in New Mexico can be measured by the local reception of his writings and other activities.

From his election as president of the Historical Society of New Mexico in 1883 to his death in 1922, Prince carried out a wide range of activities that increased popular interest in New Mexico's past among Anglos and Nuevomexicanos alike. The historical society that he led dated to 26 December 1859, when twenty-five men convened in Santa Fe to found an organization dedicated to collecting and preserving "all historical facts, manuscripts, documents, records and memoirs, relating to this Territory," including "[I]ndian antiquities and curiosities, geological and mineralogical specimens, geographical maps and information, and objects of natural History."[50] Within months of its founding, the members had established and displayed in Santa Fe "a well arranged collection of curiosities, specimens and documents, and a considerable number of books, pamphlets and written contributions."[51] The society disbanded in September 1863 at the height of the Civil War. Some of its relics and minerals were crated and stored, while others were sold to pay outstanding debts. For the next seventeen years, no comparable institution took its place, until the advent of the railroad changed that situation.[52]

In December 1880, ten months after the railway reached Santa Fe, several citizens met in the capital and proposed a "reorganization" of the historical society.[53] Concerned about the large number of Indian "relics" and "curiosities" making their way into the hands of private collectors and institutions in New York and Washington, D.C., territorial officials looked to the society to stop what they saw as the pilfering of New Mexico's cultural patrimony. On taking office in February 1881, the reinvigorated society's new president, William Gillette Ritch, took steps to do just that. "Our abiding hope should be," he declared, "as our manifest duty is, to snatch from oblivion the wonderful evidences of the prehistoric people of the Southwest."[54] Ritch launched a drive to publicize the problem and to solicit dona- tions and memberships.[55] To many officials the crisis was the result of the railway that had brought not only "progress" and "industry," but cultural predation as well.[56] Both Ritch and his successor, Prince, viewed the advent of the "Iron Steed" as a sign that a modern, indus- trial era had begun and a preindustrial one had ended.[57]

Appreciation for New Mexico's colonial past spawned a desire to preserve the objects from that period, and Prince became a preemi- nent figure in the effort. During his thirty-nine years as president of the society, he pursued a twofold agenda that aided the growing com- mercial and symbolic value of Spanish and Indian objects. First, he sought to increase the society's collection of relics by soliciting dona- tions of them, and, second, he displayed the relics in order to encour- age popular interest in New Mexico's Spanish colonial history.

Soon after taking office, Prince began accumulating Indian and Spanish "antiquities." The process of gathering such objects reveals much about perceived ethnic identities, says scholar James Clifford. By collecting the objects of "other" cultures, he writes, tourists and institutions define themselves by opposition; that is, the accumula- tion of such articles represents an act of self-demarcation because it divulges the collector's own values. Collections "embody hierarchies of value, exclusions, rule-governed territories of the self," notes Clifford. "[G]athering involves the accumulation of possessions" and reaffirms the notion that identities are defined by material cultures (that is, objects, knowledge, memories, experience).[58] But in addition to possessing symbolic value, relics also accrued commercial value.

Between 1880 and the 1920s, speculation in Indian and Spanish colonial relics led to a lucrative "curio" market that Prince, by virtue of his purchases, directly supported.[59] In his collection efforts, Prince relied on Santa Fe traders who specialized in the desired objects. In 1894, for example, he purchased from Santa Fe merchant Jake Gold sixty-five dollars worth of Spanish colonial and Mexican items, including "One old Shield; Two Matachino [sic] Frames; Four Matachino [sic] Crowns; One framed pipe; One Franciscan and Child," and several paintings.[60] That same year, Prince bought from Santa Fe curio merchant A. F. Spiegelberg fifty-nine dollars worth of relics, including six pieces of "Pajarito" pottery, two "Old Spanish" silver forks, and several "Southern Apache" and "Mexican" items.[61]

To finance these and other purchases, Prince initiated several fund drives involving mail solicitations. In 1890, for example, he wrote to nearly fifty individuals seeking donations for the purchase of a collection of "New Mexican antiquities" valued at a thousand dollars. Of those approached, sixteen (including both Anglos and Nuevomexicanos) responded with twenty-five-dollar checks, an amount that entitled them to lifetime membership in the society. Six of those contributors bore well-known Spanish surnames, such as Armijo, Otero, Montoya, and Chávez, while ten bore non-Spanish surnames, such as Hazeldine, Johnson, Browne, and Raynolds.[62] That Nuevomexicanos donated to the organization and became members suggests the extent to which they valued both the society and its drive to collect historical items. It also speaks to their ability to donate and thus to their class status, since few Nuevomexicanos could afford the membership fee. By the early 1900s, the society had procured a number of large collections, thanks both to private donations and meager appropriations from New Mexico's legislature.[63]

Another example of Nuevomexicano and Anglo fascination with the Spanish past that also dated to the years just after the railway's arrival was the "Tertio-Millennial Anniversary Celebration" in Santa Fe. Organized by Prince, it featured a series of festivities and exhibits commemorating Santa Fe's presumed 333d anniversary.[64] Though Prince miscalculated Santa Fe's founding by some fifty-odd years, his celebration drew thousands of visitors and participants to the plaza between 2 July and 3 August 1883.[65] Skeptics—including Lummis, who later berated Prince for his brash disregard for historical accuracy—argued that the celebration was little more than Prince's scheme to promote tourism and immigration to New Mexico.[66] One pamphlet hints that this may well have been the case: "The Tertio-Millennial exhibit is a collection illustrative of the growth of New Mexico from its earliest day, showing this historic land as it is today and as it was when Cabeza de Baca crossed its borders. This is the characteristic of our celebration which makes it such a novel and interesting sight and one which will be unusually attractive to eastern visitors."[67]

The 1883 celebration blended historical appreciation with tourism, and proved to be an ideal tool to market the region's cultural and natural wealth to prospective immigrants.[68] Prince believed that arousing popular interest in New Mexico and its history would lead to increased tourism, immigration, and industry.[69] A local newspaper concurred: "The celebration will excite great interest in New Mexican affairs throughout the country, and it will be of benefit not only to Santa Fe, but to the interests of the whole territory."[70]

Not by happenstance did Prince issue his *Historical Sketches of New Mexico* on the eve of the Tertio Millennial in 1883. The book offered a narrative of human "progress" in New Mexico in which the past was "divided into three epochs—the Aboriginal or Pueblo, the Spanish, and the American"—all corresponding to three distinct racial and cultural archetypes to whom he dedicated the book:

> To the Pueblos, still representing in unchanged form the aboriginal civilization which built the cities and established the systems of government and social life which astonished the European discoverers nearly four centuries ago;

> To the Mexicans, who, in generosity, hospitality, and chivalric feeling, are worthy sons of the *Conquistadores,* who, with undaunted courage and matchless gallantry, carried the cross of Christianity and the flag of Spain to the end of the earth;

> To the Americans, whose energy and enterprise are bringing the appliances of modern science and invention to develop the almost limitless resources which nature has bestowed upon us;

> To All, as New Mexicans, now unitedly engaged in advancing the prosperity, and working for the magnificent future of the Territory, of which the author is proud to be a citizen, these sketches of part of its earlier history are respectfully dedicated.[71]

To Prince, ethnic nomenclature did not correspond to national identities, but, rather, to cultural and racial ones. In invoking the term "Mexican" he referred not to Mexican citizens, but to Spanish-speaking New Mexicans whom he viewed as culturally indistinguishable from *californios, tejanos, tucsonenses,* and other Spanish-speaking peoples of the Southwest. Prince deemed New Mexico's Nuevomexicanos as "sons of the conquistadores," a characterization that seems to suggest that they traced their lineage to a romantic colonial past and were not recent Mexican migrants to the region. As if to underscore this distinction, he devoted only eight pages of three hundred to the Mexican national period (1821–48).[72] By contrast, more than two-thirds of *Sketches* deals with the "Spanish conquest," and does so in glowing, heroic terms: "The explorer of those days was traveling entirely in the dark. Nothing in more modern times has been similar to, or can again resemble, the uncertainty and romance of those early expeditions."[73] As for the Pueblo Indians, Prince portrayed them in a positive light as heirs to "the aboriginal civilization which built the cities and established the systems of government." They represented peaceful "Aztec" antecedents to Christianity and were clearly not savages but a sedentary and civilized peoples with "cities . . . government and social life."[74]

Prince's reference to "Americans" sheds light on his own identity. "Americans," he wrote, personified modernity, industriousness, and capitalist values. As a people, they possessed "energy and enterprise," and had brought to New Mexico "the appliances of modern science . . . to develop the almost limitless resources . . . [of] nature."[75] Prince celebrated the arrival of the railway and Anglo American immigrants, but his concept of progress embraced more than "Americans." "Pueblos, Americans, and Mexicans," he declared, constituted "the people of New Mexico," who one day would be "one in nationality, in purpose and in destiny."[76] That day, he added, would come when New Mexico achieved statehood. Prince's historical writings cannot be separated from his political views and, especially, his agitation for statehood that required cooperation among all New Mexicans. Nor can his racial attitudes be divorced from his promotion of tourism.

Following *Historical Sketches* Prince went into a twenty-seven-year hiatus from serious writing about the past and focused his energies on statehood, his political career, and the management of the historical society. From 1883 until the eve of statehood in 1910, the society gained visibility by emphasizing its growing collection of Spanish and Indian objects. Particularly important were its exhibits in the Governor's Palace in Santa Fe, where rooms were filled with "ancient pottery . . . stone implements and other articles illustrating the aboriginal civilization" as well as "a multitude" of newly acquired

items from the "Indigenist, Spanish, Mexican and American eras."[77]
The exhibitions attracted considerable tourist traffic that, in turn,
justified Prince's preservation efforts. "The tourist travel is a source
of large income to the Territory in various ways," he observed in the
society's 1887 annual report, "and as the passing years destroy many
of the antiquities which give New Mexico special interest to the
traveler, it is very important to preserve whatever is possible, to attract
and satisfy the antiquarian taste."[78] The society's role in advancing
tourism became eminently clear in 1893, when thousands of visitors
"from all parts of the world" came to its exhibits.[79] Within nine years,
this number grew to "more than five thousand per year," and by 1910,
that figure had doubled to nearly ten thousand.[80]

Not all these visitors came from outside New Mexico. Many local
residents, both Anglo and Nuevomexicano, viewed the society's
exhibits.[81] News of the society's collection efforts regularly appeared
in the Santa Fe *New Mexican* as well as in the Spanish-language newspapers.[82] In 1905, for example, an editorial in a Las Vegas, New
Mexico, Spanish-language newspaper urged Nuevomexicanos to
lobby the historical society for monuments to "the great men who
have figured in the history of this territory since its initial colonization . . . including the conquistador Don Juan de Oñate and the *recon-
quistador* Don Diego de Vargas."[83] This effort, declared the editorial,
required contributions from "patriotic citizens of New Mexico who
wish to honor and perpetuate the memory of . . . their most illustrious . . . forebears."[84] Such campaigns indicated that, by the early
twentieth century, at least some Nuevomexicanos were voicing
appreciation for their Spanish past.

Letters to the society also revealed the growing interest in Spanish
colonial history among both Anglo Americans and Nuevomexicanos. In 1909, H. R. Hendon of Vaughn, New Mexico, became
so intrigued by the "most valuable relics" and "small library of books
dealing with New Mexico in history" in the Governor's Palace that
he asked Prince for "a catalogue of the books, and if Coronado's
account of his expedition is among them . . . What I want to do is
to get a general view of Spanish exploration here in those times, and
also of the Indian manners and customs."[85] In the same year Nestor
Montoya, editor of Albuquerque's *Bandera Americana,* the society's
vice president in Bernalillo County, launched into a sermon to
Prince on the importance of the society's mission:

> The time has come, I think, when every true son of
> our Nuevo Mexico should take an interest in pre-
> serving its incomparable history, traditions and lore,
> of one of the most brilliant epochs in the history of
> mankind, the discovery and settlement of the New
> World. Our ancestors of Spanish, English and French
> stock made it possible for humanity to people this
> continent today with a phalanx of free Republics,
> and then why should we not be proud to keep our
> history, our names and land marks which remind us
> of that glorious epoch? More united should we be
> in this, in view of the fact, that vandals would even
> try to despoil us of our historic name.[86]

As Montoya's letter suggests, Nuevomexicanos had not only become
more appreciative of their "own history," but also more visible within
the historical society. Surviving records do not include the society's
membership lists, but they identify "life members."[87] Between 1881
and 1908, some forty-six individuals became life members by contributing twenty-five dollars or more to the society. Of these, fourteen possessed Spanish first names and/or surnames, and included
such prominent individuals as three former delegates to Congress,
Antonio Joseph, Mariano Otero, and José Pablo Gallegos.[88] The
remaining thirty-two surnames were non-Spanish, and included
William Gillette Ritch (president of New Mexico's Bureau of
Immigration) and Judge William Hazeldine.[89]

Nuevomexicano participation in the society was not limited to
membership alone, but included some who, like Montoya, became
officers or otherwise worked actively to promote the organization's
goals. Public lectures were one way of doing so, as illustrated by
Colonel José Francisco Chaves's talk in 1904 on his "Personal
Reminiscences of the Primitive Days."[90] Other speakers over the
years included Amado Chaves, Benjamin Maurice Read, Nestor
Montoya, and Jocobo Chaves.[91] Each of these individuals also held
prominent positions in northern New Mexico. Amado Chaves, for
example, was superintendent of public instruction (1891–97 and
1904–5), mayor of Santa Fe (1901–3), and Santa Fe County's representative to the territorial senate (1903–4); Benjamin Maurice Read

was a notable Nuevomexicano attorney and speaker of the New Mexico House of Representatives (1901–2).[92] In 1907, Prince invited a young professor of "Romance Languages" to speak to the society on "New Mexican Spanish." Aurelio Macedonio Espinosa eagerly accepted and delivered a "talk . . . of a popular nature" that helped instill among Nuevomexicanos a sense of ethnic pride.[93]

By 1913, Nuevomexicanos were giving society lectures nearly as often as their Anglo counterparts. That year's public meeting, held on successive evenings in the state's Hall of Representatives, featured six guest speakers, of whom three were Nuevomexicanos. One of them, Antonio Lucero—a former legislator, New Mexico's first secretary of state, and former editor of the Las Vegas, New Mexico, *La Voz del Pueblo*—addressed the meeting in Spanish, though the title and topic of his speech went unrecorded. Another, Benjamin Maurice Read, lectured in English on "Inconsistencies of History," while Antonio DeVargas recounted "The Glories of the Spanish Era."[94]

While Nuevomexicanos (read: men) rose to prominence within the society, extant records give little indication of the roles that women (Nuevomexicana or not) played in the organization. Indeed, there is no mention of women's participation until 1906, when "Miss Bertha Staab" is listed as the society's "corresponding secretary." Two years later "Mrs. Ella May Chaves" was identified as a life member, but nothing else was said about her participation.[95] In 1911, Prince reportedly established a "Ladies' Advisory Committee," but available records reveal nothing of the committee's activities.[96] The society occasionally recognized women for meritorious achievement in promoting the history of New Mexico. For example, in 1912 Matilda Coxe Stevenson, "the distinguished ethnologist," received an "honorary membership" for "making New Mexico the scene of her remarkable researches."[97] But the society membership was nearly exclusively of men through the territorial period.

As statehood approached, Prince resumed his historical research and writing. Following passage of the statehood enabling act in 1910, he authored a 128-page work entitled *New Mexico's Struggle for Statehood: Sixty Years of Effort to Obtain Self Government,* which narrated the congressional battles over the statehood question. Two years later, he issued *A Concise History of New Mexico,* which he modeled after his earlier *Historical Sketches.* His conceptual and organizational framework mirrored that in his first book.[98] Though shorter, the newer publication projected a more romantic image of Pueblo Indian and Nuevomexicano communities, past and present.[99]

> . . . the observer may in a single day visit an Indian pueblo exhibiting in unchanged form the customs of the intelligent natives of three and a half centuries ago; a Mexican town, where the architecture, the language and the habits of the people differ in no material respect from those which were brought from Spain in the days of Columbus, Cortez, and Coronado; and an American city or village, full of the nervous energy and the well-known characteristics of modern western life.[100]

While Pueblo Indians and Nuevomexicanos remained static, locked in time, "Americans," as in the earlier account, were the agents of change and purveyors of progress. This was true as well of Prince's *The Student's History of New Mexico,* a condensed textbook version designed for high school instruction and published in 1913. Though written in a simpler and more vivid style, it resembled the earlier works in content and organization. Prince actively promoted *Student's History* for high school classroom use through advertisements in the *New Mexico Journal of Education,* but it remains unknown whether the text was adopted anywhere.[101] Prince clearly intended his textbook to foment an appreciation for New Mexico's history among schoolchildren. More broadly, he viewed education as an effective means of reproducing the harmonious tri-ethnic society that he extolled in his historical and political writings. One example of that conviction was Prince's leading role in the creation of the Spanish-American Normal School in El Rito, which ostensibly was going to prepare Nuevomexicanos to teach in the rural communities where bilingual instructors were in short supply.

In 1915, Prince issued his last major monograph, *Spanish Mission Churches of New Mexico.* Written at the height of the California Mission Revival, this work argued that New Mexico, like California, possessed Spanish missions worthy of historical attention and touristic appreciation: "Outside of the boundaries of New Mexico, practically nothing is known of the far more interesting structures that render the Sunshine State [New Mexico] the paradise of the tourist, the antiquarian, and the religious enthusiast."[102]

Prince's later publications and activities until his death in 1922 were overshadowed by other developments: the establishment in 1907 of the School of American Archaeology (renamed the School of American Research in 1917), the appearance of the Spanish Colonial Arts Association in 1912, and the "revival" of the Santa Fe fiesta in 1919.[103] These events rivaled the historical society's visibility and cultural influence. This is not to say that the society diminished in size or touristic appeal. By 1921, membership was said to have grown considerably, and the annual visitors to the Governor's Palace exhibit surpassed forty thousand, double the volume of 1910.[104] Nonetheless, other organizations devoted to cultural commodification proliferated between 1909 and the 1920s, and competed with the historical society for resources, attention, and influence.

┇𝟀 The Myth of Santa Fe

As a cultural movement Hispanophilia was much larger than Lebaron Bradford Prince and Charles Fletcher Lummis. Theirs were but two early voices in what by the 1920s amounted to a chorus of worshippers of things "Spanish" or "Indian." Composed of several interconnected social networks, this movement drew together an array of individuals: novelists and poets, Indian activists, artists and architects, city boosters and elected officials, natives and newcomers, men and women, Anglo Americans and some Native Americans and Nuevomexicanos. Though these eclectic individuals were divided by their particular professional ambitions, commercial interests, and political agendas, they nonetheless shared a common conception of New Mexico as a land where tradition collided headlong with modernity, in a "a pageant of three cultures." As Hispanophiles and Indian enthusiasts streamed into places such as Santa Fe and Taos, they created what Chris Wilson calls the "modern regional tradition" by remaking their environs and by reliving the imagined past through pageants and fiestas.[105]

Women would play an ever larger role in the articulation of that tradition during the 1910s and 1920s. In her work *Engendered Encounters,* historian Margaret Jacobs has shown how "feminist primitivists" such as Mary Hunter Austin, Mabel Dodge Luhan,

Alice Corbin Henderson, Ina Sizer Cassidy, and Erna Fergusson looked admiringly on Pueblo culture and sought, variously, to preserve Pueblo traditions or to adapt them for survival within the tourist economy.[106] By the 1930s, these women and many others—including Nuevomexicanas such as Adelina (Nina) Otero-Warren, Aurora Lucero, and Fabiola Cabeza de Baca—were instrumental in the movement to preserve "Spanish colonial" village traditions.[107]

The celebration of native cultures in the early years of statehood belied the sobering reality of daily life for most Nuevomexicanos, who were all too aware of their declining political power and their hold on their land, culture, and language.

In their promotion of an idealized Spanish past, Prince and Lummis seemed, implicitly, to bemoan the inevitable decline of New Mexico's "traditional" cultures, which both viewed as casualties of the march of Anglo American "progress."[108] Anthopologist Renato Rosaldo explains this wistful sentiment as "imperialist nostalgia," noting that the agents of imperialism celebrated "the very forms of life they intentionally altered or destroyed."[109] Premised on the certain demise of Pueblo and Nuevomexicano cultures, Anglo American nostalgia contrasted sharply with Nuevomexicanos' growing determination to prevent encroachments on their land, Spanish language and traditions, and political rights. By the 1910s, Hispanophiles had succeeded in shaping many Anglo Americans' perceptions of the Southwest as "Spanish" and of Nuevomexicanos as "Spanish Americans." In 1914, a columnist for *Harper's Weekly* registered this fact, explaining: "These Spanish people of New Mexico . . . are not of the mixed breed one finds south of the Rio Grande, or even [in] Arizona. . . . Indeed, it is probable that there is no purer Spanish stock in Old Spain itself."[110]

Chapter Five

Blood of the Spirit

It must be very painful, even to our Anglo-Saxon
Americans, to live in a part of America where
Spanish tradition, blood and culture are everywhere
evident.
—*Aurelio Macedonio Espinosa, 1915*[1]

El idioma es simbolo [sic] de la raza. . . . El Pueblo
que abandona la defensa de su idioma, . . . habrá per-
dido toda su personalidad.
—*"Símbolo de Nuestra Raza"*[2]

;人 Hispanidad

If Hispanophilia involved a "foreigner's" fascination for things
Spanish, hispanidad entailed claiming ownership, most notably, of
Hispanic history, language, values, beliefs, and culture. It was to identify with these as the basis of one's identity. It referred, literally, to
one's "Hispanicity." The *Diccionario de la Lengua Española* defines "hispanidad" as "the generic character of all people of Hispanic language
and culture."[3] In its broadest sense, hispanidad was a sentiment, a sensibility, and a self-perception among Spanish-speaking peoples that
took shape in specific cultural and political contexts, and in contradistinction to "Anglo Saxon" culture. Its manifestation in New
Mexico, however, was far more complex than this.

From the 1890s through the 1930s, a loose affiliation of lettered
Nuevomexicanos, whom I shall refer to as *hispanistas,* gave voice to
this sentiment and sought, actively, to engender it among their compatriots.[4] In history texts, they exalted the conquistadores as their

171

ancestral forebears; in speeches, they defended the Spanish language as a symbol of their colonial heritage; in academic treatises, they claimed to retrace their regional idioms and folklore to the Iberian peninsula; and in grade school practices and policies, they honored and sought to preserve the cultural traditions of their students. In doing so, New Mexico's hispanistas became authors of their own heritage. In defining, defending, and deploying that heritage Nuevomexicanos did not so much conform to Anglos' fanciful expectations as they did take some degree of control over symbols of their identity.

ϟ History, Language, Culture: Señas de identidad

On a chilly February day in 1911, college student Aurora Lucero stood before an assembly of educators in Las Vegas and delivered a much-celebrated speech. With statehood imminent, she proclaimed, "Spanish Americans" had to brace themselves for heightened attacks against their language and culture. A year earlier, President William Howard Taft and congressional leaders had sought to make English the sole language of the government and of classroom instruction. That initiative, however, was turned back just weeks before Lucero's speech, when voters approved a constitution that guaranteed the rights of "children of Spanish descent" to receive instruction in their native language. Elected officials would not be required, as Washington leaders had hoped, to speak English "without the aid of an interpreter."[5]

Lucero could not fathom why some Americans, in the name of national unity, felt an urgency to banish the Spanish language from public realms. Did they not know that Spanish was the legacy of the conquistadores who had endured untold hardship to bring Christianity and "civilization" to the New World? Could they not see that Spanish would be the principal conduit of commerce with "Spanish America"? The matter, Lucero implied, boiled down to ignorance about the value of Spain's linguistic and cultural imprint on the Americas. Language and culture, as well as an attachment to land and to Catholic tradition, comprised the foundation of Spanish American identity. Anglo cultural hegemony was the social context.

> It is claimed by those who passed this [provision] that
> the Spanish-American will become a better citizen
> by depriving him of the use of his vernacular. In

resorting to such a course, it would seem that the
contrary effect might be produced ... [that] he might
be made a worse citizen. . . . Spanish is the language
of our parents. Today, it is our own, and it will be the
language of our children and our children's children.
It is the language bestowed upon us by those who
discovered the New World. We are American citizens, for certain, and . . . must learn the language of
our country. . . . [Y]et we need not negate in the
process our roots, our race, our language, our traditions, our history, or our ancestry, because we shall
never be ashamed of these. On the contrary, they
shall make us proud.[6]

Though Lucero embraced the English language with patriotic
fervor, she equally defended her "native tongue" as a sign of her
ethnic identity and difference from "Anglo Saxons." The use of two
languages was not incongruent with American citizenship, she
argued. Rather, it made for a more intelligent and prepared elec-
torate. It also promised to facilitate more trade with countries to
the south. But at a time when Progressive reformers had formulated "Americanization" programs for schoolchildren and adults,
most Americans saw a second language not as a commercial or cultural asset, but as a barrier to full integration in the body politic. In
the closing months of an arduous battle for statehood, Nuevomexicanos and Nuevomexicanas increasingly pointed to their language as an emblem of their ethnic pride and identity, and as a link
to their collective history.

Lucero's 1911 address suggests her awareness of the shifting balance of power in the territory. The previous decade had witnessed
the influx of more than 120,000 white Americans who, as discussed
previously, brought with them attitudes, beliefs, and values that they
sought to impose on "native" communities. By the time statehood
was achieved, Anglos had come to occupy key posts in government,
cultural institutions, and education. Following statehood, their grasp
on power would be expanded, but Anglos did not dislodge
Nuevomexicano políticos from all major offices. Rather, a "gentle-
men's agreement" was reached whereby Anglos and Nuevomexicanos
divided the political spoils.[7]

Between 1912 and 1938, the agreement sought to ameliorate racial tensions both within and between parties. For example, when Democrats nominated a Nuevomexicano to run for a political office, Republicans followed suit, to avoid the prospect of "race" being injected into the election. In principle, the arrangement seemed to satisfy both populations, but in practice it seldom led to an equitable distribution of power. Anglos dominated both tickets, prompting Nuevomexicano políticos to protest on several occasions. This was the case during the 1926 state Democratic convention, when Nuevomexicano delegates called for a closed-door meeting and pressured their Anglo counterparts for more equitable representation on the ballot. This strategy seemed to work, if temporarily. The scene was replayed two years later, when Nuevomexicano Democrats again pressured Anglo party leaders for a fair share of the ticket.[8] These hard-fought gains proved short-lived and were rather minimal when compared to the overwhelming disparity found in the larger political scene.

Anglo domination of politics during this period is evident in their near monopoly over the highest elected and appointed offices. They occupied six of the first seven gubernatorial terms, the sole exception coming in 1916 with the election of the Mexico-born Octaviano Larrazolo. Of the nine executives elected to office—governor, lieutenant governor, secretary of state, auditor, treasurer, attorney general, superintendent of public instruction, land commissioner, and corporation commissioner—Anglos regularly controlled all but two: auditor and secretary of state, the latter position being increasingly occupied by Nuevomexicanas. Political appointments went overwhelmingly to Anglos. Seldom did legislative elections reflect the Anglo-Nuevomexicano ratio of the state's population, although Nuevomexicanos were able to achieve greater representation in the House due to their demographic distribution and slightly more equitable districting.

In 1950 Ernest Barksdale Fincher explained Anglo political dominance as a function of Nuevomexicanos' inability to understand English and the principles of democracy. "To put it otherwise," Fincher adds, "Hispanic-Americans have not enjoyed their share of political power because they have constituted a cultural enclave which has defied incorporation."[9] Fincher's belief that Nuevomexicanos clung stubbornly to their culture and language, to the detriment of their political well-being, reflected the prevailing perception among Anglo Americans. It was informed partly by their discernment of a cultural movement that sought to preserve Nuevomexicanos' language and culture.

It was in the context of political displacement and marginalization that a growing number of educated, middle-to-upper-class bilingual Nuevomexicanos and Nuevomexicanas sought to study, document, preserve, embellish, and popularize hispanidad. From the 1890s through the 1930s, their individual and sometimes collaborative efforts stemmed from their heightened sensitivity to loss, and to their own precarious social and political standing among their Anglo counterparts. In numerous ways, hispanistas articulated and deployed their hispanidad as a defense against what they perceived as cultural erosion. Some, like the lawyer-scholar Benjamin Maurice Read or the noted linguist Aurelio Macedonio Espinosa, aggressively claimed authority over New Mexico's "Spanish" history, language, and culture. For them, the conquest and colonization of the region represented more than merely a fanciful tale of adventure, "manliness," and chivalry. To be sure, early hispanistas such as Read and Espinosa described Spanish exploits in the same masculinist terms as Hispanophiles such as Lummis—that is, they depicted the conquest as evidence of Nuevomexicanos' (read: men's) restless zeal, prowess, and virility, something that particularly resonated with Anglo Americans' preoccupation with "masculinity" in the latter decades of the nineteenth century and early years of the twentieth century.[10] Hispanistas also at times socialized or collaborated with Hispanophiles both privately and in public commemorations or ceremonial expressions of the region's Spanish legacy. But the Spanish legacy carried special significance for hispanistas like Read and Espinosa. It involved something more profound than admiration, wistful longing, or hollow consolation for Nuevomexicanos' fading political fortunes. It was a source of their historical identity and racial genealogy.

Whereas Hispanophiles simply admired, celebrated, and exploited the Spanish past for ideological, recreational, commercial, or political purposes, hispanistas claimed it as their own. They activated it, wrapped themselves in it, and used it to assert racial and civic equality with, yet difference from, the "Anglo Saxon race." It should be said, however, that hispanistas in New Mexico were not generally perceived as "anti-Yankee"—a label often given to hispanismo's proponents from Spain and Latin America, who defined themselves in opposition to "Anglo-Saxon" coldness, excessive materialism, or individualism. Nor were New Mexico's hispanistas particularly unified in their views on the "purity" of New Mexico's Spanish language or culture. Indeed, hispanistas spanned a range of ideological persuasions and included such cultural purists as Read and Espinosa, as well as such progressive educators as the feminist Nina Otero-Warren and George Isadore Sánchez. Though distinguished by their particular vocabularies of resistance, these hispanistas and their contemporaries deployed their hispanidad to denounce the continued social, cultural, political, and economic marginalization of their fellow Nuevomexicanos.

In the context of Nuevomexicanos' waning political power, hispanidad served not just individual ends, such as to reaffirm the social standing and broker position of its proponents, but also collective ends: to advance cultural cohesion and—more often than not—to gloss over stark class distinctions among Nuevomexicanos. More broadly, the deployment of hispanidad in New Mexico interfaced with cultural and political phenomena that were taking place both within the United States and abroad. New Mexico's "regional distinctiveness" responded not solely to the centrifugal forces of local politics, tourism, face-to-face relations, and social marginalization; it was also part and parcel of an ideological movement that understood Latin America to be the spiritual progeny of Spain. This movement came to be known as *hispanismo.*

ःᘁ Hispanismo and América Española

At the beginning of the twentieth century, the romantic writings that spawned popular interest in Spanish history, architecture, and traditions in the Southwest had an academic complement: hispanismo. Briefly stated, hispanismo was a movement among professional scholars who understood both Spanish and "Spanish American" history and cultures through the prism of colonialism. On the American side of the Atlantic, those who comprised and guided this movement were called hispanistas, whereas their Iberian counterparts were *hispanoamericanistas.* According to historian Fredrick B. Pike, the cohorts "shared an unassailable faith in the existence of a transatlantic Hispanic family, community, or *raza* (race)."[11] Underlying this belief, Pike continues, is the assumption that "Spaniards in discovering and colonizing America transplanted their life style, culture, characteristics, traditions, and values to the New World and then transmitted them to the aborigines whom they encountered there, to the Africans whom they imported, and to the mestizo or mixed blood peoples whom they fathered." Hispanistas believed that Spaniards (peninsulares) and Spanish Americans are members of the same race (raza), "a raza shaped more by common culture, historical experiences, traditions, and language than by blood or ethnic factors."[12] Thus, hispanismo embodied a set of beliefs and assumptions about the enduring legacy of Spain in the Americas. It was a movement that gained momentum with increasing scholarship on Latin America.[13]

In the 1880s and 1890s, a handful of historians wielding incipient "scientific" methods probed various facets of Spanish history in the Americas. The themes were rather predictable and very romantic: discovery, conquest, and exploration. Charles Gibson and Benjamin Keen posit that these themes attracted academic historians partly because "[t]hey possessed apparently controllable bibliographies; their historiographical tradition included much nonsense [that is, the Black Legend] that could be satisfactorily debunked; [and] they comprised that portion of colonial Latin American history of which everyone had heard. Conquest especially fit the familiar conception of Hispanic America as a land that had never fully emerged from the brutality of its colonial past." These scholars included such individuals as Justin Winsor, John Fiske, and John Boyd Thacher, whose multivolume works were published between 1884 and 1904.[14]

In the first two decades of the twentieth century, a critical mass of academic historians in the United States turned their attention to "Spanish America." Among them were scholars interested in Spain's imprint on regions within the United States, such as Herbert Eugene Bolton (eighteenth-century Texas), Irving B. Richman and Charles Chapman (Spanish California), and James A. Robertson and Isaac J. Cox (Louisiana). As their numbers grew and as these scholars turned their sights south to Mexico and beyond, a group of them founded the *Hispanic American Historical Review* (*HAHR*) at the 1916 meeting of the American Historical Association in Cincinnati. Its first issue appeared in 1918. The preponderance of the journal's subject matter had to do with Spain's historical legacy in the hemisphere, especially in the United States. These historians broadcast a generally positive assessment of the Spanish conquest, though they were not among the most fervent hispanistas of their day. That distinction belonged to scholars of the Spanish language.

Across the Atlantic, hispanismo had its most passionate adherents. During the years following Spain's defeat by the United States, Spanish intellectuals turned to hispanismo as a prescription for national recovery from "*el desastre del '98.*" In hispanismo, liberals (guided by a secular faith in modernization) and conservatives (tradition-bound and devout Catholics) stood united in their belief that if Spain could reach out to its "American" brethen—that is, "Spanish America"—it could redeem at least some of its former national pride and influence. Thus, such eminent thinkers as Miguel de Unamuno began to call attention to Spain's spiritual and linguistic affinities with the Americas. Language, Unamuno often said, is "the blood of the spirit."[15]

The Nuevomexicano who perhaps was the most ardent proponent of hispanismo was Aurelio Macedonio Espinosa. A professor of Romance languages at Stanford University from 1909 to 1947, Espinosa was driven by the conviction that his forebears, the conquistadores that settled New Mexico and southern Colorado, had left a linguistic and racial legacy to the people, and that the villagers of the region were their direct descendants. The evidence, he insisted, was embedded in their language and folklore. He authored nearly two hundred articles, several scholarly monographs on Spanish *cuentos* (folktales), and twenty-two textbooks on Spanish grammar, composition, and literature.[16] Espinosa's scholarship earned him both national and international scholarly recognition. From his first publication in 1907 to his death in 1958, Espinosa remained a passionate defender of the belief that Spain and Spanish America were one in spirit, language, and culture.

Espinosa was born in 1880 in El Carnero, Colorado, forty-five miles north of New Mexico, where his parents, Celso Espinosa and Rafaela Antonia Martínez, had settled just two years before his birth. Like many Nuevomexicano homesteaders of the region, they eked out a living by farming and ranching. And, like many Nuevomexicano farmers and ranchers, they claimed to be progeny of New Mexico's original Spanish settlers and conquistadores. In the words of J. Manuel Espinosa, Aurelio's son, the Espinosas were "descendants of Spanish families who had come from Spain to the Viceroyalty of New Spain in the 16th and 17th centuries and were among the first settlers of upper New Mexico."[17] The Espinosa family, in fact, traced its lineage

to Captain Marcelo Espinosa, who accompanied Governor Juan de
Oñate in his 1598 settlement of New Mexico. Rafaela Martínez's
family, likewise, believed its ancestors had come to New Mexico
"directly from Spain via New Spain in the latter part of the eighteenth century."[18] Whatever their origins, the Espinosa and Martínez
families possessed pride in their Spanish origins that they transmitted
to young Aurelio.

Aurelio's interest in language and folklore originated in his youth
and during the summers he spent in the mountains of southern
Colorado with his uncle, Ramón Martínez, a shepherd. There he
came to know the folklore of the area's Nuevomexicano shepherds
and ranchers, and "listened with interest" to their traditional cuentos, ballads, and verses.[19] As Aurelio matured, his love of folklore and
language deepened, inspiring him to study these subjects at the university level. In 1898, Aurelio enrolled in the University of Colorado,
Boulder, where he majored in philosophy and minored in Romance
languages. On graduating four years later, he accepted a professorship in modern languages at the University of New Mexico in
Albuquerque, a post he held for nearly eight years. From 1902 to
1910, he traveled extensively through northern New Mexico and
southern Colorado studying the Spanish phonology and morphol-
ogy of the region and recording folktales. Those research trips provided much of the material for his later studies of Spanish language
and folklore.[20]

In 1907, Espinosa enrolled in the University of Chicago, where,
during his summers, he pursued a doctorate in Romance languages
under philologist Karl Piestch. His 1909 dissertation, "Studies in
New Mexican Spanish," was published in three parts between 1909
and 1914 in *Revue de Dialectologie Romane*.[21] That study caught the
eye of Stanford University scholar John Ernst Matske, who offered
Espinosa a position in Stanford's department of Romance languages.
Espinosa gladly accepted the offer and remained at Stanford for
nearly forty years.

While his publications help us retrace his rise to international
fame, they say relatively little about his personal relationships with
hispanistas and Hispanophiles in New Mexico and much less about
his direct impact on the Nuevomexicanos or Anglo Americans who
read his scholarship. This absence of information is due, in part, to
the fact that his personal papers and manuscripts are in private hands

and inaccessible to researchers. Nevertheless, some materials—
including some correspondence—shed light on how Espinosa conceived of and promoted Spanishness in New Mexico, especially
during the first three decades of his career.

What we can deduce, for example, is that from 1907 to 1911,
Espinosa played a role in shaping the way some of New Mexico's
residents understood and appreciated the region's Spanish language
and folklore. He did so through talks at the Historical Society of
New Mexico and elsewhere as well as through his published writings
that emphasized the peculiarities of Spanish language in New
Mexico.[22] In a 1907 talk, Espinosa introduced the English-speaking
world (in New Mexico and abroad) to the distinctive Spanish language
and folklore of Nuevomexicanos. He emphasized three points:
Nuevomexicanos possessed a language and folklore rich in Castilian
archaisms that dated to the fifteenth and sixteenth centuries; Nuevomexicanos' geographic isolation, combined with their long occupation
of the land and resistance to Indian linguistic and cultural influences,
had perpetuated those archaisms; and while Nuevomexicanos' Spanish
contained few Indian elements, it had adopted many English words
and had also infiltrated the English language. Each of these characteristics supported Espinosa's overall contentions that Nuevomexicanos
were the descendants of the Spanish conquistadores and that their
archaic language and folklore were evidence of their Spanish identity
and cultural steadfastness. In 1907, these were rather novel ideas.[23] He
elaborated on them in a letter to Prince: "We have in N[ew] M[exico]
Spanish a mixture and confusion of the many Castilian dialects of
Spain. . . . [M]any of the original permanent settlers of N.M. came
directly from north western Spain (Galicia) and indirectly through
Mexico. You see, here linguistics comes to the aid of History. This
Galician influence . . . cannot have developed here independently,
because it is unknown in other parts of Spanish America."[24]

In other words, Galician archaisms—along with traits from
Extremadura, Castile, and Andalusia—proved Nuevomexicanos' historical and, by implication, racial and cultural link to New Mexico's
earliest Spanish settlers, particularly those who accompanied conquistadors Juan de Oñate and Diego de Vargas. In 1909, Espinosa's dissertation reaffirmed this idea, explaining that, over the course of three
centuries, those settlers had "preserved many . . . classic forms [of
Spanish] with remarkable tenacity."[25] Of the fourteen hundred dialect

forms Espinosa had discovered in the local language, he deemed a thousand to be Spanish in origin, three hundred English, seventy-five Nahuatl, and only ten "of native New Mexican Indian origin."[26]

This phenomenon was partly attributable to Nuevomexicanos' geographic isolation, Espinosa explained. Notwithstanding a twelve-year exile following the 1680 Pueblo Revolt, they had continuously occupied a region extending from Socorro, New Mexico, to Colorado's San Luis Valley. Far removed from cultural centers in Mexico and the United States, he wrote, the Spanish settlers had pre-served many of their original linguistic traits and folktales, despite the presence of two local cultural forces, the Pueblo and the Plains Indians, who, Espinosa insisted, made almost no mark on the Spaniards' language or culture.[27] In 1911 he reiterated this point, insist-ing that the "indigenous Indian elements [of New Mexico's Spanish] are unimportant, and only the Nahuatl of Mexico has exercised important influence, being the language of a semi-civilized nation."[28] Implicitly challenging Prince and Lummis, who claimed that the Pueblo Indians possessed a long history of civilization, Espinosa dis-missed the Pueblos as a semicivilized nation that had made little impact on the language of the colonizers.

At the heart of Espinosa's argument was his faith in Nuevo-mexicanos' linguistic purity, a faith that echoed older notions about purity of blood as well as the contemporary conviction, voiced by Unamuno, that language represented "the blood of the spirit."[29] Espinosa's rejection of any noticeable infiltration of Pueblo idioms into the region's Spanish language served to set Nuevomexicanos apart from their Pueblo neighbors and to reassert a distinctive culture and racial pedigree. By insisting upon Nuevomexicanos' linguistic purity, he was by implication downplaying racial mixture, or mestizaje.

In a 1911 contribution to the *Catholic Encyclopedia,* Espinosa reaffirmed his convictions by contending that most members of New Mexico's first territorial assembly "were of Spanish descent, and this has been true of all the Assemblies until the end of the cen-tury." On the arrival of the railway in 1880, he continued, "nine-tenths of the population . . . was of Spanish descent: at present (1911) this element is only about one-half, owing to the constant immi-gration from the other states of the Union."[30] Without naming the identity of immigrants from "other states," Espinosa was obviously referring to Anglo Americans.

According to Espinosa, Anglo American immigration had both positive and negative consequences for New Mexico. This "foreign race," he wrote in his 1911 encyclopedia article, had introduced "modern civilization and progress," but it also had introduced some three hundred English-dialect forms to the local language.[31] Similarly, Espinosa pointed out, Nuevomexicanos had also contributed words to the English language, a fact that deserved greater scholarly attention: "The influence of the English language on the Spanish of the entire South-west is one of the greatest importance, and of the most intense interest to the philologists and ethnologists. . . . [Yet] the Spanish language in New Mexico and the entire South-west has had a great influence on the English vernacular of these regions, and its study is of the greatest importance."

Espinosa's studies of language mixture in New Mexico came on the eve of statehood when, as mentioned, Congress and President Taft were considering adding an English-only provision to the proposed state constitution. Espinosa was among those who lobbied to preserve the use of Spanish in the courts and schools. "The scientific and comprehensive study [of] New Mexican Spanish folklore should be encouraged in every legitimate way by the learned societies and educational Institutions of New Mexico," he urged. "[L]aws of the South-west should make the study of Spanish possible in the public schools, for the benefit of the Spanish speaking children of those regions, who have no opportunity to learn to read their native tongue. To learn English no one has to forget Spanish or any other language."[32]

Espinosa's views were repeated by others, including the young suffragist Aurora Lucero, who in the 1920s became the superintendent of schools in San Miguel County and assistant professor of Spanish at New Mexico Highlands University in Las Vegas.[33] "New Mexico," she declared in her 1911 speech before the educational congress, "has seen many political and social changes, and many problems . . . solved, but on admission as a state there arises another problem[:] . . . will the Spanish language continue to be taught in public schools?"[34] The vocal opinions of individuals like Lucero and Espinosa helped persuade Congress and the president to approve a state constitution that mandated its preservation and study in New Mexico's schools and universities.

Although Espinosa's influence on language instruction and study in New Mexico is difficult to determine, his national and international influence is well documented. He rose to eminence in 1917 when, concurrent with his professorship at Stanford, he became the founding editor of *Hispania,* the official journal of the American Association of Teachers of Spanish. From that year to his departure in 1926, Espinosa authored numerous articles and edited countless contributions of others. During his tenure as editor, he also began dealing with broader issues, such as the need for the teaching of Spanish in universities and the correct terminology for referring to Latin America. His articles on these two issues speak to Espinosa's own hispanidad and to his ideas about race and language.

In September 1918, Espinosa attracted international attention with his first *Hispania* article, "The Term Latin America." It prompted a discussion about terminology, race, and history that reverberated in the pages of linguistic journals in the United States and abroad for the next five years. In that article, Espinosa decried the rising use of the term "Latin America" and insisted that the correct term when referring to the non-English-speaking countries of the Western Hemisphere was "Spanish America." During the last ten years, he noted, writers from France and the United States "have begun to use the terms Latin America [and] Latin American, for the old and proper terms Spanish America [and] Spanish American." Others had opted for another term, "Ibero America [and] Ibero American," he observed.[35] The "Latin" and "Ibero" designations were "new, improper, unjust, unscientific."[36] As editor of *Hispania,* Espinosa instructed his contributors and advertisers "to use always the old, traditional and correct terms, Spanish America, Spanish American." After all, he wrote, "What objections could any one have against this procedure?"[37] If there were any objections, they did not appear in *Hispania.*

Apparently Espinosa's opinion was widely shared. Juan Cebrián of San Francisco also protested against "Latin America." "Latin American signifies a Latin product or derivative," which implies that the people of Latin America are of French, Italian, Provencal, Rumanian, Sardinian, Spanish, or Portuguese descent. A more correct term, Cebrián insisted, was Spanish America, since the people of that region originated from "Hispania," the designation that once applied to Spain and Portugal. Italy and Rumania had not taken part in the conquest or colonization of America, and the French presence—not to mention the Dutch and Danish—on the American map was "mathematically insignificant," wrote Cebrián.

> Spain alone spilled its blood, lost its sons and daugh-
> ters, spent its wealth and intelligence, employed its
> own methods ... to conquer, civilize, and create those
> countries. Spain alone nourished them, raised them,
> guided them maternally, without the help of either
> France or Italy. . . . Spain alone gave them its language,
> laws, habits and customs, vices and virtues. . . . Once
> grown . . . those Hispanic countries followed the
> example of the United States and separated from
> their Mother Spain, but naturally conserving her lan-
> guage, laws, and customs as before.[38]

Portugal, while significant in Brazil's settlement, played a relatively
minor role in the civilizing process elsewhere, added Cebrián. Espinosa
concurred. The conquest and civilization of America was almost
wholly a Spanish affair: "Spain transplanted to those countries its own
civilization in its entirety, without any assistance." In Espinosa's words,

> today these flourishing Hispanic countries are devel-
> oping a civilization that has for its foundation the
> best of the blood and brain of old Spain. The ele-
> ments of the Indian traditions have not given worthy
> fruits. The Spaniards brought Christianity to South
> America, civilized the Indians, founded cities,
> churches, schools, developed agriculture. Nearly fifty
> million people in Spanish America today speak
> Spanish, the language of old Spain.[39]

This telling statement captures Espinosa's fervent hispanidad. It not
only reiterated his conviction that Spain—not other "Latin" countries—had conquered the New World, but it also deprecated Indian
cultures for not giving "worthy fruits." Simultaneously, it restated
Espinosa's belief that language represented a symbol of one's racial
and cultural integrity. Thus, Spanish Americans, as he called them, had
inherited and will pass on "the blood and brain of Old Spain." As for
those who sought to distinguish between Spaniards and Spanish
Americans or between Spanish Castilian and Spanish American
Castilian, they "have completely lost their heads." Differences do exist,

but they do not "constitute different languages. The language of all Spanish America . . . is *Spanish*, good *Castilian Spanish*."[40]

To Espinosa and a growing number of hispanistas the question of nomenclature took on symbolic importance, for it underscored the persistent and widespread confusion—in the United States as well as in Spain—about the historical and racial identities of Spanish-speaking peoples in the Western Hemisphere. Espinosa wished to leave no doubt that, racially, historically, and linguistically, he and, by extension, Nuevomexicanos and other Spanish-speakers were Spanish.

In the context of the second decade of the twentieth century, Espinosa's proclamations on hispanidad were charged with racial implications and even contradictions. On the one hand, his repeated dismissals of any Pueblo influence on the Spanish language of New Mexico betrayed his contempt for, or paternalistic attitude toward, Native American culture and languages. But on the other hand, Espinosa was highly sensitive to prejudice himself, especially when it was directed at Spain, "Spanish Americans," or the "Spanish race." In a 1915 newspaper editorial, he denounced an earlier editorialist for calling Spain and Portugal "miserable failures among nations." "It is poor logic and worse taste to heap insults on other races or nations simply because the ignorance of the writer deprives him of other reasons or arguments."[41] Despite Espinosa's own racial predispositions, he readily invoked a pluralist vision when it suited his agenda: to define Spanish-speaking people as a separate but equal "raza."

As Espinosa's professional network grew, he began to correspond with one of hispanismo's greatest advocates, the Spanish philologist Ramón Menéndez Pidal, who encouraged him to travel to Spain to study Spanish popular stories, or cuentos. Espinosa took his friend's advice. In 1920, sponsored by the American Folklore Society, Espinosa traveled the back roads of Spain interviewing villagers and recording nearly three hundred versions of Spanish folktales. Published in three volumes between 1923 and 1926, *Cuentos Populares Españoles* was "his most significant single contribution to Hispanic folk literature," writes his son, J. Manuel Espinosa.[42] That work, along with his article "The Term Latin America" (which was translated and published in Madrid in 1919), earned him admission to the exclusive Academia Real de la Lengua Española in 1921 as well as the commendation of Knight Commander of the Royal Order of Isabella the Catholic (the same title bestowed on Lummis five years earlier).[43]

Espinosa's visibility in Spain was matched in the United States, where he garnered numerous titles and distinctions for study of Spanish language and culture. In countless publications he made the case for the teaching of Spanish in the nation's schools and universities. "We should declare," he wrote in 1911, "that Spanish should be studied in our schools because it is the language of the Spanish people of Spain and Spanish America, a people who possess a culture inferior to none. . . . We must study Spanish literature and history in order to appreciate the great work of Spain in the civilization of the world, in order to appreciate the spirit of Spanish ideals."[44] The study of Spanish would also promote goodwill between Anglo Americans and Spanish Americans, declared Espinosa. An understanding of the art, literature, history, and life of a people will lead to an understanding of their "character and ideals." Such familiarity would bring together

> the two great civilizations of the western hemisphere, the Anglo-Saxon civilization of the north with its great material prosperity, its scientific efficiency . . . its democracy of opportunity, its love of peace and work, its wonderful educational system and its practical sense of justice, and the Spanish civilization of the south, with its love of the traditional virtues, its lofty idealism, its humanism, its love for family ties and veneration of motherhood, its artistic temperament, its deep religious instinct, and its new scientific and educational activities.[45]

In terms strikingly reminiscent of Prince's dedication of *Historical Sketches of New Mexico*, Espinosa lauded these two "civilizations," though he remained remarkably silent on the Pueblo civilization that predated the arrival of the conquistadores.[46] In fact, when he did direct his scholarly energy in the direction of Pueblo Indians, it was to demonstrate how Spanish had served as a common medium of communications among them, and how Spanish words had penetrated the Tiwa, Tewa, and Keres vocabularies.[47]

By the 1930s, Espinosa had acquired a reputation as one of the nation's leading experts on Hispanic folklore. Perhaps, more than any other individual, Espinosa succeeded in convincing a broad share of academics and the reading public that Nuevomexicanos—and, indeed, all Spanish-speaking peoples of the Americas—traced their roots to Spain. His authority on Spain's imprint in the Americas was even acknowledged by Herbert Eugene Bolton in his 1929 essay on the "significance of the Borderlands."[48] Espinosa was also elected president of the American Folklore Society (1924–25) and of the Pacific Coast Branch of the American Philological Association (1929), served on numerous editorial boards of academic journals, and was instrumental in the founding of the New Mexico Folklore Society (1931).[49] But Espinosa's fundamentalist convictions were not without skeptics. One was the young Mexico-born folklorist Arthur León Campa, who in 1930 noted the near obsession with Spanish purity among (mostly Anglo) dealers in the arts and crafts industry. "It is strange and even foolish," he wrote, "to insist that the traditional Spanish elements in New Mexico's culture should be followed to the exclusion of all the rest."[50] Whereas Espinosa succeeded in winning Anglo respect for his cultural authority, the senior statesman and lay historian Benjamin Maurice Read did not. One of the reasons was that Read directed his energies toward a Spanish-speaking popular audience, not toward the ivory tower.

☺ Reclaiming Authority over the Past

Between 1880 and 1900, more than sixty Spanish-language newspapers were begun in New Mexico. Though many of them proved short-lived ventures, their very existence gave proof to the growing literacy among Nuevomexicanos, and to a popular desire to read self-authored texts. "The Spanish-language press . . ." writes Doris L. Meyer, "was the primary vehicle for articulating and galvanizing [Nuevomexicanos'] counter-hegemonic cultural imperative."[51] As Anglo Americans streamed into the territory, they not only appropriated the land, resources, and levers of political power from the Nuevomexicano majority, and as Hispanophiles appropriated their historical narrative, some Nuevomexicanos, including Benjamin Maurice Read, began to put forth their own versions of history, and they did so in their native language.

Read was foremost among New Mexico Nuevomexicano historians between 1900 and his death in 1927. Writing in Spanish, he sought to invigorate the historical memory of his Spanish-reading audience, and to foment among Nuevomexicanos a pride in their

Spanish past; as we shall see, Nuevomexicanos responded favorably to Read's works.

Read's histories differed markedly from those of Prince and Lummis in the way they encoded a distinct sense of pride in the past, suggesting that Nuevomexicanos had begun to claim the past as their own and to use it to protest their subordination by Anglo Americans. Read, however, was not the first Nuevomexicano to narrate New Mexico's Spanish past and to encourage Nuevomexicano pride. That distinction goes to Francisco de Thoma, a relatively obscure writer who, in 1896, published the first comprehensive Spanish–language history of New Mexico following the American conquest. Thoma's *Historia popular de Nuevo México, desde su descubrimiento hasta la actualidad,* sought to make "neo-mexicanos" aware of their Spanish ancestry and history. His purpose, stated Thoma, was not to write a critical history of New Mexico,

> but, rather, to present to our people a true story, as exact as possible, of three centuries of deeds. Its principal objective: to remind the "neo-mexicanos" of the glorious achievements and painful suffering that their heroic ancestors endured [and] to arouse pride in the souls of [Nuevomexicanos] for being part of one of the most generous, noble, and valiant races of the universe—the Spanish race.[52]

As heirs to a colonial past, "Neo-Mexicanos" were obliged to learn their history, Thoma insisted. Drawing on the scholarship of Hubert Howe Bancroft, he narrated New Mexico's history in 185 pages, of which more than three-fourths dealt with the Spanish conquest and settlement. Endorsed by Archbishop P. L. Chapelle of Santa Fe, Thoma's history celebrated the missionization of the Indians. Like Prince, Thoma paid scant attention to the Mexican and U.S. periods, devoting just eleven pages to the former and twenty-five pages to the latter. It remains unknown how many copies of *Historia popular* made their way into the hands of Nuevomexicanos or how Nuevomexicanos received the work. Thoma's name does not even appear in the pages of common secondary sources, such as Ralph Emerson Twitchell's *Leading Facts of New Mexico,* published in 1917.[53] By contrast, Read's works received considerable attention from Nuevomexicanos.

Read variously labeled himself a mexicano or Spanish American, though he hailed from a mixed Mexican and Anglo American lineage. His father, Benjamin Franklin Read, was a direct descendant of George Read of Delaware, a revolutionary leader and a signer of the Declaration of Independence. Benjamin Sr. was a military officer who had aided General Stephen Watts Kearny in the taking of Santa Fe in 1846. It was there, three years later, that he married Ignacia Cano, the daughter of the once-wealthy Ignacio Cano, who had migrated north from Sonora and laid claim to the Dolores Placer. Benjamin Jr. was born in 1853. His father's death, four years later, left Ignacia alone to feed, clothe, and educate her three sons, Benjamin, Alexander, and Larkin. The younger Benjamin, fully bilingual and capable of moving within both Anglo American and Nuevomexicano social circles, earned the confidence of Governors Marsh Giddings and Lionel Sheldon, who appointed him their secretary in 1871 and 1881, respectively. In 1875, he became superintendent of public schools in Santa Fe and concurrently served as translator for the legislative assembly before being elected to that body in the 1880s.[54] In 1901, Read was elected speaker of the House of Representatives, a position he held for a single two-year term, after which he devoted his energies to historical pursuits.[55]

Read felt compelled to undertake the writing of New Mexico's past to correct the "inaccuracies" that plagued Anglo Americans' writings. With missionary fervor, he set out to expose the "truths" of New Mexico's history, expressing contempt for the "striking contradictions" in the writings of "English-speaking authors."[56] Knowing little Spanish, he wrote, they often resorted to incorrect translations of Spanish colonial documents. As a self-labeled "*historiador mexicano*," Read declared himself better equipped than "American" historians to preserve the original spirit and meaning of the primary documents. Moreover, histories written in Spanish, he insisted, best preserved the original meaning of Spanish documents.

From 1910 to 1919, during Read's most productive era, he published six books and authored dozens of articles—some in Spanish, others in English—with four of the books being particularly influential: *Guérra México-Americana* (1910), *Historia ilustrada de Nuevo México* (1910), *Illustrated History of New Mexico* (1912), and *Popular Elementary History of New Mexico* (1915). These works prompted letters of support and gratitude from Nuevomexicanos throughout New Mexico in the second decade of the twentieth century.

In Read's 249-page *Guerra México-Americana,* he boldly declared that both Mexican and American historians had failed to understand the true origins of the U.S.-Mexico War.[57] Too long, proclaimed Read, historians had fixed their attention on the immediate pretexts to war, such as Texas's struggle for independence, the role of the United States' "Manifest Destiny," and the South's desire to perpetuate slavery. The actual causes, Read explained, were to be found in the racial discord between the "Anglo-Saxon and Latin races" that dated to Spain's loss of Florida to the United States in 1819. Read's argument was simple: the "expansionist fever" that inspired Spain's colonial pursuits in America was the same that fueled the United States annexation of Texas and conquest of northern Mexico between 1846 and 1848. However, when the United States clashed with Mexico, he explained, U.S. officials invoked a rhetoric of racial superiority over the Spanish and Mexican peoples to justify their actions. Read did not denounce conquest, but rather anti-Spanish and anti-Mexican prejudice.[58] Working in the tradition of what Richard Hofstadter has called the "post-Darwinian-era" historians who professed a scientific impartiality, Read took great pains to remind his readers that he offered an objective view of history, one rooted in facts and truths. Yet he possessed an ideological agenda: to denounce Anglo Americans' prejudice and encourage Nuevomexicanos to take pride in their own conquistadorial past.[59]

When *Guerra México-Americana* appeared in 1910, Nuevomexicanos from all parts of New Mexico and southern Colorado praised Read for unearthing the "true" origins of the war. Eusebio Chacón, an attorney in Trinidad, Colorado, who later translated *Historia ilustrada* into English, applauded Read's impartiality, noting he avoided the "bombast and exageration [*sic*] which characterizes most [A]merican historians of the south-west," yet did not "lean unreasonably to the side of his mother's race. . . . He gives us the truth, plain and simple."[60] To Chacón, *Guerra's* importance lay in its being the first book written by "a native of New Mexico ... to delve into that most unpleasant subject, the period of disaster when our forefathers received such terrible chastisement from American arms."[61]

Rafael Chacón, Eusebio's father, agreed with his son, insisting that *Guerra México-Americana* ought to be read by "all Spanish-speaking

people" so that they and their children might form a "just and impartial opinion of that unequal struggle."[62] From Tierra Amarilla,
another Nuevomexicano thanked Read for undertaking the book.
"It is well-written and truthful. I believe it will sell very well, and
should find its way to every one of our homes."[63] Similarly, José
Somellera of Cuba, New Mexico, wrote that *Guerra* represented a
tremendous achievement that would forever benefit both Spanish-
speaking "Neo-Mexicanos" and "the general public."[64] Benigno
Romero of Las Vegas, New Mexico, owner of "the largest Mexican
bookstore in the United States," wrote of *Guerra:* "It fills an important void among Spanish-speaking peoples. . . . Every family of our
race [*nuestra raza*] everywhere should obtain a copy. Each and every
one of us should be proud to have a son of New Mexico produce
such a valuable work."[65]

When Margarito Romero, also of Las Vegas, read *Guerra* he
ordered another copy for his son. "This is a much-needed work for
our children," he said, "and especially for those Americans who
ignore our history."[66] In a glowing review Aurelio Espinosa praised
Read's "sound scholarship," adding, "The gross injustice on the part
of the United States, in attacking a friendly nation, for the sake of
territorial expansion, is well pointed out. Mr. Read expresses here
the opinion of the best unprejudiced minds of both the United States
and Mexico."[67]

Espinosa, then a junior professor of Romance languages at
Stanford University, congratulated Read for promoting among
Nuevomexicanos a sense of pride in their history: "You have offered
up a great work, and have done a good deed for our race. In any
case, it should be written in English, so that the Americans can read
it." Espinosa offered to translate the work for $170, but Read evi-
dently declined.[68]

Read's bicultural identity apparently gave him legitimacy in the
eyes of some Anglos. Writing in 1917, former Senator Thomas Catron
wrote an introduction for a manuscript Read was working on entitled "Sidelights of New Mexico History." Catron stated that Read was

> born, reared and educated in New Mexico, and has
> never resided elsewhere. He emanates from good
> stock. His is a lineal descendant of one of the signers
> of our Declaration of Independence. He is half of

> Anglo-Saxon blood, the other half being pure
> Castilian. He possesses in his make-up the persistence
> and determination of the Old Puritan combined
> with the enthusiasm and adventure of the Spaniard
> who opened America to the rest of the world . . .[69]

Among Anglo Americans and Nuevomexicanos alike, then, Read's credibility and authority rested on his racial and ethnic background, which presumably allowed him to write impartial history. Perceptions of Read's identity varied, however. Whereas Nuevo-mexicanos recognized him as one of their own, Anglo Americans such as Catron saw him as a mixed-blood, possessing the best traits of "Spanish" and "Anglo" Americans.

Read's second major publication, the 616-page *Historia illustrada de Nuevo México,* reinforced his reputation. The book appeared several months after *Guerra* and was reissued in 1911 with a pro-logue that—in the spirit of his earlier writings—criticized Anglo American historians for their poor scholarship.[70] The lack of agree-ment among English-speaking historians, and between "American" and "Mexican" scholars, drove Read to search for the original Spanish documents in Spain. He solicited help from Antonio Aragón Montejo of Madrid, who procured copies of colonial documents from Spain's Biblioteca Nacional.[71] Exactly what those documents dealt with Read does not state; nor does he explain their significance to his book. Although he claimed to have written a more truthful account of New Mexico's history, his version differed little from other English-language texts of the day.[72]

In Read's prologue to *Historia ilustrada* he surveyed the existing histories of New Mexico, including the works of Bancroft and Prince, both of whom he praised as sober-minded scholars. This was not his opinion, however, of the writings of Josiah Gregg and William Hart Davis, whose "venal language and slanders of New Mexico's inhabitants" had no basis in fact.[73] Davis's *El Gringo,* wrote Read, apparently was inspired by Gregg's "obscene descriptions of the sons of this land," though Read does not elaborate on those descriptions.[74] Davis's work asserted that "[t]he great mass of people are dark, a mixture, and only a few can legitimately claim to be pure-blooded Spaniards. As long as there is intermarriage there is no hope of improving the color of the people."[75]

The text of Read's *Historia ilustrada* reads much like Prince's story of civilization advancing in stages to the present day. However, Read's narration emphasized the importance of the Nuevomexicano march toward "progress" during the territorial period. The 1911 edition contained ancillary documents, including over 112 minibiographies of prominent Nuevomexicanos and thirty-four of Anglo or Euro-American residents of New Mexico. The sketches of Nuevomexicanos often underscored their "illustrious" Spanish lineage, or the fact that they were descendants of "one of the first families" to settle in New Mexico.[76] One of only six women that Read wrote biographies for was his mother, Ignacia Cano. Both Prince and Espinosa appear among these minibiographies, suggesting the high esteem in which Read held them. A. Gabriel Meléndez writes that biographical sketches such as those that appeared in Read's *Historia Ilustrada* "permitted a kind of factual conflation of the past and present through which the deeds of Neo-Mexicanos long dead might be compared to the lives of contemporary men and women," and that "biography also filled the desire to authenticate experiences compounded by the circumstances of the present day." Put another way, these biographies "authorize[d] the ethos of the group," writes Meléndez, and that ethos resonated profoundly with those who read it.[77]

Also included in the appendices of *Historia ilustrada* were two long articles that Read had recently published in the newspaper *Revista de Taos* urging Nuevomexicanos to vote for the proposed state constitution. Of his efforts "on behalf of the progress and prosperity of the sons of New Mexico," wrote Read, none had given him more satisfaction than his "humble contribution" to the statehood campaign. Although he claimed to be an avid proponent of statehood, he provided no evidence of his contribution to the effort except for the two articles that he reprinted in *Historia ilustrada*. Those articles revealed his strong support for the constitution and especially the provisions for bilingual education, which he reprinted in *Illustrated History*. Perhaps the book's greatest significance was the fact that it was written in Spanish by a Nuevomexicano and presented as a history for the Spanish-speaking people of New Mexico.

Nuevomexicano readers of *Historia ilustrada de Nuevo México* praised Read for setting the record straight about their ancestors' contributions to "civilization" and "progress." Perhaps not coincidentally, several of those correspondents were subjects of the minibiographies.

Their letters complimented Read for his objectivity, for promoting Nuevomexicano pride in the past, and for bringing Nuevomexicano history "out from obscurity." "The native sons of New Mexico," declared Isadoro Armijo, probate clerk and ex–officio recorder for Doña Ana County in July 1911, "must pride themselves on having such a dispassionate and sincere historian; a historian who will be placed on a pedestal among geniuses and *hispano-americanos,* who have struggled to erect works of both national and global importance."[78] Offering similar praise was Modesto C. Ortiz, an Albuquerque attorney: "It is a great honor for *nuestra raza,* that a son of New Mexico has produced this valiant work, such that your name will be immortalized in Spanish American minds and for future generations. . . . It will be of benefit to all of us who were once ignorant."[79] Expressing hope that Anglo Americans would read this "true" history of New Mexico, Manuel R. Otero opined that *Historia* had "set aright the 'HISTORY' of our true and beloved NEW MEXICO . . . [and given] our ancestors the place they most undoubtedly really deserve in the annals of history. May your name be in the hearts and memory of every true and loyal descendant of the Castilian race, because you are the first man who has succeeded in accomplishing what other historians have only attempted."[80]

Read helped arouse a growing sense of pride among Nuevomexicanos in their "Spanish blood" and history.[81] As pointed out in chapters 1 and 2, blood had become a metaphor for consanguinity and, therefore, a racial link to Nuevomexicanos' Spanish past. Antonio Lucero, associate editor of Las Vegas's *Voz del Pueblo,* thanked Read for making "us proud of the blood that runs through our veins . . . because this is the history of the descendants who took part in the most glorious era of history."[82] That "glorious" history involved the conquest and colonization of the land, the missionization of the Indians, and the diffusion of Spanish language and Catholic beliefs.

Not surprisingly, the Catholic church delighted in Read's rendition of the past. The archbishop of Santa Fe, Juan B. Pitaval, wrote Read to say he was "pleased to see, in your history, what the Catholic church has done for civilization in New Mexico."[83] Father P. Tommasini of San Felipe church in Old Town Albuquerque sent his payment for one of Read's works, along with a note that thanked him for "lifting from obscurity the brilliant days of the *nativos* of New Mexico."[84] Similarly, an unidentified priest at Immaculate

Conception church in Albuquerque thanked Read for promoting "our religion" in his writings.[85]

In sum, Read's two most important Spanish-language works, *Guerra México-Americana* and *Historia ilustrada,* generated considerable enthusiasm among Nuevomexicanos.[86] That many of his works were written in Spanish and accessible to a predominantly Nuevomexicano audience further suggests his desire to foster hispanidad among his readers. In emphasizing the shortcomings of English-speaking historians, he underscored his own language skills as a way of establishing his authority over the subject and allowing him to speak on behalf of the Nuevomexicano population. While Read's works gained favor among Nuevomexicanos, there is scant evidence of how Anglo Americans received his writings. The existing records suggest that his message of hispanidad—ownership of history, and resistance to social and political marginalization—did not resonate with favor among non-Nuevomexicanos. His eulogist in 1927, Paul A. F. Walter, stated that "Mr. Read's writings hardly struck a popular chord [among Anglo Americans]. . . . The fact that he thought and wrote in Spanish and insisted upon a literal translation, robbed his English work of much of the spirit and smoothness of his Spanish diction."[87] Significantly, there is a complete absence of English-language correspondence to Read regarding either *Guerra* or *Historia.* Equally telling, few Anglo Americans seem to have noted or read Read's English-language version of *Historia,* which he entitled *Illustrated History of New Mexico.* Published in 1912, *Illustrated History* was nearly identical to its Spanish counterpart, except that it had two hundred more pages of notes and appendices. Also included were a handful of tributes to the newer book.[88] None of the Anglo American tributes mentioned Read's race or heritage; rather, they congratulated him on his "painstaking labor" or his "patriotic" work on behalf of New Mexico's history.[89] On reading *Illustrated History* in 1915, Senator Thomas B. Catron wrote Read that "[y]ou have corrected much matter which had been incorrectly presented to the public . . . [and have] enlighten[ed] the people in regard to the history of New Mexico."[90] In contrast to Nuevomexicano tributes, those from Anglo Americans do not suggest that Read's history was uniquely owned by Nuevomexicanos or was part of their identity; it simply represented yet another narrative of New Mexico's past—but a narrative that possessed none of the romance or flair found in the popular histories of Prince and Lummis.

Despite the relative indifference of Anglo Americans, Read sought to disseminate his views among all schoolchildren, particularly Nuevomexicanos who could not afford his published works. To do so, he issued in 1914 a condensed, textbook version entitled *Popular Elementary History of New Mexico,* whose chief purpose was "to enable the poor and the children of our State, especially those who are the descendants of the first explorers and conquerors, to partake of the . . . marvelous deeds, the wonderful foresight, the peerless valor, and the sublime faith of the men who first visited, conquered, set-tled, and christianized this land of ours."[91] Read's publication of a textbook for the schools suggests that he was conscious of the class divisions within the Nuevomexicano community, and that he did not view the Spanish legacy as the sole property of elite Nuevomexicanos. Read may have been persuaded to produce this less expensive book by his translator, Eusebio Chacón, who told him that, as much as he enjoyed Read's work, he found the cost too expensive for the poorer Nuevomexicanos: "The high price discourages the class of people from whom I might obtain subscriptions."[92] Moreover, Read pro-fessed to be generally disinclined to distinguish between those "of pure Spanish blood" and those of mixed Spanish and Indian blood. In 1911, Mateo Luhan complained to his friends that Read had included in *Historia Ilustrada*'s minibiographies certain Nuevo-mexicanos "whose parents were not known." On hearing of Luhan's complaint, Read responded, "Such things ought to be eliminated from [the writing of] history, and the deserving individual should be written about without suffering for lack of ancestors." If historians only wrote about persons of pure Spanish lineage, contended Read, "neither Pizarro nor Alamgro [sic]—the conquistadores of Latin America—would ever have entered into the history books. By the same token, the majority of the great men, of all times and all nations, would not have been written about had historians taken into account their unknown lineage."[93]

Notwithstanding Read's desire to reach a broad audience, there is no clear evidence that Anglos or less-affluent Nuevomexicanos read his text in any appreciable numbers. The existing records include only letters from apparently professional or prominent Nuevomexicanos—doctors, merchants, lawyers, government officials, and the like. There is evidence that many school officials were aware of and thought highly of his text, but whether they introduced it into the classroom is unknown. In 1912, for example, Read advertised his *Illustrated History* in several issues of the *New Mexico Journal of Education,* often adjacent to ads announcing Prince's *A Concise History of New Mexico.*[94] Read sent a copy of *Historia* to Jesús Sánchez, superintendent of public schools in Valencia County, who proclaimed it a work of "great importance for the future of New Mexico."[95] Filadelfo Baca, assistant state superintendent of education, wrote to Read that he had "examin[ed] its [the textbook's] merits as an elementary history for our public and private schools" and found it "especially adapted and commendable for extensive use in the graded and other schools throughout New Mexico."[96] But his book was never officially adopted.[97]

By the 1920s, Nuevomexicanos throughout New Mexico had begun to look to Spanish history and language as symbols of their identity. Anglo Americans, too, began to celebrate the Spanish past by joining Nuevomexicanos in their revival—or, rather, their invention—of the "Santa Fe Fiestas," which presumably dated to Spain's reconquest of New Mexico in 1693.[98] Benjamin Maurice Read and Aurelio Espinosa had contributed to the climate of opinion fostering such an event, and Read played a personal role in the celebration. In September 1927, in a fiesta parade, he rode proudly into the plaza dressed as King Ferdinand of Spain. That was his last public appearance. A few days later, he died suddenly at the age of seventy-four.[99] Ironically, just as a new powerful myth—the Santa Fe fiesta—emerged, an individual who helped make it possible passed away.

☹ Defenders of the Mother Tongue

Because written expressions of identity were most often authored by an educated, bilingual, and professional echelon of Nuevomexicanos, it is tempting to conclude that hispanidad was a sensibility confined to elites, or that elites deployed their hispanidad to set themselves apart from working-class or impoverished compatriots. But in fact the self-described "Spanish American" professionals sought fervently to inculcate an ethnic pride among Nuevomexicanos of all classes by way of education. This effort was most evident among educators who, from the 1890s through the 1930s, fought to preserve Spanish-language instruction and to instill among schoolchildren a pride in their native language and Spanish heritage.

For much of the nineteenth century, the philosophy underpinning public education dated to early reformers such as Horace Mann. Mann viewed "common schools" as a means of eliminating social problems, particularly poverty and class divisions. By equipping students with "good work habits" and a common faith in the political system and the vote, public schools would "disarm the poor of their hostility towards the rich" and would "prevent" poverty.[100] In the early years of the twentieth century, however, public education was conceived as a vehicle for molding students into "worker-citizens" and for integrating them into the new industrial order.

With the passage of a major school law in 1891, public education in New Mexico became more accessible to families of modest or moderate means. Leaders of the territory, including Governor Lebaron Bradford Prince, viewed this achievement as one step toward preparing New Mexico for statehood. Prince called for the creation of more public schools and the establishment of a normal school for teachers, who were to receive uniform—albeit minimal—preparation, examination, and certification. Importantly, the 1891 law allowed for grade-school teachers to instruct students in either English or Spanish. Most schools and teachers taught in English, yet about one third taught in Spanish. This provision gave official sanction to the use of Spanish in public schools alongside and, sometimes, in place of English. But it was also the source of controversy for years to come.[101]

One of the most vocal advocates of this idea was New Mexico's Superintendent of Public Instruction Amado Chaves. In his 1894 report to the governor, Superintendent Chaves declared that there simply were not enough teachers who knew Spanish to adequately teach Spanish-speaking students, and that, as a result, these students were lagging behind their English-speaking classmates. He called for more bilingual teachers and, in 1896, urged that New Mexico's higher institutions require their graduates to complete a course in Spanish. He went on to say that "[i]t is a crime . . . to rob the children of New Mexico of . . . [their] language which is theirs by birthright. English and Spanish are to go hand in hand in our schools, and only the height of bigotry and supine ignorance can ever affirm that the possessor of more than one language is unfit to be a good citizen."[102] Chaves's successors, Plácido Sandoval, Manuel C. de Baca, and José Francisco Chaves, echoed this conviction. Like Amado

Chaves, they believed that English was an indispensable component of U.S. citizenship, but that citizenship was not tied to the exclusive use of the English language. A true democratic republic, they suggested in their reports to the governor, allowed for the expression of one's native language in addition to English.[103]

Beginning in 1905, Nuevomexicano superintendents were being replaced by Anglo American ones who were less receptive to bilingualism, if not wholly opposed to it. At this time, Congress was still deliberating statehood for New Mexico, and opponents such as Senator Alfred Beveridge of Indiana roundly denounced the use of Spanish in classrooms and in the courts as evidence that Nuevomexicanos were ill-prepared for self-government and hence were unfit for entry into the nation's body politic. That year Hiram Hadley became superintendent. Hadley proved exceedingly intolerant of Spanish-language instruction, arguing that the 1891 school law had been misconstrued by his predecessors as providing for bilingual instruction. In fact, he insisted, the law merely allowed for teachers' *occasional* use of Spanish with students and with their parents. Hadley's successor, James Clark, similarly opposed bilingual education and convinced the Anglo-dominated state board to deny funding for Spanish-language textbooks. Clark further mandated that schools initiate so-called "Patriotic Days" to celebrate the "great men" in U.S history and to "Americanize" Spanish-speaking children.[104]

To be certain, many Nuevomexicanos embraced the Americanizing project. But none that I could find in the course of my research embraced the English-only policies of Hadley or Clark. In fact, those policies fueled a firestorm of protest from the Nuevomexicano-controlled territorial assembly, which hastily authorized the construction of a Spanish-American Normal School to revive bilingual education and to train bilingual teachers. Founded as a symbol of Nuevomexicano's educational ambitions, the school unfortunately came to symbolize the neglect and dire reality of Nuevomexicano's education.

In 1909, the territorial legislature passed a bill sponsored by Prince that called for the creation of the Spanish-American Normal School in El Rito. For more than thirty years, this school would stand as a symbol of Nuevomexicano education. Although it was created with the noble intention of training Spanish-speaking teachers to combat the dearth of bilingual educators in rural districts, it was poorly funded and poorly attended, and in the 1920s was, effectively, transformed into a vocational school in which students handcrafted blankets, wood carvings, and furniture.[105]

As previously mentioned, when Congress added an English-only provision into the statehood authorization bill, Nuevomexicanos responded by producing a constitution that guaranteed an education in Spanish to children "of Spanish descent." After sixty-two years of petitioning Congress, New Mexico entered the Union in 1912 as the nation's only officially bilingual state. Documents would be printed in both English and Spanish; there would be no English requirement to sit on a jury and, in the spirit of the 1891 school law, teachers would need to know Spanish in school districts where Spanish was the dominant language. But the mere fact of a bilingual constitution did not ensure the future of Spanish-language instruction. The struggle to retain Spanish in the schools, to legitimize its commercial and cultural value, would continue.

When Aurora Lucero stood before the conference of educators in 1911 and gave her eloquent defense of the Spanish language, she heralded the coming of an age in which Nuevomexicanas would play a growing role in education. She was at the forefront of a cadre of educated women who were entering the classroom and administration from the second decade of the twentieth century through the 1930s. Among her peers were women who pioneered, including Adelina Otero-Warren, Fabiola Cabeza de Baca, and Cleofas Jaramillo. Lucero would help to redefine language policy and instruction in the schools, and contribute to what Sarah Deutsch and other scholars have called the "feminization of the Hispanic teaching force." In the process, she and her cohorts would invoke their hispanidad as a defense against attacks on their culture and language. The growth in numbers of women educators in New Mexico was rather remarkable after 1912, when women were granted the right to vote for and serve on school boards of education.[106]

Lucero was the daughter of Antonio Lucero, a Spanish-language newspaper publisher and New Mexico's first secretary of state. She was educated at the Loretto Academy, Highlands University, and the University of Southern California. Although Lucero was a Spanish teacher for more than thirty years (1924–54) and briefly served as superintendent of education for San Miguel County (1925–27), there are few extant records of her public service. Nevertheless, three of her speeches from 1911 were published in local newspapers, and they offer a glimpse into the bilingual and Hispanist movement of which she and numerous men and women were a part.

Those speeches—in addition to defending bilingual instruction and denouncing English-only education—were replete with both Hispanist pride and U.S. patriotism. In one, for example, she embraced statehood as the culmination of a sixty-two-year struggle to enter what she called "the sisterhood of commonwealths of this mighty union." But she also warned her audience to beware threats to their language and heritage. She pronounced that "[t]o the south [of New Mexico], are sixty million people, all descended from the Spanish Conquistadores. To the north, are to be found the homes of at least ninety million of another people, nearly all of Anglo Saxon blood, speaking an entirely different language." New Mexico, she said, was the meeting ground between these two races, whose "amalgamation" was simply a question of time. Lucero predicted that "[t]he union of the calm, businesslike spirit of the Anglo-Saxon with the sanguine, chivalrous enthusiasm of the Castillian will be such a blending of all that is best in human nature . . ." Spanish and Anglo Saxon Americans were to be united in a single citizenship, under a single flag, and they were to acknowledge and respect one another's cultures, in her view.[107]

But Lucero was keenly aware of the perils of statehood, for she knew there were those who believed one had to vanquish from the body politic all traces of culture and language that were not Anglo-Saxon. In a more immediate sense, she knew that most Anglo educators were determined to eliminate Spanish from the schools, the state constitution notwithstanding.

Though Lucero was a lifelong proponent of bilingualism, her prominence in this regard was eclipsed by that of her cousin, Adelina Otero-Warren. Born in 1881 into the same elite network of families, Adelina (or "Nina," as she preferred to be called) was educated at a private school in Saint Louis. Like Lucero, Otero met and married an Anglo American. She spent several years out of state before returning to New Mexico in 1912. Nina, however, became far more visible in politics. A leading suffragist and friend of Alice Paul, she immersed herself in political organizing and, in 1922, became the first New Mexico woman to run for Congress. Though she carried four of the five largest Nuevomexicano counties, she lost the election. By any measure, Nina Otero-Warren left the greatest imprint on the archival record of bilingual education in the state.[108]

From 1917 to 1929, she was superintendent of education for Santa Fe County. In that capacity, and later as state supervisor for the literacy classes, she published numerous pamphlets and bulletins, and delivered speeches that promoted bilingual instruction. In one pamphlet, for example, she set forth a method for teaching English to non-English-speaking adults. She explained that teachers had to understand their students' cultural and historical background and make exercises that were culturally relevant to them. Earlier, in a speech, she noted that "Bilingualism has been called a problem rather than an asset." Schools had neglected their responsibility to educate Spanish-speaking students, she said,

> by giving to our children instructional materials that is New England in content and New England centered. By trying to get them to forget their language, their heritage; by sending to us experts to measure the child's ability by New England standards, a test which all of us would be fearful of taking.[109]

To combat what she called the sense of "bewilderment" that Spanish-speaking students felt on entering school, Otero-Warren developed a curriculum that incorporated Spanish-language songs, local music, handicrafts, and Southwestern history. Otero-Warren is perhaps best remembered for her efforts to promote vocational training in traditional crafts, but her most enduring contribution to education was the "bilingual method" she developed to help students become proficient in Spanish as well as English. Considered rather "progressive" in its day, it involved teaching students to master material in English by way of graduated immersion, while separately teaching them proper Spanish grammar and composition. By 1938, this method was so widely implemented and lauded that the Taos County Teachers Association adopted a resolution calling for the direct method to be incorporated into the state's official curriculum. In justifying the resolution, County Superintendent Leonides Pacheco and County Supervisor Ruth C. Miller lamented that the "do not speak Spanish" doctrine of the schools had caused students to feel "ashamed of their language, their songs, their crafts and other home industries. We have many examples of the inhibitory effect of this method. . . . Spanish speaking students should take pride in the ability to use correct Spanish as well as English, and they should be proud of their historical and cultural heritage."[110]

Otero-Warren looked to Europe for her pedagogy and her roots. She was a fervent Hispanist and populist who believed—like her contemporary George Isadore Sánchez—that Spanish American identity cut across class boundaries, that even the poorest farmer could lay claim to a conquistadorial past. Indeed, that past was key to establishing primacy on the land, an equality with Anglo Americans and, especially, a white European heritage that would guarantee equality with other whites. But her racial cosmology was perhaps more sophisticated than that of her younger cousin. In 1930, for example, she pitched her literacy program to the Rockefeller Foundation thusly:

> In the progress of American civilization we cannot overlook the fact that the descendant of the Spanish Colonials (racially Spanish and Mexican) is a native American. And yet the Spanish-American has met the fate of all small Colonial Groups; namely, he has suffered from the inability to compete economically or industrially with the overwhelming odds of the standardized commercialism of this country. In an effort to preserve the Spanish-American people and their culture I feel this can best be accomplished through education. Heretofore, there has been a neglect of the great opportunity to incorporate the culture of these people—their arts and crafts—in our educational work. Therefore, with a combination of progressive American educational methods, together with the stimulus to preserve their culture, the Spanish-Americans can be put on a sound economic basis.[111]

As part of her educational vision to both preserve Nuevomexicanos' traditions and uplift them economically, Otero-Warren proposed to document and then incorporate Spanish colonial arts, crafts (old games, dances, religious drama), and literature into a literacy curriculum. These "hidden resources," as she called them, were rapidly being lost through neglect, largely because the Spanish language itself was viewed by many school officials as a barrier and not a means to education. Lucero and Otero-Warren pertained to a generation of Nuevomexicana educators whose story has yet to be told. Along with Fabiola Cabeza de Baca Gilbert and Cleofas Jaramillo, Lucero and Otero-Warren became, effectively, brokers between Nuevomexicano and Anglo worlds. From the 1930s through the 1950s, all of these women labored to conserve what they saw as the most enduring vestiges of their identity: their language and their folklore. Both inside the classroom and, often, in romantic and sometimes melancholy autobiographies, they also inserted their voices into the discourse of hispanidad. Yet despite their advocacy of school reforms, the "bilingual method" failed to extinguish the "do not speak Spanish" policy.[112] Indeed, the stigma associated with speaking Spanish in schools and public realms only intensified with the passing years, even as Anglo Americans and some Nuevomexicanos and Nuevomexicanas—including Otero-Warren herself—reveled in the quaintness of the Spanish heritage.

Long after George Isadore Sánchez in 1940 spelled out the mournful state of education among his "forgotten people," Nuevomexicanos remained on the margins of the body politic, still yearning for full inclusion. It remains perhaps one of the greatest ironies of New Mexico's history that despite Anglo Americans' professions of love for "all things Spanish," their adoration and tourist dollars did not translate into civic, racial, or political equality for "Spanish Americans." For, beneath the surface of Hispanophilia lurked its alter ego: contempt. Contempt for those who presumed to assert some degree of control over their own land, history, language, and destiny, and to attempt to shift the parameters of "American" citizenship. But even as early as 1930, Arthur Campa read the writing on the wall: neither Hispanophilia or hispanidad could redeem Nuevomexicanos from their marginal condition:

> That New Mexico remain different with its Indians and with its somnolent Spanish villages is the desire of those in favor of the picturesque. That it develop along definite economic lines is the desire of those who see for the state a broader future than the mere amusement of tourists. That it can develop without sacrificing the heritage of a civilization that has been

allowed to decay through neglect, isolation and stagnation, is the ideal hope of many.[113]

Figure 23. *Fiesta Jarabe*, by Luis Jiménez, 1996.
Reproduced courtesy of Luis Jiménez.

Epilogue

> Wonderful article and a lesson to all of us about wanting to be something we're not or in forgetting that part of us that isn't fashionable.
>
> —*Jerry Pusey, Oceanside*

> Thank you for an enlightening article. I am a Valdivia who argues with others here in New Mexico about the lineage issue. I tell them their ancestors would have had to fly here on a 747 more than 400 years ago to escape mixing bloodlines with so-called Mexicans. Your article is the education we all need.
>
> —*Steven Valdivia, Albuquerque*

The above two letters to the editor appeared in the *Los Angeles Times*, 21 February 2000, in response to an article by José Cárdenas ("Roots and Reality," 25 January 2000) detailing the efforts of some Latinos who had formed a genealogical society in an effort to retrace their Spanish roots.

⁂ Nostalgia Isn't What It Used to Be

Somewhere there is a black-and-white photograph of two young girls on an outdoor stage gleefully dancing the *jarabe tapatío*. One has braided black hair and is festooned in a white blouse and vivid Mexican skirt; the other is dressed as a young man, in dark pants trimmed with metal buttons and a bright satin shirt, and she sports the wide-brimmed sombrero of a *charro*. The two are facing each other and beaming with delight as relatives and neighbors look on. All are smiling or clapping. Someone has strewn a pocketful of coins across the stage, and they glisten in the afternoon sunshine. "I don't know what happened to the money," my mother says. "It never occurred to me to take the money."

The year was 1940, and the occasion was the celebration of the Coronado Cuarto Centennial, a series of statewide events that commemorated four centuries since Europeans first set foot in the region. Organized in part by a local chapter of LULAC (the League of United Latin American Citizens), the Bernalillo festivities were particularly memorable to longtime residents. Nuevomexicanos who had grown up in the vicinity were well aware that Coronado and his entourage had encamped just across the Rio Grande, at what were now mere remains of the Tiwa pueblo Kuaua. This fact of history was long a source of local pride. When the Cuarto Centennial officials came to town on 29 May 1940, to dedicate the Coronado State Monument at that site, citizens gathered excitedly to welcome Spain's ambassador to the United States, Juan Francisco de Cardenas. After several addresses had been made, Pueblo Indians performed traditional music and dances, and the fiestas began.[1]

Ostensibly, the mission of the Cuarto Centennial was to educate the local and national public about the legacy of "the first white man" to visit the region; to that end, it generally succeeded. However, the official promotional literature suggests that the underlying objective was to showcase New Mexico's history for tourists and thereby to garner revenue. Much to the dismay of state officials, the two hundred events that comprised the yearlong festivities failed to draw throngs of vacationers bearing cameras and money. True, some events lured sightseers with flamboyant reenactments of Coronado's *entrada*—for example, more than five hundred participants reenacted the historic event in an Albuquerque football stadium, to a crowd of thousands—but few of the commemorative events achieved the status of a full-fledged tourist spectacle. Festivities remained, by and large, modest affairs staged and attended by townsfolk. They drew only a fraction of the tourist traffic that planners had predicted.[2]

A few outsiders finally ventured into the far-flung communities where many events were staged—in towns such as Raton, Farmington, Tularosa, Estancia, Mesilla, and so forth. Those who did must have felt, at least in some measure, like interlopers. Such was the feeling Sarah Gertrude Knott had during the three months she toured the state as an aide to Albuquerque businessman Clinton P. Anderson, president of the organizing Coronado Cuarto Centennial Commission. Having immersed herself among nativos and Native Americans, Knott commented on how strange and yet enlightening the experience was:

> In Albuquerque I felt like the foreigner I was.
> "Natives," as the Spanish-Americans are called, and
> Indians milled through the streets. The Anglos, the
> term for all those neither Spanish-American nor
> Indian, were lost in the crowd. However, I did not
> feel foreign in spirit to the gracious, hospitable
> people. We had a common bond of love in the folk
> traditions. At the end of three months, more than
> two hundred festivals were set in Indian, Spanish-
> American, and Anglo communities throughout the
> state. I soon saw there was a vast difference between
> the traditional expressions of New Mexico and any
> other I had known. There are three distinct racial
> groups, three different philosophies of life, three sets
> of folk traditions—confusing, yet challenging.[3]

Knott's brief experience as a "foreigner" in Albuquerque is poignant testimony to the class and cultural divide that set Anglos apart from "native" communities. Generally speaking, tourists and middle-class Anglos appreciated New Mexico's "traditional expressions" within the safe and sterile confines of Santa Fe or Albuquerque, and, as Knott's statement attests, even those tourist settings attained an exotic air when "Indians" and "Spanish-Americans" outnumbered Anglos. Leaving the well-worn tourist path for more intimate environs of satellite communities along the Rio Grande was something few Anglos dared to do.

Having failed to rake in projected tourist dollars, the Coronado Cuarto Centennial's enduring impact was mostly intrinsic and not material, local and not national. It afforded Anglos and Nuevomexicanos an occasion both for historical reflection and half-serious recreation. Communities staged pageants, fiestas, and reenactments of Coronado's entrada; schoolchildren studied and dramatized various aspects of the Spanish conquest; politicians exhorted audiences to embrace equally the Indian, Spanish, and American contributions to the state; and boosters marketed New Mexico as a veritable "kaleidoscope of living history sung and danced in fiesta, religious drama, and ancient ceremonial."[4]

In 1940, New Mexico's history was indeed "living," at least in the hearts and imaginations of Cuarto Centennial participants and spectators. It was elaborated and played out in pageants, recited in classrooms, discussed in newspapers, and reconstituted in a series of official textbooks and teaching tools. The combination of festivity and instruction made the year memorable to everyone involved. To that extent, then, the Cuarto Centennial had fulfilled at least one of its objectives: to arouse historical appreciation. But more important, it reaffirmed a now pervasive claim by Nuevomexicanos to the Spanish past and symbolically revitalized their Catholic identity, attachment to the soil, and pride in their language.

⏳ The Other Cuarto Centennial

Today, one need not go far to see evidence of the Spanish legacy's continued presence and its meaning for many Nuevomexicanos. If you travel eleven miles north of Española on Highway 68 you will come upon an enormous bronze statue dedicated to Juan de Oñate. Clad in military armor and poised astride a bristling steed, Oñate bears a strong resemblance to textbook images of Hernán Cortés. His eyebrows furrowed with determination, Oñate embodies all the vigor and arrogance of the Spanish conquest. Inaugurated in 1994 in anticipation of the 1998 Cuarto Centennial of Oñate's entrada into New Mexico, the statue has generated enormous controversy in the press and has been the focus of several intense demonstrations both for and against its installation.

Those who still call themselves "Spanish Americans" have defended the Oñate statue as a tribute to their forebears and to their own identity and history. In their view, Oñate's arrival and his settlement of "New Spain" marked a major achievement in North American civilization. Protestors decried the statue as a travesty, an insult to the memory of the indigenous peoples who perished under Spain's brutal regime. They invariably retell the story of 1599. That year Oñate's army killed eight hundred Acoma Indians during a horrific battle that lasted three days, and that was launched in reprisal for the Indians having killed eleven Spanish soldiers (including Oñate's nephew). Survivors were taken captive and were forcibly marched 150 kilometers north to the Spanish settlement of San Gabriel, adjacent to present-day Española. When they arrived, Oñate ordered each Acoma male over twenty-five to have one foot severed as punishment and as an example to other natives. Oñate's "conquest," several Pueblo Indians protested, is nothing to commemorate.

Then one moonless night in January, as the Cuarto Centennial loomed near, a group of Native American activists reportedly slipped through the iron gates at the monument's entrance and, using an electric saw, cut off the right foot of the Oñate statue. They sent a local newspaper a photograph of the foot with the proclamation: "We see no glory in celebrating Oñate's fourth centennial, and we do not want our faces rubbed in it."[5]

This controversy demonstrates the emotional and political energy that resides in memory, and its potential to magnify longstanding ethnic tensions and ideological fissures in society. Debates over such monuments bring to light deep-seated assumptions, beliefs, and perceptions regarding the past, and provide a venue and a specific moment at which they might be contested. As tensions escalate, public spaces themselves often become sources of contention and disputed terrain. When spaces and landmarks are contested, so are the histories they consecrate and the community values or identities they symbolize; so, too, are the social relations of power which give them emotional meaning and political value. The Oñate statue debate is testimony to the ongoing polemic over the Spanish American identity, the polemic that is rooted in Nuevomexicanos' longing for legitimacy.

ःX The Photo

In researching this book, I once asked my mother if she sees any irony in her performance of the jarabe tapatío, the "Mexican hat dance" that grew popular following the Revolution, to celebrate the Spanish conquest. She begins to explain that, culturally, we are all "mexicanos"; we have the same values, the same religion, the same language. Then she hesitates. "I was a little girl back then, and it was just something I was asked to do. I was very happy to do it."

As she says this, an image comes to mind of the monumental statue by Luis Jiménez, *Fiesta Jarabe,* which greets visitors at the entrance of the University of New Mexico in Albuquerque. It features a dark-skinned *pareja* in festive attire, dancing with controlled passion. When it was installed in 1996, some individuals complained that the figures were too dark to be from New Mexico.

"They aren't mexicanos from here," someone once remarked to me, "*son de México*. I've never seen anyone dance the Mexican hat dance in New Mexico." I smile.

Spanish American identity in New Mexico was conceived in myth and is sustained by memory. And memories, of course, are subject to change, manipulation, distortion. Those that are incongruent with our expectations and immediate needs are often cast off into oblivion—*el olvido* or *l'oubli*. On the other hand, those that affirm our sense of self and community, and that empower us in the present or help explain our marginality, are like Jiménez's fiesta dancers: larger than life. As Latinos comprise an ever-larger proportion of the U.S. population, historians will invariably have to address the perplexities of memory in framing "Latina/o History." Until recent years, the historiography has emphasized nation-specific diasporas and narratives, broadly conceived as Mexican-American/Chicana/o, Puerto Rican, Dominican, Cuban, and so forth. But the predominant framework of Latina/o historical scholarship is yet uncertain. Which landmark events will historians consecrate in text? Which myths and memories will predominate? More important, which memories will be cast off?

:)人

I have never actually seen that photograph of my mother dressed as a charro, dancing the jarabe tapatío, and I am beginning to doubt whether one actually exists. But she insists it must. My mother distinctly recalls seeing someone in the crowd snapping photos with a Brownie camera that was popular back then. As a historian, I feel compelled to confirm or dispel her recollection with tangible evidence. But that obligation will go unfulfilled. Instead, that moment will remain preserved in her memory—and here, in these pages.

Figure 24. Matilde Elena Nieto ("La Helen"). Private collection.

Notes

Introduction

1. Rev. John Roux to Hon. Miguel A. Otero, 2 July 1898. TANM Roll #128, f1145.

2. *New York Times,* 24 August 1898.

3. Henry Wray, "America's Unguarded Gateway," *North American Review* 208 (August 1918): 213–15.

4. George Isadore Sánchez, *Forgotten People: A Study of New Mexicans* (Albuquerque: University of New Mexico Press, 1940), vii, 3.

5. In Sánchez's words, "If the romance of the Conquest is realistically meaningful, it is so because of the implications that they have upon life today." Ibid., 12–13.

6. Arthur León Campa, *Spanish Folk-Poetry in New Mexico* (Albuquerque: University of New Mexico Press, 1946), 12–13.

7. Ibid., 15.

8. In her discussion of Latino labeling, Suzanne Oboler notes that labels "presuppose the sacrificing of accuracy," and that their original meanings tend to shift over time. "Ethnic labels serve to point to practices of political inclusion or exclusion of the group's members from full participation as first-class citizens in their nation." Suzanne Oboler, *Ethnic Labels, Latino Lives: Identity and the Politics of (Re)Presentation in the United States* (Minneapolis: University of Minnesota Press, 1995), xvi–xvii. Also see Phillip B. Gonzales, "The Political Construction of Latino Nomenclatures in Twentieth Century New Mexico," *Journal of the Southwest* 35, no. 2 (1993): 158–85.

9. Carey McWilliams, *North from Mexico: The Spanish-Speaking People of the United States.* The People of the Americas Series, ed. Louis Adamic (Philadelphia: J. B. Lippincott Co., 1949), 79.

10. For these initial criticisms, see Niles Hanson, "Commentary: The Hispano Homeland in 1900," *Annals of the Association of American Geographers* 71 (June 1981): 280–82. Nostrand replied that "the spread of

'Spanish American' was part of a growing Spanish consciousness that appears to have been a latent expression and most definitely had its justification." Richard L. Nostrand, "Comment in Reply," *Annals of the Association of American Geographers* 71 (June 1981): 282–83.

11. J. M. Blaut and Antonio Rios-Bustamante, "Commentary on Nostrand's 'Hispanos' and their 'Homeland,'" *Annals of the Association of American Geographers* 74, no. 1 (1984): 157, 157–64.

12. For additional rejoinders on the Homeland Debate, see Fray Angélico Chávez, "Rejoinder," *Annals of the Association of American Geographers* 74, no. 1 (1984): 170–71; Thomas Hall, *Annals of the Association of American Geographers* 74, no. 1 (1984): 171; D. W. Meinig, *Annals of the Association of American Geographers* 74, no. 1 (1984): 171; and Marc Simmons, *Annals of the Association of American Geographers* 74, no. 1 (1984): 169–70. Simmons's rejoinder is particularly interesting because he argues Hispanos did not possess a sense of "Mexicanness" or *mexicanidad*. Rather, he said, "contemporary Hispanos may not be Spaniards, they are Spanish, for being Spanish—the concept of *hispanidad*—is a matter of culture, philosophical outlook, and personal sentiment." Ibid., 170. A dozen years after his article appeared, Nostrand published a monograph elaborating his homeland thesis: Richard L. Nostrand, *The Hispano Homeland* (Norman: University of Oklahoma Press, 1992).

13. Sylvia Rodríguez observed that the Hispano Homeland debate revealed the rather primordialist conceptions of culture that were at play. "The Hispano Homeland Debate Revisited," *Perspectives in Mexican American Studies* 3 (1992): 95–114. For a discussion of the theoretical framework that informs her ethnography, see Sylvia Rodríguez, *The Matachines Dance: Ritual Symbolism and Interethnic Relations in the Upper Rio Grande Valley* (Albuquerque: University of New Mexico Press, 1996), 10–14. For Fredrik Barth's "reactive approach to ethnicity," see Fredrik Barth, *Ethnic Groups and Boundaries: The Social Organization of Cultural Difference* (Boston: Little, Brown and Co., 1969).

14. Phillip B. Gonzales, "More Lessons from the Hispano Homeland Debate," paper presented at the National Association of Chicano Scholars, San Jose, California, 25–28 March 1993 (private manuscript); Phillip B. Gonzales, *The Protest Function of Spanish-American Identity in New Mexico*, Working Paper Series no. 111 (Albuquerque: Southwest Hispanic Research Institute, University of New Mexico, Spring 1985); Phillip B. Gonzales, "Spanish Heritage and Ethnic Protest in New Mexico: The Anti-Fraternity Bill of 1933." *New Mexico Historical*

Review 61 (October 1986): 281–99; Phillip B. Gonzales, "La Junta de Indignación: Hispano Repertoire of Collective Protest in New Mexico, 1884–1933," *Western Historical Quarterly* 31 (2000): 161–86; Phillip B. Gonzales, "The Political Construction of Latino Nomenclatures; Phillip B. Gonzales, *Forced Sacrifice as Ethnic Protest: The Hispano Cause in New Mexico and the Racial Attitude Confrontation of 1933* (New York: Peter Lang, 2001), 19–57.

15. Some important contributions include: Deena J. González, *Refusing the Favor: The Spanish-Mexican Women of Santa Fe, 1820–1880* (New York: Oxford University Press, 1999); Chris Wilson, *The Myth of Santa Fe: The Making of a Modern Regional Tradition* (Albuquerque: University of New Mexico Press, 1997); David J. Weber, *The Spanish Frontier in North America* (New Haven: Yale University Press, 1992); Sarah Deutsch, *No Separate Refuge: Culture, Class, and Gender on the Anglo-Hispanic Frontier in the American Southwest, 1880–1940* (New York: Oxford University Press, 1987); David J. Weber, *Myth and History of the Hispanic Southwest* (Albuquerque: University of New Mexico Press, 1988); John R. Chávez, *The Lost Land: The Chicano Image of the Southwest* (Albuquerque: University of New Mexico Press, 1984); Adrian Herminio Bustamante, "Los Hispanos: Ethnicity and Social Change in New Mexico" (PhD diss., University of New Mexico, 1982); David J. Weber, ed., *Foreigners in Their Native Land: Historical Roots of the Mexican Americans* (Albuquerque: University of New Mexico Press, 1973). In recent years, a number of doctoral dissertations have examined various aspects of identity, gender, sexuality, and culture in New Mexico. Some of them are: Estevan Rael-Gálvez, "Identifying Captivity and Capturing Identity: Narratives of American Indian Slavery" (PhD diss., University of Michigan, 2002); Arturo Gibert-Fernandez, "'*La Voz del Pueblo*': *Texto, identidad y lengua en la prensa neomexicana, 1890–1911*" (PhD diss., University of New Mexico, 2001); Judith S. Neulander, "Cannibals, Castes and Crypto-Jews: Premillennial Cosmology in Postcolonial New Mexico" (PhD diss., Indiana University, 2001); Pablo Reid Mitchell, "Bodies on Borders: Sexuality, Race and Conquest in Modernizing New Mexico, 1880–1920" (PhD diss., University of Michigan, 2000); Margaret Espinosa MacDonald, "'*Vamos todos a Belén*': Cultural Transformations of the Hispanic Community in the Rio Abajo Community in Belen, New Mexico from 1850 to 1950" (PhD diss., University of New Mexico, 1997); Shelley Roberts, "Remaining and Becoming: Cultural Crosscurrents in an Hispano School (Assimilation)" (PhD diss., University of Illinois, 1995).

16. Ramón A. Gutiérrez, *When Jesus Came, the Corn Mothers Went Away: Marriage, Sexuality, and Power in New Mexico, 1500–1846* (Stanford, Calif.: Stanford University Press, 1991); Ramón A. Gutiérrez, "Aztlán, Montezuma, and New Mexico: The Political Uses of American Indian Mythology," in *Aztlán: Essays on the Chicano Homeland,* ed. Rodolfo A. Anaya and Francisco Lomelí (Albuquerque: University of New Mexico Press, 1989), 170–92; Ramón A. Gutiérrez, "Unraveling America's Hispanic Past: Internal Stratification and Class Boundaries," *Aztlán* 17 (Spring 1986): 172–90; Sylvia Rodríguez, "The Hispano Homeland Debate Revisited," *Perspectives in Mexican American Studies* 3 (1992): 95–114; Sylvia Rodríguez, "Art, Tourism, and Race Relations in Taos: Toward a Sociology of the Art Colony," *Journal of Anthropological Research* 45 (Spring 1988): 77–99; Sylvia Rodríguez, "Land, Water, and Ethnic Identity in Taos," in *Land, Water, and Culture: New Perspectives on Hispanic Land Grants,* ed. Charles L. Briggs and John R. Van Ness (Albuquerque: University of New Mexico Press, 1987), 313–403.

17. Erlinda Gonzales-Berry, introduction to *Pasó por aquí: Critical Essays on the New Mexican Literary Tradition,* ed. Erlinda Gonzales-Berry (Albuquerque: University of New Mexico Press, 1989), 1–11; Erlinda Gonzales-Berry, "Which Language Will Our Children Speak," in *Contested Homeland: A Chicano History of New Mexico,* ed. Erlinda Gonzales-Berry and David R. Maciel (Albuquerque: University of New Mexico Press, 2000), 169–89; Doris L. Meyer, *Speaking for Themselves: Neomexicano Cultural Identity and the Spanish-Language Press, 1880–1920* (Albuquerque: University of New Mexico Press, 1996); A. Gabriel Meléndez, *So All is Not Lost: The Poetics of Print in Nuevomexicano Communities, 1834–1958* (Albuquerque: University of New Mexico Press, 1997); Genaro M. Padilla, *My History, Not Yours: The Formation of Mexican American Autobiography* (Madison: University of Wisconsin, 1993.

18. Genaro Padilla, "Imprisoned Narrative? Or Lies, Secrets, and Silence in New Mexico Women's Autobiography," in *Criticism in the Borderland,* ed. Hector Calderón and José Saldívar (Durham, N.C.: Duke University Press, 1991), 45.

19. Charles Montgomery, *The Spanish Redemption: Heritage, Power, and Loss on New Mexico's Upper Rio Grande* (Berkeley: University of California Press, 2002), 11–12. For a critique of Montgomery's assessment, see Phillip B. Gonzales, "Review Essay: Charles Montgomery, *The Spanish Redemption: Heritage, Power, and Loss on New Mexico's Upper Rio Grande,*" *New Mexico Historical Review* 78, no. 3 (Summer 2003); 329–37.

20. Werner Sollors views modernism as a source of "ethnicity." "Looking at ethnicity as modern does not imply that ethnic conflicts thereby appear less 'real' simply because they may be based on an 'invention,' a cultural construction. It does not suggest that ethnic consciousness is weak because there is much interaction and syncretistic borrowing at its core." Werner Sollors, introduction to *The Invention of Ethnicity*, ed. Werner Sollors (New York: Oxford University Press, 1989), xv, ix–xx. Also see Werner Sollors, *Beyond Ethnicity: Consent and Descent in American Culture* (New York: Oxford University Press, 1986), esp. 208–36.

21. This book engages a large and growing discussion on whiteness. My work is most informed by Ian Haney López's examination of popular, scientific, and legal parameters of whiteness as pertains to citizenship. What becomes clear in the case of northern New Mexico is that Nuevomexicanos were all too aware that they resided both geographically and metaphorically somewhere on the frontier between whiteness (inclusion) and Mexicanness (exclusion). Ian Haney López, *White by Law: The Legal Construction of Race* (New York: New York University Press, 1996). Other works that inform this study are: Matthew Frye Jacobson, *Whiteness of a Different Color: European Immigration and the Alchemy of Race* (Cambridge, Mass.: Harvard University Press, 1998); Karen Brodkin, *How Jews Became White Folks and What That Says about Race in America* (New Brunswick, N.J.: Rutgers University Press, 1998); Noel Ignatiev, *How the Irish Became White* (New York: Routledge, 1995); David R. Roediger, *The Wages of Whiteness: Race and the Making of the American Working Class* (New York: Verso, 1991).

22. On citizenship and the body politic, see Rogers M. Smith, *Civic Ideals: Conflicting Visions of Citizenship in U.S. History* (New Haven: Yale University Press, 1997). On "forms" of citizenship, Linda Kerber writes that U.S. citizenship is a concept that has been historically defined (or "braided") by gender, race, and class qualifications. Although, by Aristotle's definition, "'citizen' is an equalizing word," referring to "one who rules and is ruled in turn," the term has not been consistently defined or applied in the United States. Many groups have experienced distinct meanings of U.S. citizenship, states Kerber, including: "women; Africans brought enslaved and their descendants; Native Americans, who did not as a group have citizenship conferred on them until 1924 (whether or not they wanted it); other categories of involuntary immigrants [such as] people of Mexican birth or identity, who

'became' American when the United States acquired Texas, New Mexico, and other territory after the Mexican War; 'noncitizen nationals,' who lived in possessions that never became states [including] Filipinos between 1898 and 1946, Puerto Ricans between 1900 and 1917, Virgin Islanders between 1917 and 1927, persons born in American Samoa now; voluntary immigrants from Europe, all of whom were eligible for naturalization and citizenship; voluntary immigrants from Asia and elsewhere, who for long periods were ineligible for naturalization; refugees who can never return to their homelands; refugees uprooted by disruptions in which they have reason to believe the United States was complicit, for example Vietnamese 'boat people'." Linda K. Kerber, "The Meanings of Citizenship," *Journal of American History* (December 1997): 833–54. Two recent monographs on women's citizenship in the United States include Linda K. Kerber, *No Constitutional Right to Be Ladies: Women and the Obligations of* Citizenship (New York: Hill and Wang, 1998); and Candice Lewis Bredbenner, *A Nationality of Her Own: Women, Marriage, and the Law). of Citizenship* (Berkeley: University of California Press, 1998.

Chapter One

1. William W. H. Davis, *El Gringo, or New Mexico and Her People* (New York: Harper and Bros., 1857; repr., Lincoln: University of Nebraska Press, 1982), 216.

2. Fray Angélico Chávez, *Origins of New Mexico Families in the Spanish Colonial Period, in Two Parts: The Seventeenth (1598–1693) and the Eighteenth (1693–1821) Centuries* (Albuquerque: University of New Mexico in collaboration with Calvin Horn Publishers, 1973), xiv.

3. Protest rallies such as this one have been referred to by participants and, more recently, by scholars as *juntas de indignación*. Sociologist Phillip B. Gonzales describes the juntas as "a spontaneous convergence often attracting a large crowd, sometimes into the hundreds. As the proceedings commenced, a passel of officers—president, secretary, and interpreter—was immediately elected. Acting as on a sacred mission, speakers dramatized the issue in florid oratory. A resolutions committee spelled out declarations and issued demands to authorities, and these were ordered published in the press." Phillip B. Gonzales, *Forced Sacrifice as Ethnic Protest*, 37. The 1901 Las Vegas junta pública was headed by a resolutions commission composed of local citizens who signed and

submitted the resolution to be published in the local press. Signatories of the resolution included the junta leadership: José Santos Esquibel (president), Felipe Delgao y Lucero and Sabino Lujan (vice presidents), and Tranquilino Labadie (secretary). "Resoluciones de Indignación," *El Independiente*, 31 October 1901.

4. *El Independiente*, 7 November 1901, my translation. "Comienza dicha escritora por pasmarnos con decir que el hispano-americano, ó mexicano, es parte español y parte indio; que en lenguaje, costumbres, apariencia y hábitos se asemeja á sus antepasados españoles é indios. Cómo habrá torcido ella los cánones de la linguística para adunar las lenguas española ó india, es un misterio para nosotros. . . . Yo soy his-pano-americano como son los que me escuchan. En mis venas ninguna sangre circula si no es la que trajo Don Juan de Oñate, y la que trajeron después los ilustres antepsasados de mi nombre. Si en alguna parte de las Américas españolas, ó lo que antes fueron dominios españoles, se han conservado en su pureza los rasgos fisionómicos de la raza conquista-dora, esto ha sido en Nuevo México. Meszcla alguna ha dabido [*sic*], si, pero tan leve y en tan raros casos, que el decir que somos, como comu-nidad, una raza mixta, ni está comprobado por el hecho histórico, ni resiste al análisis científica. Pero si fuera verdad que somos una raza mixta, nada hay en ello de deshonroso ó degradante." Also see Chacón's speech in *La Voz del Pueblo*, 2 November 1901, as translated in Anselmo F. Arellano and Julian Josue Vigil, *Las Vegas Grandes on the Gallinas, 1835–1985* (Las Vegas, N.M.: Editorial Telaraña, 1985), 52. Unless other-wise noted, all translations hereafter are my own.

5. Benjamin Maurice Read, *Historia ilustrada de Nuevo México. Cuatro libros en un tomo* (Santa Fe: Compañía Impresora del Nuevo Mexicano, 1911), 460; Francisco A. Lomelí, *Eusebio Chacón: A Literary Portrait of Nineteenth Century New Mexico*, Working Paper no. 113 (Albuquerque: Southwest Hispanic Research Institute, Spring 1987); A. Gabriel Meléndez, *So All Is Not Lost*, 144–54.

6. Rafael Chacón recounted his lifetime of struggle and adapta-tion under the American regime in his still unpublished Spanish-lan-guage memoir. Jacqueline Dorgan Meketa, ed., *Legacy of Honor: The Life of Rafael Chacón, a Nineteenth-Century New Mexican* (Albuquerque: University of New Mexico Press, 1986); Genaro M. Padilla, *The Genealogy of a Text and a Text of Genealogy: Rafael Chacón's "Memorias,"* Working Paper no. 116 (Albuquerque: Southwest Hispanic Research Institute, University of New Mexico, Summer 1991).

7. For a discussion of Chacón's speech, see Charles Montgomery, *The Spanish Redemption: Heritage, Power, and Loss on New Mexico's Upper Rio Grande* (Berkeley: University of California Press, 2002), 64–69.

8. See note 4.

9. Uli Linke, *Blood and Nation: The European Aesthetics of Race* (Philadelphia: University of Pennsylvania Press, 1999), 3–62. In his classic early treatment of consanguinity, Lewis H. Morgan delineates the family relationships that were defined by blood, and notes that "Aryan Nations," "Romaic Nations," and "Teutonic Nations" possessed generally similar systems of bloodline classification. Lewis H. Morgan, *Systems of Consanguinity and Affinity of the Human Family* (Washington, D.C.: Smithsonian Institution, 1871), 29–32.

10. Antonio Domínguez Ortiz, *Los Judeoconversos en España y América*, Colección Fundamentos no. 11 (Madrid: Ediciones ISTMO, 1971).

11. Américo Castro, *La realidad histórica en España* (Mexico, 1954), 501, as quoted in Domínguez Ortiz, *Los Judeoconversos*, 80. Three compelling case studies of blood and identity in Spain are Pilar León Tello, *Judios de Toledo* (Madrid: Consejo Superior de Investigaciones Científicas, 1979); Luis Coronas Tejada, *Conversos and Inquisition in Jaén* (Jerusalem: Magnes Press, 1988); and Feliciano Sierro Malmierca, *Judios, moriscos e inquisición en ciudad rodrigo* (Salamanca, Spain: Ediciones de la Diputación de Salamanca, 1990).

12. Domínguez Ortiz writes that members of military cofradias "were obligated to conserve the purity of their blood, although this measure would not have the character that later would be attributed to it by incorporations called statutes. Rather, it must have been a means of the noble and militaristic minority to conserve their individuality and not be swallowed up by the masses, as had been other conquering peoples in similar circumstances." Domínguez Ortiz, *Los Judeoconversos*, 81.

13. Linda Martz, *A Network of Converso Families in Early Modern Toledo: Assimilating a Minority* (Ann Arbor: University of Michigan Press, 2003). Other recent studies on conversos, Jews, and crypto-Jews in Spain include David M. Gilitz, *Secrecy and Deceit: The Religion of the Crypto-Jews* (Albuquerque: University of New Mexico Press, 2002); Janet Liebman Jacobs, *Hidden Heritage: The Legacy of the Crypto-Jews* (Berkeley: University of California Press, 2002); Renée Levine Melammed, *Heretics or Daughters of Israel? The Crypto-Jewish Women of Castile* (New York: Oxford University Press, 1999).

14. Martz, *A Network of Converso Families;* Domínguez Ortíz, *Los Judeoconversos,* 83.

15. Martz, *A Network of Converso Families,* 25–26.

16. Ibid., 26.

17. Ibid., 33.

18. For a study of Jews in Spain during the sixteenth century, see Miguel Angel Motis Dolader, *Los judios Aragoneses en la época del descubrimiento de América* (Zaragoza, Spain: Navarro y Navarro, 1989).

19. Ibid., 135.

20. Nancy P. Appelbaum, Anne S. Macpherson, and Karin Alejandra Rosemblatt, *Race and Nation in Modern Latin America* (Chapel Hill: University of North Carolina Press, 2003); Gary B. Nash, *Forbidden Love: The Secret History of Mixed Race America* (New York: Henry Holt and Co., 1999), 46–64. Also see Carol A. Smith, Race-Class-Gender Ideology in Guatemala: Modern and Anti-Modern Forms," *Comparative Studies in Society and History* 37, no. 4 (1995): 723–49.

21. Ramón A. Gutiérrez notes that a Spaniard's national consciousness, "as a citizen of a nation-state, was weakly developed." Ramón A. Gutiérrez, "Unraveling America's Hispanic Past," 80.

22. One example of noble lineage that reached from medieval Spain to New Spain is the Military Order of Santiago, established during the twelfth century to combat the Moors and recapture the Iberian peninsula in the name of Christianity (and Saint James). This was the largest and wealthiest of a number of military orders. It incorporated more terrain, more castles, and more nobles and vassals than any of its contemporaries, and it claimed the greatest number of encomiendas. For a discussion of military orders in Mexico and New Spain, see Ignacio de Villar Villamil, *Presentación,* in *Los caballeros de las ordenes militares en méxico. Católogo biografico y geneológico,* by Leopoldo Martínez Cosio (Mexico: Editorial Santiago, 1946), vii–viii.

23. Lisbeth Haas, *Conquests and Historical Identities in California, 1769–1936* (Berkeley: University of California Press, 1995), 31; Douglas Monroy, *Thrown among Strangers: The Making of Mexican Culture in Frontier California* (Berkeley: University of California Press, 1990), 57; Martha Menchaca, *Recovering History, Recovering Race: The Indian, Black, and White Roots of Mexican Americans* (Austin: University of Texas Press, 2001), 167–69.

24. Edward H. Spicer, *Cycles of Conquest: The Impact of Spain, Mexico, and the United States on the Indians of the Southwest, 1533–1960* (Tucson: University of Arizona Press, 1962); John Huxtable Elliot,

Imperial Spain, 1469–1716 (St. Martin's Press, 1963; repr., Meridian Books, 1977), 106.

25. In 1602, King Philip II issued an order granting noble title and land in perpetuity to Juan de Oñate and "all his descendents" and heirs. This document called for the enforcement of a 1573 decree that promulgated the honorific title of "hijo dalgo" on those persons who participated in the peopling of the frontier in the name of the Crown. That order reads as follows: "That the peoplers and their legitimate children and descendents be Hijos-Dalgos in the American Indies. . . . persons of noble lineage and known origins." *Ordenanza del Rey de España Don Felipe II*. Miscellaneous manuscript (copy), vertical file, Center for Southwest Research (CSWR), University of New Mexico. According to Angélico Chávez, "[T]he term '*español*' had a particular meaning in New Spain. . . . Many of the early Spaniards . . . married Indian women, and then those *mestizo* or *coyote* children of theirs who kept intermarrying with others of pure Spanish blood (or predominantly so) were finally recognized as honest-to-goodness *españoles*. They were 'restored' Spaniards, as it were." Fray Angélico Chávez, *Chávez: A Distinctive American Clan of New Mexico* (Santa Fe: William Gannon, 1989), xiv; Elliott, *Imperial Spain*, 65–66.

26. Gutiérrez, *When Jesus Came,* 195; H. Bailey Carroll and J. Villasana Haggard, eds. *Three New Mexico Chronicles: The* Exposición *of Don Pedro Bautista Pino, 1812; the* Ojeada *of Lic. Antonio Barreiro, 1832; and the additions by Don José Agustín de Escudero, 1849* (Albuquerque: Quivira Society, 1942), 208.

27. There has been a resurgence of interest in the elaboration and visual depiction of castas dating to Magnus Mörner's classic study *Race Mixture in the History of Latin America* (Boston: Little, Brown and Co., 1967); see also Museo de Arte de Lima, *Los cuadros de mestizaje del virrey Amat: La representación etnográfica en el Perú colonial* (Lima: Museo de Arte de Lima, 1999).

28. *Diccionario de la Lengua Española* (Madrid, 1737), as translated in Gutiérrez, *When Jesus Came,* 202.

29. Gutiérrez, *When Jesus Came,* 202.

30. Hensley C. Woodbridge, "Glossary of Names Used in Colonial Latin America for Crosses among Indians, Negroes, and Whites," *Journal of the Washington Academy of Sciences* 38, no. 11 (November 15, 1948): 355.

31. Phenotype was deemed significant by Spanish authorities as a means of identifying their own soldiers prior to setting out on expeditions. For example, one year after the 1680 Pueblo Revolt, the Crown

assembled some 148 soldiers in Parral and Casas Grandes to re-"pacify" the "yndios alzados de la nueva méxico." A list of the soldiers describes their place of birth, marital status, and physical features thusly: "Francisco Xavier. 52 years old, widower, native of the kingdom of Castile, and city of Seville. Of good body (health), very grey hair, with a scar on the front left side of the forehead, etc." Others were described by their skin color: "Diego López Zambrano. 38 years old, native of New Mexico, tall, white, with a colored (dark) face." *Extracto del libro real de asientos y pagas de pobladores y soldados aviados por el ri sueldo de su magestad para la reducción de los yndios azados de la nuevo méxico.* Miscellaneous manuscript (copy), "Genealogy," vertical file, CSWR. Original document held in folders 1–4, Thomas B. Catron Papers, CSWR.

32. Caution should be exercised in interpreting these data so as not to accept Beltran's premise that race was (or is) biologically determined, strictly a function of lineage. As has already been established, race was (and remains) a socially defined means of differentiating groups of people by ascription, and thereby marginalizing them from access to certain privilege or power. Woodbridge, "Glossary of Names," 354.

33. Haas, *Conquests and Historical Identities,* 31.

34. For a study of calidad as it relates to clase and marriage patterns, see Robert McCaa, "*Calidad, Clase,* and Marriage in Colonial Mexico: The Case of Parral, 1788–90," *Hispanic American Historical Review* 64 (1984): 477–501, esp. 497–99. Also see McCaa, "Modeling Social Interaction: Marriage, Miscegenation and the Society of Castes in Colonial Spanish America," *Historical Methods* 15 (1982): 45–66.

35. Jack D. Forbes, "Black Pioneers: The Spanish-Speaking Afroamericans of the Southwest," *Phylon: The Atlanta University Review of Race and Culture* (Fall 1966): 24–26.

36. For a thorough discussion of hypergamy and hypogamy, see Gutiérrez, *When Jesus Came,* 284–97.

37. Whereas in central Mexico and the Californias, mulatos comprised approximately 20 percent of the non-Indian population in 1790, in that same year only 2.6 percent of northern New Mexico's population was enumerated as mulato. Forbes, "Black Pioneers," 23.

38. As translated in Bailey and Haggard, *Three New Mexico Chronicles,* 9. The figures for mulatos in northern New Mexico are for the region defined by Santa Fe, Tesuque, and Pecos. Alicia V. Tjarks, "Demographic, Ethnic and Occupational Structure of New Mexico, 1790," *The Americas: A Quarterly Review of Inter-American Cultural History* 35 (July 1978): 83.

39. Forbes, "Black Pioneers," 33.

40. For a discussion of ethnic nomenclature in New Mexico see Bustamante, "Los Hispanos."

41. According to Tjarks, the 1790 census was "the first one to provide specific data about sex, age, civil status, racial group, family and occupational structure of the population. Summaries of the census were formulated on the basis of the local census summaries, dividing the population by jurisdictions and classifying it by age, according to the three predominant racial groups." Tjarks, "Demographic, Ethnic and Occupational Structure," 46. Also see Sherburne F. Cook and Woodrow Borah, *Essays on Population History,* vol. 1, *Mexico and the Caribbean* (Berkeley: University of California Press, 1971), 256–57.

42. Tjarks, "Demographic, Ethnic and Occupational Structure," 83.

43. Virginia L. Olmsted, *Spanish and Mexican Colonial Censuses of New Mexico: 1790, 1823, 1845* (Albuquerque: New Mexico Genealogical Society, 1975), 1.

44. Tjarks, "Demographic, Ethnic and Occupational Structure," 82.

45. Pedro Alonso O'Crouley, *A Description of the Kingdom of New Spain, 1774* (San Francisco: John Howell Books, 1972), 18.

46. Tjarks, "Demographic, Ethnic and Occupational Structure," 79.

47. Ibid.

48. Bustamante, "Los Hispanos," 54.

49. Hubert Howe Bancroft, *History of Arizona and New Mexico* (San Francisco: The History Company, 1889; repr., Albuquerque: Horn and Wallace Publishers, 1962), 280.

50. Spanish Archives of New Mexico (SANM), microfilm rolls 14f654.

51. Quoted in Carroll and Haggard, *Three New Mexico Chronicles,* 211–62. For an overview of settlement patterns in colonial New Mexico, see Oakah L. Jones Jr., *Los Paisanos: Spanish Settlers on the Northern Frontier of New Spain* (Norman: University of Oklahoma Press, 1979). For an examination of the legal system under Spain, see Charles R. Cutter, "Community and the Law in Northern New Spain," *The Americas: A Quarterly Review of Inter-American Cultural History* 50 (April 1994): 467–80.

52. Carroll and Haggard, *Three New Mexico Chronicles,* 211–62.

53. Ibid.

54. Bustamante, "Los Hispanos," 65.

55. SANM, 20f498–99.

56. Archives of the Archdiocese of Santa Fe (AASF), microfilm rolls 54f543–54.

57. *Primer diccionario general etimológico de la Lengua Española,* as quoted in Gutiérrez, *When Jesus Came,* 191.

58. McCaa, "*Calidad, Clase,* and Marriage," 478.

59. Gutiérrez, "Unraveling America's Hispanic Past," 82.

60. Gutiérrez, *When Jesus Came,* 227.

61. Ann Twinam, "Honor, Sexuality, and Illegitimacy in Colonial Spanish America," in *Sexuality and Marriage in Colonial Latin America,* ed. Asunción Lavrin (Lincoln: University of Nebraska Press, 1989). For a discussion of the intersection between caste, class, and gender, see Asunción Lavrin and Edith Couturier, "Dowries and Wills: A View of Women's Socioeconomic Role in Colonial Guadalajara and Puebla, 1640–1790," *Hispanic American Historical Review* 59 (1979): 280–304; McCaa, "*Calidad, Clase,* and Marriage," 493.

62. McCaa, "*Calidad, Clase,* and Marriage," 493.

63. Ibid.

64. Gutiérrez, *When Jesus Came,* 297, 271–97. For an insightful discussion of class consciousness in colonial Latin America, see Magnus Mörner, "Economic Factors and Stratification in Colonial Spanish America with Special Regard to Elites," *Hispanic American Historical Review* 63 (1983): 335–69.

65. Ross Frank, *From Settler to Citizen: New Mexican Economic Development and the Creation of Vecino Society, 1750–1820* (Berkeley: University of California Press, 2000), 180. Frank prefaces this remark, stating, "The collapse of the terms describing mixed-race peoples into one non-Indian group left a bipolar system that resembled the early-eighteenth-century distinction between *vecinos* and *Naturales,* before the elaboration of mixed-race classifications. . . . [W]hile the old terms represented different racial groups, their meaning at the end of the century signified a distinction in cultural terms."

66. Myra Ellen Jenkins, "The Mexican Archives of New Mexico" (Santa Fe: New Mexico State Records Center and Archives, n.d.), 1–22; Lansing Bartlett Bloom, "New Mexico under Mexican Administration, Part 3: New Mexico as a Department, 1837–1846," *Old Santa Fe* 2 (July 1914): 35–46.

67. Draft of a letter by Melgares, Santa Fe, 18 April 1821, as cited in Marc Simmons, *Spanish Government in New Mexico* (Albuquerque: University of New Mexico Press, 1968), 213.

68. G. Emlen Hall and David J. Weber, "Mexican Liberals and the Pueblo Indians, 1821–1829," *New Mexico Historical Review* 59 (1984): 8.

69. Gutiérrez writes, "Examining the period from 1693 to 1846 as a whole, one sees major shifts in *calidad* classifications. . . . [C]ivil status dominated between 1693 and 1759, representing 70 to 90 percent of the total observations. Racial status became most important between 1760 and 1799, reaching its highest level at 78 percent during the 1760–79 period, and then tapering off. Between 1800 and 1819, race and 'no mention' each accounted for about one-third of all *calidad* assignation. Finally, after 1820 civic status was again the dominant meaning given to *calidad*." Gutiérrez, *When Jesus Came,* 192, 194.

70. From Spain's reconquest to Mexican Independence (1693–1821), 113 private and community grants were awarded, totaling over seven million acres. A much larger number of grants and acreage was apportioned to citizens during the Mexican period (1821–46). Victor Westphall, *Mercedes Reales: Hispanic Land Grants of the Upper Rio Grande Region* (Albuquerque: University of New Mexico Press, 1983), 3–6.

71. According to Hall and Weber, "Figures may be misleading, for the district covered by the census may have been larger than the boundaries of a league of an individual pueblo, and so counted people who actually lived off of pueblo land." Hall and Weber, "Mexican Liberals and the Pueblo Indians," 30–31, n. 63.

72. Ibid., 6.

73. Ibid., 13.

74. Mexican Archives of New Mexico, 42f261–62, as translated in Hall and Weber, "Mexican Liberals and the Pueblo Indians," 11, 16.

75. Hall and Weber, "Mexican Liberals and the Pueblo Indians," 16.

76. Ibid., 22.

77. Ralph Emerson Twitchell Collection, no. 254, New Mexico State Records Center and Archives (NMSRCA); Ortiz Family Papers, no. 2828, NMSRCA.

78. Ibid.

79. Chávez, *Origins of New Mexico Families,* 329–30. Also see Virginia L. Olmsted, *The Ortiz Family of New Mexico: The First Six Generations* (Albuquerque: Olmsted, 1978).

80. D. A. Brading, *The Origins of Mexican Nationalism* (Cambridge, UK: Centre of Latin American Studies, University of Cambridge, 1985); D. A. Brading, *Prophecy and Myth in Mexican History* (Cambridge, UK:

Centre of Latin American Studies, Cambridge University, 1980); D. A. Brading, *The First America: The Spanish Monarchy, Creole Patriots, and the Liberal State, 1492–1867* (Cambridge, UK: Cambridge University Press, 1991).

81. Fray Angélico Chávez, *New Mexico Roots, Ltd.* (Santa Fe: Fray Angélico Chávez, 1982), 2048–49, CSWR; AASF, 75f22–27.

82. Ruth R. Olivera and Liliene Crété, *Life in Mexico under Santa Anna, 1822–1855* (Norman: University of Oklahoma Press, 1991), 20.

83. Westphall, *Mercedes Reales.*

84. Hall and Weber, "Mexican Liberals and the Pueblo Indians," 16.

85. Josiah Gregg, *Commerce of the Prairies: The Journal of a Santa Fé Trader* (New York: Henry G. Langley, 1844; repr., Dallas: Southwest Press, 1933), 107.

86. U.S. House of Representatives, 36th Cong., 2d sess., Ex. Doc. no. 28, "Private Land Claims in New Mexico" (12 January 1861), 55.

87. Ibid., 57.

88. On the history of the Ortiz mine, see John Townley, "The New Mexico Mining Company," *New Mexico Historical Review* 46 (1971): 57–73.

89. Gregg, *Commerce of the Prairies,* 110

90. Townley, "The New Mexico Mining Company," 58–59.

91. Ibid., 59, 64.

92. In his examination of Penitente narratives, Alberto López Pulido argues that penitencia involved a range of practices including prayer, charity, and *el buen ejemplo,* or good example, but that popular depictions have tended to focus on the corporal practices as evidence of Nuevomexicanos' supposed barbarity and fanaticism. Alberto López Pulido, *The Sacred World of the Penitentes* (Washington: Smithsonian Institution Press, 2000).

93. T. M. Pearce, *New Mexico Place Names: A Geographical Dictionary* (Albuquerque: University of New Mexico Press, 1965), 144–45; Robert Julyan, *The Place Names of New Mexico* (Albuquerque: University of New Mexico Press, 1996), 323.

94. One common notion about origins and meaning of the Penitentes is that the society fulfilled certain "community functions" in the face of a rapidly shifting socioeconomic context following the Bourbon reforms of the late eighteenth century. Michael P. Carroll takes this argument one step further by hypothesizing that the Penitentes flourished in response to a "crisis of patriarchal authority" brought on

by the reforms and to "the threat that this [erosion] posed to the com-
munal/cooperative system of agriculture that was in place in northern
New Mexico. . . . The Penitentes, then, were in the first instance a social
response to a socioeconomic crisis that just happened to be dressed in
a religious cloak." Michael P. Carroll, *The Penitente Brotherhood: Patriarchy
and Hispano-Catholicism in New Mexico* (Baltimore: Johns Hopkins
University Press, 2002), 120–21. For a brief discussion of theories and
historiography relating to the Penitentes, see López Pulido, *Sacred World,*
38–59; and Carroll, *The Penitente Brotherhood,* 11–37. Also see Marta
Weigle's classic study, *Brothers of Light, Brothers of Blood: The Penitentes of
the Southwest* (Albuquerque: University of New Mexico Press, 1976).

95. Michel Foucault, *History of Sexuality,* trans. R. Hurley (New
York: Random House, 1978).

96. Gregg, *Commerce of the Prairies,* 106.

97. Ibid., 118–23.

98. Ibid., 154.

99. López, *White by Law;* Jacobson, *Whiteness of a Different Color.*

100. Jacobson, *Whiteness of a Different Color,* 226.

101. On the elaboration of ideologies of purity in the nineteenth
century, see Patrick Tort, "Le pur et le dur," in *La pureté: Quête d'absolu
au peril de l'humain,* ed. Sylvain Matton, Series Morales no. 13 (Paris:
Editions Autrements, 1993), 172–88. In their study of language and religion in the U.S. Southwest, Milo Kearney and Manuel Medrano argue
that the confluences, distinctions, and conflicts between Anglo and
Hispanic peoples can be traced to medieval Europe. Kearney and
Medrano, *Medieval Culture and the Mexican American Borderlands* (College
Station: Texas A&M University Press, 2001).

102. *El Independiente,* 7 November 1901.

Chapter Two

1. *Speech of Hon. Joseph M. Root, of Ohio, in the House of
Representatives, 15 February 1850, in the Committee of the Whole on the State
of the Union, on the Resolution Referring the President's Message to the
Appropriate Standing Committees* (Washington, D.C.: Congressional
Globe Printing Office, 1850), 2.

2. *El Nuevo Mexicano,* 5 February 1898.

3. *Congressional Globe,* 30th Cong., 1st sess., 1848, p. 99.

4. Ibid.

5. Calhoun was recorded as saying: "We make a great mistake, sirs, when we suppose that all people are capable of self-government.... None but people advanced to a very high state of moral and intellectual improvement are capable, in a civilized state, of maintaining free government." *Congressional Globe*, 30th Cong., 1st sess., 1848, p. 99. For a discussion of white racial supremacy and Anglo Saxonism, see Matthew Frye Jacobson, *Whiteness of a Different Color: European Immigration and the Alchemy of Race* (Cambridge, Mass.: Harvard University Press, 1998).

6. The United States had "incorporated" fewer than one hundred thousand Spanish-speaking Mexicans, 60 percent of whom resided in northern New Mexico. Howard Roberts Lamar, *The Far Southwest, 1846–1912: A Territorial History* (New York: W. W. Norton, 1970), 62–65.

7. On 22 July 1854, Congress established the Office of the Surveyor General, whose job it was to survey all lands in New Mexico. The resulting report eventually led Congress to confirm and patent twenty Pueblo Indian land grants between 1858 and 1864. U.S. House of Representatives, *An Act to Create a Land District in the Territory of New Mexico,* 35th Cong., 1st sess., 1858, H.R. 564; U.S. House of Representatives, *An Act to Confirm the Land Claims of Certain Pueblos and Towns in the Territory of New Mexico,* 35th Cong., 1st sess., 1858, H.R. 565. New Mexico's land issues occupy books too numerous to mention here. For a general understanding refer to Joe S. Sando, *The Pueblo Indians* (San Francisco: Indian Historian Press), 75–81; Roxanne Dunbar Ortiz, "Roots of Resistance: Land Tenure in New Mexico, 1680–1980" (PhD diss., University of California-Los Angeles, 1980); and Charles L. Briggs and John R. Van Ness, eds., *Land, Water, and Culture: New Perspectives on Hispanic Land Grants* (Albuquerque: University of New Mexico Press, 1987).

8. Sando, *The Pueblo Indians,* 74.

9. New Mexico House of Representatives, Thursday, 6 December 1853, Territorial Archives of New Mexico (TANM), reel 1, frame 260.

10. Ibid., 262–63.

11. Howard Roberts Lamar writes, "New Mexican leaders saw in civil government and statehood the chance to escape military rule, achieve autonomy for their region, and gain local office for themselves." Lamar, *The Far Southwest,* 71.

12. Petition of 14 October 1848. Quoted in LeBaron Bradford Prince, *New Mexico's Struggle for Statehood: Sixty Years of Effort to Obtain Self Government* (Santa Fe: New Mexican Printing Co., 1910), 10.

13. Ibid.

14. Ibid.

15. Ibid., 20; Lamar, *The Far Southwest,* 80–81.

16. *Speech of Hon. Joseph M. Root, 2.*

17. *California and New Mexico. Speech of Hon. James S. Green of Missouri, in the U.S. House of Representatives, February 15, 1850* (Washington, D.C.: Congressional Globe Printing Office, 1850), 4.

18. U.S. Senate, *Speech of William H. Seward, On the Admission of New Mexico. Delivered in the Senate of the United States, July 26, 1850* (Washington: Buell and Blanchard, 1850), 4.

19. Ibid.

20. Lamar, *The Far Southwest,* 9–10.

21. *Speech of William H. Seward,* 5.

22. David J. Weber, "'Scarce More Than Apes': Historical Roots of Anglo-American Stereotypes of Mexicans," in *New Spain's Far Northern Frontier: Essays on Spain in the American West, 1540–1821,* ed. David J. Weber (Albuquerque: University of New Mexico Press, 1979), 293–307.

23. U.S. Senate, *Speech of William H. Seward,* 9.

24. Ibid., 8.

25. Ibid., 14.

26. *Speech of Hon. A. W. Venable, of N. Carolina, on the Texas and New Mexico Question. Delivered in the House of Representatives, Thursday, August 15, 1850* (Washington, D.C.: Congressional Globe Printing Office, 1850), 8.

27. Lamar, *The Far Southwest,* 81; Prince, *New Mexico's Struggle,* 22–23.

28. Prince, *New Mexico's Struggle,* 23.

29. Office of the Governor, *Cuarto mensaje anual de S.E.D. Enrique Connelly a la Asamblea Legislativa de Nuevo Mejico, pronunciado diciembre, 1865* (Santa Fe: Manderfield y Tucker, Impresores, Oficina de El Nuevo Mejicano, [1865]), 18.

30. Ibid., 20.

31. Ibid., 24; U.S. House, "State Government for New Mexico. Memorial of the Assembly of New Mexico, In Regard to A State government for that Territory," 39th Cong., 1st sess. mis. doc. no. 57, 1866.

32. Gutiérrez, "Aztlán, Montezuma, and New Mexico," 175.

33. Malcolm Ebright, "New Mexico Land Grants: The Legal Background," in *Land, Water, and Culture: New Perspectives on Hispanic Land Grants,* ed. Charles L. Briggs and John R. Van Ness (Albuquerque: University of New Mexico Press, 1987), 40.

34. Lamar, *The Far Southwest,* 136–70.

35. For a careful and insightful study of the legal, gender, and social implications of the Maxwell land grant dispute, see María E. Montoya, *Translating Property: The Maxwell Land Grant and the Conflict over Land in the American West, 1840–1900* (Berkeley: University of California Press, 2002).

36. Ibid., 144.

37. Elias Brevoort, *New Mexico: Her Natural Resources and Attractions, Being a Collection of Facts, Mainly Concerning Her Geography, Climate, Population, Schools, Mines and Minerals, Agricultural and Pastoral Capacities, Prospective Railroads, Public Lands, and Spanish and Mexican Land Grants* (Santa Fe: Elias Brevoort, 1874), ix.

38. Ibid., 119.

39. Ibid.

40. Ibid.

41. Ibid., ix.

42. David R. Roediger, The *Wages of Whiteness: Race and the Making of the American Working Class* (London: Verso, 1991).

43. Reginald Horsman, *Race and Manifest Destiny: The Origins of American Anglo-Saxonism* (Cambridge, Mass.: Harvard University Press, 1981). On ethnic boundary formation and resource competition, see Edward H. Spicer and R. Thompson, eds., *Plural Society in the Southwest* (Albuquerque: University of New Mexico Press, 1972), 1–20, 21–76.

44. Historian Camille Guerin-Gonzales has documented how the term "American" came to refer to Anglo Americans, while "Mexican" was applied to both Mexican Americans and Mexican immigrants in the workplace. She writes: "The language [white Americans] used to describe their [Mexican/Mexican American] workers became a justification for discriminating against those of particular ethnic and racial groups." Camille Guerin-Gonzales, *Mexican Workers and American Dreams: Immigration, Repatriation, and California Farm Labor, 1900–1939* (New Brunswick, N.J.: Rutgers University Press, 1994), 51.

45. Quoted in Prince, *New Mexico's Struggle,* 30.

46. Rosenbaum, *Mexicano Resistance in the Southwest.*

47. Prince, *New Mexico's Struggle,* 31.

48. "Reasons Why the People Should Adopt the State Constitution," *New Mexican,* 29 May 1872. Reprinted in Prince, *New Mexico's Struggle,* 31.

49. Prince, *New Mexico's Struggle,* 30.

50. Ibid., 31.

51. Ibid., 32.

52. Ibid., 31.

53. *New Mexican*, 9 September 1871. Quoted in Oliver LaFarge, *Santa Fe: The Autobiography of a Southwestern Town* (Norman: University of Oklahoma Press, 1959), 72–73.

54. Interestingly, legislators challenged the 1870 census data on the grounds that ten thousand miners, living in the most remote regions of the territory, had gone uncounted. In this case, the population would have grown just 40 percent, not the 50 percent they had boasted. U.S. House Committee on the Territories, *Admission of New Mexico as a State; Report: [To accompany bill H.R. 2418]*, 43d Cong., 1st sess., 1874, S. Rept. 561, 2.

55. Ibid.

56. Ibid.

57. Ibid.

58. Article IX, Treaty of Guadalupe Hidalgo. As appears in Richard Griswold del Castillo, *The Treaty of Guadalupe Hidalgo: A Legacy of Conflict* (Norman and London: University of Oklahoma Press, 1990), 190.

59. *Admission of New Mexico as a State: Her Resources and Future. Speech of Hon. Stephen B. Elkins, Delegate from New Mexico, in the House of Representatives, 21 May 1874.* Report 561, 43d Cong (Washington, D.C.: Government Printing Office, 1874), 5.

60. Ibid., 23.

61. U.S. House. *Admission of New Mexico as a State*. 43d Cong., 1st sess., 1874.

62. Marion Dargan, "New Mexico's Fight for Statehood (1895–1912), [Part] 1," *New Mexico Historical Review* 14 (January 1939): 6.

63. U.S. House, *Admission of New Mexico. Memorial of the Legislative Assembly of New Mexico, asking the passage of an enabling act for admission into the Union.* 44th Cong., 1st sess., 1876, mis. doc. no. 63, 1.

64. Ibid., 2.

65. U.S. Senate, *In the Senate of the United States. Report [To accompany bill S. 229].* 44th Cong., 1st sess., 1876, Report 69; U.S. House, *New Mexico: Minority Report [To accompany bill S. 229].* 44th Cong., 1st sess., 1876, Report 503, part 2, 15.

66. U.S. House, *Minority Report,* 1876, 12.

67. Weber, "'Scarce More Than Apes,'" 293–307, 299. Reginald Horsman, "Racial Destiny and the Indians," in *Major Problems in the*

History of the American West, Documents and Essays, ed. Clyde A. Milner II (Lexington, Mass.: D. C. Heath and Co., 1989), 255. Reprinted from Horsman, *Race and Manifest Destiny,* 189–207.

68. Horsman, *Race and Manifest Destiny,* 211.

69. Reginald Horsman, "Racial Destiny and the Indians," 255.

70. U.S. House, *Minority Report,* 1876, 12.

71. As noted in chapter 1, since the early decades of the nineteenth century, the importance of race or caste designations had declined. Notwithstanding the deep division between so-called *indios* and the remaining Mexican citizenry, called *vecinos* (and sometimes *españoles*), New Mexico's social order had become defined increasingly in terms of landholdings, patronage, honor, and the regulation of marriage and sexuality. Gutiérrez, *When Jesus Came.*

72. Gutiérrez, "Aztlán, Montezuma, and New Mexico," 175.

73. U.S. House, *Minority Report,* 1876, 13.

74. Ibid., 15.

75. Prince, *New Mexico's Struggle,* 33, 58.

76. Robert W. Larson, *New Mexico's Quest for Statehood, 1846–1912* (Albuquerque: University of New Mexico Press, 1968), 132–33.

77. Ibid., 33–35.

78. Ibid., 37.

79. LeBaron Bradford Prince, "New Mexico. A Defence of the People and Country. A Reply of Chief Justice Prince to a Slanderous Letter in the *New York Times* [from the *New York Times* of 28 February 1882]," 1, L. Bradford Prince Papers, NMSRCA; "Greasers as Citizens," *New York Times,* 26 January 1882.

80. Prince, "New Mexico. A Defence of the People."

81. Ibid.

82. Ibid. The original article to which Prince was responding was the anonymously authored "Greasers as Citizens," *New York Times,* 6 February 1882. In an aggressive rebuke to Prince's defense of Nuevomexicanos, the anonymous author followed with a letter calling Prince the "Chief Justice of Greaserdom." "Greasers in New Mexico," *New York Times,* 26 March 1882.

83. Ibid.

84. The author of the February 6 article denounced Nuevomexicanas for their supposed moral laxity and sexual permissiveness: "A Mexican woman living first with this man and then with another as his de facto wife is not considered by her female neighbors

to be committing a serious impropriety, at least not such a heinous offense as should debar her from the countenance and society of others of her sex assumed to be leading a regular life. If the Mexican woman be actuated by charity in this, charity in their case covers a multitude of sins in more than one sense." "Greasers as Citizens," *New York Times,* 6 February 1882. Nuevomexicana women were the object of considerable commentary among nineteenth-century Anglo American visitors to New Mexico. Perceptions and judgments as to their sexuality, race, class, and material reveal a great deal about the workings of conquest as both racial and gendered phenomena, as Deena J. González aptly points out in *Refusing the Favor.*

85. Larson, *New Mexico's Quest for Statehood,* 144.

86. Prince, *New Mexico's Struggle for Statehood,* 40.

87. Ibid.

88. Ibid., 40–41.

89. Davis, *El Gringo,* 85–87. Quoted in Tobias Duran, "We Come as Friends: Violent Social Conflict in New Mexico, 1810–1910" (PhD diss., University of New Mexico, 1985), 192.

90. In the early months of 1888, the *New Mexican* surveyed 122 prominent citizens, such as bankers, merchants, ranchers, federal officials, and farmers. Ninety-one respondents favored statehood, according to the *New Mexican,* and twenty-one opposed statehood. A 1889 House Report cited the 1888 survey thusly: "Of the 91 in favor there were 41 Republicans, 33 Democrats, and 17 of no particular party affiliations, or whose politics were not known. Of the 31 opposed there were 11 Democrats, 10 Republicans, 6 of no particular politics, and 4 who professed to be independent." House Reports, 50th Cong., 1st sess., vol. 4, Rept. no. 1025, 15–16. Quoted in Marion Dargan, "New Mexico's Fight for Statehood (1895–1912). [Part] 3. The Opposition within the Territory (1888–1890)," *New Mexico Historical Review* 15 (April 1940): 142.

91. Archie M. McDowell, "The Opposition to Statehood within the Territory of New Mexico, 1888–1903" (PhD diss., University of New Mexico, 1939), 66.

92. As quoted in Larson, *New Mexico's Quest,* 148.

93. Ibid., 154–55.

94. Herbert H. Lang, "The New Mexico Bureau of Immigration, 1880–1912," *New Mexico Historical Review* 51 (1976): 200, 205.

95. *La Voz del Pueblo,* 23 February 1889.

96. Ibid.

97. Ibid.

98. *Santa Fe New Mexican,* 23 September 1890.

99. *La Voz del Pueblo,* 5 April 1890.

100. *La Voz del Pueblo,* 25 November 1893.

101. *La Voz del Pueblo,* Saturday, 30 January 1892. Over a month later, another editorial protested that, on occasion, Nuevomexicanos participated in the denigration of themselves and "the character and dignity of their own—*Hispano-Americanos." La Voz del Pueblo,* 13 February 1892.

102. *El Boletín Popular,* 31 August 1893.

103. The first edition of *Eco del Siglo* appeared on 9 February 1892 in Las Cruces, stating that a Spanish publication was necessary for various reasons, among them, "to establish relations with our Colleagues, and take note of acts or amendments that might affect our interests." *El Boletín Popular* began circulation in Santa Fe in 1885 as a bilingual organ of the Democratic party. Initially it opposed statehood efforts initiated by Republicans, saying that the Ring was merely seeking statehood as a means of enriching itself. See *El Boletín Popular,* 13 October 1892. By 1893, however, the newspaper appeared to support the efforts of Antonio Joseph, in combating the argument that New Mexico's "Mexican population" was still loyal to Mexico, some forty-odd years after becoming U.S. citizens. *El Boletín Popular,* 31 August 1893. Similarly, *La Voz del Pueblo* appeared to reverse its earlier opposition to statehood, which had been based on Republican plans for public education. It printed reports of ongoing accusations against Nuevomexicanos. *La Voz del Pueblo,* 2 September 1893.

104. Bustamante, "Los Hispanos," 125.

105. Phillip B. Gonzales, "The Protest Function of Spanish-American Identity in New Mexico," private manuscript.

106. *La Voz del Pueblo,* 7 October 1893.

107. Eusebio Chacón, translated speech appearing in *La Voz del Pueblo,* 2 November 1901. Reprinted in Arellano and Vigil, *Las Vegas Grandes on the Gallinas,* 52.

108. Ibid., 55.

109. Ibid., 57.

110. Ibid.

111. *La Voz del Pueblo,* 28 May 1898.

112. According to Howard Roberts Lamar, "The outbreak of the Spanish-American War meant that the United States was fighting the spiritual and cultural mother country of native New Mexicans. This proved no problem at all. In response to a call for volunteers,

Spanish-Americans as well as Americans flocked to the colors with such enthusiasm that the New Mexican companies were oversubscribed." Lamar, *The Far Southwest,* 199.

113. For an interesting discussion of racial ideas in the latter half of the nineteenth century, see Robert E. Bieder, *Science Encounters the Indian, 1820–1880: The Early Years of American Ethnology* (Norman: University of Oklahoma Press, 1986). The study of eugenics shaped government policy not only in the United States, but also in Latin America. For a stimulating discussion, see Eduardo A. Zimmerman, "Racial Ideas and Social Reform: Argentina, 1890–1916," *Hispanic American Historical Review* 71 (February 1992): 21–46.

114. Doris L. Meyer, *Speaking for Themselves: Neomexicano Cultural Identity and the Spanish-Language Press, 1880–1920* (Albuquerque: University of New Mexico Press, 1996), 6–7.

115. J. Manuel Espinosa, "Spanish Folklore in the Southwest: The Pioneer Studies of Aurelio M. Espinosa," *Americas* 35 (October 1978).

116. 57th Cong., 2d sess., House document no. 36 (4420), New Statehood Bill. *Hearings Before the Subcommittee of the Committee on Territories on House Bill 12543, to Enable the People of Oklahoma, Arizona, and New Mexico to form Constitutions and State Governments and be Admitted into the Union on an Equal Footing with the Original States. December 10, 1902. Submitted by Mr. Beveridge and ordered to be printed* (Washington, D.C.: Government Printing Office, 1902).

117. Ibid.

118. Ibid.

119. Ibid., 16

120. Ibid.

121. "Hearings on Statehood Bill," Committee on the Territories, Friday, 11 December 1903. U.S. Congressional Hearings Supplement, House Committee on the Territories (Washington, D.C.: Government Printing Office, 1904), 17.

122. Statement of Mr. Moon, "Statehood for Arizona and New Mexico," U.S. Congressional Hearings Supplement, House Committee on the Territories, 16 January 1906, 22.

123. "Hearings on Statehood Bill," Friday, 11 December 1903, 13.

124. Ibid., 15.

125. Ibid., 17.

126. Rock Island System, *New Mexico: The Land of Sunshine. Agricultural and Mineral Resources, Irrigation and Horticulture, Gold, Copper,*

Iron and Coal. A National Sanitarium. Playground of the Southwest (Chicago: Passenger Department, Rock Island System, 1904), 50.

127. Statement of R. E. Morrison, "Statehood for Arizona and New Mexico," U.S. Congressional Hearings Supplement, House Committee on the Territories, 16 January 1906, 18–19.

128. Prince to Albert Beveridge, 1 February 1905. Quoted in Larson, *New Mexico's Quest for Statehood,* 245.

129. Larson, *New Mexico's Quest for Statehood,* 244, 250.

130. The previous year Arizona's legislature, by a two-thirds majority, had imposed an English language requirement upon voters, effectively depriving two thousand citizens of suffrage. Statehood Hearing before the Committee on Territories, U.S. Senate, 18, 19, 21 February 1910, U.S. Congressional Hearings Supplement, Senate Committee on the Territories, 1910, 60–65.

131. New Mexico Constitution, Articles 7 and 12. As quoted in "Education and the Spanish-Speaking: An Attorney General's Opinion on Article XII, Section 8 of the New Mexico Constitution," *New Mexico Law Review* 3 (May 1973): 268 n 20, 372–73 n. 66–67.

132. Quoted in Larson, *New Mexico's Quest for Statehood,* 303.

Chapter Three

1. My translation. Original Spanish version appears in an interview with Macario Herrera, collected and transcribed by Yvonne Herrera and Ismael Lloyd Herrera, and published in Arellano and Vigil, *Las Vegas Grandes on the Gallinas,* 100. Unless otherwise noted, all translations are my own.

2. *La Voz del Pueblo,* 7 August 1897. As translated in Doris L. Meyer, "Early Mexican-American Responses to Negative Stereotyping," *New Mexico Historical Review* 53 (1978): 82.

3. *La Revista Católica,* 5 July 1879; 12 July 1879.

4. *Weekly New Mexican,* 14 February 1880; David F. Myrick, *New Mexico's Railroads: An Historical Survey* (Golden: Colorado Railroad Museum, 1970), 18; Lynn Perrigo, *Gateway to Glorieta: A History of Las Vegas, New Mexico* (Boulder, Colo.: Pruett Publishing Co., 1982).

5. Ibid.

6. *El Nuevo Mejicano,* 14 February 1880.

7. My discussion is inspired by the work of Edward Spicer, who applied the term to "those situations in which the sense of identity

receives some kind of expression and where individuals align themselves in some manner as members of one ethnic group or another." Spicer, "Plural Society in the Southwest," 55. Sylvia Rodríguez notes that "[e]xternally obvious ethnic markers can include language, dress, and style, while more 'subjective' ones include values, sensibilities, and manner, as well as implicit rules for identifying the ethnicity of others or of asserting one's own." Rodríguez, ""Land, Water, and Ethnic Identity in Taos," 316. Also see Fredrik Barth, *Ethnic Groups and Boundaries: The Social Organization of Culture Difference* (Boston: Little, Brown and Co., 1969).

8. Chris Wilson, *The Myth of Santa Fe*.

9. For the purpose of this study, I will employ the term "booster-ism" to refer to the self-conscious promotion and commercialization of land, climate, lifestyles, and cultures of a region through the dissemination of printed propaganda. In this case, boosterism is manifest in brochures, speeches, journal articles, and newspaper editorials printed locally or nationwide.

10. Rock Island System, *New Mexico: The Land of Sunshine*.

11. In reading these texts I approach them with the idea articulated by Chris Weedon that "Language is the place where the actual and the possible forms of social organization and their likely social and political consequences are defined and contested. Yet it is also the place where our sense of ourselves, our subjectivity, is constructed. The language that Anglo Americans used to describe 'Indians' and 'Mexicans' in New Mexico illustrates how Anglo Americans positioned and defined themselves by opposition to these two groups. As this language changes over time, it reveals changes in the way that racial perceptions changed." Weedon, *Feminist Practice and Poststructuralist Theory*, 21.

12. Myrick, *New Mexico's Railroads*, 9, 18. On the growth of railroads during the 1880s, see Victor Westphall, *The Public Domain in New Mexico, 1859–1891* (Albuquerque: University of New Mexico Press, 1965).

13. Terry John Lehmann, "Santa Fé and Albuquerque, 1870–1900: Contrast and Conflict in the Development of Two Southwestern Towns" (PhD diss., Indiana University, 1974); C. M. Chase, *Colorado and New Mexico. The Editor's Run* (Montpelier, Vt.: Argus and Patriot Steam Book and Job Printing House, 1882); *Albuquerque Illustrated* (Albuquerque: Flower and Payne, 1892); *The Educational Center of New Mexico: A Few Facts in Relation to the Educational Facilities of Albuquerque,*

With Views of School Building, Compliments of the Educators of Albuquerque (Chicago: Vandercook Engraving and Publishing Co., [1893]).

14. In his speech of 22 April 1880, Hazeldine predicted that "The invalid will seek our territory to repair his shattered health and the capitalist will come here to swell his gains. The artist will come here to paint our magnificent scenery, the miner to unearth the immense wealth now hidden in her rugged breast, the man of leisure to enjoy life in this glorious climate, where the main fact of existence is a pleasure." No longer would East Coast residents deride New Mexico as backward or savage, or not even know its location or that it was part of the United States, said Hazeldine. "Writers in leading New York papers will no longer say, as they did a few years ago, that it aught [*sic*] to be annexed to the United States. Letters will not be written asking us at what time the steamboats arrive at Santa Fe, nor will old world lawyers, in drafting legal instruments, locate New Mexico in South America, but it will be the promised land toward which the eyes of the emigrant will be longingly turned." As quoted in Victor Westphall, "Albuquerque in the 1870s," *New Mexico Historical Review* 23, no. 4 (October 1848), 266–67.

15. *El Nuevo Mejicano,* 7 February 1880.

16. Brevoort, *New Mexico,* 114.

17. Noting the impact of the railway, geographer D. W. Meinig writes, "The radical efficiency of the railroad could not but have a powerful economic effect upon what had been a remote and land-bound region. The most immediate impacts were upon the competitive commercial positions of the various towns, old and new, and upon mining and lumbering, where the large bulk and low value of the primary products had severely limited exploitation with more primitive facilities. Agriculture was less immediately responsive because it was as yet more in need of larger local systems for the transport of water than of a national system for the transport of its produce." D. W. Meinig, *Southwest: Three Peoples in Geographical Change, 1600–1970* (New York: Oxford University Press, 1971), 41.

18. Like many of his contemporaries, Brevoort espoused an understanding of the land as essentially feminine, referring to "her" resources, wealth, and fertility. Feminine representations of land have captured the attention of several scholars, including Carolyn Merchant, who writes that, in the seventeenth century, humans began to view nature as nurturing and life-giving, but also capable of wreaking havoc on mankind at a moment's notice. In the modern, mechanized world, nature needed

to be controlled, possessed, and dominated; and domination would come about through the introduction of the mighty locomotive, the plow, the pick, the surveyor's transit compass and chain, and the miner's dynamite. These implements would render her into submission and make her useful and productive. Carolyn Merchant, *The Death of Nature: Women, Ecology, and the Scientific Revolution* (San Francisco: Harper and Row, 1980), 1–9. Annette Kolodny notes that many westbound Americans viewed land as a metaphor for the female body. Annette Kolodny, *The Lay of the Land: Metaphor as Experience and History in American Life and Letters* (Chapel Hill: University of North Carolina Press, 1975), 9. Also see Kolodny, *The Land Before Her: Fantasy and Experience of the American Frontiers, 1630–1860* (Chapel Hill: University of North Carolina Press, 1984); and Vera Norwood, *Made from This Earth: American Women and Nature* (Chapel Hill: University of North Carolina Press, 1993).

19. Brevoort, *New Mexico,* ix.

20. William H. McKee, *The Territory of New Mexico, and Its Resources* (New York: Office of the American Mining Index Engraving and Printing Establishment, 1866), 12.

21. Charles P. Clever, *New Mexico: Her Resources, Her Necessities for Railroad Communication with the Atlantic and Pacific States, Her Great Future* (Washington, D.C.: McGill and Witherow, 1868), 3.

22. Samuel Woodworth Cozzens, *The Marvelous Country; Or, Three Years in Arizona and New Mexico, The Apache's Home, A Description of this Wonderful Country, Its Immense Mineral Wealth, Its Magnificent Mountain Scenery, The Ruins of Ancient Towns and Cities Found Therein, With A Complete History of the Apache Tribe, And A Description of The Author's Guide, Cochise, The Great Apache War Chief. The Whole Interspersed With Strange Events and Adventures* (Boston: Shepard and Gill, 1873); Elizabeth W. Champney, *Great-Grandmother's Girls in New Mexico, 1670–1680* (Boston: Estes and Lauriat, 1888).

23. William J. Palmer, *De la colonization du Colorado et du Nouveau-Mexique* (Paris: Typographie Lahure, 1874), 76; Charles Scheobel, "Une Expédition dans le Nouveau Mexique et l'Arizona," *Archives de la Société Américaine de France* 1 (1875): 18–30.

24. During the 1870s, in-migration to New Mexico actually increased, though the volume of people leaving the territory exceeded in-migration by some five thousand persons (tables 3.3 and 3.4). Non-native residents of New Mexico, as a proportion of total population, grew from less than 10 percent in 1870 to 23 percent in 1880 (table 3.2).

25. Whereas Brevoort viewed land as essentially feminine, he perceived his audience to be masculine, and dedicated his book to "solid men, men of means and enterprise, men desiring through safe investment alike the welfare of themselves and the growth and glory of the commonwealth, men of perception and action, everywhere." Brevoort, *New Mexico*, ix.

26. Everett S. Lee et al., *Methodological Considerations and Reference Tables*, vol. 1 of *Population Redistribution and Economic Growth, United States*, ed. Simon Kuznets and Dorothy Swaine Thomas (Philadelphia: American Philosophical Society, 1957), 278.

27. Nostrand, *The Hispano Homeland*, 139–40.

28. Deutsch, *No Separate Refuge*, 30–31.

29. Bureau of the Census, *Seventh Census of the United States, 1850*, vol. 1 (Washington, D.C., 1850), xxxvii.

30. Meinig, *Southwest;* Bureau of the Census, *Compendium of the Tenth Census, 1880*, part 1, rev. ed. (Washington, D.C.: Government Printing Office, 1885), 2–7, 43, 363, 521.

31. Richard R. Greer, "Origins of the Foreign-Born Population of New Mexico during the Territorial Period," *New Mexico Historical Review* 17 (October 1941): 287.

32. According to demographers, "in-migration" refers to total migration (national and international) into a given state or region, whereas "immigration" denotes international migration. This distinction, however, was not strictly observed, otherwise New Mexico's Bureau of Immigration should have been named Bureau of In-Migration. To remain consistent with such flexible usage, this study will employ the terms interchangeably. Lee et al., *Methodological Considerations and Reference Tables*, table P-3, 278. For a discussion on westward settlement and demography between 1870 and 1910, see Hope T. Eldridge and Dorothy Swaine Thomas, *Demographic Analyses and Interrelations*, vol. 3 of *Population Redistribution and Economic Growth, United States*, ed. Simon Kuznets and Dorothy Swaine Thomas (Philadelphia: American Philosophical Society, 1957), 4–5, 17. Regarding census bureau racial classifications, see Irene B. Taeuber, *Population Trends in the United States, 1900–1960*. Bureau of the Census Technical Paper no. 10 (Washington, D.C.: U. S. Government Printing Office, 1965), 11–12.

33. Greer, "Origins of the Foreign-Born Population," 281–87.

34. Charles Irving Jones, "William Kronig: New Mexico Pioneer, from His Memories of 1849–1860," *New Mexico Historical Review* 19 (July 1944): 185, 193–96.

35. George J. Sánchez, *Becoming Mexican American: Ethnicity, Culture and Identity in New Mexico, 1900–1945* (New York: Oxford University Press, 1993), 87–88.

36. George J. Sánchez notes that "Midwestern migrants to California brought with them a familiar Protestant world view. This pietistic perspective emphasized faith in a transcendent God, concentrated on the immediacy of personal conversion, and adhered to strict codes of proper behavior to insure individual salvation and prosperity." Sánchez, *Becoming Mexican American,* 91.

37. Among many Anglo Americans, migration was believed to be the engine of economic growth and prosperity on "the frontier." Where Anglo American pioneers went, civilization and prosperity followed. This thinking was captured by Frederick Jackson Turner in his landmark 1893 essay "The Significance of the Frontier in American History." Turner's "frontier thesis" professed that "the existence of an area of free land, its continuous recession, and the advance of American settlement westward, explain American development." Such settlement gave birth to democratic institutions and prosperity through the exploitation of the land. Equally important, the frontier fashioned a particular American ethos, characterized by rugged individualism. "In the crucible of the frontier," wrote Turner, "the immigrants were Americanized, liberated, and infused into a mixed race." According to Turner, American individualism and democratic institutions were shaped by the harsh environment of the frontier and then regenerated. As American civilization vanquished the savage environment, the frontier receded, and the process moved westward. Frederick Jackson Turner, "The Significance of the Frontier in American History," in *Proceeding of the Forty-First Annual Meeting of the State Historical Society of Wisconsin,* Madison, Wisc., 1894, 79–112, reprinted in *Major Problems in the History of the American West: Documents and Essays,* ed. Clyde A. Milner II (Lexington, Mass.: D. C. Heath and Co., 1989), 2, 13.

38. Sánchez contrasts Mexican "circular migration" with European "chain migration." Sánchez, *Becoming Mexican American,* 132–33. For insightful studies of U.S. immigration patterns, see John Bodnar, *The Transplanted: A History of Immigrants in Urban America* (Bloomington: Indiana University Press, 1985); Alejandro Portes and Robert L. Bach, *Latin Journey: Cuban and Mexican Immigrants in the United States* (Berkeley: University of California Press, 1985); Douglass Massey et al., *Return to Aztlán: The Social Process of International Migration from Western Mexico* (Berkeley: University of California Press, 1987).

39. Brevoort, *New Mexico,* ix.

40. Simon Kuznets, introduction to Eldridge and Thomas, *Demographic Analyses and Interrelations,* xxiii.

41. According to Herbert H. Lang, New Mexico's "Anglo-American population was the key to long-desired statehood, and statehood was inseparably intertwined with economic progress." Herbert H. Lang, "The New Mexico Bureau of Immigration, " 195.

42. Myrick, *New Mexico's Railroads,* 8–9.

43. *Weekly New Mexican,* 22 March 1880.

44. As quoted in Carey McWilliams, *North from Mexico,* 119.

45. *Revista Católica,* n.d., as translated in Arellano and Vigil, *Las Vegas Grandes,* 42.

46. Lang, "The New Mexico Bureau," 193, 212 n. 3.

47. *Weekly New Mexican,* 27 March 1880.

48. Walter John Donlon, "LeBaron Bradford Prince, Chief Justice and Governor of New Mexico Territory, 1879–1893" (PhD diss., University of New Mexico, 1967).

49. Ireneo L. Chávez, *Compiled Laws of New Mexico, 1884* (Santa Fe: n.p., 1885), 628.

50. *Nature's Sanitarium: Las Vegas Hot Springs, Las Vegas, New Mexico, on the Line of the Atchison, Topeka and Santa Fe Railroad* (Chicago: Rand McNally, 1883), 3, as quoted in Marta Weigle, "From Desert to Disney World: The Santa Fe Railway and the Fred Harvey Company Display the Indian Southwest," *Journal of Anthropological Research* 45 (Spring 1989): 120.

51. The literature on tourism is too vast to adequately discuss here. This study is informed by the work of Scott Norris, ed., *Discovered Country: Tourism and Survival in the American West* (Albuquerque: Stone Ladder Press, 1994); JoAnn Martin, "Contesting Authenticity: Battles over the Representation of History in Morelos, Mexico," *Ethnohistory* 40 (Summer 1993): 438–65; Thomas J. Schlereth, *Cultural History and Material Culture: Everyday Life, Landscapes, Museums* (Charlottesville: University Press of Virginia, 1992); Malcolm Crick, "Representation of International Tourism in the Social Sciences: Sun, Sex, Sights Savings, and Servility," *Annual Review of Anthropology* 18 (1989): 307–44; Valene L. Smith, ed., *Hosts and Guests: The Anthropology of Tourism,* 2d ed. (Philadelphia: University of Pennsylvania Press, 1989); Caroline B. Brettell, "Introduction: Travel Literature, Ethnohistory, and Ethnography," *Ethnohistory* 33 (1986): 127–38; Francis Jennings, "A Growing Partnership: Historians, Anthropologists and American Indian History," *Ethnohistory* 29 (1982): 21–34.

52. Gutiérrez, "Aztlán, Montezuma, and New Mexico," 172; Bureau of Immigration, *Report of the Bureau of Immigration, February 16, 1884* (Santa Fe: New Mexican Printing Co., 1884).

53. Bureau of Immigration, *Santa Fé: Ancient and Modern, Including Its Resources and Industries, with Numerous Illustrations, and a Map of the County,* by William Gillette Rich (Santa Fe, Bureau of Immigration, 1885), 12.

54. Jerry L. Williams and Steve Fox, "The Healthseeker Era, 1880–1940," in *New Mexico in Maps,* ed. Jerry L. Williams (Albuquerque: University of New Mexico Press, 1986), 129.

55. Quoted in Brevoort, *New Mexico,* 27.

56. Williams and Fox, "The Healthseeker Era," 127–31; Judith L. DeMark, *Chasing the Cure: A History of Healthseekers to Albuquerque, 1902–1940,* History of Albuquerque Exhibits series, vol. 4 (Albuquerque: The Albuquerque Museum, 1981).

57. Rock Island System, *New Mexico: The Land of Sunshine.* Other health-oriented brochures include *New Mexico Health Resorts* (n.p., 1899); *Facts and Figures Concerning Santa Fe, New Mexico, as a Sanitarium, from Writings of Henry F. Lyster, M.D. (Detroit), and Others* (n.p., [1894]). Two studies of New Mexico's healthseeker era are: Barton Harry Barbour, "In Search of Better Health: James Ross Larkin on the Santa Fe Trail, 1856–57" (MA thesis, University of New Mexico, 1988); and Judith R. Johnson, "Health Seekers to Albuquerque, 1880–1940" (MA thesis, University of New Mexico, 1983).

58. William Gillette Ritch, "Chronological Annals of New Mexico, Etc.," in *Resources of New Mexico, Prepared Under the Auspices of the Territorial Bureau of Immigration for the Territorial Fair, To Be Held at Albuquerque, New Mexico, October 3, 4, 5, 6, 7, 8, 1881* (Santa Fe: New Mexican Book and Job Printing Department, 1881), 29.

59. Lang, "The New Mexico Bureau," 202–3.

60. Bureau of Immigration, *Illustrated New Mexico, Historical and Industrial,* by William Gillette Ritch (Santa Fe: Bureau of Immigration, 1885); Bureau of Immigration, *Santa Fé: Ancient and Modern*61. Bureau of Immigration, *Santa Fé: Ancient and Modern,* 55.

62. Ibid.

63. Bureau of Immigration, *Aztlán: The History, Resources and Attractions of New Mexico, Embellished with Maps and Seventy-Five Characteristic Illustrations,* by William Gillette Ritch. 6th ed. (Boston: D. Lothrop and Co., 1885).

64. Gutiérrez, "Aztlán," 181–82.

65. For an informative discussion of the Montezuma Legend, see Richard J. Parmentier, "The Mythological Triangle: Poseyemu, Montezuma, and Jesus in the Pueblos," in *Handbook of North American Indians,* vol. 9, ed. Alfonso Ortiz (Washington, D.C.: Smithsonian Institution, 1979), 609–22.

66. Gutiérrez, "Aztlán," 184; Enrique R. Lamadrid, "Ig/Noble Savages of New Mexico: The Naturalization of 'El Norte' into 'the Great Southwest.'" Working Paper Series no. 121 (Albuquerque: Southwest Hispanic Research Institute, University of New Mexico, 1992).

67. Lynn I. Perrigo, "The Original Las Vegas," unpublished manuscript (Albuquerque: Center for Southwest Research, University of New Mexico).

68. Miguel Antonio Otero, *My Life on the Frontier,* vol. 1, *1864–1882, Incidents and Characters of the Period When Kansas, Colorado, and New Mexico Were Passing Through the Last of Their Wild and Romantic Years* (New Mexico: Press of Pioneers, 1935), 280–86, cited in Chávez, *The Lost Land,* 58.

69. Albert Hurtado, *Indian Survival on the California Frontier* (New Haven: Yale University Press, 1988); Haas, *Conquests and Historical Identities.*

70. Keith Basso, "History of Ethnological Research," in *Handbook of North American Indians,* vol. 9, ed. Alfonso Ortiz (Washington, D.C.: Smithsonian Institution, 1979), 14–15. Also see Marc Simmons, "History of the Pueblos Since 1821," in *Handbook of North American Indians,* vol. 9, ed. Alfonso Ortiz (Washington, D.C.: Smithsonian Institution, 1979), 219.

71. Bureau of Immigration, *Santa Fé: Ancient and Modern,* 57.

72. Simmons, "History of the Pueblos," 219.

73. Dean McCannell, *The Tourist: A New Theory of the Leisure Class* (New York: Schocken Books, 1976), 5. Also see Dennison Nash, "Tourism as a Form of Imperialism," in *Hosts and Guests: The Anthropology of Tourism,* ed. Valene L. Smith, 2d ed. (Philadelphia: University of Pennsylvania Press, 1989); and Bieder, *Science Encounters the Indian.*

74. McCannell, *The Tourist,* 5.

75. James Clifford, *The Predicament of Culture: Twentieth-Century Ethnography, Literature, and Art* (Cambridge, Mass.: Harvard University Press, 1988).

76. *Souvenir of Las Vegas, New Mexico: The Leading City of the Territory* (Chicago: Rand, McNally, 1893), 6.

77. Rock Island System, *New Mexico: Land of Sunshine,* 47.

78. Marta Weigle, "From Desert to Disney World."

79. Two insightful essays on the impact of tourism on Native American resources are Mark Spence, "Dispossessing the Wilderness: Yosemite Indians and the National Park Ideal, 1864–1930," *Pacific Historical Review* 65 (February 1996): 28–59; and Kerwin L. Klein, "Frontier Products: Tourism, Consumerism, and the Southwestern Public Lands, 1890–1990," *Pacific Historical Review* 62 (1993): 39–71.

80. T. C. McLuhan, *Dream Tracks: The Railroad and the American Indian, 1890–1930* (New York: Harry N. Abrams, 1985), 18.

81. McLuhan continues: "The adoption of the Indian proved to be an important step for the Santa Fe Railway in its synthesis of corporate image making and primitive culture.... [I]ts promotional themes transformed the Indians into symbolic reductions of the American heritage." Ibid., 19.

82. A former quartermaster of the U.S. Army recalled his first impression of the locomotive plowing through the countryside: "I stood on the absolutely level plateau at the mouth of the Pawnee Fork where that historic creek debouches into the great river. The remembrance of that view will never pass from my memory, for it showed a curious temporary blending of two distinct civilizations. One, the new, marking the course of empire in its restless march westward; the other, that of the aboriginal, which, like a dissolving view, was soon to fade away and be forgotten." Henry Inman, *The Old Santa Fé Trail: The Story of a Great Highway* (New York: Macmillan Co., 1897; repr., Topeka: Crane and Co., 1899), 488.

83. Susan E. Wallace, *The Land of the Pueblos* (Troy, N.Y.: Nims and Knight, 1889), 5. Wallace's writings on New Mexico were originally published in various newspapers and journals including the *Atlantic Monthly*.

84. In 1902, 1903, and 1906, bills were introduced in Congress proposing to admit New Mexico and Arizona as a single state named Montezuma. Larson, *New Mexico's Quest for Statehood*, 149, 206, 224.

85. *New Mexican*, 15 June 1906.

86. Bureau of Immigration, *Aztlán*, 240.

87. Charles W. Greene, *A Complete Business Directory of New Mexico, and Gazetteer of the Territory for 1882* (Santa Fe: New Mexican Printing and Publishing Co., 1882), 11.

88. Noble L[ovely] Prentis, *South-Western Letters* (Topeka: Kansas Publishing House, 1882), 41.

89. Ibid., 52.

90. Albert R. Greene, *Wonderland: The Story of Ancient and Modern New Mexico* (n.p., 1883), 5, 16.

91. Ibid., 58.

92. Bureau of Immigration, "Despacho de emigración y sus trabajos," in *New Mexico,* ed. H. C. Burnett (Santa Fe: Bureau of Immigration, 1886), 15.

93. Horatio O. Ladd, *The Story of the States: New Mexico* (Boston: D. Lothrop Co., 1891), 262–63.

94. Ibid., 435.

95. Ibid., 453. Horatio Ladd was a main promoter of education in New Mexico. In 1889, he founded the Ramona Indian School for girls, which the bureau described as "a beautiful and characteristic memorial to Helen Hunt Jackson." Ladd also founded the Indian school for boys in Santa Fe two years later. Bureau of Immigration, *New Mexico. Its Resources, Climate, Geography and Geological Condition. Official Publication of the Bureau of Immigration,* ed. Max Frost (Santa Fe: New Mexican Printing Co., 1890).

96. Helen Hunt Jackson, *Ramona: A Story* (n.p., 1884; repr., with a foreword by Michael Dorris, New York: Signet Classic Printing, 1988).

97. On Hispanophobia, see David J. Weber, "Blood of Martyrs, Blood of Indians: Toward a More Balanced View of Spanish Missions in Seventeenth-Century North America," in *Columbian Consequences,* ed. David Hurst Thomas (Washington, D.C.: Smithsonian Institution Press, 1990): 429–48.

98. Bureau of Immigration, *New Mexico. Its Resources, Climate, Geography and Geological Condition,* 104–5.

99. Bureau of Immigration, *New Mexico. The Resources and Prospects of Her Counties, with Special Reference to Advantages for Investment in All Localities. Where Her Colonies Should Settle, and What Avocations Will Prove Profitable* (Santa Fe: Bureau of Immigration, 1893), 340–41.

100. Bureau of Immigration, *New Mexico. Its Resources, Climate, Geography, Geology, History, Statistics, Present Condition and Future Prospects,* ed. Max Frost (Santa Fe: New Mexico Printing Co., 1894), 4.

101. Ibid., 3–4.

102. Many publications during Frost's tenure made little mention of history. They simply pointed out the material resources of the territory. Bureau of Immigration, *Facts and Figures Concerning New Mexico* (Santa Fe: New Mexican Printing Co., 1891); Bureau of Immigration, *New Mexico, The Coming Country. Budget of Information Concerning the Natural Resources and Advantages of New Mexico. Facts and Figures for the Public. A Concise Statement Carefully Prepared for the Delectation of the Homeseeker—An Inviting Field for Capital—The Coming Country of the South and West* (Santa

Fe: New Mexican Printing Co., 1891); *Programme of Excursion to Santa Fe, New Mexico, Tendered to the Delegates of the Fourth National Irrigation Congress and Their Wives, by the Territory and Citizens of Santa Fe, September 19th, 1895* (Santa Fe: New Mexican Print, [1895]); Bureau of Immigration, *New Mexico, 1898: Climate, Mineral Springs, Schools,* bulletin no. 1 (Santa Fe: New Mexican Printing Co., 1898); Bureau of Immigration, *Socorro County, New Mexico: The Largest County in the Territory. Possesses Great Mineral Riches. Stock Ranges as Large as a European Kingdom. Fertile Valleys and Canyons. Mild and Equitable Climate,* bulletin no. 11 (Santa Fe: New Mexican Printing Co., 1901).

103. Chávez, *Lost Land,* 92.

104. Nostrand, *Hispano Homeland,* 16.

105. Bureau of Immigration, *The Land of Sunshine: A Handbook of the Resources, Products, Industries and Climate of New Mexico,* ed. Max Frost and Paul A. F. Walter (Santa Fe: New Mexico Bureau of Immigration, 1906), 329; Bureau of Immigration, *Facts and Figures.*

106. Ten years earlier, in his colorful "sketch of the early Spaniards," Walter W. Storms noted that "there were mythical stories of how an early Montezuma had once passed down the valley of the Rio Grande, building a town in a single night where he stopped. . . . [B]eautiful stories," he opined, "but not history. . . . The Pueblo civilization was not so far advanced as the Aztec; still, the New Mexican villages were free from that awful abomination that blackened the pages of Aztec history—the practice of sacrificing men as victims on the altars of their gods. The missionaries who accompanied Coronado and the later Spanish invaders, found the Indians easy converts to the Christian faith." Walter W. Storms, *The Story of New Mexico, Briefly Told. With a Sketch of the Early Spaniards, and an Outline of the Territorial Civil Government* (Terre Haute, Ind.: Inland Publishing Co., 1896), 23.

107. Bureau of Immigration, *Santa Fe County: The Heart of New Mexico, Rich in History and Resources,* ed. Max Frost and Paul A. F. Walter, (Santa Fe: New Mexico Bureau of Immigration, 1906), 111; George B. Anderson, *History of New Mexico: Its Resources and People,* 2 vols. (Los Angeles: Pacific States Publishing Co., 1907); H. B. Hening and E. Dana Johnson, comps., *Albuquerque* (Albuquerque: Albuquerque Morning Journal, 1908).

108. Edith M. Nicholl, *Observations of a Ranchwoman in New Mexico* (New York: Macmillan Co., 1898), 38; Edith M. Nicholl, *The Desert and the Rose* (Boston: Cornhill Co., 1921).

109. *New Mexican,* 26 April 1898.

110. *New Mexican,* 10 May 1902.

111. Rock Island System, *Land of Sunshine,* 50.

112. Ibid., 51.

113. Monroy, *Thrown Among Strangers,* 264–65.

114. Marta Weigle and Peter White, *The Lore of New Mexico* (Albuquerque: University of New Mexico Press, 1988), 55.

115. Ibid., 57.

116. The Denver and Rio Grande Railroad published 250,000 copies of its tourist handbook between 1885 and 1896. Denver and Rio Grande Railway, *Tourists' Hand-Book: Descriptive of Colorado, New Mexico and Utah* (n.p., 1885); Denver and Rio Grande Railway, *Spanish and Indian New Mexico* (Denver: Chain and Hardy, n.d.).

117. Bureau of Immigration, *The Land of Sunshine,* 5.

118. Lang, "New Mexico Bureau of Immigration," 200, 205.

119. Ibid., 199.

120. Bureau of Immigration, *Biennial Report of the Bureau of Immigration of the Territory of New Mexico, For the Two Years Ending November 30th,* by Max Frost (Santa Fe: New Mexican Printing Co., 1902), 7. Also see Bureau of Immigration, *Informe del Buró de Inmigración, desde abril, 1897, hasta enero 1898* (Santa Fe: Compañía Impresora del Nuevo Mexicano, 1899).

121. Lang, "New Mexico Bureau of Immigration," 211.

122. For further reading on the impact of immigration to New Mexico, see Alvar W. Carlson, *The Spanish-American Homeland: Four Centuries in New Mexico's Río Arriba* (Baltimore: Johns Hopkins University Press, 1990); Walter Nugent, "The People of the West since 1890," in *The Twentieth-Century West: Historical Interpretations,* ed. Gerald D. Nash and Richard W. Etulain (Albuquerque: University of New Mexico Press, 1989), 35–69; Boyd C. Pratt, Charles D. Biebel, and Dan Scurlock, with Vernon J. Glover, *Trails, Rails, and Roads: The Central New Mexico East-West Transportation Corridor Regional Overview* (Santa Fe: New Mexico Historic Preservation Division, 1988); William J. Parish, "The German Jew and the Commercial Revolution in Territorial New Mexico, 1850–1900," *New Mexico Quarterly* 25 (Autumn 1959): 307–32.

123. La Voz del Pueblo, 15 February 1896. As translated in Doris L. Meyer, "Early Mexican-American Responses to Negative Stereotyping," New Mexico Historical Review 53 (1978): 87.

124. *El Nuevo Mundo,* 29 May 1897.

125. Ibid.

126. Ibid.

127. Ibid.

128. *La Voz del Pueblo,* 7 August 1897.

129. Ibid.

130. *La Voz del Pueblo,* 2 November 1901. As translated and quoted in Arellano and Vigil, *Las Vegas Grandes,* 54–55.

131. Bureau of Immigration, *Why New Mexico Is Entitled to Statehood: We Have the People, the Land, the Water, the Mines, the Coal, Flocks and Herds, Splendid Schools, Clean Local Government, Our People Are Industrious, Progressive Americans* (Santa Fe: n.p., 1910). Also see the pamphlet of 1909 that trumpeted "More than 90 per cent of [San Juan County] is American born and there is no foreign element in the entire county." Bureau of Immigration, *San Juan County, New Mexico. The Land of Sunshine. The Land of Opportunity* (Santa Fe: n.p., 1909), 13.

132. Bureau of Immigration, *Santa Fe County, New Mexico: A Country Rich in Attractions for the Sight Seeker, the Health Seeker, the Wealth Seeker and Home Seeker,* by Paul A. F. Taylor, (Santa Fe: New Mexican Printing Co., 1909), 19.

133. Weigle and White, *The Lore of New Mexico,* 437.

134. *La Voz del Pueblo,* 2 December 1911.

135. Rock Island System, *New Mexico: The Land of Enchantment,* 47.

Chapter Four

1. Charles Fletcher Lummis to Arturo Cuyás, 14 March 1916, Charles Fletcher Lummis Manuscript Collection, Southwest Museum, Los Angeles (hereafter LMCSM).

2. David J. Weber, *The Spanish Frontier in North America,* 335.

3. Charles Fletcher Lummis, *The Spanish Pioneers,* 8th ed. (Chicago: A. C. Motley and Co., 1920), 18.

4. Lummis's book is given reviews in Spain, Argentina, and Cuba, and other countries of Latin America. "[I]t is gratifying to know that the good seeds you have sown have been spread broadcast and not fallen on barren ground." Cuyás to Lummis, 9 June 1916, LMCSM. After conferring knighthood on Lummis, King Alfonso XIII of Spain sent Lummis an autographed photo, via the Spanish ambassador to the United States, Juan Riaño, who wrote, "You do justice to the Spanish

explorers who conquered the New World and laid the foundation of civilization." Juan Riaño to Lummis, 15 October 1918, LMCSM.

5. Lummis to Arturo Cuyás, 7 March 1914, Southwest Museum, Los Angeles.

6. For a discussion of both the "Hispanophobia" that permeated Anglo American texts into the twentieth century and the "Hispanophilic sentiment" that suffused the works of Herbert Howe Bancroft, Bret Harte, Helen Hunt Jackson, Gertrude Atherton, and others, see Weber, *The Spanish Frontier in North America*, 335–60.

7. Lummis, *Spanish Pioneers,* 52.

8. "Nostalgia for a vanquished Hispanic past resembled a similar shift in Anglo-Americana attitudes toward Indians," writes David J. Weber, "[w]hen writing about Hispanics, for example, the first generation of Anglo Americans in California to take the Indian's side." Weber, *The Spanish Frontier in North America*, 343.

9. *Diccionario de la Lengua Española,* 15th ed. (Madrid: Talleres Calpe, 1925).

10. Prince to Edgar Lee Hewett, 28 February 1909, Southwest Museum, Los Angeles.

11. Weber, *The Spanish Frontier,* 336.

12. The term "White Legend" is most often attributed to historian Benjamin Keen, who, in 1962, questioned aloud whether a *leyenda blanca* had not been perpetuated by scholars who saw in Fray Bartolomé de las Casas ample evidence of "Spanish altruism and tolerance" in Spain's treatment of native peoples in the New World. That query sparked a particularly lively debate between Keen and Lewis Hanke (the object of Keen's query) in the pages of the *Hispanic American Historical Review.* Keen's "White Legend" reference was made in his introduction to Edward Gaylord Bourne, *Spain in America, 1450–1580* (New York: Harper and Bros., 1904; reprinted with a new introduction and supplementary bibliography by Benjamin Keen, New York: Barnes and Noble, 1962), x. Also see Charles Gibson and Benjamin Keen, "Trends of United States Studies in Latin American History, *Hispanic American Historical Review (HAHR)* 62, no. 4 (July 1957): 855–77; Lewis Hanke, "More Heat and Some Light on the Spanish Struggle for Justice in the Conquest of America," *HAHR* 44, no. 3 (August 1964): 293–340; Benjamin Keen, "The Black Legend Revisited: Assumption and Realities," *HAHR* 49 (November 1969): 703–19; Lewis Hanke, "A Modest Proposal for a Moratorium on Grand

Generalizations: Some Thoughts on the Black Legend," *HAHR* 51, no. 1 (February 1971): 112–27.

13. William P. DuVal to President James Monroe, Pensacola, 10 September 1822, in Carter, comp. and ed., *Territorial Papers of the United States,* 22:532, as cited in Weber, *The Spanish Frontier,* 338.

14. Senate, *Speech of William H. Seward, On the Admission of New Mexico, July 26, 1850* (Washington: Buell and Blanchard, 1850), 4.

15. Jackson, *Ramona;* Harriet Beecher Stowe, *Uncle Tom's Cabin* (1852; repr., Cambridge, Mass.: Harvard University Press, 1962).

16. Helen Hunt Jackson, *A Century of Dishonor* (New York: Harper, 1881); Cuyás, 7 March 1914, Southwest Museum, Los Angeles.

17. James W. Byrkit, *Charles Lummis: Letters from the Southwest, September 20, 1884 to March 14, 1885* (Tucson: University of Arizona Press, 1989), xi–xii, xlvi.

18. Lummis to Leader, 25 November 1884, quoted in ibid., 108.

19. Lummis to Leader, El Rito, 1 December 1884, quoted in ibid., 123.

20. Lummis to Leader, Santa Fe, 25 November 1884, quoted in ibid., 120.

21. Lummis to Leader, Santa Fe, 25 December 1884, quoted in ibid., 192.

22. Lummis to Leader, Santa Fe, 25 November 1884, quoted in ibid., 112.

23. Charles Fletcher Lummis, *Tramp across the Continent* (New York: Charles Scribner's Sons, 1892), 275.

24. Lummis to Leader, Santa Fe, 25 November 1884, quoted in Byrkit, *Letters from the Southwest,* 112–13.

25. Lummis to Leader, El Rito, 1 December 1884, quoted in Byrkit, *Letters from the Southwest,* 131–32.

26. Ibid., 124.

27. Lummis to Leader, San Mateo, 1 January 1885, quoted in Byrkit, *Letters from the Southwest,* 217.

28. Marc Simmons, *Two Southwesterners: Charles Lummis and Amado Chaves* ([Cerrillos, N.M.]: San Marcos Press, 1968), 14.

29. Ralph Emerson Twitchell, *The Leading Facts of New Mexican History,* vol. 5 (Cedar Rapids, Iowa: Torch Press, 1917), 124, n. 891.

30. Simmons, *Two Southwesterners,* 18.

31. Charles Fletcher Lummis, *Pueblo Indian Folk-Stories* (New York: Century Co., 1910; repr., with an introduction by Robert F. Gish, and titled

Pueblo Indian Folk-Tales, Lincoln: University of Nebraska Press, 1992), 5.

32. Ibid., xxv–vi.

33. Jose Felipe Abeita to Lummis, 15 June 1905, LMCSM; Lummis to Abeita, 7 September 1905, LMCSM.

34. Abeita to Lummis, 14 April 1906, LMCSM; Abeita to Lummis, 21 May 1906, LMCSM.

35. Ibid., 95.

36. Lummis to the *Chillicothe Leader,* El Rito, 1 December 1884, quoted in Byrkit, *Letters from the Southwest,* 124.

37. Lummis, *A Tramp across the Continent,* 113.

38. Ibid., 137.

39. Ibid., 195.

40. Herbert Howe Bancroft, *California Pastoral, 1769–1848* (San Francisco: n.p., 1888), 179, quoted in David J. Langum, "From Condemnation to Praise: Shifting Perspectives on Hispanic California," *California History* 61 (Winter 1983): 284.

41. Jackson, *Ramona.*

42. Chávez, *The Lost Land,* 87.

43. David J. Weber, "The Spanish Legacy in North America and the Historical Imagination," *Western Historical Quarterly* 61 (1992): 11–12.

44. Lummis, *The Spanish Pioneers,* 18.

45. Ibid., 11–12.

46. Ibid., 23.

47. Ibid., 149.

48. Ramón A. Gutiérrez, "Charles Fletcher Lummis and the Orientalization of New Mexico," in *Nuevomexicano Cultural Legacy: Forms, Agencies, and Discourse* (Albuquerque: University of New Mexico Press, 2002), 15, 11–27.

49. Genaro M. Padilla, *My History, Not Yours: The Formation of Mexican American Autobiography* (Madison: University of Wisconsin Press, 1993), 208.

50. Records of the New Mexico Historical Society (RNMHS), 1f6–8.

51. Historical Society of New Mexico, *Inaugural Address Delivered by Hon. W. G. Ritch at the Adobe Palace, February 21, 1881* (Santa Fe: New Mexican Book and Job Printing Department, 1881), 10.

52. *Constitution,* RNMHS, 1f1–9.

53. Historical Society, *Inaugural Address,* 17–20.

54. Ibid., 11–13.

55. Pamphlet, 1882, RNMHS, 2f3.

56. Historical Society, *Inaugural Address,* 13–14.

57. Ibid., 12–13.

58. James Clifford, "On Collecting Art and Culture," in *Out There: Marginalization and Contemporary Cultures,* ed. Russell Ferguson et al. (New York: New Museum of Contemporary Art, 1990), 143.

59. Merchants often approached Prince offering to sell him relics. In a letter dated 31 December 1890, J. J. Leeson of Socorro, New Mexico, urged Prince to purchase a "lot of pottery, beads, hammers . . . skeletons and other curiosities" for $100, saying, "I consider this cheap. If they were mine, three-hundred dollars could not purchase them." Leeson to Prince, 31 December 1890, RNMHS, 2f7.

60. Miscellaneous receipt, RNMHS, 2f540. In 1862, Jake Gold established a business dealing in Indian and Spanish antiquities. His letterhead proclaimed him a "Dealer in Ancient and Modern Aztec and Pueblo Pottery, Navajo Blankets, Turquois [*sic*], Old Spanish Relics, Mexican Hair Bridles, Chains and Whips, Indian Views, Cactus Cane, and All Sorts of Indian Curiosities." RNMHS, 2f576.

61. Miscellaneous receipt, RNMHS, 2f538.

62. RNMHS, 2f228. Another circular, dated 21 July 1913 and signed by Prince, was sent to "just a few individuals that I think will be interested," appealing for additional support to purchase display cases for the Palace of the Governors. RNMHS, 2f256.

63. RNMHS, 2f47. That both Nuevomexicanos and Anglos viewed such items as historically symbolic and contributed to the commodification of things "Spanish" and "Indian" runs counter to the assertions of some Chicana and Chicano scholars—John Chávez foremost among them—who argue that such commodification represented a predominantly Anglo American endeavor. Rather, it was a joint endeavor that speaks to a mutual fascination with the Spanish past. Chávez, *The Lost Land,* 87. Also see Gonzales-Berry, *Paso por aqui,* and Padilla, *My History, Not Yours,* esp. 202–13.

64. Folder 2, L. Bradford Prince Papers, New Mexico State Records Center and Archives. Hereafter referred to as Prince Papers.

65. RNMHS, 2f488. Also see "Official Invitation" in folder 2, Prince Papers.

66. La Farge, *Santa Fe,* 120.

67. *Santa Fe New Mexican,* 3 July 1883, as quoted in La Farge, *Santa Fe,* 120–21.

68. RNMHS, 2f488.

69. Pamphlet, RNMHS, 2f3.

70. *Santa Fe New Mexican*, 3 July 1883. Quoted in La Farge, *Santa Fe*, 121.

71. Prince, *Historical Sketches*, 11, 3.

72. Russell S. Saxton, "Ethnocentrism in the Historical Literature of Territorial New Mexico" (PhD diss., University of New Mexico, 1980), 105–6.

73. Prince, *Historical Sketches*, 16–17.

74. Ibid., 11.

75. Ibid., 3.

76. Ibid.

77. Historical Society of New Mexico, *Official Report of the Historical Society of New Mexico* (Santa Fe: New Mexican Printing Co., 1887), 1–4.

78. Ibid., 3.

79. Historical Society of New Mexico, *Report of the Historical Society of New Mexico* (Santa Fe: New Mexican Printing Co., January 2, 1893).

80. Historical Society of New Mexico, *Informe Bienal de la Sociedad Historica de Nuevo Mexico. Diciembre 1, 1904* (Santa Fe: Compañia Impresora del Nuevo Mexicano, 1905), 5; Historical Society of New Mexico, official reports, 1898, 1904, and 1912.

81. Historical Society of New Mexico, *Official Report*, 1912. The record does not indicate whether or how many Native Americans visited the museum or participated in the historical society.

82. Miscellaneous newspaper clippings, RNMHS, 2f746–54.

83. Undated newspaper clipping, RNMHS, 2f754. Also see a similar editorial, 13 August 1905, that appeared in an unnamed Las Vegas newspaper. Miscellaneous newspaper clipping, RNMHS, 2f747.

84. Unidentified newspaper clipping, RNMHS, 2f754.

85. H. R. Hendon to Prince, 27 January 1909, RNMHS, 2f128.

86. Nestor Montoya to Prince, 30 January 1909, RNMHS, 2f132.

87. Historical Society of New Mexico, *Constitution*, RNMHS, 1f1–9.

88. Also included in that list was Félix Martínez. C. E. Hodgin, "The Early School Laws of New Mexico," *Bulletin*. University of New Mexico Educational Series, vol. 1 (Albuquerque: University of New Mexico, 1906), 36.

89. Historical Society, *Official Report,* 1912, 3.

90. Historical Society, *Official Report,* 1904, 6.

91. Titles of their lectures are not given. Historical Society, *Official Report,* 1906 (Santa Fe: New Mexican Printing Co., 1906), 8.

92. Hodgin, "The Early School Laws," 35.

93. Aurelio Macedonio Espinosa to Prince, 15 January 1907, RNMHS.

94. Twitchell, *The Leading Facts,* 156 n. 914; Historical Society of New Mexico, *Official Reports of the Society, 1912 and 1913,* Historical Society of New Mexico Publications no. 19 (Santa Fe: New Mexican Printing Co., 1914), 9.

95. Twitchell, *The Leading Facts,* 4; Historical Society, *Official Report,* 1906.

96. Prince to "Madame," 26 January, 1911, RNMHS, 2f185.

97. Historical Society of New Mexico, *Official Report of the Society,* 1912, Historical Society of New Mexico Publications no. 18 (Santa Fe: New Mexican Printing Co., 1913), 5.

98. Prince, *Concise History,* 20.

99. Ibid., 10–11.

100. Ibid., 20.

101. Ibid.

102. Lebaron Bradford Prince, *Spanish Mission Churches of New Mexico* (Grand Rapids, Iowa: Torch Press, 1915), 7.

103. Weigle and White, *The Lore of New Mexico,* 437.

104. Miscellaneous newspaper clipping, 19 February 1921, RNMHS, 1f753.

105. Chris Wilson, *The Myth of Santa Fe,* see esp. 110–55. For a thorough description of how Anglos "discovered" Spanish culture by manufacturing traditions such as the Santa Fe Fiesta, see Montgomery, *The Spanish Redemption,* 128–57.

106. Margaret D. Jacobs, *Engendered Encounters: Feminism and Pueblo Cultures, 1879–1934* (Lincoln: University of Nebraska Press, 1999). Also see Barbara A. Babcock, "Mudwomen and Whitemen: A Meditation on Pueblo Potteries and the Politics of Representation," in *Discovered Country: Tourism and Survival in the American West* (Albuquerque: Stone Ladder Press, 1994), 180–95; Marta Weigle, "Selling the Southwest: Santa Fe InSites," in *Discovered Country;* Louise Lamphere, "Women, Anthropology, Tourism, and the Southwest," *Frontiers: A Journal of Women's Studies* 12, no. 3 (1992): 5–11; Lamphere,

"Gladys Reichard Among the Navajo," *Frontiers* 12, no. 3 (1992): 79–115; and Marta Weigle, "Exposition and Mediation: Mary Colter, Erna Fergusson, and the Santa Fe/Harvey Popularization of the Native Southwest, 1902–1940," *Frontiers* 12, no. 3 (1992): 117–50. For two recent works on white women and their roles in commodifying Native American culture, see Flannery Gaussoin Burke, "Finding What They Came for: The Mabel Dodge Luhan Circle and the Making of a Modern Place, 1912–1930" (PhD diss., University of Wisconsin, 2002); and Erika Marie Bsumek, "Making 'Indian-Made': The Promotion, Consumption and Construction of Navajo Ethnic Identity, 1880–1935" (PhD diss., Rutgers State University, 2000).

107. On Mary Hunter Austin's role in the promotion of Hispanophilia, see Dennis Peter Trujillo, "Commodification of Hispano Culture in New Mexico: Tourism, Mary Austin, and the Spanish Colonial Arts Society" (PhD diss., University of New Mexico, 2003). Nuevomexicanas' participation in the "revival" of the Spanish colonial arts and crafts movement is discussed in Montgomery, *The Spanish Redemption,* 158–89.

108. For a discussion of declining Native American populations, see Hurtado, *Indian Survival.*

109. Renato Rosaldo, *Culture and Truth: The Remaking of Social Analysis* (Boston: Beacon Press, 1989), 69, 81.

110. McGregor [pseud.?], "Our Spanish-American Fellow Citizens," *Harper's Weekly,* 20 June 1914, quoted in Chávez, *Lost Land,* 92.

Chapter Five

1. Aurelio Macedonio Espinosa, "Guinea-Hen Intelligence," [May 30, 1915], exemplar found in Read Collection, NMSRCA.

2. "Símbolo de Nuestra Raza," *El Eco del Valle,* 22 July 1909. Quoted in Lynne Marie Getz, *Schools of Their Own: The Education of Hispanos in New Mexico, 1850–1940* (Albuquerque: University of New Mexico Press, 1997), 20.

3. My use of the term here is rather anachronistic, since it was not widely employed in New Mexico during the period in question. *Diccionario de la Lengua Española,* 715.

4. My use of the term "hispanista" is intentionally anachronistic and narrow. I employ it to describe Nuevomexicanos who began to study their own language, history, and folklore between the 1890s and

1930s, and who professed a certain degree of authority over these subjects. In 1956, the Spanish Royal Academy defined "hispanista" as "A person versed in the Spanish language and culture. This label is commonly given to those who are not Spaniards." ("*Persona versada en la lengua y cultura españolas. Se da comúnmente este nombre a los que no son españoles.*") Real Academia Española, *Diccionario de la Lengua Española* (Madrid: Talleres Espasa Calpe, 1956). More recently, the Academy has broadened its definition to include any person "who professes to study of, or is versed in, Hispanic languages, literatures or cultures." ("*Persona que profesa el estudio de lenguas, literaturas o cultura hispánicas, o está versada en ellos.*"); Real Academia Española, *Diccionario de la Lengua Española,* 22d ed. (Madrid: Talleres Espasa Calpe, 2002).

5. New Mexico Constitution, Articles VII and XII. Quoted in "Education and the Spanish-Speaking: An Attorney General's Opinion on Article VII, Section 8 of the New Mexico Constitution," *New Mexico Law Review* 3 (May 1973): 268 n. 20, 372–73 n. 66–67.

6. Aurora Lucero, "Defensa de Nuestro Idioma. Discurso, en inglés, pronunciado por la señorita Aurora Lucero, en el Concurso Interescolástico Territorial, aquí en Las Vegas. Ha sido muy comentado por la prensa," *La Voz del Pueblo,* 25 February 1911.

7. Ernest Barksdale Fincher, *Spanish-Americans as a Political Factor in New Mexico, 1912–1950* (New York: Arno Press, 1974), 244–60.

8. Ibid., 248–51.

9. Ibid., 286.

10. Ramón A. Gutiérrez, "Charles Fletcher Lummis," 14–15. Also see E. Anthony Rotundo, *American Manhood: Transformations in Masculinity from the Revolution to the Modern Era* (New York: Basic Books, 1993). In 1960, John Francis Bannon collected a number of writings that explore whether the Spanish conquest came to embody manliness, honor, and virtue, or avarice and savagery. John Francis Bannon, *The Spanish Conquistadores: Men or Devils?* (New York: Holt, Rinehart and Winston, 1960).

11. Fredrick B. Pike, *Hispanismo, 1898–1936: Spanish Conservatives and Liberals and Their Relations with Spanish America* (Notre Dame, Ind.: University of Notre Dame Press, 1971), 1.

12. Ibid.

13. Ricardo Pérez Monfort, *Hispanismo y falange: Los sueños imperiales de la derecha española y México* (México: Fondo de Cultura Económica, 1992), 15.

14. Charles Gibson and Benjamin Keen, "Trends of United States Studies in Latin American History," *Latin American Historical Review* 62, no. 4 (July 1957): 855–56.

15. Miguel de Unamuno, "Comunidad de la lengua," in *Temas argentinos* (Buenos Aires: Institución Cultural Españala, 1943), p. 164. As quoted in Pike, *Hispanismo*, 135.

16. George E. McSpadden, "Aurelio M. Espinosa (1880–1958)," *Hispania* 42 (March 1959): 20–21.

17. Espinosa, "Spanish Folklore in the Southwest," 221.

18. J. Manuel Espinosa, "Part One: Aurelio M. Espinosa: New Mexico's Pioneer Folklorist," in *The Folklore of Spain in the American Southwest: Traditional Spanish Folk Literature in Northern New Mexico and Southern Colorado,* by Aurelio Macedonio Espinosa, ed. J. Manuel Espinosa (Norman: University of Oklahoma Press, 1985), 10.

19. Ibid., 13.

20. In the course of his travels, he discovered a handwritten manuscript of a folk play that, Espinosa concluded in his first publication, an article entitled "Los Comanches," revealed many of the peculiarities of hispanos' Spanish language. Ibid., 26–27; Aurelio Macedonio Espinosa, *Los Comanches,* Bulletin no. 45, Language Series no. 1 (Albuquerque: University of New Mexico, 1907).

21. J. Manuel Espinosa, "Part One," 14–15.

22. Espinosa to Prince, 15 January 1907, RHSNM, Center for Southwest Research, University of New Mexico, 2f51–55.

23. Espinosa insisted that "The Spanish language as spoken to-day by nearly one quarter of a million people in New Mexico and Colorado, is not a vulgar dialect, as many misinformed persons believe, but a rich archaic Spanish dialect, largely Castilian in source." Aurelio Macedonio Espinosa, *The Spanish Language in New Mexico and Southern Colorado,* Historical Society of New Mexico Publications no. 16 (Santa Fe: New Mexican Printing Co., 1911), 1–2.

24. Espinosa to Prince, 15 January 1907.

25. Aurelio Macedonio Espinosa, *Studies in New Mexican Spanish: Part I, Phonology,* University of New Mexico Bulletin, Language Series no. 1 (Albuquerque: University of New Mexico, 1909), 55–56.

26. Ibid., 56–57, n. 2.

27. Ibid., 56.

28. Espinosa, "Spanish Language in New Mexico," 1.

29. Miguel de Unamuno, "Comunidad de la lengua," in *Temas*

argentinos (Buenos Aires: Institución Cultural Española, 1943), p. 164. As quoted in Pike, *Hispanismo,* 135.

30. Charles George Herbermann et al., eds. *The Catholic Encyclopedia,* vol. 11 (New York: Encyclopedia Press, 1911), 2.

31. When the United States conquered the region in 1846, Espinosa stated, "The people joyfully accepted American rule, and swore obedience to the Stars and Stripes. . . . [A]fter existing under Spanish institutions for nearly three centuries, [hispanos were] brought under the rule of a foreign race and under new and unknown institutions." Ibid.

32. Espinosa, "Spanish Language in New Mexico," 1–2.

33. There is no indication that Espinosa ever directly influenced Lucero, or vice versa.

34. Aurora Lucero, *La Voz del Pueblo,* 25 February 1911.

35. Aurelio Macedonio Espinosa, "The Term Latin America," *Hispania* 1 (September 1918): 135.

36. Ibid., 142.

37. Ibid., 143.

38. Ibid., 136–37.

39. Ibid., 139.

40. Ibid., 141.

41. Miscellaneous newspaper clipping, Prince Papers, NMSRCA.

42. J. Manuel Espinosa, "Part One: Aurelio M. Espinosa: New Mexico's Pioneer Folklorist," 22.

43. Aurelio Macedonio Espinosa, *América Española o Hispano América: El término "America Latina" es erróneo,* trans. Felipe M. de Setién (Madrid: Comisaría Regia del Turismo y Cultura Artistica, 1919).

44. Espinosa further insisted that "Spanish language is the language of millions of people of Europe and America who are the standard bearers of a great civilization that has developed in Spanish America a great European culture modeled after that of Old Spain, and that this culture deserves the close attention and study of the educated American. Spanish studies, linguistic, literary, historical, social, and what not, are now carried on in this country with increasing vigor and enthusiasm." Aurelio Macedonio Espinosa, "On the Teaching of Spanish," *Hispania* 4 (December 1921): 267–84.

45. Ibid., 279–80.

46. Lebaron Bradford Prince, *Historical Sketches of New Mexico from the Earliest Records to the American Occupation* (New York: Leggat Brothers, 1883), 3.

47. Aurelio Macedonio Espinosa, "Spanish Tradition among the Pueblo Indians," in appendix B of Aurelio Macedonio Espinosa, *The Spanish Folklore of Spain*, ed. J. Manuel Espinosa (Norman: University of Oklahoma Press, 1985), 240–50.

48. Herbert Eugene Bolton, "Defensive Spanish Expansion and the Significance of the Borderlands," in *The Trans-Mississippi West*, ed. James F. Willard and Colin B. Goodykoontz (Boulder: University of Colorado Press, 1930), 39; as noted in J. Manuel Espinosa, "Part One: Aurelio M. Espinosa," 24.

49. Espinosa's fundamentalist conviction about Nuevomexicanos' Spanish cultural purity perhaps had no more devout worshippers than among members of the Spanish Colonial Arts Society, founded in 1925 by mostly Anglo artists, writers, and philanthropists who saw in the arts and crafts an opportunity for uplifting Nuevomexicanos. For more on the society's commodification of things Spanish, see Montgomery, *The Spanish Redemption*, 171–77.

50. Arthur León Campa, "Federal Emergency Relief Administration (FERA) Project #S-A1-17," Southwest Museum, Los Angeles, 4.

51. Doris L. Meyer, *Speaking for Themselves: Neomexicano Cultural Identity and the Spanish-Language Press, 1880–1920* (Albuquerque: University of New Mexico Press, 1996), 8, 12.

52. Francisco de Thoma, *Historia popular de Nuevo México, desde su descubrimiento hasta la actualidad* (New York: American Book Co., 1896), 5.

53. Twitchell, *The Leading Facts of New Mexican History*.

54. Paul A. F. Walter, "Benjamin M. Read," *New Mexico Historical Review* 2 (October 1927): 394–97.

55. In addition to writing histories, Read occasionally participated in meetings of the Historical Society of New Mexico. On 28 May 1911, for example, Read presented a paper entitled "Inconsistencies of History" at a public meeting of the society. Historical Society of New Mexico, "Report of the Historical Society," *Old Santa Fe* 1 (July 1913): 107.

56. Benjamin Maurice Read, *Illustrated History of New Mexico* (Santa Fe: New Mexican Printing Co., 1912), 5.

57. Benjamin Maurice Read, *Guerra México-Americana* (Santa Fe: Compañía Impresora del Nuevo Mexicano, 1910), 3–6.

58. Read's reason for writing *Guerra México-Americana* is clearly stated in the opening pages: "This being the first historical work written by a native son of New Mexico, by a descendent of both races—the Anglo-Saxon and the Latin—I take great pride in presenting it . . . for the

benefit of the maltreated Latin race, the race of my mother. . . . I seek not glory, but the satisfaction of contributing something—however humble—to rendering historical justice, of which the descendants of the brave *conquistadores* have been deprived." Read, *Guerra Mexico-Americana,* 6.

59. Hofstadter writes that "[i]t was science that, in the post-Darwinian era, had the prestige; and all the social disciplines—anthropology, economics, politics, the new field of sociology, as well as history—were at pains to modernize themselves by bringing their methods into harmony with evolutionary methods, and at the same time to strengthen their status in the academy by affirming whenever possible their scientific character." Richard Hofstadter, *The Progressive Historians: Turner, Beard, Parrington* (Chicago: University of Chicago Press, 1967), 167.

60. Eusebio Chacón, manuscript, Trinidad, Colorado, 24 August 1910, Read Collection, NMSRCA.

61. Ibid.

62. Rafael Chacón to Read, Trinidad, Colorado, 25 August 1910, Read Collection, NMSRCA.

63. Hernández to Read, 28 July 1910, Read Collection, NMSRCA.

64. "Opinión del Dr. José Somellera, 22 November 1910," Read Collection, NMSRCA.

65. Benigno Romero to Read, [ca. 1910], Read Collection, NMSRCA.

66. Margarito Romero to Read, 2 August 1910, Read Collection, NMSRCA.

67. Espinosa agreed with Read's assessment that "American pioneers like Kit Carson, St. Vrain . . . never any trouble with the honest and good hearted New Mexicans of 60 years ago. . . . [As] true Spaniards, they [Nuevomexicanos] rebelled against the impertinent insults of men like C. Bent." Espinosa manuscript, September 1910, Read Collection, NMSRCA.

68. Espinosa to Read, 29 July 1910, Read Collection, NMSRCA. In 1911 Espinosa wrote to Read to congratulate him on his *Historia Ilustrada:* "Would that other historians of our people work in the same fashion! . . . [You] expound on the truths and deeds (so well documented and proven) that make the enemies of our race and our people blush. The *nuevo-mejicanos* of 1846 and 1848 were generous and gentlemenly . . . but they did not know how to tolerate insults, for never have the sons of Spain tolerated insults. Again, I congratulate you and hope you continue with

your studies for the honor and benefit of the *pueblo nuevo mejicano.*" Espinosa to Read, 15 July 1911, Read Collection, NMSRCA.

69. T. B. Catron, manuscript, Santa Fe, 23 November 1917, Read Collection, NMSRCA.

70. Read, *Historia Ilustrada de Nuevo México,* 8.

71. Ibid., 9.

72. Further illustrating Read's compunction for what he called historical accuracy, in a letter to C. M. Light, who had purchased a copy of *Illustrated History,* Read criticized English-speaking historians who "do not understand the Spanish language enough to disentangle the abreviations [*sic*] and peculiar Spanish of 400 yeras [*sic*] ago and, consequently, they fabricate and cover their fabrications with literary embelishments [*sic*]." Read to C. M. Light, 13 December 1913, Read Collection, NMSRCA.

73. Read, *Historia Ilustrada de Nuevo México,* 29–30.

74. Ibid., 30.

75. William W. H. Davis, *El Gringo, or New Mexico and Her People* (1857, rprt., New York: Arno Press, 1973). Quoted in Duran, "We Come as Friends," 192.

76. Read, *Historia ilustrada,* 539.

77. A. Gabriel Meléndez, introduction to *The Biography of Casimiro Barela,* by José E. Fernández (Albuquerque: University of New Mexico Press, 2003), xv. Commenting specifically on Read's book, Meléndez also notes that "the inclusion of this [biographical] material in a book of history was a strategy meant to reverse the intensive negativism of the eastern press toward New Mexico and Neo-Mexicanos." Ibid., xvi.

78. Isadore Armijo to Read, Las Cruces, New Mexico, 14 July 1911, Read Collection, NMSRCA.

79. Modesto C. Ortiz to Read, Albuquerque, 12 June 1911, Read Collection, NMSRCA. Juan Casados wrote that he loved *Historia* because it was so "invaluable, magnificent, and interesting . . ." Similarly, "Mr. Gallegos" of Santa Rita, New Mexico, was pleased to read "the true history of our country." Juan P. Casados to Read, Reyes, New Mexico, 16 September 1911, Read Collection, NMSRCA; Gallegos to Read, 15 September 1910, Read Collection, NMSRCA.

80. Manuel R. Otero to Read, Santa Fe, 11 January 1912, Read Collection, NMSRCA.

81. In 1917, E. V. Chavez, an attorney in Los Angeles, thanked Read for sending him a copy of *Historia ilustrada:* "My heart fills with pride

on seeing one of my compatriots and blood brothers rise to such distinction [with this work], and reach new heights in the history of our beloved *patria*." E.V. Chávez to Read, Los Angeles, 19 April 1917, Read Collection, NMSRCA.

82. Antonio Lucero to Read, 30 April 1911, Read Collection NMSRCA.

83. Archbishop John B. Pitaval to Read, Santa Fe, 17 April 1911, Read Collection, NMSRCA.

84. P. Tommasini, S.J., to Read, Old Albuquerque, New Mexico, 28 August 1911, Read Collection, NMSRCA.

85. [s.n.] to Read, Albuquerque, 28 November 1911, Read Collection, NMSRCA.

86. Several individuals viewed Read's writings as important to their families. D. Martinez Jr., of Velarde, New Mexico, wished that "every home in the territory" would own Read's *Historia ilustrada.* Similarly Antonio Lucero, associate editor of Las Vegas's *Voz del Pueblo,* wrote that he wished that text "were placed in the hands of every Spanish American family both in New Mexico and Southern Colorado so that our people might learn more about the history of their ancestors and feel justly proud of their achievements." D. Martinez Jr. to Read, Velarde, New Mexico, 22 May 1911, Read Collection, NMSRCA; Lucero to Read, 11 August 1911, Read Collection, NMSRCA.

87. Walter, "Benjamin M. Read," 396.

88. Read, *Illustrated History,* 806.

89. Read, *Illustrated History,* 812, 807.

90. Sen. Thomas B. Catron to Read, 4 January 1915, Read Collection, NMSRCA.

91. Benjamin Maurice Read, *Popular Elementary History of New Mexico* (Cedar Rapids, Iowa: Torch Press, 1914), 7.

92. Chacón to Read, Trinidad, Colorado, 5 April 1911, Read Collection, NMSRCA.

93. Read to Mateo Lujan, 22 May 1911, Read Collection, NMSRCA.

94. *New Mexico Journal of Education* 9 (October 15, 1912): 30.

95. Jesus C. Sánchez to Read, 20 May 1911, Read Collection, NMSRCA.

96. Baca further commended Read for his expert translations of the "Castilian language" documents, full of "provincialisms and abbreviations, as used in the epoch of the Spanish Conquistadores." Read's

"conversations with . . . the sons of the Conquistadores," Baca continued, gave Read an "advantage over other writers of New Mexican history." Filadelfo Baca to Read, Santa Fe, 26 July 1916, Read Collection, NMSRCA.

97. By 1919, his most productive years behind him, Read wrote one last major manuscript. "Historia de Nuevo México en las guerras de la Unión Americana, 1855–1919" was his final effort to prove hispanos' valor and loyalty in battle, from "the war with the Indians" to the Great War. For many Spanish Americans, wrote Read, the United States' war with Spain in 1898 was "the supreme test" of their loyalty, because they had been called on "to fight against their own blood and lineaje." Benjamin Maurice Read, "Nuevo México en la Guerras de la Unión Americana, 1855–1919," unpublished manuscript, Read Collection, NMSRCA.

98. Weigle and White, *The Lore of New Mexico,* 415.

99. By strange coincidence, Prince's wife, who had paraded as Queen Isabella years earlier, died within days after her appearance. Walter, "Benjamin M. Read," 396–97.

100. Horace Mann, "Twelfth Annual Report to the Board of Education," in *Life and Works of Horace Mann,* vol. 4 (Boston: Lee and Shephard, 1891), 251, as quoted in Edward Stevens Jr., George H. Wood, and James J. Sheehan, *Justice, Ideology, Education: An Introduction to the Social Foundations of Education,* 4th ed. (Boston: McGraw Hill, 2002), 123.

101. Getz, *Schools of Their Own,* 16.

102. *Annual Report of the Territorial Superintendent of Public Instruction* (Santa Fe: New Mexican Printing Co., 1896), 8–9.

103. The 1890s might be thought of as the apex of Nuevomexicano control over the public school system. During that decade, Nuevomexicanos (that is, men) occupied the post of superintendent of public instruction, being appointed by the territorial governor. Uniformly, these men acknowledged that the acquisition of English was of primary importance to the education of Spanish-speaking children, for it was the de facto language of the nation's citizenry, they said. Yet they also agreed that Spanish should be taught simultaneously, at least until the Spanish-speaking student could master English.

104. Getz, *Schools of Their Own,* 17–21.

105. Montgomery, *The Spanish Redemption,* 178.

106. Deutsch, *No Separate Refuge,* 67–68.

107. Aurora Lucero, "Shall the Spanish Language Be Taught in the Schools of New Mexico," undated publication in possession of author.

108. For a more detailed description of Lucero's activism on behalf of Spanish-language instruction, see Getz, *Schools of Their Own,* 40–47. Also see Charlotte Whaley, *Nina Otero-Warren of Santa Fe* (Albuquerque: University of New Mexico Press, 1994).

109. Untitled notes for a speech delivered at Taos, 18 February 1938, Bergere Family Papers, NMSRCA.

110. Lionides Pacheco and Ruth C. Miller, "The Bi-Lingual Method and the Improvement of Instruction," February 1938, Bergere Family Papers, NMSRCA.

111. Adelina Otero-Warren to Hermon M. Bumpus, 30 January 1930, Bergere Family Papers #41, NMSRCA.

112. For a critical examination of how Jaramillo, in particular, deployed the Spanish heritage, see Padilla, *My History, Not Yours,* 196–227.

113. Arthur León Campa file no. 970.61, "FERA Project #S-A1-17," 1Southwest Museum, Los Angeles.

Epilogue

1. The League of United Latin American Citizens (LULAC) reportedly sponsored "Spanish-American folk dances . . . in every community where there is a Lulac council," including Bernalillo, Las Vegas, Albuquerque, and other communities. "Coronado Folk Festival Groups Named in Many Communities," *Albuquerque Journal,* 24 December 1939. La Sociedad Folklórica of Santa Fe formed a Coronado Cuarto Centennial committee, chaired by none other than Aurora Lucero-White. That committee planned events such as stagings of "Los Moros y Cristianos" and "Los Matachines," two New Mexico dance-drama traditions that celebrate the Spanish conquest and conversion of non-Christian peoples. "Folklorica Adopts Plan for Part in Coronado Cuarto Centennial," *New Mexico Examiner,* 25 February 1940.

2. Joseph A. Bursey, director of the state tourist bureau, in 1937 projected that the festivities would attract six million visitors to the state, and garner sixty million dollars in revenue. "Return on Investment in State Cuarto Centennial Expected by Its Backers," *Raton Range,* 13 January 1937. For an excellent summary of the state's Coronado Cuarto Centennial Committee formation and activities, see Denise Pan, "Commercializing the Spanish Past: The Coronado Cuarto Centennial, 1935–1940," *Explorations in American History,* Occasional Paper no. 8, ed.

Sandra Varney MacMahon and Louis Tanner (Albuquerque: University of New Mexico Center for the American West, 1995), 81–109.

4. Sarah Gertrude Knott, "North of the Border," *Survey Graphic* 29, no. 6 (June 1940): 339.

4. Ibid.

5. James Brooke, "In New Mexico, Hispanic Pride Clashes With Indian Anger," *New York Times,* 8 February 1998.

Bibliography

Newspapers

Albuquerque El Defensor del Pueblo
Albuquerque El Nuevo Mundo
Albuquerque La Bandera Americana
Las Cruces El Defensor del Pueblo
Las Cruces El Eco del Siglo
Las Vegas El Independiente
Las Vegas La Voz del Pueblo
Las Vegas La Revista Católica
New York Times
Santa Fe El Boletín Popular
Santa Fe El Nuevo Mexicano
Santa Fe La Aurora
Santa Fe Herald
Santa Fe The New Mexican
Santa Fe Weekly New Mexican

Archival Materials and Manuscripts

Archives of the Archdiocese of Santa Fe (AASF).
Álvarez, Manuel. Collection. New Mexico State Records Center and Archives, Santa Fe.
Austin, Mary. Mary Hunter Austin Collection. Huntington Library, Pasadena.
Bergere, A. M. Bergere Family Papers. New Mexico State Records Center and Archives, Santa Fe.
Catron, Thomas B. Catron Papers. Center for Southwest Research, University of New Mexico, Albuquerque.
Castañeda, Carlos E. Carlos Eduardo Castañeda Papers. University of Texas, Austin.
Coronado Cuarto Centennial Commission. New Mexico Coronado

Cuarto Centennial Commission Collection. Center for
Southwest Research, University of New Mexico, Albuquerque.

Historical Society of New Mexico. Historical Society of New
Mexico Records Collection (microform). Center for Southwest
Research, University of New Mexico, Albuquerque.

Larrazolo, Octaviano A. Octaviano A. Larrazolo Papers. Center for
Southwest Research, University of New Mexico, Albuquerque.

Lummis, Charles Fletcher. Charles Fletcher Lummis Manuscript
Collection. Southwest Museum, Los Angeles.

Menéndez Pidal, Ramón. Ramón Menéndez Pidal Collection.
Fundación Menéndez Pidal, Madrid.

Mexican Archives of New Mexico (microform). New Mexico State
Records Center and Archives, Santa Fe.

Ortiz Family. Ortiz Family Papers. New Mexico State Records
Center and Archives, Santa Fe.

Otero, Miguel Antonio. Governor Miguel A. Otero Papers. New
Mexico State Records Center and Archives, Santa Fe.

Prince, Lebaron Bradford. L. Bradford Prince Papers. New Mexico
State Records Center and Archives, Santa Fe.

Read, Benjamin Maurice Benjamin Maurice Read Collection, New
Mexico State Records Center and Archives, Santa Fe.

Sánchez, George Isadore. George Isadore Sánchez Papers. Benson
Library, University of Texas, Austin.

Spanish Archives of New Mexico (microform). New Mexico State
Records Center and Archives, Santa Fe.

Territorial Archives of New Mexico (microform). New Mexico State
Records Center and Archives, Santa Fe.

Twitchell, Ralph E. Ralph Emerson Twitchell Collection. New
Mexico State Records Center and Archives, Santa Fe.

Warshaw Collection. Smithsonian Archives, Smithsonian Institution,
Washington, D.C.

Government Publications

New Mexico

Bureau of Immigration. *Resources of New Mexico.* Santa Fe: New
Mexican Book and Job Printing Department, 1881.

———. *Report of the Bureau of Immigration, February 16, 1884.* Santa Fe:
New Mexican Printing Co., 1884.

————. *Aztlán: The History, Resources and Attractions of New Mexico, Embellished with Maps and Seventy-Five Characteristic Illustrations.* By William G[illette] Ritch. 6th ed. Boston: D. Lothrop and Co., 1885.

————. *Illustrated New Mexico, Historical and Industrial.* By William G[illette] Ritch. Santa Fe: Bureau of Immigration, 1885.

————. *Santa Fé: Ancient and Modern, Including Its Resources and Industries, with Numerous Illustrations, and a Map of the County.* By W[illiam] G[illette] Ritch. Santa Fe, 1885.

————. "Despacho de emigración y sus trabajos." In *New Mexico,* ed. H. C. Burnett. Santa Fe: Bureau of Immigration, 1886.

————. *New Mexico.* Edited by H. C. Burnett. Santa Fe: Bureau of Immigration, 1886.

————. *New Mexico: Its Resources, Climate, Geography and Geological Condition.* Edited by Max Frost. Santa Fe: New Mexican Printing Co., 1890.

————. *Facts and Figures Concerning New Mexico.* Santa Fe: New Mexican Printing Co., 1891.

————. *New Mexico, The Coming Country. Budget of Information Concerning the Natural Resources and Advantages of New Mexico. Facts and Figures for the Public. A Concise Statement Carefully Prepared for the Delectation of the Homeseeker. An Inviting Field for Capital. The Coming Country of the South and West.* Santa Fe: New Mexican Printing Co., 1891.

————. *New Mexico. The Resources and Prospects of Her Counties, with Special Reference to Advantages for Investment in All Localities, Where Her Colonies Should Settle and What Avocations Will Prove Profitable.* Santa Fe: Bureau of Immigration, 1893.

————. *New Mexico. Its Resources, Climate, Geography, Geology, History, Statistics, Present Condition and Future Prospects.* By Max Frost. Santa Fe: New Mexico Printing Co., 1894.

————. *New Mexico, 1898: Climate, Mineral Springs, Schools.* Bulletin no. 1. Santa Fe: New Mexican Printing Co, 1898.

————. *Informe del Buró de Inmigración, desde abril, 1897, hasta enero 1898.* Santa Fe: Compañía Impresora del Nuevo Mexicano, 1899.

————. *Socorro County, New Mexico: The Largest County in the Territory. Possesses Great Mineral Riches. Stock Ranges as Large as a European Kingdom. Fertile Valleys and Canyons. Mild and Equitable Climate.* Bulletin no. 11. Santa Fe: New Mexican Printing Co., 1901.

————. *Biennial Report of the Bureau of Immigration of the Territory of New Mexico, For the Two Years Ending November 30th.* By Max Frost. Santa Fe: New Mexican Printing Co., 1902.

————. *The Land of Sunshine: A Handbook of the Resources, Products, Industries and Climate of New Mexico.* Edited by Max Frost and Paul A. F. Walter. Santa Fe: New Mexico Bureau of Immigration, 1904, 1906.

————. *Santa Fe County: The Heart of New Mexico, Rich in History and Resources.* Edited by Max Frost and Paul A. F. Walter. Santa Fe: New Mexico Bureau of Immigration, 1906.

————. *San Juan County, New Mexico. The Land of Sunshine. The Land of Opportunity.* [Santa Fe], 1909.

————. *Santa Fe County, New Mexico: A Country Rich in Attractions for the Sight Seeker, the Health Seeker, the Wealth Seeker and Home Seeker.* By Paul A. F. Walter. Santa Fe: New Mexican Printing Co., 1909.

————. *Why New Mexico Is Entitled to Statehood: We Have the People, the Land, the Water, the Mines, the Coal, Flocks and Herds, Splendid Schools, Clean Local Government, Our People Are Industrious, Progressive Americans.* [Santa Fe], 1911.

Office of the Governor. *El cuarto mensaje anual de S.E.D. Enrique Connelly a la Asamblea Legislativa de Nuevo Méjico, pronunciado diciembre, 1865.* Santa Fe: Impresores, Oficina de El Nuevo Mejicano, [1865].

————. *Message of Governor L. Bradford Prince to the Thirtieth Legislative Assembly of New Mexico, December 28, 1892.* Santa Fe: New Mexican Printing Co., 1892.

————. *Message of Governor Miguel A. Otero to the Thirty-Third Legislative Assembly of New Mexico.* Santa Fe: New Mexican Printing Co., 1899.

United States

Bureau of the Census. *Seventh Census of the United States, 1850.* Vol. 1. Washington, D.C., 1850.

————. *Compendium of the Tenth Census, 1880.* Part 1. Rev. ed. Washington, [D.C.]: Government Printing Office, 1885.

————. *Population Trends in the United States, 1900–1960.* Bureau of the Census Technical Paper no. 10. By Irene B. Taeuber. Washington, D.C.: Government Printing Office, 1965.

Bureau of the Census. *U.S. Census of Population, 1850–1910.*
Washington, D.C.: Government Printing Office, various dates.

Congress. House of Representatives. *California and New Mexico. Speech of Hon. James S. Green of Missouri, February 15, 1850.* [Washington, D.C., 1850].

———. *Speech of Hon. A. W. Venable of N. Carolina on the Texas and New Mexico Question, Delivered in the House of Representatives, Thursday, August 15, 1850.* Washington, D.C.: Congressional Globe Printing Office, 1850.

———. *Speech of Hon. James A. Seddon of Virginia, August 13, 1850.* Washington, D.C.: Congressional Globe Printing Office, 1850.

———. *Speech of Hon. Joseph M. Root of Ohio, February 15, 1850, in the Committee of the Whole on the State of the Union, on the Resolution Referring the President's Message to the Appropriate Standing Committees.* Washington, D.C.: Congressional Globe Printing Office, 1850].

———. *An Act to Create a Land District in the Territory of New Mexico.* 35th Cong., 1st sess. 1858.

———. *An Act to Confirm the Land Claims of Certain Pueblos and Towns in the Territory of New Mexico.* 35th Cong., 1st sess. H.R. 565. 1858.

———. "Private Land Claims in New Mexico." 36th Cong., 2d sess. Ex. Doc. 28. 12 January 1861.

———. "State Government for New Mexico. Memorial of the Assembly of New Mexico, In Regard to a State government for that Territory." 39th Cong., 2d sess. Mis. Doc. 57. 1866.

———. *Admission of New Mexico as a State: Her Resources and Future. Speech of Hon. Stephen B. Elkins, Delegate from New Mexico, in the House of Representatives, May 21, 1874.* Report 561. 43d Cong., 1st sess. Washington, D.C.: Government Printing Office, 1874.

———. "Admission of New Mexico. Memorial of the Legislative Assembly of New Mexico Asking the Passage of an Enabling Act for Admission into the Union." 44th Cong., 1st sess. Mis. Doc. 63. 1876.

———. Committee on the Territories. *Hearings on House Bill 12543, December 10, 1902.* 57th Cong., 2d sess. Doc. 36. 1902.

———. Committee on the Territories. *Hearings on Statehood Bill, December 11, 1903.* Washington, D.C.: Congressional Hearings Supplement, 1904.

———. Committee on the Territories. *Hearings on Statehood, January 16, 1876.* Washington, D.C.: Congressional Hearings Supplement, 1906.

Congress. Senate. *Congressional Globe,* 30th Cong., 1st sess. 1848.

———. *Speech of William H. Seward on the Admission of New Mexico, July 26, 1850.* Washington: Buell and Blanchard, 1850.

———. Committee on the Territories. *Admission of New Mexico as a State. [To accompany bill H.R. 2418].* 43d Cong., 1st sess. S.R. 561. 1874.

———. *New Mexico: Minority Report [To accompany bill S. 229].* 44th Cong., 1st sess. S.R. 503. 1876.

———. *Report [To accompany bill S. 229].* 44th Cong., 1st sess. S.R. 69. 1876.

———. Committee on the Territories. *Statehood Hearings, February 18–21, 1910.*

Articles, Books, Monographs, Dissertations, and Pamphlets

Acuña, Rodolfo. *Occupied America: The Chicano's Struggle toward Liberation.* San Francisco: Harper and Row, 1972.

Albuquerque Illustrated. Albuquerque: Flower and Payne, 1892.

Alonso, José Ramón. *Norteamérica, hispanidad.* Colección Tiempos Actuales. Edited by Francisco Daunis. Barcelona, Spain: N.p., 1965.

Altamira [y Crevea], Rafael. *La política de España en América.* Valencia, Spain: Editorial Edeta, 1921.

———. "El Primer Congreso Internacional de Hispanistas." *Hispania* 2 (October 1919): 169–73.

———. *España en América.* Valencia, Spain: F. Sempere y Compañía, 1908.

Anderson, Benedict. *Imagined Communities: Reflection on the Origin and Spread of Nationalism.* New York: Verso, 1991.

Anderson, George B. *History of New Mexico: Its Resources and People.* 2 vols. New York: Pacific States Publishing Co., 1907.

Annual Report of the Territorial Superintendent of Public Instruction. Santa Fe: New Mexican Printing Co., 1896.

Appelbaum, Nancy P., Anne S. Macpherson, and Karin Alejandra Rosemblatt. *Race and Nation in Modern Latin America.* Chapel Hill: University of North Carolina Press, 2003.

Arellano, Anselmo F. *Los pobladores nuevo mexicanos y su poesía, 1889–1950.* Albuquerque: Pajarito Publications, 1976.

Arellano, Anselmo F., and Julián Josue Vigil. *Las Vegas Grandes on the Gallinas, 1835–1985.* Las Vegas, N.M.: Editorial Telaraña, 1985.

Babcock, Barbara A. "Mudwomen and Whitemen: A Meditation on Pueblo Potteries and the Politics of Representation." In *Discovered Country: Tourism and Survival in the American West,* ed. Scott Norris, 180–95. Albuquerque: Stone Ladder Press, 1994.

———. "'A New Mexican Rebecca': Imaging Pueblo Women." *Journal of the Southwest* 32 (1990): 400–437.

Bancroft, Hubert Howe. *History of Arizona and New Mexico.* San Francisco: History Company, 1889. Reprint, Albuquerque: Horn and Wallace, 1962.

———. *California Pastoral, 1769–1848.* San Francisco: N.p., 1888.

Bannon, John Francis. *The Spanish Conquistadores: Men or Devils?* New York: Holt, Rinehart and Winston, 1960.

Barbour, Barton Harry. "In Search of Better Health: James Ross Larkin on the Santa Fe Trail, 1856–57." MA thesis, University of New Mexico, 1988.

Barrera, Mario. *Race and Class in the Southwest: A Theory of Racial Inequality.* Notre Dame, Ind.: University of Notre Dame Press, 1979.

Barth, Fredrik. *Ethnic Groups and Boundaries: The Social Organization of Culture Difference.* Boston: Little, Brown and Co., 1969.

Basso, Keith. "History of Ethnological Research." In *Southwest,* vol. 9 of *Handbook of North American Indians,* ed. Alfonso Ortiz, 14–21. Washington, D.C.: Smithsonian Institution, 1979.

Bataille, Gretchen M. Introduction to *Native American Representations: First Encounters, Distorted Images, and Literary Appropriations,* ed. Gretchen M. Bataille, 1–7. Lincoln: University of Nebraska Press, 2001.

Beltrán, Aguirre. *Colección Larrauri Montaño.* N.p., 1946.

Bieder, Robert E. *Science Encounters the Indian, 1820–1880: The Early Years of American Ethnology.* Norman: University of Oklahoma Press, 1986.

Blaut, J. M., and Antonio Rios-Bustamante. "Commentary on Nostrand's 'Hispanos' and their 'Homeland.'" *Annals of the Association of American Geographers* 74, no. 1 (1984): 157, 157–64.

Bloom, Lansing Bartlett. "New Mexico under Mexican

Administration, Part 1: New Mexico as a Department, 1837–1846." *Old Santa Fe* 1 (July 1913): 1–35.

————. "New Mexico under Mexican Administration, Part 3: New Mexico as a Department, 1837–1846." *Old Santa Fe* 2 (July 1914): 35–46.

Bodine, John J. "A Tri-Ethnic Trap: The Spanish Americans in Taos." In *Spanish-Speaking People in the United States: Proceedings of the 1968 Annual Spring Meeting of the American Ethnological Society,* ed. June Helm, 145–53. Seattle: University of Washington Press, 1968.

————. "Attitudes and Institutions of Taos, New Mexico: Variables for Value System Expression." PhD diss., Tulane University, 1967.

Bodnar, John. *The Transplanted: A History of Immigrants in Urban America.* Bloomington: Indiana University Press, 1985.

Bolton, Herbert Eugene. "Defensive Spanish Expansion and the Significance of the Borderlands." In *The Trans-Mississippi West,* ed. James F. Willard and Colin B. Goodykoontz. Boulder: University of Colorado Press, 1930.

Bonilla y San Martín, Adolfo. "América 'española.'" *Raza Española* 1 (1919): 95–101.

Bourne, Edward Gaylord. *Spain in America, 1450–1580.* New York: Harper and Bros., 1904; reprinted with a new introduction and supplementary bibliography by Benjamin Keen, New York: Barnes and Noble, 1962.

Bradfute, Richard Wells. "The Court of Private Land Claims and the Adjudication of Spanish and Mexican Land Grant Titles, 1891–1904." PhD diss., University of Colorado, 1973.

Brading, D. A. *The First America: The Spanish Monarchy, Creole Patriots, and the Liberal State, 1492–1867.* Cambridge, UK: Cambridge University Press, 1991.

————. *The Origins of Mexican Nationalism.* Cambridge, UK: Centre of Latin American Studies, Cambridge University, 1985.

————. *Prophecy and Myth in Mexican History.* Cambridge, UK: Centre of Latin American Studies, Cambridge University, [1980].

Bredbenner, Candice Lewis. *A Nationality of Her Own: Women, Marriage, and the Law of Citizenship.* Berkeley: University of California Press, 1998.

Brettell, Caroline B. "Introduction: Travel Literature, Ethnohistory, and Ethnography." *Ethnohistory* 33 (1986): 127–38.

Brevoort, Elias. *New Mexico: Her Natural Resources and Attractions, Being a Collection of Facts, Mainly Concerning Her Geography, Climate, Population, Schools, Mines and Minerals, Agricultural and Pastoral Capacities, Prospective Railroads, Public Lands, and Spanish and Mexican Land Grants.* Santa Fe: Elias Brevoort, 1874.

Briggs, Charles L., and John R. Van Ness, eds., *Land, Water, and Culture: New Perspectives on Hispanic Land Grants.* Albuquerque: University of New Mexico Press, 1987.

Brodkin, Karen. *How Jews Became White Folks and What That Says about Race in America.* New Brunswick, N.J.: Rutgers University Press, 1998.

Brooke, James. "In New Mexico, Hispanic Pride Clashes With Indian Anger." *New York Times,* 8 February 1998.

Bsumek, Erika Marie. "Making 'Indian-Made': The Promotion, Consumption and Construction of Navajo Ethnic Identity, 1880–1935." PhD diss., Rutgers State University, 2000.

Burke, Flannery Gaussoin. "Finding What They Came for: The Mabel Dodge Luhan Circle and the Making of a Modern Place, 1912–1930." PhD diss., University of Wisconsin, Madison, 2002.

Bustamante, Adrián Herminio. "Los Hispanos: Ethnicity and Social Change in New Mexico." PhD diss., University of New Mexico, 1982.

Byrkit, James W. *Charles Lummis: Letters from the Southwest, September 20, 1884 to March 14, 1885.* Tucson: University of Arizona Press, 1989.

Camarillo, Albert. *Chicanos in a Changing Society: From Mexican Pueblos to American Barrios.* Cambridge, Mass.: Harvard University Press, 1979.

Campa, Arthur León. *Spanish Folk-Poetry in New Mexico.* Albuquerque: University of New Mexico Press, 1946.

———. "Federal Emergency Relief Administration (FERA) Project #S-AI-17," Southwest Museum, Los Angeles.

Carlson, Alvar W. *The Spanish-American Homeland: Four Centuries in New Mexico's Río Arriba.* Baltimore: Johns Hopkins University Press, 1990.

Carroll, H. Bailey, and J. Villasana Haggard, trans. and eds. *Three New Mexico Chronicles: The Exposición of Don Pedro Bautista Pino, 1812; the Ojeada of Lic. Antonio Barreiro, 1832; and the Additions by Don José Agustín de Escudero, 1849.* Albuquerque: Quivira Society, 1942.

Carroll, Michael P. *The Penitente Brotherhood: Patriarchy and Hispano-Catholicism in New Mexico.* Baltimore: Johns Hopkins University Press, 2002.

Castro, Américo. *La realidad histórica en España.* México: N.p., 1954.

Cebrián, Juan C. "A la Academia." *Boletín de la Real Academia de la Historia* (October–December 1926): 3–11.

———. "On Italian and Spanish in American Education." *Hispania* 3 (1920): 5–9.

———. "El apelativo 'Iberoamericano.'" *Raza española* 1 (1919): 102–4.

Champney, Elizabeth W. *Great-Grandmother's Girls in New Mexico, 1670–1680.* Boston: Estes and Lauriat, 1888.

Chang, Susanna W. "Hispanic and Anglo Attributions Related to Ethnic Labels in New Mexico." MA thesis, University of New Mexico, 1994.

Chase, C. M. *Colorado and New Mexico. The Editor's Run.* Montpelier, Vt.: Argus and Patriot Steam Book and Job Printing House, 1882.

Chaves, Amado. *The Defeat of the Comanches in 1717.* Historical Society of New Mexico Publications no. 8. Santa Fe: New Mexican Printing Co., 1906.

Chávez, Fray Angélico. *Chávez: A Distinctive American Clan of New Mexico.* Santa Fe: William Gannon, 1989.

———. "Rejoinder." *Annals of the Association of American Geographers* 74, no. 1 (1984): 170–71

———. *New Mexico Roots, Ltd.* Santa Fe: Fray Angélico Chávez, 1982.

———. *Origins of New Mexico Families in the Spanish Colonial Period, In Two Parts: The Seventeenth (1598–1693) and the Eighteenth (1693–1821) Centuries.* Albuquerque: University of New Mexico Press in collaboration with Calivin Horn Publishers, 1973.

Chávez, Ireneo L. *Compiled Laws of New Mexico, 1884.* Santa Fe: N.p., 1885.

Chávez, John R. *The Lost Land: The Chicano Image of the Southwest.* Albuquerque: University of New Mexico Press, 1984.

Clancy, Frank W. *In Memory of L. Bradford Prince, President of the Society.* New Mexico Historical Society Publications no. 25. Santa Fe, 1923.

Clever, Charles P. *New Mexico: Her Resources, Her Necessities for Railroad Communication with the Atlantic and Pacific States, Her Great Future.* Washington, D.C.: McGill and Witherow, 1868.

Clifford, James. "On Collecting Art and Culture." In *Out There: Marginalization and Contemporary Cultures,* ed. Russell Ferguson et al., 141–69. New York: New Museum of Contemporary Art, 1990.

————. *The Predicament of Culture: Twentieth-Century Ethnography, Literature, and Art.* Cambridge, Mass.: Harvard University Press, 1988.

Comaroff, Jean, and John Comaroff. *Of Revelation and Revolution: Christianity, Colonialism, and Consciousness in South Africa.* Vol. 1. Chicago: University of Chicago Press, 1991.

Comas, Juan. *Ensayos sobre indigenismo.* México: Instituto Indigenista Interamericano, 1953.

"Coronado Folk Festival Groups Named in Many Communities." *Albuquerque Journal,* 24 December 1939.

Cook, Sherburne F., and Woodrow Borah, *Essays on Population History: Mexico and the Caribbean.* Vol. 1. Berkeley: University of California Press, 1971.

Cozzens, Samuel Woodworth. *The Marvelous Country; Or, Three Years in Arizona and New Mexico, the Apache's Home, a Description of this Wonderful Country, Its Immense Mineral Wealth, Its Magnificent Mountain Scenery, the Ruins of Ancient Towns and Cities Found Therein, with a Complete History of the Apache Tribe, and a Description of the Author's Guide, Cochise, the Great Apache War Chief, the Whole Interspersed with Strange Events and Adventures. Illustrated With Upwards of One Hundred Engravings.* Boston: Shepard and Gill, 1873.

Crick, Malcolm. "Representation of International Tourism in the Social Sciences: Sun, Sex, Sights Savings, and Servility." *Annual Review of Anthropology* 18 (1989): 307–44.

Cutter, Charles R. "Community and the Law in Northern New Spain." *The Americas* 50 (April 1994): 467–80.

Dargan, Marion. "New Mexico's Fight for Statehood (1895–1912), 1." *New Mexico Historical Review* 14 (January 1939): 1–33.

————. "New Mexico's Fight for Statehood (1895–1912), 2." *New Mexico Historical Review* 14 (January 1939): 121–42.

————. "New Mexico's Fight for Statehood (1895–1912), 3. The Opposition within the Territory (1888–1890)." *New Mexico Historical Review* 15 (April 1940): 133–87.

Davis, William W. H. *El Gringo, or New Mexico and Her People.* 1857. Reprint, New York: Arno Press, 1973.

————. *The Spanish Conquest of New Mexico.* Doylestown, Pa., 1869.

DeMark, Judith L. *Chasing the Cure: A History of Healthseekers to Albuquerque, 1902–1940.* History of Albuquerque Exhibits Series. Vol. 4. Albuquerque: The Albuquerque Museum, 1981.

Denver and Rio Grande Railway. *Spanish and Indian New Mexico.* Denver: Chain and Hardy, n.d.

————. *Tourists' Hand-Book: Descriptive of Colorado, New Mexico and Utah.* N.p., 1885.

Deutsch, Sarah. *No Separate Refuge: Culture, Class, and Gender on an Anglo-Hispanic Frontier in the American Southwest, 1880–1940.* New York: Oxford University Press, 1987.

Diccionario de la Lengua Española. 15th ed. Madrid: Talleres Calpe, 1925.

Dolader, Miguel Angel Motis. *Los judios Aragoneses en la época del descubrimiento de América.* Zaragoza, Spain: Navarro y Navarro, 1989.

Domínguez Ortiz, Antonio. *Los Judeoconversos en España y América.* Collección Fundamentos no. 11. Madrid: Ediciones ISTMO, 1971.

Donlon, Walter John. "LeBaron Bradford Prince, Chief Justice and Governor of New Mexico Territory, 1879–1893." PhD diss., University of New Mexico, 1967.

Duran, Tobias. "We Come as Friends: Violent Social Conflict in New Mexico, 1810–1910." PhD diss., University of New Mexico, 1985.

Ebright, Malcolm. "New Mexico Land Grants: The Legal Background." In *Land, Water, and Culture: New Perspectives on Hispanic Land Grants,* ed. Charles L. Briggs and John R. Van Ness, 50–64. Albuquerque: University of New Mexico Press, 1987.

"Education and the Spanish-Speaking: An Attorney General's Opinion on Article VII, Section 8 of the New Mexico Constitution." *New Mexico Law Review* 3 (May 1973): 268 n. 20, 372–73 n. 66–67.

Educational Center of New Mexico: A Few Facts in Relation to the Educational Facilities of Albuquerque, with Views of School Building, Compliments of the Educators of Albuquerque. Chicago: Vandercook Engraving and Publishing Co., [1893].

Eldridge, Hope T., and Dorothy Swaine Thomas. *Demographic Analyses and Interrelations.* Vol. 3 of *Population Redistribution and Economic Growth, United States,* ed. Simon Kuznets and Dorothy Swaine Thomas. Philadelphia: American Philosophical Society, 1957.

Elliot, John Huxtable. *Imperial Spain, 1469–1716.* New York: St. Martin's Press, 1963.

Enciclopedia Universal Europeo-Americana. Madrid: Espasa–Calpe, 1933.

Espasa diccionario de la lengua española. Madrid: Espasa–Calpe, 1999.

Espinosa, Aurelio Macedonio. *The Folklore of Spain in the American Southwest: Traditional Spanish Folk Literature in Northern New Mexico and Southern Colorado.* Edited by J. Manuel Espinosa. Norman: University of Oklahoma Press, 1985.

—————. *España en Nuevo Méjico: Lecturas elementales sobre la historia de Nuevo Méjico y su tradición española.* New York: Allyn and Bacon, 1937.

—————. *España: Lecciones elementales sobre la historia de la civilización española.* New York: Oxford University Press, 1937.

—————. *The Spanish Republic and the Causes of the Counter-Revolution.* San Francisco: Spanish Relief Committee, 1937.

—————. "New Mexican Versions of the Tar-Baby Story." *New Mexico Quarterly* 1 (February 1931): 85–104.

—————. "La ciencia del folklore." *Archivos del Folklore* 3 (Havana, 1929): 3–16.

—————. "The Language of the Cuentos Populares Españoles." *Language* 3 (September 1927): 189–98.

—————. "Spanish Folk-Lore in New Mexico." *New Mexico Historical Review* 1 (April 1926): 135–55.

—————. "A Folk-Lore Expedition to Spain." *Journal of American Folklore* 34 (April–June 1921): 127–42.

—————. "On the Teaching of Spanish." *Hispania* 4 (December 1921): 269–84.

—————. *América Española o Hispano América: El término "América Latina" es erróneo.* Traducción de Felipe M. de Setién. Madrid: Comisaría Regia del Turismo y Cultura Artística, 1919.

—————. "The Term Latin America." *Hispania* 1 (September 1918): 135–43.

—————. "New Mexico." In *The Catholic Encyclopedia: An International Work of Reference on the Constitution, Doctrine, Discipline, and History of the Catholic Church,* ed. Charles George Herbermann et al. Vol. 11, 1–5. New York: Encyclopedia Press, 1911.

—————. *The Spanish Language in New Mexico and Southern Colorado.* Historical Society of New Mexico Publications no. 16. Santa Fe: New Mexican Printing Co., 1911.

———. *Studies in New Mexican Spanish: Part I, Phonology.* University of New Mexico Bulletin, Language Series no. 1. Albuquerque: University of New Mexico, 1909.

———. *Los Comanches.* Bulletin no. 45. Language Series no. 1. Albuquerque: University of New Mexico, 1907.

Espinosa, Manuel J. "Part One: Aurelio M. Espinosa: New Mexico's Pioneer Folklorist." In *The Folklore of Spain in the American Southwest: Traditional Spanish Folk Literature in Northern New Mexico and Southern Colorado.* By Aurelio Macedonio Espinosa. Edited by J. Manuel Espinosa. Norman: University of Oklahoma Press, 1985.

———. "Additional Hispanic Versions of the Spanish Religious Ballad 'Por el rastro de la sangre.'" *New Mexico Historical Review* 56 (October 1981): 249–367.

———. "Spanish Folklore in the Southwest: The Pioneer Studies of Aurelio M. Espinosa." *Americas* 35 (October 1978): 219–37.

———. *Inter-American Beginnings of U.S. Cultural Diplomacy, 1936–48.* Cultural Relations Programs of the U.S. Department of State. Historical Studies no. 2. Washington, D.C.: Government Printing Office, 1976.

Estrada, Ramón. *Justicia tardía pero satisfactoria.* Madrid: Ministerio de Marina, 1925.

Facts and Figures Concerning Santa Fe, New Mexico, As a Sanitarium, from Writings of Henry F. Lyster, M.D. (Detroit), and Others. N.p., [1894].

Fincher, Ernest Barksdale. *Spanish-Americans as a Political Factor in New Mexico, 1912–1950.* New York: Arno Press, 1974.

Fitz-Gerald, John D. "The Bilingual-Biracial Problem of Our Border States." *Hispania* 4 (October 1921): 175–86.

Fleming, Robert E. *Charles F. Lummis.* Western Writers Series. Boise, Idaho: Boise State University Press, 1981.

"Folklorica Adopts Plan for Part in Coronado Cuarto Centennial." *New Mexico Examiner,* 25 February 1940.

Forbes, Jack D. "Black Pioneers: The Spanish-Speaking Afroamericans of the Southwest." In *Historical Themes and Identity: Mestizaje and Labels,* ed. Antoinette Sedillo López, 20–33. New York: Garland Publishing, 1995.

Foucault, Michel. *History of Sexuality.* Translated by R. Hurley. New York: Random House, 1978.

———. *The Archaeology of Knowledge, and the Discourse on Language.* New York: Pantheon, 1972.

Frank, Ross. *From Settler to Citizen: New Mexican Economic Development and the Creation of Vecino Society, 1750–1820*. Berkeley: University of California Press, 2000.

García, Mario T. *Mexican Americans: Leadership, Ideology, and Identity, 1930–1960*. New Haven: Yale University Press, 1989.

Getz, Lynne Marie. *Schools of Their Own: The Education of Hispanos in New Mexico, 1850–1940*. Albuquerque: University of New Mexico Press, 1997.

Gibson, Arrell Morgan. *The Santa Fe and Taos Colonies: Age of the Muses, 1900–1942*. Norman: University of Oklahoma Press, 1983.

Gibson, Charles, and Benjamin Keen. "Trends of United States Studies in Latin American History." *Hispanic American Historical Review* 62, no. 4 (July 1957): 855–56.

Gibert-Fernandez, Arturo. "'*La Voz del Pueblo*': *Texto, identidad y lengua en la prensa neomexicana, 1890–1911*." PhD diss., University of New Mexico, 2001.

Gilitz, David M. *Secrecy and Deceit: The Religion of the Crypto-Jews*. Albuquerque: University of New Mexico Press, 2002.

Gonzales, Phillip B. "Review Essay: Charles Montgomery, *The Spanish Redemption: Heritage, Power, and Loss on New Mexico's Upper Rio Grande*." *New Mexico Historical Review* 78, no. 3 (Summer 2003): 329–37.

———. *Forced Sacrifice as Ethnic Protest: The Hispano Cause in New Mexico and the Racial Attitude Confrontation of 1933*. New York: Peter Lang, 2001.

———. "La Junta de Indignación: Hispano Repertoire of Collective Protest in New Mexico, 1884–1933." *Western Historical Quarterly* 31 (2000): 161–86.

———. "More Lessons from the Hispano Homeland Debate." Paper presented at the National Association of Chicano Scholars, San Jose, California, 25–28 March 1993 (private manuscript).

———. "The Political Construction of Latino Nomenclatures in Twentieth-Century New Mexico." *Journal of the Southwest* 35, no. 2 (1993): 158–85.

———. "Spanish Heritage and Ethnic Protest in New Mexico: The Anti-Fraternity Bill of 1933." *New Mexico Historical Review* 61 (October 1986): 281–99.

———. *The Protest Function of Spanish-American Identity in New Mexico*. Working Paper Series no. 111. Albuquerque: Southwest Hispanic

Research Institute, University of New Mexico, Spring 1985.
Gonzales-Berry, Erlinda. "Which Language Will Our Children Speak? The Spanish Language and Public Education Policy in New Mexico, 1890–1930." In *The Contested Homeland: A Chicano History of New Mexico,* ed. Erlinda Gonzales-Berry and David R. Maciel. Albuquerque: University of New Mexico Press, 2000.

———, ed. *Pasó por aquí: Critical Essays on the New Mexican Literary Tradition, 1542–1988.* Albuquerque: University of New Mexico Press, 1989.

González Calleja, Eduardo, and Fredes Limón Nevado. *La hispanidad como instrumento de combate: Raza e imperio en la prensa franquista durante la guerra civil española.* Consejo Superior de Investigaciones Científicas. Centro de Estudio Históricos. Madrid: Consejo Superior de Investigaciones Científicas, 1988.

González, Deena J. *Refusing the Favor: The Spanish-Mexican Women of Santa Fe, 1820–1880.* New York: Oxford University Press, 1999.

González, Nancie L. *The Spanish-Americans of New Mexico: A Heritage of Pride.* Albuquerque: University of New Mexico Press, 1967.

Greene, Albert R. *Wonderland: The Story of Ancient and Modern New Mexico.* N.p., 1883.

Greene, Charles W. *A Complete Business Directory of New Mexico, and Gazetteer of the Territory for 1882.* Santa Fe: New Mexican Printing and Publishing Co., 1882.

Greer, Richard R. "Origins of the Foreign-Born Population of New Mexico during the Territorial Period." *New Mexico Historical Review* 17, no. 4 (October 1941): 281–87.

Gregg, Josiah. *Commerce of the Prairies: The Journal of a Santa Fé Trader.* New York: Henry G. Langley, 1844. Reprint, Dallas: Southwest Press, 1933.

Griswold del Castillo, Richard. *La Familia: Chicano Families in the Urban Southwest, 1848 to the Present.* South Bend, Ind.: University of Notre Dame Press, 1984.

Guerin-Gonzales, Camille. *Mexican Workers and American Dreams: Immigration, Repatriation, and California Farm Labor, 1900–1939.* New Brunswick, N.J.: Rutgers University Press, 1994.

Gutiérrez, Ramón A. "Charles Fletcher Lummis and the Orientalization of New Mexico," in *Nuevomexicano Cultural Legacy: Forms, Agencies, and Discourse.* Albuquerque: University of New Mexico Press, 2002.

————. *When Jesus Came, the Corn Mothers Went Away: Marriage, Sexuality, and Power in New Mexico, 1500–1846.* Stanford, Calif.: Stanford University Press, 1991.

————. "Aztlán, Montezuma, and New Mexico: The Political Uses of American Indian Mythology." In *Aztlán: Essays on the Chicano Homeland,* ed. Rodolfo A. Anaya and Francisco Lomelí, 170–92. Albuquerque: Academia/El Norte Publications, 1989.

————. "Unraveling America's Hispanic Past: Internal Stratification and Class Boundaries." *Aztlán: A Journal of Chicano Studies* 17 (Spring 1986): 172–90.

Haas, Lisbeth. *Conquests and Historical Identities in California, 1769–1936.* Berkeley: University of California Press, 1995.

Hagan, William T. *Theodore Roosevelt and Six Friends of the Indians.* Norman: University of Oklahoma Press, 1997.

Hall, Emlen G., and David J. Weber. "Mexican Liberals and the Pueblo Indians, 1821–1829." *New Mexico Historical Review* 59 (1984): 5–32.

Hall, Thomas. *Annals of the Association of American Geographers* 74, no. 1 (1984): 171.

Hanke, Lewis. "A Modest Proposal for a Moratorium on Grand Generalizations: Some Thoughts on the Black Legend." *Hispanic American Historical Review* 51, no. 1 (February 1971): 112–27.

————. "More Heat and Some Light on the Spanish Struggle for Justice in the Conquest of America." *Hispanic American Historical Review* 44, no. 3 (August 1964): 293–340.

Hanson, Niles. "Commentary: The Hispano Homeland in 1900." *Annals of the Association of American Geographers* 71 (June 1981): 280–82.

Hening, H. B., and E. Dana Johnson, comps. *Albuquerque.* Albuquerque: Albuquerque Morning Journal, 1908.

Herbermann, Charles George, et al., eds. *The Catholic Encyclopedia.* Vol. 11. New York: Encyclopedia Press, 1911.

Historical Society of New Mexico. *Records of the New Mexico Historical Society, 1859–1959.* Santa Fe: Archives Division, State of New Mexico Records Center, 1969.

————. "Report of the Historical Society." *Old Santa Fe* 1 (July 1913): 107.

————. *Official Report of the Historical Society of New Mexico.* Santa Fe: New Mexican Printing Co., 1887.

————. *Official Reports of the Society, 1912 and 1913.* Publications Series no. 19. Santa Fe: New Mexican Printing Co., 1914.

————. *Official Report.* Publications Series no. 17. Santa Fe: New Mexican Printing Co., 1912.

————. *Official Report of the Society, 1912.* Historical Society of New Mexico Publications no. 18. Santa Fe: New Mexican Printing Co., 1913.

————. *Official Report.* Santa Fe: New Mexican Printing Co., 1906.

————. *Informe Bienal de la Sociedad Historica de Nuevo Mexico.* Diciembre 1, 1904. Santa Fe: Compañia Impresora del Nuevo Mexicano, 1905.

————. *Official Report of the Historical Society.* Santa Fe: New Mexican Printing Co., 1904.

————. *Report of the Historical Society of New Mexico.* Santa Fe: New Mexican Printing Co., 1898.

————. *Report of the Historical Society of New Mexico.* Santa Fe: New Mexican Printing Co., 2 January 1893.

————. *Inaugural Address Delivered by Hon. W. G. Ritch at the Adobe Palace, February 21, 1881.* Santa Fe: New Mexican Book and Job Printing Department, 1881.

Hobsbawm, Eric, and Terence Ranger, eds. *The Invention of Tradition.* Cambridge, UK: Cambridge University Press, 1983.

Hodgin, C. E. "The Early School Laws of New Mexico." *Bulletin.* University of New Mexico Educational Series. Vol. 1. Albuquerque: University of New Mexico, 1906.

Hofstadter, Richard. *The Progressive Historians: Turner, Beard, Parrington.* Chicago: University of Chicago Press, 1967.

Horsman, Reginald. "Racial Destiny and the Indians." In *Major Problems in the History of the American West: Documents and Essays,* ed. Clyde A. Milner II, 226–62. Lexington, Mass.: D. C. Heath and Co., 1989.

————. *Race and Manifest Destiny: The Origins of American Anglo-Saxonism.* Cambridge, Mass.: Harvard University Press, 1981.

Huhndorf, Shari M. *Going Native: Indians in the American Cultural Imagination.* Ithaca, N.Y.: Cornell University Press, 2001.

Hundley, Norris C. Jr. *The Great Thirst: Californians and Water, 1770s–1990s.* Berkeley: University of California Press, 1992.

Hurtado, Albert. *Indian Survival on the California Frontier.* New Haven: Yale University Press, 1988.

Ignatiev, Noel. *How the Irish Became White.* New York: Routledge, 1995.

Inman, Henry. *The Old Santa Fé Trail: The Story of a Great Highway.* New York: Macmillan Co., 1897. Reprint, Topeka: Crane and Co., 1899.

Jackson, Helen Hunt. *Ramona: A Story.* N.p., 1884. Reprinted with a foreword by Michael Dorris. New York: Signet Classic Printing, 1988.

———. *A Century of Dishonor.* New York: Harper, 1881.

Jacobs, Janet Liebman. *Hidden Heritage: The Legacy of the Crypto-Jews.* Berkeley: University of California Press, 2002.

Jacobs, Margaret D. *Engendered Encounters: Feminism and Pueblo Cultures, 1879–1934.* Lincoln: University of Nebraska Press, 1999.

Jacobson, Matthew Frye. *Whiteness of a Different Color: European Immigration and the Alchemy of Race.* Cambridge, Mass.: Harvard University Press, 1998.

Jenkins, Myra Ellen. *The Mexican Archives of New Mexico.* [Santa Fe]: New Mexico State Records Center and Archives, n.d.

Jennings, Francis. "A Growing Partnership: Historians, Anthropologists and American Indian History." *Ethnohistory* 29 (1982): 21–34.

Johnson, Judith R. "Health Seekers to Albuquerque, 1880–1940." MA thesis, University of New Mexico, 1983.

Jones, Charles Irving. "William Kronig: New Mexico Pioneer, from His Memories of 1849–1860 (Continued)." *New Mexico Historical Review* 20 (January 1945): 271–311.

———. "William Kronig: New Mexico Pioneer, from His Memories of 1849–1860." *New Mexico Historical Review* 19 (July 1944): 188–97.

Jones, Oakah L. Jr. *Los Paisanos: Spanish Settlers on the Northern Frontier of New Spain.* Norman: University of Oklahoma Press, 1979.

Julyan, Robert. *The Place Names of New Mexico.* Albuquerque: University of New Mexico Press, 1996.

Kearney, Milo, and Manuel Medrano. *Medieval Culture and the Mexican American Borderlands.* College Station: Texas A&M University Press, 2001.

Keen, Benjamin. "The Black Legend Revisited: Assumption and Realities." *Hispanic American Historical Review* 49 (November 1969): 703–19.

Kerber, Linda K. *No Constitutional Right to Be Ladies: Women and the Obligations of Citizenship.* New York: Hill and Wang, 1998.

————. "The Meanings of Citizenship." *Journal of American History* (December 1997): 833–54.

Klein, Kerwin L. "Frontier Products: Tourism, Consumerism, and the Southwestern Public Lands, 1890–1990." *Pacific Historical Review* 62 (1993): 39–71.

Knott, Sarah Gertrude. "North of the Border." *Survey Graphic* 29, no. 6 (June 1940): 339.

Kolodny, Annette. *The Land Before Her: Fantasy and Experience of the American Frontiers, 1630–1860.* Chapel Hill: University of North Carolina Press, 1984.

————. *The Lay of the Land: Metaphor as Experience and History in American Life and Letters.* Chapel Hill: University of North Carolina Press, 1975.

Ladd, Horatio O. *The Story of the States: New Mexico.* Boston: D. Lothrop Co., 1891.

LaFarge, Oliver. *Santa Fe: The Autobiography of a Southwestern Town.* Norman: University of Oklahoma Press, 1959.

Lamadrid, Enrique R. "Ig/Noble Savages of New Mexico: The Naturalization of 'El Norte' into 'the Great Southwest.'" Working Paper Series no. 121. Albuquerque: Southwest Hispanic Research Institute, University of New Mexico, 1992.

Lamar, Howard Roberts. *The Far Southwest, 1846–1912: A Territorial History.* New York: W. W. Norton, 1970.

Lamphere, Louise. "Women, Anthropology, Tourism, and the Southwest." *Frontiers: A Journal of Women's Studies* 12, no. 3 (1992): 5–11.

————. "Gladys Reichard among the Navajo." *Frontiers: A Journal of Women's Studies* 12, no. 3 (1992): 79–115.

Lang, Herbert H. "The New Mexico Bureau of Immigration, 1880–1912." *New Mexico Historical Review* 51 (1976): 193–214.

Langston, La Moine. "Arizona's Fight for Statehood in the Fifty-Seventh Congress." MA thesis, University of New Mexico, 1939.

Langum, David J. "From Condemnation to Praise: Shifting Perspectives on Hispanic California." *California History* 61 (Winter 1983): 282–91.

Lanning, John Tate. *The Royal Protomedicato: The Regulation of the Medical Professions in the Spanish Empire.* Durham, N.C.: Duke University Press, 1985.

Larson, Robert W. *New Mexico Populism: A Study of Radical Protest in*

a Western Territory. Boulder: Colorado Associated University
Press, 1974.

————. *New Mexico's Quest for Statehood, 1846–1912.* Albuquerque:
University of New Mexico Press, 1968.

Lavrin, Asunción, and Edith Couturier, "Dowries and Wills: A View of
Women's Socioeconomic Role in Colonial Guadalajara and
Puebla, 1640–1790." *Hispanic American Historical Review* 59 (1979):
280–304.

Lee, Everett S., et al. *Methodological Considerations and Reference Tables.*
Vol. 1 of *Population Redistribution and Economic Growth, United
States,* ed. Simon Kuznets and Dorothy Swaine Thomas.
Philadelphia: American Philosophical Society, 1957.

Lehmann, Terry John. "Santa Fé and Albuquerque, 1870–1900:
Contrast and Conflict in the Development of Two Southwestern
Towns." PhD diss., Indiana University, 1974.

Linke, Uli. *Blood and Nation: The European Aesthetics of Race.*
Philadelphia: University of Pennsylvania Press, 1999.

Lomelí, Francisco A. *Eusebio Chacón: A Literary Portrait of Nineteenth
Century New Mexico.* Working Paper no. 113 Albuquerque:
Southwest Hispanic Research Institute, Spring 1987.

López, Ian Haney. *White by Law: The Legal Construction of Race.* New
York: New York University Press, 1996.

López Pulido, Alberto. *The Sacred World of the Penitentes.* Washington:
Smithsonian Institution Press, 2000.

Los Ríos de Lampérez, Blanca de. "Nuestra raza." *Raza española* 1
(1919): 7–12.

Los Ríos de Lampérez, Blanca de, et al. *Nuestra raza es española, ni
latina ni ibera.* Madrid: E. Maestre, Pozas, 1926.

Lucero, Aurora. "Defensa de Nuestro Idioma. Discurso, en inglés, pronunciado por la señorita Aurora Lucero, en el Concurso
Interescolástico Territorial, aquí en Las Vegas. Ha sido muy
comentado por la prensa." *La Voz del Pueblo,* 25 February 1911.

Lucero, Aurora. "Shall the Spanish Language Be Taught in the Schools
of New Mexico." Undated publication in possession of author.

Lucero-White, Aurora. *Los Hispanos: Five Essays on the Folkways of the
Hispanos as Seen through the Eyes of One of Them.* Denver: Sage
Books, 1947.

Lummis, Charles Fletcher. *Pueblo Indian Folk-Stories.* New York:
Century Co., 1910. Reprinted with an introduction by Robert F.

Gish and titled *Pueblo Indian Folk-Tales.* Lincoln: University of Nebraska Press, 1992.

————. *Los exploradores españoles del siglo XVI: Vindicación de la acción colonizadora española en América.* 7th ed. Barcelona: Araluce, 1925.

————. *The Spanish Pioneers.* 8th ed. Chicago: A. C. McClurg and Co., 1920.

————. "Porfirio Díaz." *Harper's Weekly* 48 (December 17, 1904): 1950–52.

————. "The Man of Mexico." *Outlook* 69 (November 2, 1901): 536–45.

————. "The Mexican Wizard." *Land of Sunshine* 11 (November 1899): 309–16.

————. *The Awakening of a Nation.* New York: Harper's, 1898.

————. "The Spanish-American Face." *Land of Sunshine* 2 (January 1895): 21–22.

————. *The Land of Poco Tiempo.* New York: Scribner's, 1893.

————. *A Tramp Across the Continent.* New York: Charles Scribner's Sons, 1892.

————. *A New Mexico David and Other Stories and Sketches of the Southwest.* New York: Scribner's, 1891.

————. *Some Strange Corners of Our Country.* New York: Century Company, 1891.

Lux, Guillermo. *Politics and Education in Hispanic New Mexico: From the Spanish-American Normal School to the Northern New Mexico Community College.* El Rito: Northern New Mexico Community College, 1984.

MacDonald, Margaret Espinosa. "'*Vamos todos a Belén*': Cultural Transformations of the Hispanic Community in the Rio Abajo Community in Belen, New Mexico from 1850 to 1950." PhD diss., University of New Mexico, 1997.

Maddox, Charles Edgar. "The Statehood Policy of Albert J. Beveridge: 1901–1911." MA thesis, University of New Mexico, 1938.

Malmierca, Feliciano Sierro. *Judios, moriscos e inquisición en ciudad rodrigo.* Salamanca, Spain: n.p., 1990.

Mann, Horace. "Twelfth Annual Report to the Board of Education." In *Life and Works of Horace Mann.* Vol. 4. Boston: Lee and Shephard, 1891.

Marcial Dorado, Carolina. "Una española en California." *Hispania* 2 (October 1919): 286–90.

Martin, JoAnn. "Contesting Authenticity: Battles over the Representation of History in Morelos, Mexico." *Ethnohistory* 40 (Summer 1993): 438–65.

Martz, Linda. *A Network of Converso Families in Early Modern Toledo: Assimilating a Minority.* Ann Arbor: University of Michigan Press, 2003.

Massey, Douglass, et al., *Return to Aztlán: The Social Process of International Migration from Western Mexico.* Berkeley: University of California Press, 1987.

McCaa, Robert "Calidad, Clase, and Marriage in Colonial Mexico: The Case of Parral, 1788–90." *Hispanic American Historical Review* 64 (1984): 477–501.

————. "Modeling Social Interaction: Marriage, Miscegenation and the Society of Castes in Colonial Spanish America." *Historical Methods* 15 (1982): 45–66.

McCannell, Dean. *The Tourist: A New Theory of the Leisure Class.* New York: Schocken Books, 1976.

McDowell, Archie M. "The Opposition to Statehood within the Territory of New Mexico, 1888–1903." PhD diss., University of New Mexico, 1939.

McGregor [pseud.?]. "Our Spanish-American Fellow Citizens." *Harper's Weekly,* 20 June 1914.

McKee, William H. *The Territory of New Mexico, and Its Resources.* New York: Office of the American Mining Index Engraving and Printing Establishment, 1866.

McLuhan, T. C. *Dream Tracks: The Railroad and the American Indian, 1890–1930.* New York: Harry N. Abrams, 1985.

McSpadden, George E. "Aurelio M. Espinosa (1880–1958)." *Hispania* 42 (March 1959): 20–21.

McWilliams, Carey. *North from Mexico: The Spanish-Speaking People of the United States.* Edited by Louis Adamic. Philadelphia: J. B. Lippincott Co., 1949.

Meier, Matt S. *Mexican American Biographies: A Historical Dictionary, 1836–1987.* New York: Greenwood Press, 1988.

Meinig, D. W. *Annals of the Association of American Geographers* 74, no. 1 (1984): 171.

————. *Southwest: Three Peoples in Geographical Change, 1600–1970.* New York: Oxford University Press, 1971.

Meketa, Jacqueline Dorgan, ed. *Legacy of Honor: The Life of Rafael*

Chacón, a Nineteenth-Century New Mexican. Albuquerque: University of New Mexico Press, 1986.

Melammed, Renée Levine. *Heretics or Daughters of Israel? The Crypto-Jewish Women of Castile.* New York: Oxford University Press, 1999.

Meléndez, A. Gabriel. Introduction to *The Biography of Casimiro Barela,* by José E. Fernández. Albuquerque: University of New Mexico Press, 2003.

——. *So All Is Not Lost: The Poetics of Print in Nuevomexicano Communities, 1834–1958.* Albuquerque: University of New Mexico Press, 1997.

Menchaca, Martha. *Recovering History, Recovering Race: The Indian, Black, and White Roots of Mexican Americans.* Austin: University of Texas Press, 2001.

Merchant, Carolyn. *The Death of Nature: Women, Ecology, and the Scientific Revolution.* San Francisco: Harper and Row, 1980.

Metzgar, Joseph V. "The Ethnic Sensitivity of Spanish New Mexicans: A Survey and Analysis." *New Mexico Historical Review 49* (January 1974): 49–73.

Meyer, Carter Jones. "Saving the Pueblos: Commercialism and Indian Reform in the 1920s." In *Selling the Indian: Commercializing and Appropriating American Indian Cultures,* ed. Carter Jones Meyer and Diana Royer, 190–211. Tucson: University of Arizona Press, 2001.

Meyer, Doris L. *Speaking for Themselves: Neomexicano Cultural Identity and the Spanish-Language Press, 1880–1920.* Albuquerque: University of New Mexico Press, 1996.

——. "Early Mexican-American Responses to Negative Stereotyping." *New Mexico Historical Review 53* (1978): 75–91.

Mitchell, Pablo Reid. "Bodies on Borders: Sexuality, Race and Conquest in Modernizing New Mexico, 1880–1920." PhD diss., University of Michigan, 2000.

Monroy, Douglas. *Thrown Among Strangers: The Making of Mexican Culture in Frontier California.* Berkeley: University of California Press, 1990.

Montejano, David. *Anglos and Mexicans in the Making of Texas, 1836–1986.* Austin: University of Texas Press, 1987.

Montgomery, Charles. *The Spanish Redemption: Heritage, Power, and Loss on New Mexico's Upper Rio Grande.* Berkeley: University of California Press, 2002.

Montoya, María E. *Translating Property: The Maxwell Land Grant and the Conflict over Land in the American West, 1840–1900.* Berkeley: University of California Press, 2002.

Morgan, Lewis H. *Systems of Consanguinity and Affinity of the Human Family.* Washington, D.C.: Smithsonian Institution, 1871.

Mörner, Magnus. "Economic Factors and Stratification in Colonial Spanish America with Special Regard to Elites." *Hispanic American Historical Review* 63 (1983): 335–69.

———. *Race Mixture in the History of Latin America.* Boston: Little, Brown and Co., 1967.

Museo de Arte de Lima. *Los cuadros de mestizaje del virrey Amat: La representación etnográfica en el Perú colonial.* Lima: Museo de Arte de Lima, 1999.

Myrick, David F. *New Mexico's Railroads: An Historical Survey.* Golden: Colorado Railroad Museum, 1970.

Nash, Dennison. "Tourism as a Form of Imperialism." In *Hosts and Guests: The Anthropology of Tourism,* 2d ed., ed. Valene L. Smith, 37–52. Philadelphia: University of Pennsylvania Press, 1989.

Nash, Gary B. *Forbidden Love: The Secret History of Mixed Race America.* New York: Henry Holt and Co., 1999.

Nature's Sanitarium: Las Vegas Hot Springs, Las Vegas, New Mexico, on The Line of the Atchison, Topeka and Santa Fe Railroad. Chicago: Rand McNally, 1883.

Neulander, Judith S. "Cannibals, Castes and Crypto-Jews: Premillennial Cosmology in Postcolonial New Mexico." PhD diss., Indiana University, 2001.

New Mexico Health Resorts. N.p., 1899.

Nicholl, Edith M, *The Desert and the Rose.* Boston: The Cornhill Co., 1921.

———. *Observations of a Ranchwoman in New Mexico.* New York: Macmillan Co., 1898.

Norris, Scott, ed., *Discovered Country: Tourism and Survival in the American West.* Albuquerque: Stone Ladder Press, 1994.

Norwood, Vera. *Made from This Earth: American Women and Nature.* Chapel Hill: University of North Carolina Press, 1993.

Nostrand, Richard L. *The Hispano Homeland.* Norman: University of Oklahoma Press, 1992.

———. "Hispano Cultural Distinctiveness: A Reply." *Annals of the Association of American Geographers* 74 (1984): 164–69.

————. "Comment in Reply." *Annals of the Association of American Geographers* 71 (June 1981): 282–83.

————. "The Hispano Homeland in 1900." *Annals of the Association of American Geographers* 70 (September 1980): 382–96.

Nugent, Walter. "The People of the West Since 1890." In *The Twentieth-Century West: Historical Interpretations,* ed. Gerald D. Nash and Richard W. Etulain, 35–70. Albuquerque: University of New Mexico Press, 1989.

O'Crouley, Pedro Alonso. *A Description of the Kingdom of New Spain, 1774.* San Francisco: John Howell Books, 1972.

Oboler, Suzanne. *Ethnic Labels, Latino Lives: Identity and the Politics of (Re)Presentation in the United States.* Minneapolis: University of Minnesota Press, 1995.

Olivera, Ruth R., and Liliene Crété. *Life in Mexico under Santa Anna, 1822–1855.* Norman: University of Oklahoma Press, 1991.

Olmsted, Virginia L. *The Ortiz Family of New Mexico: The First Six Generations.* Albuquerque: Olmsted, 1978.

————, trans. and comp. *Spanish and Mexican Colonial Censuses of New Mexico: 1790, 1823, 1845.* Albuquerque: New Mexico Genealogical Society, 1975.

Ortiz, Roxanne Dunbar. *Roots of Resistance: Land Tenure in New Mexico, 1680–1980.* Chicano Studies Research Center, University of California, Los Angeles; American Indian Research Center, University of California, Los Angeles, [1980].

Otero, Miguel Antonio. *My Nine Years as Governor of the Territory of New Mexico, 1897–1906.* Albuquerque: University of New Mexico Press, 1940.

————. *My Life on the Frontier.* Vol. 1, *1864–1882, Incidents and Characters of the Period When Kansas, Colorado, and New Mexico Were Passing Through the Last of Their Wild and Romantic Years.* New Mexico: Press of Pioneers, 1935.

Pacheco, Lionides, and Ruth C. Miller. "The Bi-Lingual Method and the Improvement of Instruction." February 1938, Bergere Family Papers, NMSRCA.

Padilla, Genaro M. "Rediscovering Nineteenth-Century Mexican-American Autobiography." In *Memory, Narrative, and Identity: New Essays in Ethnic American Literatures,* ed. Amritjit Singh, Joseph T. Skerrett Jr., and Robert E. Hogan, 205–31. Boston: Northeastern University Press, 1994.

—. *My History, Not Yours: The Formation of Mexican American Autobiography.* Madison: University of Wisconsin Press, 1993.

—. "Imprisoned Narrative? Or Lies, Secrets, and Silence in New Mexico Women's Autobiography." In *Criticism in the Borderland,* ed. Hector Calderón and José Saldívar. Durham, N.C.: Duke University Press, 1991.

—. *The Genealogy of a Text and a Text of Genealogy: Rafael Chacon's "Memorias."* Working Paper no. 116. Albuquerque: Southwest Hispanic Research Institute, University of New Mexico, Summer 1991.

Palmer, William J. *De la colonization du Colorado et du Nouveau-Mexique.* Paris: Typographie Lahure, 1874.

Pan, Denise. "Commercializing the Spanish Past: The Coronado Cuarto Centennial, 1935–1940." In *Explorations in American History.* Occasional Paper no. 8, ed. Sandra Varney MacMahon and Louis Tanner. Albuquerque: University of New Mexico Center for the American West, 1995.

Parish, William J. "The German Jew and the Commercial Revolution in Territorial New Mexico, 1850–1900." *New Mexico Quarterly* 25 (Autumn 1959): 307–32.

Parmentier, Richard J. "The Mythological Triangle: Poseyemu, Montezuma, and Jesus in the Pueblos." In *Southwest,* vol. 9 of *Handbook of North American Indians,* ed. Alfonso Ortiz, 609–22. Washington, D.C.: Smithsonian Institution, 1979.

Pearce, T. M. *New Mexico Place Names: A Geographical Dictionary.* Albuquerque: University of New Mexico Press, 1965.

Pérez Monfort, Ricardo. *Hispanismo y falange: Los sueños imperiales de la derecha española y México.* México: Fondo de Cultura Económica, 1992.

Pérez Villanueva, Joaquín. *Ramón Menéndez Pidal: Su vida y su tiempo.* Madrid: Espasa-Calpe, 1991.

Perrigo, Lynn. *Gateway to Glorieta: A History of Las Vegas, New Mexico.* Boulder, Colo.: Pruett Publishing Co., 1982.

—. "The Original Las Vegas." Unpublished manuscript. Albuquerque: Center for Southwest Research, University of New Mexico.

Pike, Fredrick B. "Hispanismo and the Non-Revolutionary Spanish Immigrant in Spanish America, 1900–1930." *Inter-American Economic Affairs* 25 (Autumn 1971): 3–30.

Ponce, Merrihelen. *The Lives and Works of Five Hispanic New Mexican Women Writers, 1878–1991.* Working Papers Series no. 119. Albuquerque: Southwest Hispanic Research Institute, University of New Mexico, 1992.

Portes, Alejandro, and Robert L. Bach. *Latin Journey: Cuban and Mexican Immigrants in the United States.* Berkeley: University of California Press, 1985.

Pratt, Boyd C., Charles D. Biebel, and Dan Scurlock, with contributions by Vernon J. Glover. *Trails, Rails, and Roads: The Central New Mexico East-West Transportation Corridor Regional Overview.* [Santa Fe]: New Mexico Historic Preservation Division, 1988.

Prentis, Noble L[ovely]. *South-Western Letters.* Topeka: Kansas Publishing House, 1882.

Prince, Lebaron Bradford. *The Spanish Mission Churches of New Mexico.* Grand Rapids, Iowa: Torch Press, 1915.

———. *The Student's History of New Mexico.* Denver: Publishers Press, 1913.

———. *A Concise History of New Mexico.* Cedar Rapids: Torch Press, 1912.

———. *New Mexico's Struggle for Statehood: Sixty Years of Effort to Obtain Self Government.* Santa Fe: New Mexican Printing Co., 1910.

———. *Historical Sketches of New Mexico from the Earliest Records to the American Occupation.* New York: Leggat Brothers, 1883.

Programme of Excursion to Santa Fe, New Mexico. Tendered to the Delegates of the Fourth National Irrigation Congress and Their Wives, by the Territory and Citizens of Santa Fe, September 19th, 1895. Santa Fe: New Mexican Print, [1895].

Rael-Galvez, Estevan. "Identifying Captivity and Capturing Identity: Narratives of American Indian Slavery." PhD diss., University of Michigan, 2002.

Read, Benjamin Maurice. *Popular Elementary History of New Mexico.* Cedar Rapids, Iowa: Torch Press, 1914.

———. *Illustrated History of New Mexico.* Translated by Eleuterio Baca. Santa Fe: New Mexican Printing Co., 1912.

———. *Historia ilustrada de Nuevo México.* Cuatro libros en un tomo. Santa Fe: Compañía Impresora del Nuevo Mexicano, 1911.

———. *A History of Education in New Mexico: Pertinent Advice to Students. Education and Its Relations to the Discovery, Conquest,*

Civilization and Colonization of New Mexico. The Minister of God and the Teacher. Santa Fe: New Mexican Printing Co., 1911.

————. *Guerra México-Americana.* Santa Fe: Compañía Impresora del Nuevo Mexicano, 1910.

————. "Nuevo México en la Guerras de la Unión Americana, 1855–1919." Unpublished manuscript, Read Collection, NMSRCA.

Real Academia Española, *Diccionario de la Lengua Española,* 22d ed. Madrid: Talleres Espasa Calpe, 2002.

————. *Diccionario de la Lengua Española.* Madrid: Talleres Espasa Calpe, 1956.

"Return on Investment in State Cuarto Centennial Expected by Its Backers." *Raton Range,* 13 January 1937.

Ritch, William Gillette. "Chronological Annals of New Mexico, Etc." In *Resources of New Mexico, Prepared under the Auspices of the Territorial Bureau of Immigration for the Territorial Fair, To Be Held at Albuquerque, New Mexico, October 3, 4, 5, 6, 7, 8, 1881.* Santa Fe: New Mexican Book and Job Printing Department, 1881.

Roberts, Shelley. "Remaining and Becoming: Cultural Crosscurrents in an Hispano School (Assimilation)." PhD diss., University of Illinois, 1995.

Robinson, Cecil B. *Mexico and the Hispanic Southwest in American Literature.* Tucson: University of Arizona Press, 1977.

Rock Island System. *New Mexico: The Land of Sunshine. Agricultural and Mineral Resources, Irrigation and Horticulture, Gold, Copper, Iron and Coal. A National Sanitarium. Playground of the Southwest.* Chicago: Passenger Department, Rock Island System, 1904.

Rodríguez, Sylvia. *The Matachines Dance: Ritual Symbolism and Interethnic Relations in the Upper Rio Grande Valley.* Albuquerque: University of New Mexico Press, 1996.

————. "The Hispano Homeland Debate Revisited." *Perspectives in Mexican American Studies* 3 (1992): 95–114.

————. "Art, Tourism, and Race Relations in Taos: Toward a Sociology of the Art Colony." *Journal of Anthropological Research* 45 (Spring 1988): 77–99.

————. "Land, Water, and Ethnic Identity in Taos." In *Land, Water, and Culture: New Perspectives on Hispanic Land Grants,* ed. Charles L. Briggs and John R. Van Ness, 313–403. Albuquerque: University of New Mexico Press, 1987.

Roediger, David R. *The Wages of Whiteness: Race and the Making of the American Working Class.* New York: Verso, 1991.

Rosaldo, Renato. *Culture and Truth: The Remaking of Social Analysis.* Boston: Beacon Press, 1989.

Rosenbaum, Robert J. *Mexicano Resistance in the Southwest: "The Sacred Right of Self Preservation."* Austin: University of Texas Press, 1984.

Rotundo, E. Anthony. *American Manhood: Transformations in Masculinity from the Revolution to the Modern Era.* New York: Basic Books, 1993.

Sánchez, George Isadore. *Forgotten People: A Study of New Mexicans.* Albuquerque: University of New Mexico Press, 1940.

Sánchez, George J. *Becoming Mexican American: Ethnicity, Culture and Identity in New Mexico, 1900–1945.* New York: Oxford University Press, 1993.

Sánchez, Joseph P. *The Spanish Black Legend / La leyenda negra española: Origins of Anti-Hispanic Stereotypes / Orígenes de los esteriotipos anti-hispánicos.* Spanish Colonial Research Center Publication Series no. 2. Albuquerque, 1990.

Sando, Joe S. *The Pueblo Indians.* San Francisco: Indian Historian Press, 1976.

Sarber, Mary A. *Charles F. Lummis: A Bibliography.* Tucson: University of Arizona Graduate School Library, 1977.

Saxton, Russell S. "Ethnocentrism in the Historical Literature of Territorial New Mexico." PhD diss., University of New Mexico, 1980.

Scheobel, C[harles]. "Une Expédition dans le Nouveau Mexique et l'Arizona." *Archives de la Société Américaine de France* 1 (1875): 18–30.

Schlereth, Thomas J. *Cultural History and Material Culture: Everyday Life, Landscapes, Museums.* Charlottesville: University Press of Virginia, 1992.

Sears, John F. *Sacred Places: American Tourist Attractions in the Nineteenth Century.* New York: Oxford University Press, 1989.

Seed, Patricia. *To Love, Honor, and Obey in Colonial Mexico: Conflicts over Marriage Choice, 1574–1821.* Stanford, Calif.: Stanford University Press, 1988.

Simmons, Marc. "Commentary on Nostrand's 'Hispanos' and Their 'Homeland.'" *Annals of the Association of American Geographers* 74 (1984): 157–64.

———. *Annals of the Association of American Geographers* 74, no. 1 (1984): 169–70

————. "New Mexico's Spanish Exiles." *New Mexico Historical Review* 69 (1984): 67–79.

————. "History of the Pueblos since 1821." In *Handbook of North American Indians*. Vol. 9. ed. Alfonso Ortiz. Washington, D.C.: Smithsonian Institution, 1979.

————. *New Mexico: A History*. New York: W. W. Norton, 1977.

————. *Spanish Government in New Mexico*. Albuquerque: University of New Mexico Press, 1968.

————. *Two Southwesterners: Charles Lummis and Amado Chaves*. [Cerrillos, N.M.]: San Marcos Press, 1968.

Simmons, Marc, et al. "Rejoinders." *Annals of the Association of American Geographers* 74 (1984): 169–71.

Smith, Anthony. *The Ethnic Revival*. Cambridge, UK: Cambridge University Press, 1981.

Smith, Carol A. "Race-Class-Gender Ideology in Guatemala: Modern and Anti-Modern Forms." *Comparative Studies in Society and History* 37, no. 4 (1995): 723–49.

Smith, Rogers M. *Civic Ideals: Conflicting Visions of Citizenship in U.S. History*. New Haven: Yale University Press, 1997.

Smith, Valene L., ed. *Hosts and Guests: The Anthropology of Tourism*. 2d ed. Philadelphia: University of Pennsylvania Press, 1989.

Sollors, Werner. Introduction to *The Invention of Ethnicity*, ed. Werner Sollors. New York: Oxford University Press, 1989.

————. *Beyond Ethnicity: Consent and Descent in American Culture*. New York: Oxford University Press, 1986.

Souvenir of Las Vegas, New Mexico: The Leading City of the Territory. Chicago: Rand, McNally, 1893.

Spence, Mark. "Dispossessing the Wilderness: Yosemite Indians and the National Park Ideal, 1864–1930." *Pacific Historical Review* 65 (February 1996): 28–59.

Spicer, Edward H. *Cycles of Conquest: The Impact of Spain, Mexico, and the United States on the Indians of the Southwest, 1533–1960*. Tucson: University of Arizona Press, 1962.

Spicer, Edward H., and R. Thompson, eds. *Plural Society in the Southwest*. Albuquerque: University of New Mexico Press, 1972.

St. Michael's College. *Seventy-Five Years of Service, 1859–1934: An Historical Sketch of Saint Michael's College*. Santa Fe: Saint Michael's College, 1934.

Stevens, Edward Jr., George H. Wood, and James J. Sheehan. *Justice, Ideology, Education: An Introduction to the Social Foundations of Education.* 4th ed. Boston: McGraw Hill, 2002.

Storms, Walter W. *The Story of New Mexico, Briefly Told. With a Sketch of the Early Spaniards, and an Outline of the Territorial Civil Government.* Terre Haute, Ind.: Inland Publishing Co., 1896.

Stowe, Harriet Beecher. *Uncle Tom's Cabin.* 1852. Repr., Cambridge, Mass.: Harvard University Press, 1962.

Taeuber, Irene B. *Population Trends in the United States, 1900–1960.* Bureau of the Census Technical Paper no. 10. Washington, D.C.: U.S. Government Printing Office, 1965.

Tejada, Luis Coronas. *Conversos and Inquisition in Jaén.* Jerusalem: Magnes Press, 1988.

Tello, Pilar León. *Judios de Toledo.* Madrid, Spain: Consejo Superior de Investigaciones Científicas, 1979.

Thoma, Francisco de. *Historia popular de Nuevo México: Desde su descubrimiento hasta la actualidad.* New York: American Book Co., 1896.

Thompson, Mark. *American Character: The Curious History of Charles Fletcher Lummis and the Rediscovery of the Southwest.* New York: Arcade Publishing, 2001.

Thornton, Russell. *American Indian Holocaust and Survival: A Population History Since 1492.* Norman: University of Oklahoma Press, 1987.

Tjarks, Alicia V. "Demographic, Ethnic and Occupational Structure of New Mexico, 1790." *The Americas: A Quarterly Review of Inter-American Cultural History* 35 (July 1978): 45–88.

Tort, Patrick. "Le pur et le dur." In *La pureté: Quête d'absolu au peril de l'humain,* ed. Sylvain Matton, Series Morales no. 13. Paris: Editions Autrements, 1993.

Townley, John. "The New Mexico Mining Company." *New Mexico Historical Review* 46 (1971): 57–73.

Townley, John M. "Mining in the Ortiz Mine Grant Area, Southern Santa Fe County, New Mexico." MA thesis, University of Nevada, 1968.

Trujillo, Dennis Peter. "Commodification of Hispano Culture in New Mexico: Tourism, Mary Austin, and the Spanish Colonial Arts Society." PhD diss., University of New Mexico, 2003.

Turner, Frederick Jackson. "The Significance of the Frontier in American History." In *Proceeding of the Forty-First Annual Meeting of the State Historical Society of Wisconsin,* 79–112. Madison, Wisc.,

1894. Reprinted in *Major Problems in the History of the American West: Documents and Essays,* ed. Clyde A. Milner II, 2–34. Lexington, Mass.: D. C. Heath and Co., 1989.

Twinam, Ann. "Honor, Sexuality, and Illegitimacy in Colonial Spanish America." In *Sexuality and Marriage in Colonial Latin America,* ed. Asunción Lavrín, 118–55. Lincoln: University of Nebraska Press, 1989.

Twitchell, Ralph Emerson. *The Leading Facts of New Mexican History.* 5 vols. Cedar Rapids, Iowa: Torch Press, 1917.

Unamuno, Miguel de. "Comunidad de la lengua." In *Temas argentinos.* Buenos Aires: Institución Cultural Española, 1943.

Van Den Berghe, Pierre L. *The Quest for the Other: Ethnic Tourism in San Cristóbal, México.* Seattle: University of Washington Press, 1994.

Vigil, Maurilio E. *Defining Our Destiny: The History of New Mexico Highlands University.* Las Vegas: New Mexico Highlands University, 1993.

Villar Villamil, Ignacio de. "Presentación." In *Los caballeros de las ordenes militares en México, Católogo biográfico y geneológico,* by Leopoldo Martínez Cosio. México: Editorial Santiago, 1946.

Wallace, Susan E. *The Land of the Pueblos.* Troy, N.Y.: Nims and Knight, 1889.

Walter, Paul A. F. "Benjamin M. Read." *New Mexico Historical Review* 2 (October 1927): 394–97.

Weber, David J. *The Spanish Frontier in North America.* New Haven: Yale University Press, 1992.

———. "The Spanish Legacy in North America and the Historical Imagination." *Western Historical Quarterly* (February 1992): 5–24.

———. "Blood of Martyrs, Blood of Indians: Toward a More Balanced View of Spanish Missions in Seventeenth-Century North America." In *Columbian Consequences,* ed. David Hurst Thomas, 429–48. Washington, D.C.: Smithsonian Institution Press, 1990.

———. *Myth and History of the Hispanic Southwest.* Albuquerque: University of New Mexico Press, 1988.

———. "'Scarce More Than Apes': Historical Roots of Anglo-American Stereotypes of Mexicans." In *New Spain's Far Northern Frontier: Essays on Spain in the American West, 1540–1821,* ed. David J. Weber, 293–307. Albuquerque: University of New Mexico Press, 1979.

————, ed. *Foreigners in their Native Land: Historical Roots of the Mexican Americans.* Albuquerque: University of New Mexico Press, 1973.

Weedon, Chris. *Feminist Practice and Poststructuralist Theory.* Oxford, UK: B. Blackwell, 1987.

Weigle, Marta. "Selling the Southwest: Santa Fe InSites." In *Discovered Country,* ed. Scott Norris, 210–24. Albuquerque: Stone Ladder Press, 1994.

————. "From Desert to Disney World: The Santa Fe Railway and the Fred Harvey Company Display the Indian Southwest." *Journal of Anthropological Research* 45 (Spring 1989): 115–37.

————. *Santa Fe and Taos: The Writer's Era, 1916–1941.* 1st ed. Santa Fe: Ancient City Press, 1982.

————. *Brothers of Blood: The Penitentes of the Southwest.* Albuquerque: University of New Mexico Press, 1976.

Weigle, Marta, and Peter White. *The Lore of New Mexico.* Albuquerque: University of New Mexico Press, 1988.

Westphall, Victor. *Mercedes Reales: Hispanic Land Grants of the Upper Rio Grande Region.* Albuquerque: University of New Mexico Press, 1983.

————. *The Public Domain in New Mexico, 1859–1891.* Albuquerque: University of New Mexico Press, 1965.

————. "Albuquerque in the 1870s." *New Mexico Historical Review* 23 (October 1948): 253–68.

Whaley, Charlotte. *Nina Otero-Warren of Santa Fe.* Albuquerque: University of New Mexico Press, 1994.

Whitman, Walt. *The Complete Poetry and Prose of Walt Whitman as Prepared by Him for the Deathbed Edition.* Vol. 2. New York: Pellegrini and Cudahy, 1948.

Williams, Jerry L., and Steve Fox. "The Healthseeker Era, 1880–1940." In *New Mexico in Maps,* ed. Jerry L. Williams, 129–31. Albuquerque: University of New Mexico Press, 1986.

Wilson, Chris. *The Myth of Santa Fe: Creating a Modern Regional Tradition.* Albuquerque: University of New Mexico Press, 1997.

Woodbridge, Hensley C. "Glossary of Names Used in Colonial Latin America for Crosses among Indians, Negroes, and Whites." *Journal of the Washington Academy of Sciences* 38, no. 11 (15 November 1948): 353–61.

Zimmerman, Eduardo A. "Racial Ideas and Social Reform: Argentina, 1890–1916." *Hispanic American Historical Review* 71 (February 1992): 21–46.

Index